Chang Tso-lin
in Northeast China, 1911-1928

Chang Tso-lin
in Northeast China, 1911-1928

China, Japan, and the Manchurian Idea

GAVAN MCCORMACK

Rev'a
JAS 38.3 (May '79), 563-65
by G Kaye Falconeri

Stanford University Press, Stanford, California   1977

The photographs on pp. 136–38 are taken from
a film "Fengtien Forces, 1924–25," with the kind
permission of the Imperial War Museum, London.
The frontispiece picture is from Putnam Weale
(B. Lennox Simpson), *Why China Sees Red* (New York,
1925), by permission of Macmillan London and
Basingstoke. The pictures on p. 135 are (top) from
O. D. Rasmussen, *Tientsin: An Illustrated Outline
History* (Tientsin, 1925); and (bottom) from
Hakuunsō Shujin, *Chō Sakurin* (Tokyo, 1928).

Stanford University Press
Stanford, California
© 1977 by the Board of Trustees of the
Leland Stanford Junior University
Printed in the United States of America
ISBN 0–8047–0945–9
LC 76–48028

Published with the assistance of
the Andrew W. Mellon Foundation

Acknowledgments

Harold Kahn first introduced me to the study of Chinese history when I attended his lectures in London in 1964. He has taught me a good deal since then, about many things as well as Chinese history, and has been not only friend and mentor but also a model of scrupulous, sensitive, and committed scholarship.

Professor W. G. Beasley guided this book through its early stages till it was first drafted as a doctoral dissertation for London University in 1974. From him I learned many invaluable lessons on the methodology of research and historical writing.

During my two spells of research in Tokyo, in 1969–70 and in 1973, Professor H. Kōhachiro Takahashi extended me his unique hospitality and guidance. From him I was privileged to be able to imbibe something of the rich spirit of the Japanese intellectual tradition.

Many others have helped in the preparation of this manuscript, either in reading and commenting on some part or the whole of it, or in discussing aspects of the history of the period—or in some cases their own recollections of it. My sincere thanks to the following: Andō Hikotarō, Mark Elvin, Etō Shinkichi, Etō Toyoji, Jon Halliday, Imai Seiichi, Inaba Masao, Itō Takeo, Owen Lattimore, Machino Tatsuyu, Matsuzawa Tetsunari, Andrew Nathan, Jim Raphael, Stuart Schram, James Sheridan, and Ronald Suleski. Needless to say, I alone am responsible for the final product which is this book.

This research has been supported at various stages by the School of Oriental and African Studies (London University), the London-Cornell Project, Nomura Zaidan, and Leeds University. The Institute of Social

Science of Tokyo University generously provided me with facilities for my research while I was in Japan.

I am grateful to Andrew Forbes and Peter Hotson for help in the preparation of maps, and to Fawzia Ali for the typing.

Finally, for help in innumerable ways, and, despite all the other demands on her as artist and mother, for brewing the beer and pickling the daikon that sustained us both while this book was being written, my thanks to my wife, Yoshinaga Fusako.

G.M.

Leeds University
July 1976

Contents

Chang Tso-lin
in Northeast China, 1911-1928

Introduction

Chang Tso-lin was a tiny, frail-looking, mustachioed illiterate, leader of an obscure frontier bandit gang, who used to dream, in the intervals between opium pipes and all-night gambling sessions, of becoming emperor of China. Unlike many others who may have shared this dream, Chang came close to accomplishing it, since he was also perhaps the greatest of that strange group of men known as the warlords. As such, he was deeply involved in the military and political history of the early Chinese republic. At the same time, because his power was based in China's vast Northeastern region, the region that China's neighbors, Japan and Russia, designated as Manchuria, he was also inextricably involved in the development of that contradiction between China and Japan that a decade after his death was to plunge both countries and eventually the whole of Asia into war. His importance should therefore be manifest; yet he has been little studied. This book, therefore, while structured around the chronological development of Chang's career, focuses attention on the two main themes of warlordism and Japanese imperialism in republican China. Through this focus, however, we believe also that it is possible to deepen our understanding of the social and economic dynamics in the early development of what is now one of China's key centers of industrialization.

The issues are undoubtedly complex; relevant scholarly literature is scarce, and some of the judgments are therefore tentative. We hope at least that they will serve to open debate on important and neglected matters. The introductory comment that follows is designed to establish the setting and the protagonists, and to draw attention to some of the major historical issues involved in consideration of these themes.

THE SETTING: NORTHEAST CHINA OR "MANCHURIA"?

The township of Shan-hai-kuan, which lies about 250 miles northeast of Peking by rail, at the point where the Great Wall comes down to the sea at the Gulf of Pechihli, is the normal point of entry into what the Chinese know either as the Three Eastern Provinces (Tung-san-sheng) or simply as the Northeast (Tung-pei). Together the three provinces of Liaoning (formerly Fengtien), Kirin, and Heilungkiang constitute an area roughly equal to that of France and Germany combined.

Historically this territory has been occupied by three main ethnic and cultural groups, much of its history having been the product of the clash between them: to the south, the agricultural plains of the Liao River Valley were settled early by Han Chinese, and a close relationship was maintained with the rest of North China either by land via Shan-hai-kuan or by sea across the Pohai Gulf to Shantung; to the east and southeast were Tungusic peoples, who lived as hunters and fishermen, practicing a Shamanistic religion, in the forests and along the banks of the Yalu, Tumen, and Ussuri rivers (which presently constitute the international boundaries dividing China from Korea and the Soviet Union); the western and northwestern plains and grasslands were the home of the nomadic, herd-grazing Mongolian peoples.[1]

There was constant tension and interaction not only among these three peoples but also between the region as a whole—when one or other was able to achieve hegemony over it—and the rest of China. Thus several important Chinese dynasties—the Liao, Chin, and Yuan, as well as the last of all, the Ch'ing—arose from bases in the same general area, although at the same time there was a constant northward diffusion of Chinese cultural influences. Conquering tribes from the North themselves succumbed in time to the blandishments of Chinese culture. In the Ming dynasty (1368–1644), the Tungusic peoples in the area east of what would now be Liaoning and Kirin provinces, known then as the Juchen, were divided administratively into three segments, one of which, the Juchen of Chien-chou, repeating this cyclical historical pattern, gradually began to gain ascendancy.* From the late sixteenth to the early seventeenth century the Juchen tribes were unified; in 1616 their leader, Nurhachi, was proclaimed em-

---

*Chien-chou was the administrative name for part of Fengtien province from at least the T'ang dynasty (Lee, p. 227).

peror; in 1621 the Ming administrative centers of Shenyang and Liao-yang were captured; and, after Nurhachi's death, his son Abahai succeeded in transferring the capital of the new dynasty, the Ch'ing, to Peking in 1644 and in establishing control over the whole country.[2]

The name "Manchu" (*Man-chou* in Chinese) was adopted by Abahai only in 1635.[3] This word, Tibetan in origin, meant "oriental brightness," and was originally an honorific title bestowed on the sons of Nurhachi by Mongol lamas.[4] Under Abahai it came to be used as a collective name for the Juchen tribes and, according to a leading Chinese scholar, also for Mongols and Chinese settlers who accepted Nurhachi's leadership. It thus did not denote any distinct ethnic group or race, and by the time the Ch'ing dynasty was proclaimed in Peking, the Manchus had already acquired "all the Chinese ideas about government, morals and education."[5]

After its adoption by Abahai, the term "Manchu" came to be used as part of an assertion of separateness and distinctness from China. A typical example of its use is in the title of a work commissioned by the Ch'ien-lung emperor in the eighteenth century, the *Man-chou yuan-liu k'ao* (a study into the origins of Man-chou), which was a deliberate attempt to establish the non-Chineseness of the ruling house by assertion of a history and civilization comparable to the Chinese.[6] The series of attempts by the Manchu to stave off total assimilation and an end to the formal basis of power and privilege in China are well known.[7] Yet, even at the time of the establishment of the Ch'ing dynasty, Han Chinese heavily outnumbered the tribal followers of Nurhachi, perhaps by as much as two to one, in their homelands in the Northeast.[8] For a time the Manchus encouraged Han Chinese immigration into the Northeast, although early in the eighteenth century they switched to a policy of prohibition as part of the same attempt to maintain exclusive Manchu control. In the mid-nineteenth century, however, initially for financial reasons, they began again to open large tracts of land for sale to Chinese, and the French traveler Abbé Huc, who visited the area in 1844–46, wrote: "You may now traverse Mantchouria to the river Amour without being at all aware that you are not travelling in a province of China."[9] Thereafter powerful strategic considerations also came into play, as the cession of large areas north of the Amur and east of the Ussuri underlined the importance of populating and developing the Northeast lest it be completely lost to Russia. The restrictions on Chinese immigration were gradually phased out area by area till the last was lifted in 1904.[10] At the beginning of this century, as the Ch'ing dynasty was drawing to a close, probably 80 percent of the estimated population of 14 million was Chinese.[11] The Manchu were by then a small minority, but because they constituted an important and readily identifiable group, it is convenient to continue to describe them as Manchu.

However, it is precisely at the time when the Manchus were losing importance and—because of assimilation, intermarriage, and Sinicization— actually disappearing as a separate group that the word "Manchuria" began to assume importance. Because of the associations of separateness and non-Chineseness that accrued to it, it formed a convenient vehicle for the nineteenth century imperialistic ambitions of Russia and Japan. As Robert H. G. Lee in his book *The Manchurian Frontier in Ch'ing History* observes, "The term Manchuria or *Man-chou* is a modern creation used mainly by Westerners and Japanese."[12] It was the apparently innocuous convention of referring to the Northeast as "Manchuria" that allowed the idea to develop that it was not part of China and that prepared the way for severance from China and the eventual establishment of the Japanese puppet state of Manchukuo in 1932. Actually the word "Manchuria," as a geographical or geopolitical term, appears not to have had any precise meaning, since the three provinces that had been described as "Manchuria" to 1931 were expanded to four, with the inclusion of Jehol, to make up the new state, providing further illustration of the primarily political and imperialistic nature of the word. However common the word "Manchuria" is in Western writing, therefore, its positively imperialistic overtones are clear, and to refer to "China and Manchuria," for example, as many scholars still do, is as misleading, question-begging, and incorrect as it is to refer to "China and Taiwan." Since it is difficult, if not impossible, to purge the word altogether of its positively imperialistic associations, this book adopts the practice of "rectification of names," using the word "Manchuria" only in inverted commas or in quotation marks, otherwise replacing it with the simple and precise term "Three Eastern Provinces," or, where precision is less important, "the Northeast," both expressions being direct translations of the terms used by the Chinese.

There are other problems of nomenclature too, since in a number of cases the names by which towns, and even provinces, were known in the early part of this century were subsequently changed. Since many of the offices and institutions dealt with in this book were identified by the place-names then current, we have as a general rule continued to refer to places by their old names. Thus the provinces of Liaoning and Hopei, for example, will be referred to throughout by the names by which they were known between 1911 and 1928: Fengtien and Chihli. The sole exception to this rule is the capital of Fengtien province, the city that has been variously known as Fengtien, Ch'eng-te, and Shenyang (from 1929). It was in fact officially known between 1923 and 1929 as Fengtien *shih*, or Fengtien city.[13] Consequently, to avoid confusion between the name of the province and that of its capital, the latter will be referred to here as Mukden, which is both the old "Manchu" name for it and the name by which it was known in the West right up till the time of the establishment of the People's Republic in 1949.

At the beginning of this century, the population of the Northeast was spread very thinly throughout the three provinces: farming communities in the river valleys and more accessible areas; bandits, lumbermen, gold prospectors, seekers of ginseng root, and dealers in elkhorn and furs scattered throughout the mountainous or inhospitable hinterland.[14] Construction of the railways played a decisive part in throwing the frontier open to settlement and development. Grains once fed to the pigs could be transported to market and sold as cash crops for export. Development skills, labor, and capital quickly poured in, mainly from Russia and Japan, but also, of course, from China itself. The main section of a British-built railway line between Peking and Mukden was completed in 1903 as far as Hsin-min-t'un, and after interruption occasioned by the Russo-Japanese War of 1904–5, the line was completed in 1907. The 2,500-kilometer Chinese Eastern Railway network, which formed a T-shaped grid across the north and down through the heart of the three provinces, was completed by Russia in 1903. Shortly after its completion, Russian plans had to be greatly revised because of defeat in the Russo-Japanese War. In the Portsmouth Treaty of 1905, the Russian-leased territory in the Kwantung Peninsula and all Russian rights in the section of the Chinese Eastern Railway south of Changchun were transferred to Japan. By the Treaty of Peking which followed, the Chinese government gave formal consent to the transfer.

To administer its gains, the Japanese set up two major new institutions: the South Manchuria Railway Company, a semigovernmental organization that from its inception with a capitalization of 200 million yen was Japan's largest company, and a Kwantung Government administration, initially under a Governor-General, responsible for the administration of the leased territories and also for the policing of the railway lines. The South

Manchuria Railway Company, often simply known by its abbreviated Japanese name Mantetsu, was very much more than a mere railway company. Indeed its first president, Gotō Shimpei, took as his model the East India Company, an organization that was of course involved in the whole range of colonial activity.[15] Mantetsu's major activities, apart from its obvious railway focus, were in the towns that had grown up on lands adjacent to the railways, and in which, following Russian precedent, the company claimed virtually exclusive administrative authority. Residents of these areas paid a local tax to the company, which ran services such as gas, electricity, water, schools, hospitals, and hotels, and it was within these so-called Japanese settlements that the main Japanese business, banking, and industrial concerns came to be concentrated. There were also, however, other lands run by the company, outside these towns, that were either directly assumed from the Russians in 1905 or else acquired, sometimes in very cloudy and uncertain circumstances, during or after the war.[16] These included the enormous coal deposits at Fu-shun and elsewhere in the vicinity of Mukden, the iron at An-shan, and various port and harbor works at An-tung and Ying-k'ou. The interests of the company were so great, in short, that it constituted an *imperium in imperio*, greatly limiting and conditioning the sovereignty of successive Chinese administrations in the Northeast. One scholar concludes from this:"De facto and increasingly from 1905, Manchuria was a piece of colonial property, probably even more effectively so than India or Java. . . . Manchuria was in many ways the kind of *tabula rasa* where a developmental blueprint could most easily and quickly be translated into reality by a determined manager with technology, organization, and capital to invest."[17] Although such a formulation appears to us to go too far, it is indisputable nevertheless that Japanese wealth, resources, and potential military might were always greater by far than those of any Chinese authority in the Northeast, and the latter can therefore not be studied without due consideration of the workings of the Japanese connection. That Japanese control was not absolute, however, and that the Chinese authorities were often far from being puppets are points that should become clear in the course of this book.

In the period with which we are mainly concerned, 1911–28, the economic importance of the three Northeastern provinces to both China and Japan increased enormously, and since contention for this wealth was a prime factor conditioning their relations, a sketch of some of the main economic developments is appropriate at this point. The economy of the region began by being closely tied to the demand in Japan, and after 1908 in Europe also, for the soya bean, an enormously valuable and versatile crop that was used either in the form of oil for lighting, household, or industrial purposes or as cake for fodder or fertilizer. Its production increased fourfold between 1907 and 1927, from 39.9 million to 158 million bushels, by which time nearly half the world's supply of soya was coming from Northeast China's three provinces.[18] Though the foreign trade of the region's ports was a mere 3.5 percent of that of the country as a whole in 1903, by 1928 its proportion was up to 32.5 percent, of which the major item continued to be soya, accounting for 59 percent of the total export value down to 1931.[19] Furthermore, though the balance of trade in the early years was occasionally unfavorable, from 1920 it registered every year a healthy surplus, in marked contrast with the situation in the rest of China. Thus, while a favorable 1913 balance of three million taels in the three Northeastern provinces rose by 1928 to 105 million, in the same period the deficit in the rest of China increased from 169 to 310 million taels.[20] But perhaps the most significant index of the growing importance of the Northeast to the economy of China as a whole is provided by the following figures, in which the economic weight of the single province of Fengtien in 1929 is measured against the country as a whole. It accounted then for 33.0 percent of total coal output, 32.7 percent of total iron output, 21.7 percent of railway mileage, 21.5 percent of foreign trade, 21.5 percent of power capacity, and 85.5 percent of bean production. Its population, however, was a mere 3.2 percent of the country's total.[21]

In reading these figures, however, one must understand that the major cause, controller, and beneficiary of this development was not China but Japan. The major coal and iron mines, trunk railway lines, foreign trading and shipping companies, and much of the electric power supply system were Japanese. As far as trade is concerned, Japan's share of the external trade of the three provinces rose from 32 percent in 1908 to 39 percent in 1927, an increase in value of about eight and a half times; trade between the three provinces and the rest of China, however, shrank in the same period from 39 percent to 22 percent of the total, which meant an increase in value of only about four times.[22] Most, or about 85 percent, of Japan's foreign investment in 1927 was concentrated in China, and about 80 percent of that sum, just under 700 million yen, was invested in the three provinces of the Northeast.[23] By far Japan's largest single overseas investment, was, of course, the South Manchurian Railway Company, origi-

8

Number of Factories and Capital Invested in the Industrial
Sector in the Three Eastern Provinces, 1932

Category	Number of factories	Percent of whole	Capital (million yen)	Percent of whole
Metal industry	248	6%	34.61	14%
Machine tools	223	6	27.65	11
Ceramics	510	13	18.29	8
Spinning	800	21	23.92	10
Chemicals	641	17	60.02	25
Foodstuffs	712	18	48.88	20
Miscellaneous	749	19	28.95	12
TOTAL	3,883	100%	242.32	100%
Japanese capital	727	18%	154.37	64%
Chinese capital	3,081	80	67.98	28
Other foreign capital	75	2	19.97	8

SOURCE: Nishimura Shigero, "Dai kakumei-ki ni okeru Tōsanshō, rōdō mondai o chūshin ni" (The Three Eastern Provinces during the Great Revolution), Ajia seiji gakkai, ed., *Ajia kenkyū*, Oct. 1972, p. 33.

nally capitalized at 200 million yen but increased in 1920 to 440 million.[24] Throughout the industrial sector of the economy, however, Japanese influence was dominant. Table I relates to the year 1932, but indicates the accumulated result of the tendencies at work in the period with which this book is concerned. The fact that 64 percent of the capital invested in the industrial sector was Japanese is the most striking indication of the extent of Japanese influence and control.

In the dual economy of the Northeast the Chinese sector was inferior, a fact that was of the utmost political significance. The contradiction between Japanese power and Chinese sovereignty became acute as the nationalist movement matured throughout China in the 1920s, and as the Chinese population increased dramatically; in the period 1922–30, during which the Chinese government took active steps to promote and encourage colonization and settlement and for which reliable statistics are available, more than five million immigrants entered the Northeast, of whom just under three million were permanent settlers.[25]

THE PROTAGONISTS: CHINESE WARLORDISM AND JAPANESE IMPERIALISM

The subject of Chinese warlordism has been explored by a number of monographs, published and unpublished, since the appearance in 1966 of James Sheridan's pioneering study of Feng Yü-hsiang.[26] Sheridan's work

still provides the best simple definition of the term and an excellent general
account of what has become known as the warlord period. The term "warlord," he says, in Chinese history "ordinarily designates a man who was
lord of a particular area by virtue of his capacity to wage war. A warlord
exercised effective governmental control over a fairly well-defined region
by means of a military organization that obeyed no higher authority than
himself. From 1916 to 1928, virtually all of China was divided among such
regional militarists, big and small."[27]

Chang Tso-lin first came to prominence in Fengtien province because of
his role in crushing the republican revolutionaries there in 1911–12.[28] In
1916 he became military and civil governor of the province; within three
years he had extended his control over Kirin and Heilungkiang also, and
thus established a grip over the whole Northeast that was not broken, and
was only once even seriously challenged, during his lifetime. Beginning in
1918 he also expanded his power sporadically, both west into inner Mongolia and south into the North China plains and beyond. Early in 1925 he
became the major power in North China as a whole, and although he suffered some reverses thereafter, it was his forces, and his regime in Peking
from 1926, against which the Kuomintang's Northern Expedition under
Chiang Kai-shek was mainly launched. He was, in the last resort, the final
and main enemy of the revolutionary armies. He was, by any account, a
major warlord.

Although Chang's "ability to wage war" was fundamental to his success, no less so was his ability to maintain an effective peace over the
territories he ruled, and to extract from them the revenues necessary to
sustain his extensive military campaigns without goading their populations
to rebellion. The instrument that served him to both these ends was the
Fengtien clique, sometimes also known as the Mukden clique. The clique
was, of course, a common organizational form in Chinese military politics
of the time, but it is a kind of organization most difficult to define. Its unity
was not the ideological unity of a political party, nor was it that of a ritual-
ized brotherhood such as in a secret society. It was indeed a makeshift,
lacking any ideological unity, lacking the sense of shared coherent purpose
that more recent military regimes have derived from their experience of
colonialism or their common professional training, and lacking even a
leader of obvious charismatic proportions—for few would make such a
claim for Chang Tso-lin.

The very word "clique," with its primary English associations of exclu-

siveness, is scarcely appropriate to an organization so diffuse and so lacking in clear-cut purpose, program, or definition. There are, however, two
defining characteristics to which attention may be drawn. First is the sense
of provincial, or rather regional, solidarity that members shared as against
the rest of the country. But this must be qualified by several observations:
first, that membership was by no means confined to those born in the province; second, that unlike other parts of the country where regional loyalties
had deep historical roots, most members of the Fengtien clique were
settlers of first, or at most second generation, if not actually themselves
immigrants from Shantung and Chihli (Hopei); and third, that alongside the
sense of shared provincial identity there existed a drive within the Fengtien
clique that was perhaps stronger than in the case of any other warlord
clique to transcend regional origins and impose a unity on the country as a
whole. This latter may be explained in historical terms as stemming from a
consciousness of the strategic advantages enjoyed by the Northeast and
demonstrated by the unifiers of the country who had arisen there in the
past, particularly since it was the collapse of the last of these, the Ch'ing
dynasty, that provided the occasion for the rise of the Fengtien clique.
Within the clique there were, as will become clear, both a "mainstream"
faction, intent upon conquest and unification of the country as a whole, and
an "anti-mainstream" faction, which preferred to avoid the often expensive and risky burdens of unification campaigns and to concentrate more or
less exclusively on developing and exploiting the riches of the Northeast,
maintaining merely a sufficient military establishment to defend the frontiers and maintain order within them.

The second defining characteristic of the clique is that its internal structure was hierarchical and essentially feudal. In the absence of any fixed
institutional arrangements about the location of power and the mode in
which it should be exercised, personal relationships were paramount. The
clique, or the faction, as some prefer to call it, was, in social science terms,
a "leader-centered, dyadically-structured, clientilism-based structure."[29]
If it was represented in the form of a pyramid, then Chang Tso-lin stood at
its pinnacle, reserving to himself final authority in all fields, and confirmed
in his authority by the allegiance of a group of close aides and advisors
immediately beneath him, a group made up of senior military men, and a
few key civil officials such as the governor and advisers on foreign affairs
and railway matters. It was this group that was responsible for organizing,
administering, taxing, and policing the masses that made up the base of the

pyramid. The clique, because of its peculiar structure, had a strictly limited capacity to withstand stress or to undertake determined action. As Nathan puts it: "Factions enjoy less power capability than formal organizations because of the limitations on their extent, coordination, and control of followers implied by their basis in the clientilist tie, their one-to-one communications structure, and their tendency toward breakdown." [30]

Generally speaking, the particularistic connections that enable factions or cliques to cohere may be of considerable variety, [31] ranging from close family ties at the center through relationships of shared provincial or local origin, patron-protégé links of various kinds (teacher-student, boss-henchman, and so on) to shared institutional affiliation, past or present—as, for example, in the same school, university, military academy, office, or gang. However, whereas personal attachments of one or other of these kinds constituted the principal structural bonds that held the Fengtien clique together, it should be understood that personal loyalty was rarely absolute. Indeed, it was frequently no more than the product of the conviction that such personal attachment was the precondition for office and therefore for the rewards that flow from office, or even occasionally the best means—because the only means—of promoting the development of the region and the welfare of its people. Thus the clique was most homogeneous and united when it was successful and expanding, most susceptible to fissiparous internal pressures in times of defeat or of serious reverses and contractions in the sphere of its jurisdiction. The transformation of the Fengtien clique from its original nucleus of Chang and a handful of old bandit comrades into the powerful military machine and civilian bureaucracy that from the mid-1920's made serious bid to conquer all China forms an important theme in this study.

Sheridan has advanced the general proposition concerning the warlords that "none of them represented any important segment of the population, nor were their struggles the expression of genuine national or social movements." [32] Study of the Fengtien clique suggests that although this is undoubtedly true of the warlords individually, in the case of Chang Tso-lin in particular the clique as a whole may not be dismissed so simply. Since there was at the time no other path of professional advancement either for soldier or bureaucrat than through attachment to it, its makeup was extremely heterogeneous. Whereas Chang's interests were undoubtedly served first, the clique was responsible for many developments, not all of which can be dismissed as retrogressive. As it expanded greatly, especially in the mid-1920's, it took under its wing many who were influenced to a greater or lesser degree by the new currents of the time—nationalism, anti-imperialism, industrialization. Thereafter it functioned as the forum through which contending forces strove to press their cause on Chang, who was undoubtedly arbiter of last resort, but who allowed at times considerable autonomy to lower echelons of his administration so long as they functioned consistently with the few broad policy guidelines that he determined. The existence of opposing elements within the clique was widely recognized at the time, sometimes under the general terms "new men" and "old men," sometimes "civilian" and "military," sometimes "Japan-trained" as against "locally educated." The existence of these complexities suggests that it is necessary to look carefully at the Fengtien clique to see whether genuine national and social forces, even in embryonic form, may not have been at work within it.

The Japanese involvement in Northeast China, and with Chang and his Mukden clique, was many-faceted.[33] A consideration of Japanese policy from the narrow perspective involves a study of the diplomatic historical record, and of the conventional dichotomy that draws a line between the foreign ministries of Shidehara Kijūrō (1924–27) and Tanaka Giichi (1927–28), attributing to the former the characteristics of caution and negativeness, diplomatic internationalism, and a broad general concern with the exigencies of China policy as a whole; and to the latter, boldness and positiveness, a predilection for unilateral and military solutions, and a preoccupation with the exigencies of policy toward the Northeast to the virtual exclusion of that toward China as a whole. Here it will be argued that of greater significance than the difference between the two were the continuities underlying them both, deriving from conventions established before the time of either, at latest by the years of the Hara ministry (1918–21). At the root of all thinking about the Northeast from that time were the assumptions of its separateness from the rest of China—an assumption reinforced by the linguistic convention of referring to "China" and "Manchuria" as distinct and separate entities—and of the paramount importance of the rights acquired there by Japan as a result of the Russo-Japanese War.

Second, it is necessary to look at other lines of bifurcation in Japanese policy: between civilian and military on the one hand, and between China-based officers and officials and their home-based superiors on the other. This is necessary because Japan's actions in the Mukden Incident of September 1931 and the sequence of events leading up to the China war in

1937 are sometimes accounted for as a consequence of a breakdown either in the chain of authority between Tokyo and China, or in communications between military and civilian wings of the Japanese government. Conspicuous differences, it must be conceded, did often exist at both of these levels, but they too must be seen in the light of the overall structure of Sino-Japanese relations. Although the Japanese Ministry of Foreign Affairs, particularly between 1920 and 1928, issued repeated protestations of its neutrality and absolute nonintervention in the internal affairs of China, it was directing itself primarily externally, in effect pledging compliance with international opinion in the post–World War I climate and, after 1921, the post–Washington Conference climate, of democracy, internationalism, and, as far as China was concerned, the "open door." In doing so it was intent on maintaining a diplomatic and internationally acceptable stance. However, at the same time, there was another theme constantly reiterated in Tokyo that was primarily internally directed, that formed the basic assumptions of the officials and officers concerned with executing Japanese policy in China, and that was unchallenged by civilians and militarists alike: the inviolability of Japan's treaty rights and special interests in "Manchuria." When those rights and special interest were threatened, and when diplomatic processes were exhausted, intervention was assumed to be unavoidable. The fact that intervention on a large scale took place at several crucial stages, and minor interventions almost constantly, without any positive initiatives from Tokyo to prevent or put an end to them, indicates that nonintervention and intervention were seen as different expressions of the same China policy. Differences between civil and military wings of the Japanese government, or between Tokyo and its officers and officials in the field in China, were an occasional but by no means a necessary expression of this "two-faced" quality of Japanese policy.

The other important point to observe in the Japanese involvement is that of the relation between warlordism and imperialism—in particular, between Chang Tso-lin and Japan. This study makes clear that Chang was by no means simply a puppet in the service of Japanese interests. The strength of anti-Japanese and nationalist sentiment within the Fengtien clique was considerable, and Chang, particularly in his later years, was clearly affected by it. At the same time, his position in relation to Japan was highly vulnerable. Japanese power in the Northeast was in most respects greater than his own, and he could ignore the fact only at his peril. Furthermore, in the last resort, his security in the ongoing Chinese civil war positively depended on Japanese good will, to earn and retain which had to be a constant concern. Inevitably torn between these contradictory pressures, Chang therefore presents an ambiguous image. He became in fact the focus of the three main forces at work in the China of his day: Chinese tradition, represented in its most attenuated and debased form in warlordism; Chinese nationalism; and imperialism, especially Japanese imperialism. In relation to Japanese imperialism, Chang was therefore more than a mere puppet but less than a nationalist. It is clear, however, that the failure of Chang and the other warlords to achieve unification of the country, and their squandering of enormous resources to the point of pillaging the local economy in pursuit of every conceivable source of revenue to finance their inconclusive warfare, left China weak and divided, and made resistance to Japanese imperialist inroads all the more difficult.

CHAPTER ONE

Chang Tso-lin: Bandit to Governor

CHANG TSO-LIN: THE EARLY YEARS

The major Chinese figure of the period 1911–28 in the Northeast of China was undoubtedly Chang Tso-lin, with whose career we are here primarily concerned. He was a remarkable man, most successful of all the so-called warlords who dominated parts of China and contended for mastery over all of it in this period; yet a most enigmatic figure, whose life and character, for all the details that may be pieced together, must remain in the end largely a mystery. Although a modest corpus of literature has grown up about his peers and contemporaries—Yüan Shih-k'ai, Feng Yü-hsiang, Wu P'ei-fu, Yen Hsi-shan, and others—Chang has been but little studied.[1] There is no full-scale biography of him in any Western language; much of the Chinese literature about him is in the style of historical romance—an almost inextricable blend of fact and legend; and, although there are various biographies of him in Japanese, none has been published since 1928, the year of his death.

It is particularly in relation to the early years of Chang's life that reliable historical evidence is scarce.[2] Even about the date of his birth there has been wide disagreement; various authorities have suggested 1873, 1875, or even as late as 1879.[3] There can be no certainty about this, but the best authority seems to support the view that he was born in 1875. He was born on the 12th day of the second month according to the old lunar calendar, in the vicinity of Hai-ch'eng, a township about 130 kilometers south of Mukden that later developed into an important station on the South Manchurian Railway line. His grandfather had fled from his village in Chihli (now Hopei) during a famine in 1821, and, defying the then prohibition, moved into the Northeast. His father was a sometime gambler, bandit, and vagabond, and Tso-lin and his elder brother, Tso-fu, were raised largely by their

mother, apparently in very straitened circumstances. When he was around
10 years of age, however, his father died, and his mother remarried, this
time to a somewhat more prosperous and settled figure, a horse doctor,
after which the boys were better looked after. At 16, Chang Tso-lin left his
family to commence work as an errand boy in a local inn. When he was just
20 years of age, in 1894, the Sino-Japanese War broke out. Much of it was
fought in southern Fengtien province, and Chang became a soldier in a
cavalry unit of the Chinese forces. When the main Chinese armies withdrew in the spring of the following year at the end of the war, Chang
returned to his village and at 22 he "entered the greenwood." He became,
in other words, a bandit.

Banditry was a phenomenon common enough all over China, particularly in the time of upheaval such as that in which Chang Tso-lin was born,
but there were also in the Northeast certain peculiar features stemming
from the nature of the frontier society. "Squatters who failed to hit it off on
coming into contact with officials or the community in a new area or who
were driven away for attempted encroachment on local interests, then often
became outlaws. The history of spontaneous colonization in Manchuria
and Mongolia is closely interwoven with the history of banditry. Indeed the
pioneers were often squatters, wanderers and outlaws by turn."[4] Opium,
with which banditry was often closely associated, played the role in the
colonization of the Northeastern provinces of China that was played by
gold in places like California and Australia, drawing to unsettled, frontier
regions "men of adventure and enterprise." According to Lattimore, more
villages were founded in this area by such bandit groups than anywhere
else in the world: they were the "effective advance guard of normal settlement and exploitation," so that the bandit life that Chang Tso-lin chose is
not necessarily to be seen as the essentially predatory banditry of "social
disintegration and despair" common elsewhere in China.[5] The "hung-hu-
tzu" (Red Beards), as the bandits in the Northeast were popularly known,
often enjoyed quite wide popular support and somewhat of a "Robin
Hood" reputation for killing the rich and helping the poor (sha-fu chi-
p'in). Their reputation among the people was at least probably no worse
than that of regular army detachments, and a recent Chinese study of "the
people's revolutionary movement in the Northeast" quotes with approval
the popular adage: "When the bandits come, people send out presents of
food and drink; when the soldiers come, they point them the wrong way at
the crossroads."[6] Generally, however, bandits were bandits, in China as

elsewhere; they lived by raiding, robbing, or murdering the wealthy, be they landlords, usurers, businessmen, or even successful bandit rivals; sometimes by trading in opium; sometimes by plundering whole villages or towns; and sometimes by kidnaping travelers or rich men and holding them for ransom.[7]

There is little reliable evidence on what exactly Chang's band did, or how typical it was. Chang's reputation was that of "a good man with a gun, gifted with exceptional leadership ability, possessed both of bold originality and of diplomatic finesse. He knew how to choose the right moment to fight and the right moment to negotiate." [8]

From the beginning his closest comrades-in-arms were some young men from neighboring villages, Chang Ching-hui and Chang Tso-hsiang, the three being bound by an oath of blood brotherhood, the former to Chang as "elder brother," the latter as "younger brother." [9] When Chang's band was once outnumbered in a clash with a rival band, another chieftain, T'ang Yü-lin, came to Chang's aid, after which an offensive-defensive alliance was set up linking the two. Both were then operating in the vicinity of Pa-chiao-t'ai, in the country to the west of the Liao River.[10]

After the Boxer disturbances of 1900, the Ch'ing hold over local administration throughout the country was further weakened; so that the only real authority in the Northeast was that of the Russians, who sent a virtual army of occupation there, and the local hung-hu-tzu. The hung-hu-tzu consequently were wooed both by the Ch'ing authorities and by the Russians. In 1903 Chang was approached by the Prefect of Hsin-min and persuaded to ride into the town at the head of his force to assume the post of commander of the local garrison.[11] At the time there were about 230 men under his command. Shortly afterward he came under pressure from the Russians to assist them, and when the war between Russia and Japan broke out in 1904, he performed various services—scouting, intelligence—for the Russian army.[12] In this he seems to have been exceptional, since most of the other bandit leaders favored the Japanese from the start. It is also possible, however—and there is some reason for thinking—that he was playing a double game: not only aiding the Russians but cooperating with some elements of the Japanese forces at the same time.[13] When the Japanese army took Hsin-min, he was captured and sentenced to death as a Russian agent, but the evidence that he had given some cooperation to the Japanese, plus the belief that he could still be usefully employed by them, worked in his favor. A certain Japanese lieutenant, Idokawa Tatzuzō, relates being struck by his appearance—"his mien gentle as a woman but his speech and manner bold and direct"—and, thinking he might be worth saving, recommended mercy. Eventually this recommendation was adopted, and by an extraordinary coincidence the decisive role in determining his fate was played by the then Chief of Operations in the Japanese Army, Lieutenant Colonel Tanaka Giichi. Twenty-three years later, when the same Tanaka was Japanese Premier, Chang's murder by another Japanese officer marked the culminating point in his "positive" policy toward China. Throughout Chang's career the Japanese connection was important, but never more so than at the very beginning and very end of that career.[14]

After the war Chang's band continued to behave only partly as an official force, partly remaining true to its extralegal origins. Early in 1907 Chang invited to a banquet in Hsin-min a rival leader named Tu Li-shan, possibly the most powerful hung-hu-tzu in the whole Liaohsi (west of the Liao River) region. Ostensibly the meeting was to discuss the possibility of Tu also entering government service; in mid-feast, however, Tu and all his bodyguard were seized and murdered, his hoard of some four million gold roubles, plus weapons and horses, were then confiscated, and many of his men too went over to Chang.[15]

The administrative changes that the Ch'ing court adopted in the wake of the Russo-Japanese War gave Chang further opportunity for advancement. Foreign encroachment and domestic anarchy engendered a sense of crisis in which wide-ranging reforms were seen as unavoidable. The Manchus at this eleventh hour ordered that the Three Eastern Provinces' administration be brought in line with that of the rest of China; civil governors were appointed to each, under the overall jurisdiction of a governor-general possessed of extremely wide powers, and the military organization was completely revamped. The newly appointed Governor-General, Hsü Shih-ch'ang, moved up several important "New Army" units of the Peiyang Army—its crack 3d Division and two newly created mixed brigades (the 1st and 2d), while at the same time reorganizing the "old" provincial army units scattered throughout the Northeast.[16] Chang Tso-lin's garrison posting at Hsin-min was highly convenient, since, pending completion in 1907 of the final section of the Peking–Mukden railway, from Hsin-min to Mukden, all communications and officials passing between Peking and Mukden or other points further north had to cross his bailiwick. From his strategically advantageous position Chang made use of simple, but evidently effective, ingratiating gestures, such as the gift of his best horse and provision of an armed escort to Mukden for the passing Fengtien military commander Chang Hsi-luan in 1906, and a substantial bribe (10,000 taels) to him the following year, to win rapid promotion in the course of the military reorganization.* In 1907 he was moved to Cheng-chia-t'un in the Mongolian frontier region at the head of five battalions of troops, and expanded his force to seven battalions, moving farther north into the Mongolian frontier at T'ao-nan the following year when Chang Hsi-luan's reorganization plans were put into operation. In this reorganization all the Fengtien provincial army forces were regrouped into five route armies (hsün-fang-tui). Chang assumed immediate command of the forward route, Wu Chün-sheng of the rear, Feng Te-lin of the left, and Ma Lung-t'an of the right. The center route, based in the Mukden and T'ieh-ling area, was initially under the command of a certain Liu, but it too was to become part of Chang's direct command during the revolutionary disturbances of the autumn of 1911. When Chang moved to Cheng-chia-t'un in 1907, it is significant that the five battalions set up under him were commanded by himself and four of his oldest ex-bandit comrades—his blood brothers Chang Ching-hui and Chang Tso-hsiang, T'ang Yü-lin, the ally whose timely aid had once saved Chang's life, and Tsou Fen, one of his earliest henchmen. When he moved to T'ao-nan, he assumed control over two additional battalions that had been under the command of Sun-Lieh-ch'en, with his overall strength rising to 3,500 men.[17] All of these men were to remain close to Chang throughout his subsequent rise, at the core of what became known as the Mukden clique.

As elsewhere in China, it was the wide-ranging reform program adopted in the Northeast after the Russo-Japanese War that laid the ground for the Revolution of 1911—although the forces of revolution accomplished less there than, given their apparent strength, they might have been expected to. In the event, the major beneficiary of the aborted revolution was Chang Tso-lin.

*Sonoda, Kaiketsu Chō Sakurin, pp. 47–48; Wang, Tung-pei, p. 9. By some accounts Chang remained a bandit till 1906, when persuaded by Chang Hsi-luan to enter government service (T'ien Pu-i teng, p. 62). Since T'ien agrees that Chang and his men were at that time stationed at Hsin-min, the difference relates only to the status of his force. What seems most likely is that Chang did actually enter government service in 1903, but functioned in the lawless years spanning the Russo-Japanese War more or less as a law unto himself, and that his unit then was substantially reorganized and expanded in the reforms initiated by Chang Hsi-luan.

In the military changes referred to above, the New Army units, moved to
the Northeast in the effort to restore order and put down the hung-hu-tzu,
were all commanded by Japanese-trained officers, graduates of the military
academy (the Shikan Gakkō) in Tokyo. All were members of Sun Yat-
sen's Revolutionary Alliance (T'ung-meng-hui), which had been set up in
Tokyo in 1905.[18] Likewise the officers appointed to staff the reorganized
Three Eastern Provinces Military Academy in Mukden were predominantly
revolutionary and in the position to exercise wide influence.[19] A Northeastern branch of the T'ung-meng-hui was set up in 1907 and, apart from its
strength in the army, was very influential in the newly established schools
and in the production of newspapers. T'ung-meng-hui organizers directed
their propaganda impartially at two groups that were modern (the students
and soldiers of the New Army) and one that was very traditional (the hung-
hu-tzu), evidently appraising the latter highly for the potential military role
it might play. The constant military pressure applied to these bandits by the
Ch'ing from 1907 on made them so susceptible to the revolutionary appeal
that 36 bandit leaders actually entered into alliance with the T'ung-meng-
hui.[20]

The bandits were not the only group with a well-established tradition of
armed resistence to the Ch'ing in the years leading up to the 1911 Revolution. In Taiping and Boxer times they seem to have spearheaded that resistance,[21] but the rapid social and economic change in the Three Eastern
Provinces after 1905, particularly the growth in population and the com-
mercialization of the economy consequent upon the completion of the railway network, meant that Ch'ing policies of rationalization and reorganization, and the tax increases that were necessary to pay for them, stimulated
opposition on a broad scale.

Tax increases led to a rising in the Ying-k'ou area in 1906, and the
addition of stiff "local" taxes to the normal tax burden in the Mukden and
Liao-yang area the following year stimulated protests involving some
30,000 people. In rural areas, opposition focused on the land surveys, from
which greatly increased tax assessments were being made, and in the urban
areas on the surtaxes known as the police levy and the school levy, as well
as on increased commodity taxes on items such as fish and salt.[22] The
quasi-autonomous village self-defense organization set up during the
breakdown of authority at the time of the Boxer and Russo-Japanese wars,
the Village Federations (Lien-chuang-hui), provided a readymade organizational structure for this resistance, and Chuang-ho and Fu-chou on the

eastern side of the Liaotung Peninsula became its focal points. Rebellion there in the summer of 1911 was only put down after a detachment of 1,000 troops had been sent in and fought a ten-day-long battle with the insurgents. Eventually suppressed, the smoldering resentments of the area were quickly rekindled in the disturbances that followed the October 1911 revolutionary outbreaks on the Yangtze.[23]

THE REVOLUTION IN THE NORTHEAST

These armed units, estimated to possess about 4,000 rifles among them, together with the bandit groups allied to the T'ung-meng-hui and the well-trained and -equipped 30,000-man New Army force, added up to an apparently formidable military strength on the revolutionary side at the time when news of the revolution broke in the Northeast.[24] In Mukden, where the fate of the Northeast was decided, the Provincial Assembly provided the forum within which currents of change and reaction met and contended. It had been set up only two years previously and represented a major fruit of the late Ch'ing reforms. Progressive elements from educational and military circles there gathered under the leadership of Chang Yung, a wealthy Manchu aristocrat and seasoned revolutionary who had already spent three years in prison for his part in a bomb incident in 1905. A reformist group of constitutionalist gentry was loosely gathered around the Assembly President, Wu Ching-lien; and a diehard conservative faction had been organized by Yüan Chin-k'ai.[25] Yüan Chin-k'ai, a Confucian scholar and originally teacher in an old-style academy in Mukden, was later to emerge as one of the outstanding civilian political leaders in Fengtien under Chang Tso-lin.

The New Army in the Northeast was made up of two divisions, the 6th under Wu Lu-chen, and the 10th under Chang Shao-tseng, and a mixed brigade, the 2d, under Lan T'ien-wei. The military advantage that this formidable force should have conferred on the revolutionary cause was, however, much reduced by the fact that when the revolution broke out on the Yangtze on October 10, the 20th Division was already in Chihli, having been ordered south to take part in autumn exercises due to be held at Yung-p'ing, about 80 kilometers south of the Great Wall.[26] The 6th Division was also ordered south, and its commander, Wu Lu-chen, complied, evidently believing that he would thus be in a better position to put pressure on Peking.[27] In the latter part of October the maneuvers of these two divisions did indeed help to put the regime into a critical position: Chang's 20th

Northeast China in the 1920's

Area of map on facing page

0   300 Miles

0   300 Kilometers

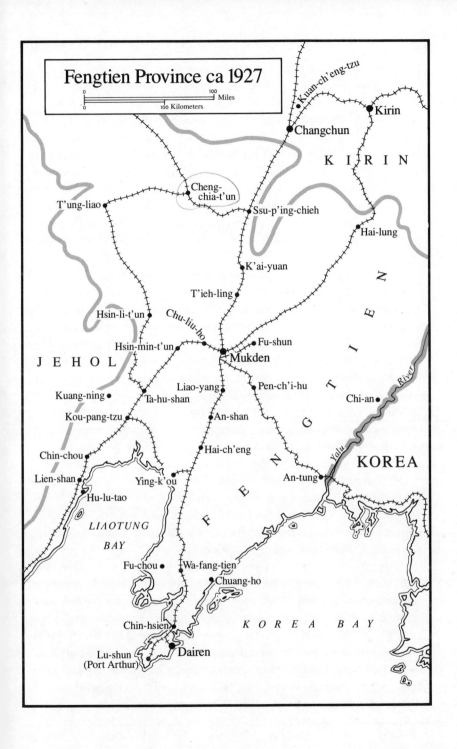

Fengtien Province ca 1927

Kuan-ch'eng-tzu

Kirin

Changchun

KIRIN

Cheng-
chia-t'un

T'ung-liao

Ssu-p'ing-chieh

Hai-lung

K'ai-yuan

T'ieh-ling

Hsin-li-t'un

Chu-liu-ho

Fu-shun

Hsin-min-t'un

Mukden

JEHOL

Liao-yang

Pen-ch'i-hu

Chi-an

River

Kuang-ning

Ta-hu-shan

Kou-pang-tzu

An-shan

FENGTIEN

Chin-chou

Hai-ch'eng

KOREA

Lien-shan

Ying-k'ou

An-tung

Yalu

Hu-lu-tao

LIAOTUNG
BAY

Fu-chou

Wa-fang-tien

Chuang-ho

KOREA BAY

Chin-hsien

Lu-shun
(Port Arthur)

Dairen

Division, commanding the northeastern approaches to the capital at Luan-chou, refused orders to move to the relief of the imperial armies on the Yangtze, and Wu's 6th Division, when ordered to move against the re-volutionaries who had caused Shansi province to declare independence, proceeded only as far as Shih-chia-chuang, at the intersection of the Peking–Hankow railway with the branch line to Shansi, thus threatening the supply lines of the imperial forces.[28] In Mukden itself there remained only the 2d Mixed Brigade of Lan T'ien-wei, whose barracks quickly be-came a center of revolutionary organization and excitement. All three commanders were signatories of a telegram calling on the Ch'ing to estab-lish a constitution and concede responsible parliamentary government within the year.[29]

However, the balance of forces in the North shifted very rapidly with the emergence from retirement of Yüan Shih-k'ai on November 2 and his ac-ceptance of the court's commission as Prime Minister with full powers to deal with the crisis. Wu Lu-chen and Chang Shao-tseng were both removed at once from their commands and on November 7 Wu was assassinated by a Ch'ing agent.[30] As a result, the importance of Lan T'ien-wei's brigade in Mukden was enhanced. Lan and his comrades hoped, however, that force would not be necessary to achieve their goals. Their favored plan, drawn up around November 6, was for a bloodless coup to dispose of Governor-General Chao Erh-hsün, and to declare independence of the court in Peking under Lan T'ien-wei as military governor and Wu Ching-lien as civil gov-ernor. Having consolidated the Northeast as a revolutionary base they could then send troops south against Peking. Various detachments of Liaotung rebels were commissioned as official units in the National Revo-lutionary Army, and November 11 was fixed as the day for the meeting of officers, officials, and notables on the premises of the Provincial Assembly, where the planned coup was to take place.[31]

Delay, and the hope that violence would not be necessary to attain their ends, were fatal to the revolutionaries. The Governor-General, working in consultation with Yüan Shih-k'ai, was able to subvert the revolutionary command of Lan's mixed brigade by working through a "loyalist" artil-lery officer, Nieh Ju-ch'ing, and to prepare for the planned confrontation in the Assembly chamber by summoning to Mukden the provincial army forces of Chang Tso-lin. At 36 years of age, Chang thus moved to the center of the political stage in the Northeast, and he remained based in Mukden for almost the whole of his subsequent career.[32]

The confrontation, when it came in the Assembly chamber on November 11, was brief and dramatic, but for all these reasons anticlimatic. Lan had already taken refuge in the Japanese quarter when the meeting began. His cannon, deployed by Nieh Ju-ch'ing, were trained on the doors of the Assembly building, while uniformed men of Chang Tso-lin's ringed it inside. When a revolutionary spokesman tried to interrupt the opening address of the Governor-General, Chang Tso-lin drew his revolver and threatened to shoot him. The revolutionary challenge at once subsided: Chao was elected president of a Peace Preservation Association (Pao-an-hui), and Nieh, who formally assumed command of all the troops in the province, Chang Tso-lin becoming his deputy. The revolutionary leader, Chang Yung, evidently did not despair even then of achieving something through peaceful means, since he became one of the association's vice-presidents.[33] He retained close contact with both Chao Erh-hsün and Chang Tso-lin, though he also took the main initiative a few days later, on the 17th, in organizing a United Progressive Association (Lien-ho chi-chin-hui), which he hoped would serve as a united front of the various revolutionary organizations.[34] Even after the opening of hostilities by various revolutionary groups in the Liaotung Peninsula on November 20—hostilities that quickly spread throughout the peninsula and drew a response even in Mukden itself— Chang Yung continued to meet with and appeal to Chao to sever relations with the Ch'ing. There is no evidence to suggest that he conceived of the revolution as meaning anything more than that.[35]

While Lan remained in Mukden, fearful of provoking Japanese intervention by moving openly against Chao and Chang Tso-lin, and continuing to hope for concessions from them, a number of battles were fought and rebels in various parts of the Northeast were either isolated or defeated, or neutralized by negotiations. When a provisional republican government under Sun Yat-sen was set up at Nanking in the New Year period of 1912, the importance of quickly sending relief to the forces struggling in the Northeast was realized. Lan T'ien-wei, then in Shanghai, was appointed military governor and was dispatched by sea at the head of a small naval flotilla to link up with the rebels of Liaotung. Before it landed in late January, however, the revolutionary position in Fengtien had deteriorated further. Early in the month the major local commander, Ku Jen-i, succumbed to the blandishments of the negotiators sent him by the Governor-General and accepted a sum of 10,000 taels in order to reconstitute his men as the official army garrison for the Chuang-ho area.[36] Then, on January

23, Chang Yung was murdered by Chang Tso-lin's troops, by prearrangement with Chao, on emerging from a dinner engagement with Yüan Chin-k'ai—thus paying with his life the penalty for his naïveté and continued hope for a bloodless revolution. A reign of terror followed in Mukden, in which Chang Tso-lin's men killed somewhere between 100 and 300 revolutionary figures.[37] When Lan T'ien-wei's little flotilla landed, therefore, the revolutionaries in the Northeast had lost their main leadership and coordinating center. Above all they had lost the initiative to the enemy. It is remarkable under the circumstances that they fought back so well: Wa-fang-tien was captured on February 10; T'ieh-ling was captured and held for three days from the 15th; K'ai-yüan for four days from the 21st.[38]

These victories are so much more surprising when it is recalled that the emperor had stepped down and handed over power to Yüan Shih-k'ai on February 12, whereupon hostilities in the country at large had virtually ceased. On February 17 Lan received positive orders to withdraw his force, however, and did so a few days later, abandoning the Liaotung rebels.[39] The hopelessness of their position was underlined by the fact that Lan's forces also faced the threat of Japanese intervention: he was first "warned" of the consequences of any infringement of the "neutral zone" adjacent to the Japanese-administered Kwantung territory, then was issued a specific demand that he withdraw.[40] The rebel areas in Liaotung were soon completely pacified, and conservative "republican" forces were left triumphant in the Northeast.

Chang Tso-lin was technically the second-in-command of the army in Fengtien but actually, because of his local power base, he was second to none. Ochiai Kentarō, Japanese consul general in Mukden, reckoned that Chang's power was greater even than that of the Governor-General.[41] Given the extent of Japanese interests in the Northeast, it was a matter of some importance therefore to determine how to react to his rise. On January 26 Chang proclaimed to Ochiai that from his point of view nothing could be worse than to have southern (republican) control extend to the Northeast.[42] One alternative to which Chang gave serious consideration was that of an independent loyalist stronghold based in the old Manchu capital at Mukden. With military backing from Chang, it seemed at least feasible, and contacts were opened between Chang and Kawashima Naniwa, the principal Japanese plotter for the restorationist cause, through a Japanese adviser then attached temporarily to Chang, Captain Machino Takema.[43] The talks were unproductive, however, at least partly because of uncertainty about the official Japanese position on these schemes, an uncertainty that the involvement of other Japanese with the revolutionaries fighting against Chang's men only served to heighten.[44] Chang did, nevertheless, persist with a staunchly monarchist position, even after Yüan Shih-k'ai had come to terms with the revolutionaries—news that Chang greeted with a call for a southern expedition to punish him and restore the throne.[45] He was only persuaded to swallow his initial bitter abhorrence for the republic when messengers from Yüan arrived the following day bearing the clinching argument—a substantial sum of money.[46]

CHANG'S RISE IN THE THREE EASTERN PROVINCES

Fengtien

In 1912 Chang's soldiers were reorganized and expanded into a division, the 27th, remaining in Mukden. An old bandit comrade, Feng Te-lin, commanded a second Fengtien division, the 28th, stationed at Kuang-ning in the west of the province, near the Mongolian border.[47] Under the patronage of the military governor, Chang Hsi-luan, who was his sworn "father," Chang continued quietly to consolidate his power in the province. When Chang Hsi-luan retired in August 1915, however, Chang's claim to succeed him was ignored. Yüan Shih-k'ai preferred to appoint a close follower from Hupei, Tuan Chih-kuei, no doubt largely with a view to ensuring the support of the Northeast in the enthronement attempt he was then planning. Formally, Tuan's position was the equal of the old viceroy, since he was not only Fengtien military governor but also supervisor of Kirin and Heilungkiang; in practice, he lacked any independent power base, and his fortunes were intimately tied up with those of his declining Peking patron. Chang's strength, by contrast, was local, and in Mukden itself was unchallenged. Chang was also supposed to have been a supporter of Yüan Shih-k'ai, but he avoided any involvement in the campaign to have him declared emperor. Instead he agitated for a "Fengtien for the Fengtienese," thus intimidating Tuan and frustrating Yüan to the point where eventually, on April 16, Tuan fled to Peking, leaving Yüan little alternative but to appoint Chang his official successor, military and civil governor of Fengtien province.[48] These offices, known in Chinese as chiang-chün and hsun-an-shih at the time of Chang's appointment, were renamed tu-chün and sheng-chang in the reforms of July 1916, which followed Yüan Shih-k'ai's death. The formal title of the office of military governor varied at different times during the next decade, but the word *tuchün* continued to be used in popular parlance, and indeed it even passed into English usage as a word synonymous with warlord.*

Chang's appointment came at a fateful time. Since the summer of 1915, a plan had been gathering support in army and navy circles in Tokyo to overthrow Yüan Shih-k'ai. On March 7, 1916, the plan was finally ratified at cabinet level. As part of the plan, army backing was given to the plan of the Manchu supporter, Kawashima Naniwa, to use the Mongol loyalist armies of Prince Babojab, backed by Japanese arms and adventurers, to restore the Ch'ing emperor in a domain that was to include the Three Eastern Provinces, Mongolia, and North China.[49] A special Foreign Office representative, Morita Kanzō, was sent out to swing reluctant diplomatic officials behind the plan, and the Governor-General of Kwantung province ordered all consuls in the Northeast to turn a blind eye to the activities of Japanese involved in the plotting.[50] However, around the time of Chang Tso-lin's appointment to governorship of the province, opposition to this plan began to crystalize around a proposal from Yada Shichitarō, consul general at Mukden.

Yada also favored promotion of an independent "Manchuria-Mongolia," but argued that Japanese interests would be better served by encouraging Chang Tso-lin to take the steps necessary to set it up, rather than by becoming involved with Manchu restorationists plots.[51] His plan quickly drew support from Foreign Minister, Ishii Kikujirō, Army Deputy Chief of Staff Tanaka Giichi, and other important officials. However, their support was not without reservations, understandable in view of the fierce opposition Chang had expressed only a year previously to the "21 Demands" by which Japan, through the issue to Yüan Shih-k'ai in January 1915 of a series of requests in the form of a virtual ultimatum, greatly expanded its various interests and privileges in China.[52] Doubts on this score were set aside, however, possibly discounted as demonstrating no more than Chang's opportunism, and on April 10 Tanaka instructed the deputy chief of staff in the Kwantung Army to approach Chang in the utmost secrecy and discuss a secessionist regime. Negotiations were

---

*Asano, pp. 31–32; Sonoda, *Kaiketsu Chō Sakurin*, p. 96. Particularly from 1922 there was a tendency to avoid use of the word *tuchün* because of the perjaorative associations it had acquired in popular usage. Despite the changes in official nomenclature to *tuli* in some provinces from December 1922, or to *tupan*, more generally from December 1924, in an attempt to confer a refurbished image on the office, it remained in fact the same office and continued generally to be known as *tuchün*. In the Inner Mongolian subprovincial special areas (*t'e pieh ch'ü-yü*), which did not attain full provincial status until 1928, the military governor continued to be known throughout this period as *tutung*.

opened through a trusted adviser of Chang's, Yü Ch'ung-han. Yü, born in Liao-yang *hsien* in 1871, had begun his career as a *hsiu-ts'ai*, or provincial examination graduate, under the Ch'ing. He went to Japan in 1891 and spent a number of years as an instructor of Chinese at Tokyo Foreign Language University, studying Japanese and Russian at the same time. During the Russo-Japanese War he served the Japanese forces as an interpreter, and from early in the republic he became an adviser on foreign affairs to the Chinese authorities in Mukden. Having thus come into contact with Chang, he remained thereafter close to him, serving him in effect as "foreign minister" in many of the diplomatic negotiations in which Chang subsequently became involved.[53]

Though the second plan, originally proposed by Yada, was adopted, the first, with which it was quite inconsistent, was not canceled. Japanese policy was confused, but significantly there was no dissent at any level from the proposition that an "independent" (Japanese-protected) "Manchuria-Mongolia" should be promoted. The differences lay between those who favored a monarchist and those who favored a militarist basis for constructing such a state. Before the difference could be resolved, the plotting suddenly erupted into action. On May 26, 1916, Mitsumura Yutaka, a 25-year-old Japanese second lieutenant, put a bomb under his coat and threw himself at what he took to be Chang Tso-lin's carriage in a street in Mukden. Mitsumura belonged to the wing of the Japanese military that was plotting the Manchu restoration. He was opposed not only to the usurper Yüan Shih-k'ai but also to Chang Tso-lin for having apparently abandoned his earlier loyalist principles. Chang escaped unhurt from the attack, but knowing the perpetrators were Japanese, he lost interest in the talks that Yü Ch'ung-han was engaged in, and soon they were suspended.[54]

Yüan Shih-k'ai, who had been sadly disappointed at the hostile response from the country to the announcement of his imperial pretensions, suddenly died on June 6, 1916. One immediate consequence was that the Japanese government's March decision to use Mongolian armies to overthrow him and restore the Ch'ing dynasty lapsed. Instead, Japanese support was given to the new President, Li Yüan-hung, and, from July 1917, to the Anhwei clique of Tuan Ch'i-jui and Hsü Shu-cheng.[55] This was one of the two rival groups into which Yüan's Peiyang Army split soon after his death, and which began very soon to contend against each other and against Chang's Fengtien clique for dominance. Some aspects of Japanese involvement with the Anhwei clique are dealt with below. Not until the defeat of the Anhwei clique in the Anhwei-Chihli war of 1920 did Japanese attention at the highest levels turn again seriously to the question of aid for Chang Tso-lin.

Involvement by Japanese army officers and adventurers with the Babojab cause did not cease, however, with the attempt on Chang's life and the death of Yüan. Babojab's 3,000 Mongolian cavalrymen began to move south and east from their Hai-la-erh encampment on July 1916, and by August 14 they had reached Kuo-chia-tien on the South Manchuria Railway line about 200 kilometers north of Mukden. Arms, ammunition, and reinforcements were quickly dispatched to them from co-conspirators in Dairen. The change of circumstances in China and the change of line in Tokyo meant, however, that Babojab's enterprise was of much more limited scope than originally planned. Other Northeastern units of what was dubbed the Imperialist Army did not mobilize. The Mongols suffered from fatigue and shortage of food. As the battle with a Chinese army under Chang Ching-hui turned against the ''Imperialists,'' the Japanese military authorities called a halt to the hostilities and negotiated a safe withdrawal for the Mongolians under Japanese protection. Once they were well removed from the area of prime Japanese interest along the railway line, Japanese protection was withdrawn and Babojab himself was killed in the battles that ensued with pursuing Chinese forces in early October. The Mongol army was completely dispersed.[56]

The difficulties implicit in relating to the enormous concentration of Japanese economic and military power in Northeast China were thus brought home to Chang within months of his assumption of office as Governor of Fengtien. The fate of Babojab, once he had outlived his usefulness to the Japanese, may have served Chang as a useful political lesson. But just as important political lessons of another kind had to be learned if Chang was to transform his military retinue of ex-bandits and frontiersmen into the kind of political force capable not only of winning power in Fengtien but also of retaining and exploiting it there—and perhaps of expanding it to bid for wider leadership. Chang showed early signs of readiness to learn these lessons.

Late in 1916 he came under attack from two of his former bandit comrades: Feng Te-lin was a man whom Chang always referred to deferentially as "elder brother" but who was dissatisfied with the meager post he was awarded ("military affairs assistant" or *chün-wu pang-pan*) under Chang in 1916; and Tang Yü-lin was a bandit associate of Chang's from around the turn of the century, who had followed him into government service as a battalion commander in 1903 and had risen eventually to be chief of Chang's secret police. For his work in this latter capacity he was known as the "toad general." The campaign against Chang was organized by Feng and pitched on several different grounds. The basis was constitutional in Peking, where Feng attacked him as an autocrat who refused to convene or consult the Provincial Assembly, which, though supposed to meet annually, had in fact not done so for three years. The basis was almost the opposite in Mukden, where he strove to split Chang's followers by canvassing support for T'ang Yü-lin in a jurisdictional dispute between him and Wang Yung-chiang, who had been appointed all-province police chief in November 1916.[57] Wang's career was in marked contrast to that of Feng and T'ang. He had begun as a *kung-sheng*, or licentiate of the provincial examinations under the Ch'ing, thereafter earning rapid promotion through positions as magistrate, police chief, and tax bureau chief in various parts of the province before being appointed to this post.[58] He has won Chang's favor because of his reputation as a gifted bureaucrat, and had likewise impressed him in 1911–12 by the ruthlessness and efficiency he had demonstrated when called on by Chao Erh-hsün to assume responsibility in several of the important military campaigns against the revolutionaries.[59] Immediately after his appointment in November 1916, he challenged the powers of the secret police by arresting an old friend of T'ang's who had enjoyed his protection in operating a large-scale gambling business in Mukden.[60]

Chang enjoyed good political connections in Peking, and with his purely formal concession on the issue of reconvening the Assembly, the campaign against him there fizzled out. The difficulties in Mukden were potentially much more serious, however. To the surprise of many, Chang refused the pleas of T'ang and Feng for intervention against Wang, a decision that pushed them to the brink of rebellion. Eventually the pressure of superior military force, and the failure to induce other defections among Chang's lieutenants, forced them to back down. In June 1917, Feng and T'ang finally lost all political credibility by attaching themselves closely to the short-lived imperial restoration campaign under Chang Hsün. T'ang escaped when the campaign collapsed, but Chang Tso-lin had to intercede with Peking to spare the life of the captured Feng Te-lin.[61]

The outcome of the affair was that Chang's direct military power was expanded by two divisions: first, Feng's 28th, which was transferred directly to Chang's command; then, by the creation of an additional, 29th, division being authorized by Peking.[62] His most likely potential rival for dominance of the province, Feng Te-lin, was effectively eliminated, though once it was clear that neither he nor T'ang Yü-lin represented any further threat to him, Chang was prepared to be magnanimous to them; by 1919 both were back in Chang's camp as advisers, Feng presently as assistant governor of Mukden and Chin-chou.[63] Finally, and most important, Chang had shown readiness to allow free reign in the administration of provincial affairs to qualified and competent civil officials, as well as a determination not to brook any interference with that administration by the unsophisticated, often ex-bandit comrades with whom he had ridden to power. Among men of his background, Chang's ability to attract the loyal services of talented bureaucrats like Wang Yung-chiang, Yü-Ch'ung-han, and Yüan Chin-k'ai was unique. The services they performed for him were vital, Wang in financial affairs, Yü in foreign relations, and Yüan in domestic political affairs generally. Clearly there was friction in the relationship with Chang—Yüan left him several times during his career and Wang and Yü both eventually resigned, the former in 1926 and the latter in 1927—but on the whole they performed faithfully the invaluable service of running the machinery of government for him. Various examples of the services they performed are dealt with below, but at this stage the importance of Wang Yung-chiang in particular should be understood.

When Chang took office as Civil and Military Governor of the province in April 1916, it was running an annual deficit of between 2 and 3 million yüan, and owed 10 million to foreign and Shanghai banking concerns. His first nominee as Treasurer, a man named Wang Shu-i, was not able to improve on this situation; in fact, under him the indebtedness increased. After repeated clashes with Chang he soon resigned, and Wang Yung-chiang was appointed to the post in May 1917. Wang Yung-chiang immediately ordered a severe shake-up of the administration and a crackdown on malpractices, especially in the collection of revenues, together with a thoroughgoing rationalization of the business enterprises run by the government. Till his new measures could begin to show effect, he contracted a 3 million yen loan with the Japanese Bank of Chōsen in 1918, but was able to repay this by October of the following year. The accumulated deficit of his predecessors was also quickly wiped out and, by 1921, converted into a balance of 10 million yüan in the treasury.[64] This prosperity was of course the product not only of Wang's strict supervision of the administration, but also of the natural wealth of the provinces and the gradual development of its resources. Its continuation, therefore, depended on there being no serious interruption to the peace and political stability of the Northeast. However, decisions affecting this were quite beyond his jurisdiction. Indeed, it was Wang's financial wizardry that gave Chang the strength to expand militarily, just as in turn it was the military campaigns Chang embarked on that eventually wrought havoc with all Wang's plans.

Heilungkiang

Heilungkiang province is the vast expanse of Chinese territory roughly 200,000 square miles, lying to the south of the Amur or Heilung River, and therefore having a long frontier with Russia. It was the last part of China to be opened to regular settlement and cultivation, beginning only in 1850; because of its severe climate and the continuing possibilities of settlement in other, more accessible, parts of Fengtien and Kirin, it was populated very slowly and retained later than elsewhere a pristine Manchu-dominated social structure, with only an extremely weak Chinese gentry elite. Like Kirin province, it was always subordinate under the Ch'ing to the overall Northeastern jurisdiction of the Governor-General or Viceroy in Mukden. Again like Kirin, it gained briefly a formal equality of status with Fengtien under a military governor after the Revolution of 1911, but Chang Tso-lin quickly moved to reestablish traditional Fengtien dominance once he was ensconced in Mukden.

Just as Chang Tso-lin gradually consolidated his military dominance over Fengtien after 1911 but did not formally accede to the governorship until 1916, so likewise in Heilungkiang did Hsü Lan-chou. Hsü was a Chihli man by origin, graduate of the Hunan Army College (Hunan-lu-chün hsueh-t'ang), who first came to the province in 1907 and who, from 1914, commanded the province's major military force, the 1st Division.[65] By June 1917, his position appeared impregnable, and acting apparently on this belief, Hsü gave Pi Kuei-fang, third in the line of tuchün appointed by Peking since 1912, just 24 hours to leave the province.[66] Pi obligingly withdrew, leaving Hsü in de facto control as civil and military governor. Almost immediately, however, Hsü declared his support for the Ch'ing restorationist coup engineered by Chang Hsün in July 1917, though he changed his mind very quickly, declaring his allegiance to the republic again as it became clear the restoration cause was doomed to fail.[67]

This provided the pretext for his enemies to attack him and demand his

removal, and for Chang Tso-lin first to supply military pressure in the guise
of mediation, then to use his influence in Peking to have his own nominee,
Pao Kuei-ch'ing, appointed on July 26 to fill the tuchün position in Hsü's
stead. Pao was a man from the same village as Chang, and was soon further
tied to him by marriage alliance. He was also a powerful figure in his own
right—a direct protégé within the Peiyang Army of Tuan Ch'i-jui, and
from August 1915 National Director of Military Training Schools. With
such connections his appointment was not to be easily resisted. On September 23, 1917, Hsü yielded to the order for his transferral to Chang's
direct command in Fengtien; Pao's appointment took effect, and Chang
Tso-lin's political and military influence extended for the first time into
Heilungkiang. Hsü Lan-chou, like Chang's defeated protagonists in Fengtien province, was later rehabilitated, took part in the southern military
campaigns of 1918, still later becoming chief of the general staff and one of
Chang's senior advisers.[68]

Chang's dominance over Heilungkiang was established quickly and apparently with ease. Unlike the situation in neighboring Kirin, there is no
record of any significant opposition from within the province. Two years
later, when Sun Lieh-ch'en assumed office there in August 1919 as part of
a reshuffle of top posts in the Northeast, he took with him a military chief
of staff, chief secretary, treasurer, and police chief, all of whom were
Fengtien men and close associates of Chang Tso-lin.[69] This appears to
have been a fairly typical mechanism for the assertion of Chang's control over the other two provinces of the Northeast. Furthermore, in
Heilungkiang in particular the sense of provincial identity was extremely
weak, so that official posts in both civil and military wings of the government came to be dominated by Fengtien men. (See Chapter 3, p. 85.)

Kirin

Kirin province bore many similarities to adjacent Heilungkiang. Although its 81,000 square miles were rich in mining, forest, and agricultural
possibilities, its population until World War I was only a little over 5 million, and its potential was only beginning to be tapped. As in
Heilungkiang, the collapse of Ch'ing authority was followed by a brief
period of uncertainty, during which it was ruled by a locally entrenched
militarist, Meng En-yüan, who attempted to establish control there, as
Chang Tso-lin did in Fengtien. Though he made greater efforts than Hsü
Lan-chou in Heilungkiang to resist the thrust of Chang's ambition, in the

Harry Tso hin   Davar McCormack

Studies of Manchuria coming of age
    new J. & W. scholarship based on the
    availability of reprints of supreb (?) primary
    source mats. & analysis

    hist'l decolonization — no mean task since
    the best mats are in J. w/ an unavoidable
    J. bias/ premise or, at best, non-Ch
    premise
    — as measured by the no. of times a Ch-lang
        source is cited in the fn's.
    — a ratio of 10:1 (?) to J. sources. (& Western?)

    So not only did Japan dominate the essential trade
    & ind'l sector of the NE prov. but also the scholarship
        & research / surveys
    — the poverty of good Ch lang source mats
        & secondary studies

in/ amid all this,   How does one make today
it nevertheless "that'll" a history of war & diplomacy (s p.152
An trad'l histories perhaps a necessary phase — but
hopefully one to be quickly superseded by studies / proving war?
or more substantial matters — the local eco. & trade networks
& relig'n, multiple currency systems, id'n, land holding + property
The people of trade, say bears, is not once mentioned, but so
   h
having read this one wonders "Where are the people?" How did
the live — & how did their lives contrib to the oft-repeated
claim that the NE was rich — ... ?

a major achievement in untangling web of intrigue & shifting alliances
that was warlord - imp'st politics of China's warlord period

(a prob. of false expectations)

"the Manchurian idea" of Japan — in the subtitle — yet
a major disappointment that it was not dev'd. & given short shrift

- the reader gets only the vaguest notion that
  some J. mil. & civilian officials held to this
  idea — but no knowledge / info about its
  evolution

    - surprising given its prominent mention in sub
  - we merely are informed that it exists, or illus. by periodic ex.
    but that hardly justifies its

Reading the intro one is excited by the thought
a new stage in the of this work studies of
China's NE may be coming of age. yet the text itself
is quite conventional history: wars & diplomacy.
To the extent
I suppose that the latter is a precondition to
understanding the former in an environment of
intense mil + pol struggle, this book has rendered
a major service. But it also highlights the
length to which "deeper" studies of the NE's local society
& economy are needed.   & not just from Tokyo, & not justify the am
                           not just in China but from in Tokyo, der the Ft & cabinet
                                (J. power   century
                                (J.d. analysis & sources)

the Japanese involvement ∧ characterized ∧ persuasively
as "complexity" (133, 179-80
                                        ambitions p. 175
"J. plotting & interference" 130 (narrow self-interest & aggrand
intervention to CTL vs Russ Jt. 184-85   "officially sanctioned plotting" 256
"imp'list aggression" 215
war of Jap'sm/corruption 227
   essential consistency of ~)

Salience of honor of the J. position — (any J. Interpreter note
on this?) since the Hara cabinet of 1918-21 ??

CTL: "reasons for success" 152, 251

warlord politics — useful passing references & analysis though
various available citing recent studies.
                    double bind/problematic
Chang TL caught in the dilemma bc two forces; rampant
bent on unifying China against warlord competitors   ambitions were
+ J. invasion bent on manipulate power holders to main
maintaining the special its & interests by manipulat
power holders, at min., to maintain law & order and, at max
to exact from the concessions beyond the letter of past agmts.

activing suppression by Chang & overlord of the rising

tide of nat'ism ep 1925 summed up in the

mores blatant case of Chang Tsung-ch'ang in

ch # pp 155-56

eg Tso-lin - w/o inherent limitation "origin" or "ideology"

relations from the For Min's Archives

wartime pear - what boundary of 閉東 lased here?

les. How Chang was as much out of touch w/ the rise of Ch nat'ism

as was his J. patrons - an anti-J. nat'ism "failing" remedied/rectified we

Hsueh-liang became a torch bearer in 1935 & 1936

leading up to the dramatic Sian Incident of Dec. 1936

by Hsueh-liang's pivotal role in pressuring

CKS to resist the invaders who had crossed

him of his homeland

policy: its executors analyzed pp 225 ff

int/conscious on ends/rts : despised on means only 233-34

"china's rights for quick cash (not it) 1837, 244

raising the g. of the "legality" of treaties extracted under duress

w/ unpopular shortlived dictatorial gov'ts/regimes with shortlived

w/ J. - clash of final auth : the unreconcilable logic

of @ position 241 ±, 257

Chang Tso-lin, as ~~first~~ ~~noted~~ chief most noted benefactor + most noted then prime ~~and~~ victim of J. imp'ism in China, hovers like a phantom in modern Chinese studies. Heretofore, the paucity of solid factual studies of Chang Tso-lin into Chinese in power, + his location in the "peripheral "Northeast of its exceptional J. presence/or not ~~and~~ of ~~China~~ have led even students of China's early Republican period warlord to ~~neglect~~ avoid / give short shrift to the case? omit or Chang.

This book brings that era to an end, for now there can be no excuses.

[Check "warlord lit" cited p 269, n 26

Chin, Jerome. "Defining Ch warlords + their factions,"
        Bull of the SOAP, 31, pt 3 (1968), 563-600

Ch'i-Hsi-sheng Warlord Pol. in China 1916-1928
        (Stanford 1976)
            The Ch Warlord System (Wash DC 1969)

Pye, Lucien Warlord Politics: Conflict + Coalition —
        (NY 1971)

This book does more than that. It is an attempt at but I see + simplify the study of China's NW, pointing out how most non-Ch scholars unthinkingly usually adopt have generally/unthinkingly adopted the term rectify the long- for term "Manchuria" to refer to the area. To do this is no mean task, however, since the best research mat of a "Manchuria" under Jap domination — inc'd by the very plotters/protagonists Thus the mats. are hardly bias-free. But they do have the virtue, fully exploited by the Cormack, of making the pattern of J. thinking ("plotting" + "intervention" + "imperialist aggression" — all the Cormack's words) clear.

end he too succumbed to superior force and was replaced by a line of nominees of Chang, who ruled the province as an appendage of Fengtien until the time of the Japanese takeover in 1931.

Meng En-yüan was a common soldier who rose through the ranks after becoming a protégé of Yüan Shih-k'ai at the Hsiao-chan Military Academy in Tientsin late in the Ch'ing period. In 1904 he became a brigade commander in Kirin, later a division commander (the 23d), and in June 1913 assumed full command of all Kirin armies under the title Kirin *hu-chün-shih* (Defense Army Commissioner). A year later he became military governor of the province. One, not necessarily reliable, account has it that Meng was able to write only the character *hu*, meaning tiger, and that while he amused himself with music and women the internal affairs of the province were left to his son-in-law, Lu Ch'eng-wu, and the external affairs to his nephew, Kao Shih-pin.[70]

Like Feng Te-lin in Fengtien and Hsü Lan-chou in Heilungkiang, Meng was an early supporter of the imperial restoration sponsored by Chang Hsün in July 1917, and like them he quickly regretted it. Chang Tso-lin's secret requests for Meng's removal were answered on October 18, when Meng was ordered by Tuan Ch'i-jui to return to Peking to make way for a close subordinate of Tuan's, T'ien Chung-yü. Four days later Meng declared his province independent and, when a punitive expedition was organized by Chang Tso-lin, prepared for an early military showdown. That it did not come to this was due partly to the fact that T'ien, who had no base in the province or prospect of easily establishing one there, thought better of accepting the appointment, thus allowing the office temporarily to revert to Meng. And partly it was due to Chang Tso-lin's reluctance to risk an armed flare-up in the Northeast at a time when his power had only just been established in much of it—particularly on behalf of a powerful subordinate of Tuan Ch'i-jui and with no great advantage for himself. Meng won further respite with his dispatch in December 1917 of an expedition in support of the "moderate" Chinese Eastern Railway administration of General Horvath against the threat of a Red takeover. The seizure of part of the line and the policing duties thereafter undertaken by his 35,000 troops won favor from Peking and an appreciative cable from Chang Tso-lin asking that he be retained in office.[71]

By June 1919, when Chang reopened the attack, however, the situation had changed appreciably. Chang's control by this time was firmly established over both Fengtien and Heilungkiang, and in September 1918 he had been appointed inspector general of the Three Eastern Provinces (Tung-san-sheng hsün-yüeh-shih), for reasons to be discussed in the following chapter. It was an undefined position, yet one that implied recognition by the central government of Chang's primary interest in the area and his right to be consulted on major decisions affecting it; and it was sufficient in practice to justify his insistence on supervising and interfering in the affairs throughout the Northeast more or less as he wished. Chang felt on stronger ground, therefore, when he issued an open letter on June 11, 1919, asking Peking to dismiss Meng on grounds of financial irregularities in the affairs of the province, and to replace him with the commander of Chang's 27th Division, Sun Lieh-ch'en. Since Peking was reluctant to do this, fearing it might arouse strong opposition in Kirin against Fengtien domination, a compromise agreement was reached with Chang, whereby Pao Kuei-ch'ing was to be moved from Heilungkiang to Kirin, and replaced in Heilungkiang by Sun Lieh-ch'en. Meng was again ordered back to Peking, and again preparations were made on both sides toward a military show-down.[72]

In June, as the crisis began to develop, Meng announced to the Provin-cial Assembly his intention to resist. At the same time he stated that rather than let the province fall into the hands of a "certain ambitious fellow from a certain place"—a clear reference to Chang—"it would be better to hand it over completely to the Kwantung government."[73] This clear preference for Japanese rule rather than rule by Chang Tso-lin raises the question of Meng's relationships with Japan. Kirin province was obviously important to Japan, not only strategically, because of its borders with both Korea and Russia, but also in terms of all kinds of economic interests either acquired or sought there, principally in railways, forests, and mines. This is clear from the degree of importance attached to Kirin in the "21 Demands" and subsequent treaties of 1915, and in the Nishihara loans of 1918. Thus, when Chang Tso-lin, as inspector general, laid claim to jurisdiction over all three of the Northeastern provinces, and his relations with Meng began to deteriorate, evidently toward warfare, in mid-1919, the situation pre-sented peculiar problems for Japan. Morita Kanzō, Japanese Consul Gen-eral in Kirin, wrote two letters at this time to his home government, first pointing out that

it would be extremely worrisome for our Manchurian policy if the present advan-tageous position of Meng being interposed between Chang [Tso-lin] and Pao [Kuei-ch'ing] [Fengtien and Heilungkiang tuchün] were to break down completely and Chang were to display his true character, since he holds a position in every respect unfavorable to our interests.

Second, he noted that, should there be a changeover,

however friendly to Japan Meng's replacement may be, not only will this inevitably cause setbacks in the joint [Sino-Japanese] enterprises that till now have been connected with Meng, but we can hardly expect that he will be as easy for us to manipulate as the naïve Meng. It is because Meng has been extremely well disposed to us for some years now, and has pushed the irresolute Governor Kuo [Tsung-hsi], that we have been able to set up a variety of joint enterprises, and have others in the pipeline now. I think it would be extremely disadvantageous for us to allow this situation, in which there has been considerable economic development, to break down. . . . I personally think it would be a matter for some regret if we were to stand by while a fine old fellow like Meng, who comes to us with his tail wagging, is done away with and Chang is allowed to fulfill his ambitions.[74]

The reference to "joint enterprises" needs a little explanation. The Terauchi ministry in Japan resolved in July 1917, as briefly mentioned above, to pursue a China policy based primarily on support and aid to the Anhwei-based warlord faction of Tuan Ch'i-jui.[75] In pursuit of this policy it initiated an extremely vigorous phase of economic, political, and military expansion in China by means of loans and military aid to the government set up by Tuan in August 1917, and by simultaneously encouraging private Japanese investment in "joint ventures" with Chinese capitalists, above all in Kirin province. The latter part of the strategy was in conformity with the recommendations offered by Tanaka Giichi upon his return in July 1917 from a tour of China. Tanaka argued that "the vehicle of Sino-Japanese cooperation and growth would be joint stock enterprises, in which Japan would contribute the capital and technicians."[76] As a vehicle of economic penetration it was by no means new, but the emphasis accorded it as an instrument of government policy was; accordingly, the number of joint ventures recorded shows a rapid increase from 1917.[77] Many were "joint" only in name, since the contribution on the Chinese side often amounted to no more than the actual property interest in the forest, mine, or whatever, which Japanese companies by themselves were legally unable to acquire—the provisions of the 1915 treaties supposedly granting them this privilege in "Manchuria" and eastern Inner Mongolia notwithstanding, since official opposition rendered them a dead letter. Bribery, or the offer of lucrative sinecure posts on the boards of such companies to influential Chinese gentry or political figures, could usually be relied on to secure the interests the Japanese desired, and in this respect the relationship with Meng En-Yüan was evidently a highly satisfactory one. Just prior to the initiation of Chang Tso-lin's 1919 campaign to dislodge Meng, for example—on May 28, 1919—the Secretary of the Kirin provincial government's Department of Industry signed over lumber rights for *all* the forests of Meng-chiang hsien in the southern part of the province to a joint Sino-Japanese company called the China Forest Lumber Company. The million yüan nomially subscribed by the Chinese side came from a simultaneous Japanese loan of 2 million yüan—the purpose of the additional million being unspecified but perhaps easily conjectured.[78] This company is mentioned only as an example. Other enterprises, which Morita referred to as being in the pipeline, were considerable: a light railway to link Kirin city with Harbin had been agreed on with the local authorities in Kirin but was awaiting formal approval from the authorities in Peking; another project from Changchun to Nung-an was under discussion; other extensive ventures in lumber and paper manufacturing involved, on the Chinese side as interested parties, not only Meng En-yüan, the civil governor, and leading gentry figures in Kirin, but also the President of the Republic, Hsü Shih-ch'ang, and various leading officials, particularly those connected with the Communications clique in Peking.[79] (For discussion of this latter, see p. 54.)

The extent of the Japanese stake demanded careful consideration of protective measures as the 1919 crisis between Chang and Meng appeared to be developing toward war. Not all Japanese officials echoed the line of supporting Meng that Morita, with his close involvement with him, thought advisable, although there was, on the other hand, little support for Chang either. Through Consul General Akatsuka Shōsuke in Mukden, Chang was advised that he should be careful not to let any misunderstanding arise over Japan's special position in the Northeast. Uchida Yasuya, the foreign minister, sent instructions in two dispatches, of June 23d and 28th, on how Japanese officials on the spot should respond to the crisis. They struck a somewhat ambiguous note: on the one hand, proclaiming that the matter of the appointment of regional Chinese tuchün was an internal Chinese affair, in which Japan had no desire to interfere; on the other, instructing that representations should be made to the Chinese government toward arriving at a satisfactory settlement of the problems, since disturbance of the peace in an area in which there were a considerable number of Japanese residents and substantial Japanese interests could not be tolerated.[80] Uchida here articulated, in fact, the formula under which successive interventions in Chinese affairs were rationalized throughout the following decade: neutrality, coupled with an emphasis on Japanese rights and interests that were to be preserved inviolate, regardless of changes in the Chinese political situation.

Uchida's instructions plunged Japanese representatives on the spot into a flurry of activity designed to secure the latter objective, without conspicuously contravening the former. For his part, Meng suggested that if the Japanese could secure him a reprieve for six months or a year, then allow him to save face by drawing his troops away to a new post elsewhere, say Jehol, the time might profitably be spent in setting up the joint ventures the Japanese were concerned about, incorporating conditions advantageous to Japan, and thus "not allowing the treasurehouse of Kirin to pass to Chang Tso-lin."[81] However, while Japanese mediation toward some such end was in progress, the affair reached an unexpected and sudden dénouement.

On July 19, 1919, Meng's Kirin provincial troops clashed with Japanese troops from the Japanese railway zone at a place called Kuan-ch'eng-tzu, about three kilometers northwest of Changchun. Eighteen Japanese were killed and 17 wounded as a result. Peking was seriously embarrassed, and though the origins of the incident were obscure, the chain of command led to Meng and his chief of staff, Kao Shih-pin. In the Sino-Japanese negotiations that opened at Changchun shortly afterward, their stepping down became the precondition of settlement.[82] Meng therefore retired, his personal wealth assured, to Tientsin. Something of the flavor of personal relationships between protagonists in warlord feuds of this time may be understood from the fact that enroute he was feasted for several days in Mukden by Chang Tso-lin.[83] His departure, however, left the province in a severe financial crisis, since he was believed to have carried off most of its reserves with him when he left, and since he had financed his resistance against Chang simply by issuing the necessary funds from the provincial bank regardless of the reserves. In 1918 the issue of notes was nearly four times what it had been in 1917. As a result, the value of the notes, measured in exchange terms against the Japanese gold yen, declined from an average of 19 *tiao* in 1918 to an average of 33 in 1919. The rate of decline not only was not arrested, but increased further thereafter.[84] As for Kao Shih-pin, he was merely shifted to another appointment—and lived, indeed, to rebel against Chang again, a few years later.

The resolution of the immediate political difficulties still left the status of

Japanese economic interests in some doubt, though not for long. Pressure applied jointly to the new tuchün by both Chinese and Japanese officials, who were interested in promoting the joint ventures, soon elicited the desired statement of commitment to their support from Pao Kuei-ch'ing. Even Hsü Shih-ch'ang, the President of the Republic, joined in urging him to "look after" the interests of the companies concerned; leading political figures in Peking approached the Japanese minister there, asking him to see that appropriate steps were taken in Kirin so that Pao would not be swayed by popular opposition to the joint ventures; and in Kirin itself Morita put the Japanese point to Pao repeatedly. Eventually, on August 13, he secured from Pao the promise that Japan "could be completely assured" of his support. To demonstrate his sincerity, he took steps on the same day to see that a promised series of articles did not appear in the local paper, the *Min-shih pao*, which, it was claimed, would expose the corrupt nature of the joint ventures.[85] The immediate outcome of the affair was thus quite satisfactory to Japan, although hostility to Japanese penetration in the province ran deep, and popular opposition to planned developments continued throughout the following decade to provide serious problems for the Japanese. Chang Tso-lin's satisfaction at the outcome was also tempered by awareness that the anti-Japanese sentiments of the province were almost equally matched by its anti-Fengtien spirit—in other words, the frontier tradition of independence and autonomy expressed itself in opposition to any and every infiltration by nonnatives of the province, and since Chang was seen not only as an outsider from Fengtien but also as a cat's-paw of Japanese expansion, he was doubly reviled.

Furthermore, his agent, Pao, was a man of mixed political attachments, tied to Chang by provincial origins and marriage alliance, but also to Tuan Ch'i-jui as protégé. He was thus from the beginning not simply Chang's man in Kirin, and he succeeded gradually in greatly strengthening his position vis-à-vis Chang. Shortly after his appointment, combining in himself also the roles of Chinese Eastern Railway commissioner and commander in chief of the Railway Defense Corps, he played an important role in expanding Chinese control of that railway at the expense of the Russian Whites (whom his predecessor, Meng, had two years previously aided in securing the line against the then Red threat), and also in reasserting Chinese authority over Harbin. He thus established himself in a strong position for dealing directly with the central government in military, transport, and foreign affairs, and to that extent undermined the office and the

ambition of Chang as inspector general of the three Northeastern provinces.[86]

Pao's position vis-à-vis Peking was weakened, however, by the acute
difficulties he experienced in dealing with the Japanese problem. The question of economic penetration and the reaction it excited in Kirin has already
been mentioned. The problems stemming from the large Korean minority
in Kirin in the context of the Korean independence movement struggle,
which began to develop from March 1919, were just as acute. Repression
in Korea, then known as Japan's colony of Chōsen, had the effect of turning the mountainous border area across the Tumen River in Kirin into an
important base area for Korean liberation fighters. There in comparative
immunity they were able to establish camps and supply depots, recruitment
and training centers. In June 1919, just before Pao took up his Kirin
appointment, the Japanese consulate general at Chien-tao was attacked and
partly burned. Other incidents followed, leading to an increase in the
number of Japanese policemen attached to consular offices adjacent to the
border. In 1920, when the situation became so serious that the idea of a
full-scale Japanese troop dispatch across the border to deal with the trouble
was mooted, the same resistence that had been shown in 1919 to the joint
Sino-Japanese ventures quickly developed again in Kirin, led by Hsü Ting-
lin, civil governor of Kirin, himself.[87] Hsü was also believed by the
Japanese to be attempting to combat their economic plans for the province
by encouraging American investment there, even to the extent of securing
American funds for the construction of a railway from Kirin to the Korean
border, a line regarded as crucial to Japanese economic and military
planning, and one for which unsecured loan funds had been advanced in
1918.[88] Under pressure from the Japanese, Chang Tso-lin therefore had
Hsü dismissed from office on September 2, 1920, at the same time sending
word to Tokyo that he personally welcomed any dispatch of Japanese
troops, though adding that he might, nevertheless, have to issue some
public protest about it.

In September and October 1920 came two attacks on the township of
Hun-ch'un, in the course of which most of the Japanese consular office was
burned and a number of Japanese killed. This was despite the Chinese
troop reinforcements sent up from Kirin after the first attack on September
12, and indeed the Japanese view was that these "bandit suppression
forces" were actually in collusion with the rebels.[89] After a cabinet decision on October 7, the Japanese approached the Chinese authorities, seek-

ing approval of their plan to dispatch a military expedition to the area. The
response in both Peking and Mukden was devious: Chang gave his private
consent to the consul general in Mukden, but then for the record, and as he
had intimated he might do, cabled Peking recommending that it should be
refused.[90] The foreign minister in Peking initially announced his refusal of
the request, but when the Japanese insisted they would have to go ahead
quickly, he entered negotiations on terms for a "joint expedition."[91] These
were agreed to by late October, and a force of some 3,000 Japanese troops,
air force included, moved across the border, thereafter patrolling a vast
stretch of country, establishing field telephones and a telegraph and telephone system linked with their Korean network. Most of the Japanese force
was withdrawn early in 1921, but substantial units of military police were
thereafter attached to all consular offices in the area.[92] The initiative that
Chang seized in settling this Korean affair, and his apparent sympathy with
Japanese aims, meant that when Pao Kuei-ch'ing retired ill to Tientsin in
March 1921, there was no opposition either in Peking or in Tokyo to
Chang's man, Sun Lieh-ch'en, taking over the provinces.[93] With Sun's
appointment, Chang's control over the three provinces of the Northeast
was complete in fact as well as in name.

One question remains about this affair: was Chang's public expression of
opposition to the Japanese dispatch of troops into Kirin merely a face-
saving gesture, and his private expression of consent actually the indication
of his true sentiments? Alternatively, could it be that Chang himself opposed any extension of Japanese influence in his territory, but knowing
open opposition to the point of arousing Japanese antagonism would be
fatal, cunningly tried to make the Japanese believe that if he occasionally
gave voice to anti-Japanese sentiments it was simply because he had to in
order to placate mass opinion? His record to this point did not point to any
clear-cut answer. In 1915 he had urged Yüan Shih-k'ai to resist Japanese
pressures and yield "not so much as an iota" in the negotiations arising out
of the Japanese "21 Demands" of January of that year.[94] In 1916 he himself negotiated briefly with the Japanese when it seemed they might be
prepared to supply him with arms and aid, and when he was still in the
process of establishing his hold over Fengtien province. (See above, p.
28.) In 1919 he took severe repressive measures against any flare-up of
anti-Japanese demonstrations in the Northeast in the course of the May
Fourth Movement;[95] and in 1920 he quickly suppressed the movement,
throwing its leaders into prison, when the Japanese troop dispatch into

Kirin sparked unprecedented opposition in Mukden, expressed through numerous circular protest telegrams and demonstrations by students, particularly those of the Mukden Higher Normal School, outside the Provincial Assembly.[96] He could, perhaps, have hardly done less, since he had a high-level mission under Yü Ch'ung-han actually in Tokyo at the time trying to negotiate a Japanese military assistance program. But whereas he had to suppress the demonstrations in order not to antagonize the Japanese, he had to do so with care and expedition, for the course of the May Fourth Movement the previous year showed how quickly anti-Japanese passions could turn against Chinese suspected of traitorous connivance with Japanese. At the same time, for Chang to appear too solicitous to satisfy a Japanese constituency carried the further risk of strengthening the Japanese impression of him as "a clerk in the branch office," thus leading them to make demands on him that would become more and more difficult to meet.[97] There were pitfalls whichever way he chose to turn, and there was little indication that he had as yet any fixed policy to deal with the problem of Japan.

Balance Sheet

Chang thus succeeded in building up his "Mukden clique" from a nucleus of sworn blood brothers operating as mounted bandits along the frontiers of the decaying Ch'ing empire in the chaotic years spanning the turn of the century into a complex and formidable group. By 1920 the clique had become a most catholic organization, in which unruly frontiersmen rubbed shoulders with modern army officers fresh from the best military academies of both China and Japan, and with Confucian scholars and sophisticated bureaucrats. The chemistry of transformation working within Chang's entourage was a familiar one within Chinese history, as the vigor and dynamism of iconoclastic rebel groups were mellowed in the process of winning the support from scholars necessary to administer and govern the empire. For Chang the economic strength made possible by the services of his civilian aides was particularly important. None of his rivals could command either material or human resources to match those supporting the campaigns that Chang now began to launch. The aura of success associated with the rapid growth of his power, first within Fengtien province, then the Northeast as a whole, and then southward and westward into the rest of the country, helped to attract to him the services of the ambitious and the able. The fact that he seemed to have succeeded in winning a degree of recognition and understanding from Japan also no doubt helped his rise. However, in tracing the vicissitudes of Chang's fortunes from this point until his death in 1928, it will be apparent that contradictions existed in fact at each of these levels, internally within the Mukden clique itself, and externally between it and the interests of Japanese imperialism, and also between it and the forces of Chinese nationalism and social revolution beginning to develop in the South.

Three Provinces, Six Provinces, or All China?

EXPANSION AND THE JAPANESE INTEREST

Paralleling Chang's rapid rise in the Northeast, to a power in no way inferior to that of the old Ch'ing viceroys, went an increasingly deep involvement in the politics of Peking and the affairs of the nation as a whole. This involvement was both necessary to his achievement of dominance in the Northeast and at the same time the cause of his ultimate downfall.

To the Japanese, Chang strove to establish that he was the powerful figure who would assure the Three Eastern Provinces of order and stability and safety for Japanese residents and investments, who would offer resistance to the encroachments of bolshevism or the other powers, and who was, therefore, the man they must support. At the same time, once his hold there became established, the temptation to use his geographical, economic, and military base in the Northeast as a springboard to the achievement of mastery over China as a whole was irresistible. The difficulty of pursuing both these goals at once was intractable.

SOUTHERN ADVANCES

"Unification" Expedition, 1918

Chang's armies first went south in the spring of 1918, and were involved thereafter in a constant cycle of advance and retreat till their final retreat in the face of the Kuomintang's Northern Expedition in 1928. Chinese military politics of this period are almost infinitely complex, as any student of its interminable wars, shifting alliances, and feuding factions is aware. Here only such detail is included as concerns the career of Chang Tso-lin or the Japanese involvement with him, or as is necessary background to these themes.

After the death of Yüan Shih-k'ai in June 1916, the Peiyang Army, which he had created and, from 1912, used as the instrument for imposing administrative unity on the country, began to break up. The tensions that had been held in check by personal dominance and the network of loyal subordinates he had relied on began to surface, ushering in the 12-year interregnum of "warlordism" proper, in which successive weak central governments, backed by one or other military factions, strove vainly to impose unity over various rival, semi-independent, regional military regimes. It is fortuitous that the consolidation of Chang's personal hold over the strategically important Fengtien province was accomplished almost contemporaneously with the opening of this unsettled period, and his dominance over all three Northeastern provinces was established a few years later. His involvement in Southern affairs was a product initially of the desire for political support in establishing himself in the Northeast, though it developed very soon into an end in itself.

After Yüan's death, parliament reconvened briefly, but was dissolved in mid-1917 in the course of the abortive attempt at restoration of the Ch'ing emperor by Chang Hsün. The Peiyang Army militarists and politicians who ousted Chang Hsün made no attempt to reconvene parliament. Instead they set up a Provisional National Council and after appropriate preparations held elections in May and June of 1918 for a new parliament. Dissident members of the 1912 parliament, however, gathered in Canton, where a rival, military government was set up under Sun Yat-sen on August 31, 1917. In October and November 1917, a brief and inconclusive war was fought between the two sides in Hunan and Szechwan. In its aftermath the leading Northern militarist Tuan Ch'i-jui was forced to resign as Premier, and the issue of the right tactics to follow to achieve the unification of the country became a focus for the emerging factional differences in the Peiyang Army group—Tuan's group continuing to favor unification of China by force, and as a parallel strategy, participation in the European war. The two were closely related aims in that Tuan had, from February 1917, been promised substantial Japanese aid in the event of a declaration of war on Germany, and the additional benefits such a declaration seemed likely to lead to—cancellation of the Boxer indemnity payments to Germany and Austria-Hungary, suspension of payments to the Allies, and a possible agreement on tariff increases—were also very positive inducements, since they appeared to offer the prospect of decisive financial and military dominance over his rivals for power in China.[1] Tuan's rival faction within the Peiyang Army, the Chihli-based clique led by Feng Kuo-chang, favored unification of the country by peaceful negotiation and opposed participation in the war.[2] Chang Tso-lin's first involvement in central political affairs was in the context of this deepening rift. During the Fengtien political crisis of 1917, Chang had enjoyed important political support in Peking from Tuan's right-hand man, Hsü Shu-cheng, often known as "Little Hsü." Hsü had been just two years senior to Chang's Chief of Staff, Yang Yü-t'ing, at the Japanese Military Academy, the Shi-kan Gakkō in Tokyo, and Yang became the intermediary between the two. Thus it was Yang who appeared on Chang's behalf at a Tientsin conference of tuchün supporting Tuan's position in December 1917.[3]

This relationship gave Chang the means whereby to benefit, indirectly but substantially, from the deliberate Japanese policy of sponsorship of Tuan determined by the Terauchi ministry in July 1917, and the enormous Japanese aid that began to be funneled to him through semi-official and business channels, even earlier the same year.* Part of this aid was in the form of a consignment of 17 million yen worth of weapons shipped to China in February 1918, in fulfillment of an agreement negotiated the previous December between the Chinese Ministry of War and the Japanese Taihei Kumiai,[4] the latter a semi-official Japanese arms export consortium set up in 1908 at the suggestion of then War Minister Terauchi jointly by three of the largest trading companies, Mitsui, Okura, and Takada.[5] The arms were ostensibly to facilitate Chinese participation in the Great War, to which China was committed by its declaration of August 14.[6] Actually, however, they were all seized by a detachment of Chang's troops acting on an agreement with Tuan, while they lay on board ship in harbor at Ch'in-huang-tao. Carried off to Mukden, they helped supply Chang's rapidly expanding Northeastern armies. Protests from Peking were ignored, the action being explained on grounds that the arms were to outfit a Northeastern expeditionary force to help unify the country.[7]

From March 16 a 50,000 man force, comprising most of the 27th, 28th, and 29th divisions, with several newly formed mixed brigades, began to march south in fulfillment of this pledge. Camped outside Peking, it issued a series of demands partly in the interests of the unification to which the Anfu leaders aspired and partly a reflection of the predominantly North-

*The decision to support Tuan was taken in Chōshu clique circles in August 1916, after a visit to Peking by Nishihara Kamezō, close adviser to Terauchi Masatake; Terauchi was then Korean Governor-General, and became Premier in October. An agreement on a five million yen loan from three Japanese banks to Tuan's government was signed on January 8, 1917. It was the first of many. Morley, p. 14; Hatano, *Chūgoku kindai gunbatsu no kenkyū*, p. 319.

eastern concerns of Chang: on the one hand, restoration of Tuan as Premier, censure of the tuchün who opposed him, and military expansion; on the other hand, the establishment of an office of "inspector general" (*hsün-yüeh-shih*) over the Three Eastern Provinces—in other words, Peking recognition of Chang's claims to dominate the entire Northeast.[8] Feng Kuo-chang, then President, was no longer able to resist, particularly since the leading Chihli militarists, Ts'ao K'un and Wu P'ei-fu, had by this time been converted to the cause of war, possibly by promises of the rewards it would bring them, and Ts'ao had accepted overall command of the expeditionary force on January 30.[9] Tuan Ch'i-jui resumed the premiership on March 23, and part of the Northeastern force was dispatched, under Hsü Shu-cheng's command, to aid the main expedition into Hunan.[10] It was, however, a short-lived campaign. Chang had little stomach for fighting on such a remote front, and became suspicious that he was being used by Tuan and Hsü to further ambitions that conformed less and less to his own. He particularly regretted the assumption of overall command of his troops by Hsü. With the expedition bogged down in Central China in mid-1918, Chang therefore ordered his troops to withdraw, giving as reason the need for strengthened defenses in the Russian border area. Before actually pulling out, however, he made sure that his office of "inspector general" was confirmed by the "new" parliament, which was dominated by Tuan and his supporters organized in the newly formed "Anfu clique," * and succeeded in extracting from the treasury half a million yüan to cover the expenses of his expedition. This first phase of Chang's involvement in the affairs of the nation as a whole ended with his withdrawal in December 1918.[11] He had lost nothing by it; indeed, on the contrary he had gained considerably in experience and political weight in Peking, and, above all, he had gained the formal recognition of his Northeastern claims that helped his gradual takeover of Kirin province in the crisis of the following year.

The only aspect of the affair that might have given Chang pause for sober reflection was the warning delivered to him on his return to Mukden by Japanese Consul General Akatsuka Shōsuke, in which it was made clear that the Japanese government did not approve of his Southern entanglements and ambitions:[12]

---

* "Anfu Club" was the name given to the organization of Anhwei- and Fukien-based militarists and politicians set up in March 1918 to further the interests of Tuan in the National Assembly elections of June 1918 (Li Chien-nung, pp. 383–84; Ch'i, p. 27).

The Three Eastern Provinces are intimately related to Japan. For the man responsible for the maintenance of peace and order there to absent himself unnecessarily from the area and send his army to the center of China is an act likely not only to hinder the unification of China as a whole but also to interfere with the maintenance of order in the Three Eastern Provinces. . . . I would urge you to refrain from such behavior.

This was the first of a series of attempts by Japan, which continued for the whole of Chang's subsequent career, to persuade him to confine his attention to the Northeast. However, since extensive Japanese financial and military backing had made possible the 1918 campaign in the interests of unification under Tuan, it was perhaps not unreasonable for Chang to hope that he might win such support for himself in the future.*

The Anhwei-Chihli War, 1920

After the failure of the North-South peace conferences early in 1919, differences within the Peiyang warlord group continued to intensify, eventually erupting in open warfare, in the summer of 1920. The rivalries that produced this warfare, though expressed in terms of differing views on political issues such as the tactics to be followed in pursuing national unification, were in large part the expression of a politically neutral power struggle, as the various cliques and factions maneuvered for advantage with an eye to the rewards it was anticipated would follow from national unification.[13]

Despite attacks launched on it in the course of the May Fourth Movement in 1919, the Anfu clique continued to enjoy formidable strength, derived partly from its dominance in the "new" parliament elected in 1918, and partly from its military strength, particularly as represented by

---

*Between the reinstatement of Tuan cabinet on March 23, 1918, and the collapse of the Terauchi ministry in Japan just over four months later, 152.4 million yen was supplied in Japanese loans to Tuan (Usui, *Nihon to Chūgoku*, p. 135). On the Japanese side, much of it was negotiated through Nishihara Kamezō, hence "Nishihara loans"; on the Chinese side, much of the money went to military and political expenses in the interest of the Tuan faction, and little if any on the purposes to which nominally the loans were directed—the development of forests, mines, railways, etc. (Hatano, *Chūgoku kindai gunbatsu no kenkyū*, n. 60). In addition to financial aid, Tuan also built up the War Participation Army, a force of three divisions and four mixed brigades that was probably the best equipped in the country, entirely with Japanese aid under Japanese advisers and instructors. This was in accordance with the Military Assistance Agreement of July 31, which followed the Sino-Japanese Joint Defensive Military Agreement of May 16, 1918. Full text of agreement in Morley, pp. 363–65 (see also pp. 113–21, 162–64); Usui, *Nihon to Chūgoku*, p. 135; Li Chien-nung, p. 383.

the Japanese-trained and -financed Frontier Defense Army (originally the War Participation Army, set up after the declaration of war on Germany in 1917). However, as typical of faction-dominated politics, its strength was the stimulus that united its enemies and led to its downfall. In Central China, Chihli leaders Ts'ao K'un and Wu P'ei-fu felt threatened by Anhwei moves to neutralize or displace them there, while Chang Tso-lin felt that the Anhwei advances into Mongolia threatened his own ambitions in the same direction. Hsü Shu-cheng had won what appeared to be a considerable triumph in November 1919 in having the Government of Outer Mongolia rescind its declaration of independence—though, as it turned out, the triumph was short-lived.[14] An anti-Anhwei alliance between the Chihli leaders and Chang Tso-lin was thus a natural development. Jointly they constituted a bloc of eight provinces as opposed to the five led by Anhwei. Between June 19 and early July 1920, Chang was in and around Peking, ostensibly to mediate between the Chihli and Anhwei factions, actually to discuss with Ts'ao and Wu the terms on which they were to cooperate against Anhwei. On July 13 Chang ordered his forces to begin moving south.[15]

Since Japan had been closely associated with Anhwei, particularly with Tuan Ch'i-jui, while being also deeply interested in Chang and the Northeast, the gradual build-up toward war could not be a matter of indifference. The policy of support for Tuan and the Anhwei clique had been decided in the time of the Terauchi cabinet in July 1917, and the accumulated Japanese commitment was not something easily reversed, despite the switch from oligarchic to party political cabinet with the accession of Hara Kei's Seiyūkai ministry in September 1918. Thus it was agreed in 1919 by the cabinet and the Genrō* (Yamagata Aritomo) that, despite pronouncements of neutrality and nonintervention in Chinese affairs, "secretly, the pro-Japanese elements should be supported to the utmost and made not to lose hope," to which end an expenditure of "between five to six and ten million yen a year" might be necessary.[16] As the crisis of 1920 developed, there is no evidence of any positive secret initiatives by Japan, but, although nonintervention and neutrality were the watchword, both in the Hara ministry's public statements and in its official instructions to representatives in China, it was in an impossible quandary.

*Genrō: A small, extra-constitutional but highly important group of "elder statesmen," of which at this point Prince Yamagata was most important.

The Frontier Defense Army, which was directly controlled by Tuan Ch'i-jui, was a Japanese creation: though Japan did nothing, it could still not avoid implication by proxy in any war in which this force was involved; but equally it could not avoid the charge of involvement, on the opposite side, if it took any positive steps to compel its nonparticipation in such a war. The declaration of neutrality, coupled with the refusal or inability to counteract the long liaison with Tuan, did therefore work to Tuan's advantage. Both the Army Minister and the Foreign Minister were agreed that Japan should do nothing to prevent the involvement of the Japanese-sponsored force in the civil war.[17]

But if noninvolvement worked to the advantage of Tuan (however little actual good it did him), it also worked to help Chang, since there was no attempt to implement the interdiction on Southern involvement hinted at in the warning from Consul General Aksatsuka in December 1918. Thus, while Tokyo did its best to abstain from any compromising action, local Japanese officers in China maintained very close relations with Chang, and Chang in turn made every effort to ingratiate himself with Japan: it was at this time that he agreed to dismiss from office the civil governor of Kirin, Hsü Ting-lin, who was suspected of opposition to Japanese plans for the development of that province, and that he also suggested to senior Kwantung Army officers that his absence in the event of war would be a good opportunity for Japan to extend its policing operations in "North Manchuria."[18] That he enjoyed a substantial measure of understanding and cooperation from local Japanese officers in the Kwantung Army may be inferred from a postwar Kwantung Army report on "Circumstances of the Dispatch of the Fengtien Army and Railway Transportation," and one authority has concluded that a secret understanding must have existed between Chang, the Kwantung Army, and Army General Staff Headquarters in Tokyo.[19]

It is just as likely, however, that local Kwantung Army initiatives were taken in the absence of any coherent policy in Tokyo, for which the failure of Japanese intelligence to predict the outbreak of hostilities, Chang's involvement in them, and above all, their likely outcome, were in turn responsible. The information from Chang's adviser, Machino, who was with him in Peking in late June and early July, was that Chang would not move his forces at all, would not involve himself in the war beyond the extent of issuing telegrams from Mukden, and that Anhwei, having superior arms and funds at its disposal, would quickly be victorious.[20] Machino's report was dated July 11. On the 12th, the actual day Chang and Ts'ao K'un jointly declared war on Anhwei, Obata Yūkichi, the Minister in Peking, reported for the first time that Chang seemed likely to move.[21] Two days later the troop trains from the Northeast began to roll. By July 22 the war was over; the Anhwei forces had been defeated by the combined armies of Chihli and Fengtien, and the Anhwei leadership was in refuge in the Japanese legation.[22]

This was, from the Japanese point of view, an inexplicable and, apparently, a virtually unforeseen development. One can only surmise that the scale of involvement with the Anhwei clique politically, and with the Frontier Defense Army militarily, was such as to blind the Japanese officials concerned to the changes in the actual balance of power. Certainly the notion that the relationship between two Japanese protégés, viewed as complementary representatives of the Japanese interest in quite different parts of China—Chang in the Northeast and Tuan in North China—might develop in an antagonistic direction did not occur to Japanese intelligence until it was obvious. The assumption that Northeastern policy was and should be something distinct from general China policy, the "Manchurian idea" in fact, was already deep in Japanese thinking. The outcome was that Japan was left with its China policy in shreds. The long and extensive involvement with the Anhwei clique was brought to this ignominious end without any serious attention being paid to what might replace it.[23] Further, the situation was much more complicated than it had been when the Terauchi cabinet decision to support Tuan Ch'i-jui was taken: the Peiyang Army group was splintered, apparently irrevocably, and prolonged feuding and division seemed likely; Chang Tso-lin's Northeastern frontier force had demonstrated its strength not just as a local faction but also as a potential contender for national power; the parliament was split; the other great powers, recovering from their European war preoccupations, were returning vigorously to contest the dominance that Japan had seized in China between 1914 and 1918; and, perhaps most important of all, Chinese nationalism had emerged from 1919 as a powerful, unpredictable new factor to be taken into account. The real question presented for Japanese policy by Chang's rise, however, was whether the integration of Northeastern affairs with those of the rest of China would be in the Japanese interest or not. To understand the issue, the extent of Chang's rise to power in the aftermath of this war must be understood.

POSTWAR PROBLEMS

The Fengtien-Chihli Rivalry

Chang's arrival as a major new political and military force in China was evident from the moment he arrived in Peking, very much the "man of the hour," to discuss with his ally, Ts'ao K'un, the disposition of the country's affairs.[24] After their joint victory over Anhwei, there was not a lot that united them, but they dictated certain basic points to Hsü Shih-ch'ang and the restored Premier, Chin Yün-p'eng: they were to be consulted on future government policies and on important appointments, they were to have the right to nominate to office in their own special areas and the right of veto outside them, and jointly they would "advise" provinces not accepting orders from the central government.[25] Their informal power was clearly to be much more substantial than that exercised by the actual holders of central government office. But in the absence of any agreement on general political principles, rivalry, jealousy, and mutual recrimination soon soured their relationship.

Chang's gains appeared initially the greater. The three-division Frontier Defense Army, which had been set up in September 1918 as the War Participation Army, was proved in the war to be an ineffective fighting force, but it was nevertheless the best equipped in China, thanks to the 20 million yen Japanese loan with which it was established (see p. 49n). Most of its equipment was seized by Chang, as well as other evidence of the affluence accruing from the lavish Japanese funding Anhwei had enjoyed—motorcars, airplanes, etc.[26] Second, with the cessation of hostilities in July, Chang withdrew to the Northeast only 40,000 of his 70,000-man force, having his chief of staff, Ch'in Hua, appointed on August 14 to the important post of commander of the military police in the capital area (*ching-tsin hsien-ping ssu-ling*).[27] Third, he also used his political influence in Peking to have his old blood brother and close confidant, Chang Ching-hui, appointed commander of the 16th Division and *tutung* (equivalent of tuchün) of the Inner Mongolian special area of Chahar.[28]

However, the Peking government was unable to tackle any of the issues it had supposedly been set up to resolve—national unification, military retrenchment, and administrative reform—and it was chronically short of funds. The instability of the Chihli-Fengtien alliance made progress on any of these difficult. In mid-April 1921, a long, seven-week round of conferences and negotiations opened in Tientsin between Chang, Ts'ao, and other leading military and political figures, in an attempt to resolve some of the difficulties.[29] Little of consequence was actually accomplished. On the central problem, national unification, nothing was agreed beyond the issue of a declaration of opposition to the assumption of the office of president by Sun Yat-sen in Kwangtung and to the Southern parliament.[30] Otherwise there were two main developments: the Chin cabinet was reorganized, principally through the exclusion of the Communications clique representatives, Yeh Kung-ch'o and Chou Tzu-ch'i, and agreement was reached between Chang and Ts'ao on the area within which each would agree to the territorial expansion of the other.[31] Both of these points call for some clarification.

The Communications clique was that group of officials within the Ministry of Communications (established in 1906) that developed in the late Ch'ing period around the person of Liang Shih-i, with administrative interests in railways, shipping, postal, telegraph, and telephone services, and financial interests mediated through the Communications Bank (established in 1907).[32] It continued through the early years of the republic to exercise a powerful political influence owing to the patronage of Yüan Shih-k'ai, but his death in 1916 set it adrift from the political power nexus necessary to its mode of operation. To make up for this, an accommodation was gradually worked out, till October 1918 with the Anhwei clique, then, after the defeat of Anhwei in 1920, with Chang's Fengtien clique, thus linking Chang's military and political power to its financial and bureaucratic expertise.[33] The ousting of Yeh and Chou from the Chin cabinet in April 1921 therefore represented a weakening of Chang's political pull in Peking, but it was compensated by the territorial gains he made.

Whereas Chihli control was confirmed over the two provinces of Shensi and Kansu, to which Ts'ao K'un nominees were appointed tuchün, Chang Tso-lin was declared development commissioner (*ching-lüeh-shih*) for Mongolia and Sinkiang, with explicit authority over the three special areas of Jehol, Chahar, and Suiyuan.[34] In September 1920, Chang's lieutenant, Chang Ching-hui, was appointed to rule Chahar; another subordinate, Chi Chin-ch'un, commander of the 28th Division, took office in Jehol in September of the following year, after a delay apparently caused by the fact that part of the deal for the removal of the aged incumbent, Chiang Kuei-t'i, was that he should be allowed to get in the year's opium harvest and thus recoup the amounts owed him and his men from the central government; and in Suiyuan Ma Fu-hsiang was appointed—though not a direct subordinate of Chang's, he was loosely affiliated to him and had no ties with his rivals.[35]

Chang also received three million yüan from the treasury and was authorized to set up four new army brigades so that he might lead an expedition to retake the Outer Mongolian capital, Urga, from the White Russian armies of Baron Nikolaus von Ungern-Sternberg, who had captured it in early February and proclaimed its independence in the name of the Living Buddha.[36] Ungern-Sternberg, "half Magyar, half Russian, [who] was married to a Manchurian princess, and was deeply versed in Buddhist mysticism,"[37] was bent on the creation of a Buddhist empire embracing Mongolia and Tibet, as well as on the restoration of the Grand Duke Michael as "All-Russian Emperor." Announcing his intention "to exterminate commissars, communists and Jews with their families,"[38] he launched a bloody reign of terror in Urga. Chang Tso-lin, as a result, was able to represent his projected Mongolian advances as those of a liberator.

In the early summer of 1921, Chang drew up plans for his expedition. Under Chang's personal command, 30,000 of his men were to take part in the march on Urga. He was to leave Mukden on July 26, travel by rail to Man-chou-li, and then march accross country following the banks of the Kerulen River for the 970 miles to Urga. Once the "mad Baron" was overthrown, Chang was to proceed by car across the Gobi for a triumphant return to Peking. The whole operation was to take a mere three months. The scale of the plan was sufficient to win Chang an additional grant of two million yüan toward his expenses. However, because of the rapid change in the situation both in Mongolia and in China itself, the operation never took place.[39]

Late in June Ungern-Sternberg's forces met a series of reverses at the hands of a combined Red Army–Mongolian force. They eventually fled, Ungern-Sternberg himself being captured and executed, and a People's Government was proclaimed on July 10.[40] In China itself the fragile balance of power between the joint victors of the 1920 war was gravely upset at about the same time. In the immediate postwar settlement, Chang's power—which, however considerable in geographical extent, was still confined largely to the frontier regions—was balanced against that of Chihli in the central part of China by the existence of a loose alliance with Wang Chan-yüan, inspector general of Hunan and Hupei. Consequently, when Wang was overthrown in August 1921 and replaced by Ts'ao K'un's subordinate, Wu P'ei-fu, the delicate equilibrium between Fengtien and

Chihli was upset, and Chang's attention was diverted from the uncertain prospects of an expedition into Outer Mongolia to apparently more urgent matters that were closer at hand.[41]

At this stage Chang had two main options: to prepare to fight Chihli for mastery over all or at least the North of China, or to abandon, at least for the moment, his wider ambitions and concentrate on consolidating his hold over the vast bloc of territory he already controlled. It was a choice with which Japanese policy and Chang's conception of his relation to Japan were closely connected, since the three provinces and three special administrative areas he controlled corresponded closely to the "Man-Mō," the "Manchuria-Mongolia" that the more aggressive of Japan's imperialists had dreamed of creating as a Japanese dependency in 1911 and again in 1916. At the same time the danger that involvement in the affairs of Central and Southern China would lead to the introduction of complicated warlord and political struggles in the Northeast, thus damaging Japanese interests there, had prompted the Akatsuka warning to Chang of December 1918 to set aside any Southern aspirations (see above, pp. 48–49).

Overtures to Japan and the "Eastern Conference" of 1921

How then did Japan react to Chang, and Chang to Japan, after the Anhwei-Chihli war in 1920? Chang did his best from the outset to represent himself to Japan as the new Tuan Ch'i-jui, worthy of at least as much support and aid as a candidate for the unification of China under benevolent Japanese auspices as Tuan had received.[42] He was, perhaps naturally, anxious that "Japanese support be not inconclusive as it was in the case of Tuan."[43] His Chihli rivals, by contrast, he insisted were mere cat's-paws of the European and American powers. Wu P'ei-fu's proposal for the calling of a "national convention" (*kuo-min ta-hui*) he cited in particular as evidence that he had been won over by the Southerners (the Nationalists in Canton) and by Europeans and Americans. In the future, he stressed to his Japanese adviser, Machino Takema, it would be necessary "for these bad elements to be annihilated and the people delivered from servitude to Europe and America."[44] At press conferences he held in Tientsin and Peking in July and August 1921, he stressed to the Japanese reporters that, whereas Wu P'ei-fu and other Chihli figures were "just puppets of politicians and of Americans such as Legation Secretary Tenny and Presidential Adviser Anderson," he, Chang, was concerned above all with Japanese interests, and hoped in the near future to be able to visit Japan. His meeting with American press and agency representatives, on the other hand, ended in hostile exchanges.[45]

On the Japanese side voices favoring support for Chang on these terms, i.e. as a new "strong man" candidate for unifier of China, were strongest among those closest to him—his adviser, Machino, and senior Kwantung Army Officers. They appear to have accepted without question his assurances that he would promote as strongly as possible a pro-Japan policy throughout China and restrict European and American penetration, and that to succeed he needed strong Japanese support.[46] Military opinion in China as a whole was also in general agreement on the desirability of support for Chang when canvassed on this specific issue in a dispatch from Army Staff Headquarters in mid-August 1920.[47] The only note of caution was sounded by Major General Banzai Rihachirō, which was perhaps understandable in view of his close association with the disastrous pro-Tuan line, for he had been the senior Japanese officer attached to the War Participation Army.

However, one crucial problem divided Japanese thinking: whether to see Chang as a local pro-Japanese official in the Northeast or as a prospective unifier of the country. Major General Satō Yasunosuke, who was sent to Mukden in October 1920 especially to talk to Chang, reported to Premier Hara and the army authorities that in his opinion Chang should be aided only insofar as he confined himself to the former role, since any attempt by him to expand southward would be likely to lead to complications with the other powers.[48] A contrary view was expressed by Nagao Hanpei, a senior official who had been Japanese representative on the inter-allied board that had been running the Chinese Eastern Railway since January 1919. In an opinion evidently prepared for War Minister Tanaka in mid-December 1920, he argued for an openly declared policy of support for Chang, which he thought would be acceptable to the other powers if the urgency of the struggle against bolshevism was sufficiently stressed; and once Chang's power was consolidated in the Northeast, he thought it might easily—and to Japan's advantage—be extended over Mongolia and over the whole of China north of the Yangtze.[49]

Already in June 1919, as noted above, the Hara ministry had decided that, although for public consumption it was necessary to proclaim "a neutral and impartial attitude toward the North and South,"[50] in fact "the pro-Japanese elements should be supported to utmost, and made not to lose hope" (see above, p. 50). By the autumn of 1920 Chang appeared to be the leading figure among "pro-Japanese elements." In November Chang sent Yü Ch'ung-han, his trusted adviser on Japanese affairs, to Tokyo to ask for Japanese support "both tangible and intangible." Among those Yü met were Prime Minister Hara, War Minister Tanaka Giichi, Foreign Minister Uchida Yasuya, and the Chief of the General Staff, General Uehara Yūsaku.[51] Yü was well received, and although no specific decisions on military or other aid were recorded, the entry in Hara's diary is significant: "Chang is trying to extend his influence with Japanese backing. Since it is also important for us to treat Chang well in order to expand in the Three Eastern Provinces, it just happens that the interests of both sides can be reconciled.[52]

The position of the Hara cabinet was spelled out in greater detail and more clearly at the Eastern Conference in May 1921. After full consultation with the civil and military officials of the departments concerned with the implications of postwar changes in the situation in Northeast China ("Manchuria"), Korea, Siberia, and Shantung, two major decisions were taken following this conference with reference to "Manchuria and Mongolia" and to Chang Tso-lin.[53] The former affirmed that dealings with the other powers concerning these areas should be predicated on the fact of special Japanese interests and position, both as spelled out in the existing treaties and as stemming from considerations of their propinquity to Japan. The latter was concerned with how these interests were to be maintained and protected—the answer, in short, being through Chang Tso-lin: "In general the [Japanese] empire should offer Chang Tso-lin aid both direct and indirect in reorganizing and developing the civil affairs and military preparedness of the Three Eastern Provinces and in establishing his firm authority over the region."

This important general principle was qualified only by the rider that such aid would not be forthcoming were Chang to seek "the assistance of the [Japanese] empire in order to accomplish his ambition in central political affairs." On this point, in other words, the cabinet accepted the advice of Satō Yasunosuke rather than that of Nagao Hanpei. Chang was to receive Japanese favor as ruler in the Northeast, not as candidate for the unification of China. He was not to be a second Tuan Ch'i-jui after all.

Five specific clauses were attached to this general resolution, of which the two relating to the way in which military and civil aid were to be channeled to Chang are for our purposes most important. Direct supply of arms was ruled out because of the "Embargo on the Sale of Arms to China," which Japan along with the other major powers had signed in

1919, but in clause III of the resolution it was noted that this could be circumvented by aiding Chang in the establishment of an arsenal and thus helping him to become self-sufficient in weapons. The stipulation about financial aid in clause IV is most instructive and is worth quoting in full:

> While the imperial government is not unwilling to give friendly consideration to financial aid according to circumstances, it is important to do so by means of economic loans, especially by adopting the form of investment in joint enterprises, in order to avoid the suspicion of the powers and the jealousy of the central government. If Chang Tso-lin too will strive increasingly to promote the reality of Sino-Japanese cooperation, exerting himself, for example, in relation to the lease of land, the management of mines and forests, and other such promising enterprises, and if he will apply every effort to implementing the principle of so-called coexistence and coprosperity and devise methods of joint control both in already existing and in newly to be set up Sino-Japanese joint venture companies, then the finances of the Three Eastern Provinces can be made to flourish of their own accord and in an inconspicuous way.

The importance of the principles set out at the Eastern Conference of 1921 is considerable. It has been given much less attention by scholars than the much better known Eastern Conference of 1927, which is often held to have heralded a new, positive policy toward China. The fact is, however, that the points clearly set out here—insistence on Japan's special rights and interests in "Manchuria-Mongolia," support and aid for Chang Tso-lin as the actual power holder there but discouragement of any attempt by him to unify China as a whole, and the belief that Chang in return for Japanese aid should preserve the peace and promote Japanese enterprise—are points constantly reiterated by Japanese policymakers throughout Chang Tso-lin's career in the Northeast, up to and beyond the Eastern Conference of 1927.

"MANCHURIA-MONGOLIA"?

Chang's readiness to forgo ambitions toward conquest of China as a whole and his readiness to satisfy Japanese developmental blueprints for the Northeast were points on which Japan was never able to gain complete satisfaction. In 1921, when Chang did appear to hesitate between persisting in his rivalry with the Chihli clique for dominance over North China—and ultimately all China—and withdrawing from central affairs to go his own way in the North and Northeast, there is little to indicate that he was thinking along the same lines as the Japanese, not at least in any more than geographical terms, for he was in effect, from the autumn of 1921, the ruler of the three provinces and the three special administrative areas that were to the Japanese "Manchuria-Mongolia." He did, however, give serious consideration to the idea of withdrawal, at least temporarily, from the contest within the passes, in order to consolidate and coordinate the vast gains he had already made by establishing an autonomous, if not independent regime. In the first place, a number of steps were taken toward coordinating communications, finance, and civil administration to match the military unity of the area under his command. Certain of the revenues collected in all the six provinces and special administrative areas (salt tax, tobacco tax) were ordered remitted directly to Mukden rather than, as previously, to Peking.[54] The policy of placing Chang's retainers in all important posts in the newly acquired territories was followed, and a grandiose scheme for railway construction was mooted at policy conferences in Mukden.[55] Other ideas were that the so-called "special areas" should be elevated to proper provincial status, that a unified six-province currency and banking system should then be instituted throughout, and that military organization and training should likewise be coordinated, with central facilities at Mukden.[56] According to one source, part of the planned unification consisted in having the expenses of the entire territory met in accordance with the following apportionment: central government, 40 percent; the three provinces, 40 percent; the three special areas, 20 percent. Armaments and military supplies were to be provided 50 percent from the arsenal in Mukden and 50 percent from local sources.[57]

A striking and important fact to note, however, is that these plans for independence from Peking were not couched in terms of the Japanese notion of "Man-Mō" (Manchuria-Mongolia), nor indeed did they refer even to the concept of "Manchuria" in order to legitimize or promote the idea of independence. References to the independent territory envisaged seem to have been simply to a nameless unit composed of six provinces.

In September 1921, Chang cabled his deputies, Sun Lieh-ch'en in Kirin and Wu Chün-sheng in Heilungkiang, specifically to see how they felt on the idea of independence. In view of the Mongolian disturbances, the instability of the government of Peking, and the fact of secret foreign aid being given to the powers of North and South, should they not declare independence, he asked, expel the foreigners, and borrow money abroad on the security of the territory to buy arms and raise troops to defend it?[58] Beginning September 22, Sun, Wu, and others of Chang's lieutenants arrived in Mukden for talks that continued for close to a month.[59] Outright independence was evidently rejected—it was difficult, after all, to see how it might be possible to "expel the foreigners," particularly if it was necessary at the same time to rely on them for loan funds—but increasing independence of action was nevertheless stressed. There are no firsthand reports of the proceedings of this conference, but circumstantial evidence suggests the adoption of a strategic concept rather along the lines of the following proposal, which was apparently submitted to Chang Tso-lin earlier in the year by General Chang Huan-hsiang in Harbin:[60]

Our system of counter-acting Japan in this direction should consist in creating collisions of interest as strong and frequent as possible between America and Japan. The granting to America of concessions and trade privileges, the conclusion of secret trade conventions, the attraction of American capital for industrial and commercial purposes—form a rough canvas of means for combatting the Japanization of Manchuria.

In late 1921 and early 1922 there were several straws in the wind to suggest that this point had been made. The new Kirin tuchün, Sun Lieh-ch'en, was proving just as obstreperous in negotiations over various joint Sino-Japanese ventures as had his predecessor. It was said of him: "Not only does Sun abhor the invasion of Japanese influence and keep drawing out the negotiations, but he tends to welcome the gradual infiltration of American influence." [61] Chang himself had in 1920 for the first time taken on an American, the ex–U.S. consul general, E. Carleton Baker, as commercial adviser.[62]

Given the priority attached in Japanese circles to expansion of Sino-Japanese joint ventures, the failure to make the hoped-for progress in this sphere was most significant. On March 14, 1922, in the Peking newspaper *Cheng-yen pao*, which was the Peking organ of the Mukden clique, an article appeared entitled "Inspector General Chang forbids all Japanese joint ventures in the Three Eastern Provinces." [63] The text included the following sentences:

Since the 21 Demands of 1915 were set up by force, [Japan] sees the Three Eastern Provinces as its own territory; the more it takes the more it demands. . . . As for the enterprises that are seizing rights under the name of Sino-Japanese joint ventures, there is no need for a single one of them. The authorities of the Three Eastern Provinces realize that Japan cannot be greatly trusted. All joint ventures that have not yet been set up are to be forbidden; laws are to be set to cancel those that have already been established.

There was doubt among Japanese officials about how this story was to be interpreted: though to some it seemed clear that Chang had taken a definite

anti-Japanese turn, to others it meant only that he was engaging in a propaganda exercise to strengthen his chances as potential unifier of China by
overcoming his image as a Japanese puppet.[64] The seeds of doubt were
sown, however. Even Chang's generally fulsome biographer, Sonoda,
writing late in 1921, noted that, whereas Chang understood Japan's position in the Northeast and acted as a Japanese lobbyist, yet "he exacts his
price on Japan anyway. If he thought pro-Americanism would be advantageous to him, he would be pro-American."[65] This perspective may have
been closest to the truth.

THE FIRST FENGTIEN-CHIHLI WAR, 1922

Peking: The Die Is Cast

However, both Japanese designs and Chang's rather different ideas of
autonomous development in Northeast China and Inner Mongolia were
frustrated by the course of events in 1922. Chang found himself increasingly involved in Peking politics, and the stakes for which he was playing
were too substantial for him to easily relinquish the game. In November
1921, the Peking government faced an acute financial crisis. Police and
soldiers in the capital area had been unpaid for seven months, and when a
run occurred on the Bank of China and the Bank of Communications at the
same time, the existing government of Chin Yün-peng was reduced to im-
potence.[66] Liang Shih-i, then managing director of the Bank of Communications, invited Chang to intervene. This he did in no uncertain terms. He
first agreed to advance an emergency loan of four million yüan to tide over
the immediate crisis; then, after consultations in Peking with Ts'ao K'un
and the resignation of Chin's cabinet, he engineered the establishment of a
joint Mukden and Communications Clique cabinet under Liang as Premier
on December 25.[67] The outcome was that Chang gained control over the
finances of the central institutions—Treasury, Bank of China, and Bank of
Communications—as well as a standard of formal legitimacy that appeared
likely to be useful in the anticipated showdown with Chihli.

Domestic Allies

His achievements in Peking were matched by a complex set of negotiations throughout the country aimed at constructing the alliances that would
ensure his eventual triumph over the Chihli clique, particularly over the
forces of Wu P'ei-fu, then a rapidly rising subordinate of Ts'ao K'un in
Central China. The anti-Wu alliance was constructed on the broadest pos-

sible basis: the Fengtien and Communications cliques, which were more or less formally linked in the cabinet; minor leaders of the old Anfu clique, who were almost immediately pardoned by the new cabinet, and the principals, Tuan Ch'i-jui and Hsü Shu-cheng, who escaped from their refuge in the Japanese Ministry in early February, probably with the help of Japanese army officers, and quickly resumed political activity in the Japanese concession in Tientsin; also the tuchün of Honan, Anhwei, and Chekiang; and, most unlikely ally, the father of the republic, Sun Yat-sen.[68] Sun's involvement merits some explanation.

In April 1921, Chang had joined in denouncing the Southern parliament in Canton and Sun Yat-sen's assumption of the presidency there,[69] and in August of the same year Sun described Chang as "the head of a gang of murderers," who "obeys Tokyo in all important matters which concern Japan." [70] By December, however, as Chang was engaged in his maneuvers in Peking, there were rumors about possible approaches to Sun,[71] which led to some anxious speculation in Japanese circles. Foreign Minister Uchida wrote to the Japanese Minister in Peking: [72]

Since there is some tendency for the Japanese position in Manchuria and Mongolia to have been much strengthened as a result of the Washington Conference, may it not be that Chang, fearful of future Japanese development in Manchuria, is planning to make some contact with Sun Yat-sen, raise the argument against the so-called 21 Demands, promote anti-Japanese feeling throughout China, and through the Liang cabinet, to unify North and South?

In fact, Chang sent delegates to see Sun some time in February 1922, a visit that was reciprocated by the dispatch of C. C. Wu from Canton to Mukden about the same time.[73] From this time till Sun Yat-sen's death, relations remained close and apparently friendly between Sun and Chang, despite the vast difference in their positions. Given the physical distance between them, it was obviously both possible and politic for them to unite against a common enemy. It may even be that Sun saw some politically redeeming qualities in Chang, who was, on the face of it, the epitomy of the feudal and reactionary forces he was committed to eliminate. The Dutch socialist Hendricus Sneevliet, who had a number of contacts with Sun between 1921 and 1923 under the name by which he was known in the Comintern, Maring, suggests that it was more than a mere marriage of convenience: [74]

In Sun's opinion Chang Tso-lin, who seemed to the Chita Russians to be purely a Japanese tool, was in reality opposing the Japanese on every hand, building rival railways, port development, etc. Sun Yat-sen kept a permanent personal representative at Mukden; for a long time Wang Ching-wei supervised these connections.

The new alliance drew support in some unlikely places. The London *Times* correspondent wrote from Peking on March 9:[75]

Wu P'ei-fu has no published programme to justify his going into battle, but, curiously enough, Chang Tso-lin, the whilom bandit chief, now champions constitutionalism and provincial autonomy, as well as the recall of the old and twice disbanded parliament, which has long been quartered in Canton. Chang Tso-lin and Tuan Ch'i-jui, as political bedfellows with Sun Yat-sen, may do more to unify China than if opposed in the field.

Japanese Allies

Despite the various indications of an independent attitude toward Japan, Chang continued his efforts to secure Japanese aid, particularly arms and ammunition. In the first two weeks in January 1922, feelers were put out through Chang's adviser, Machino, to the Japanese minister in Peking,[76] and through Yü Ch'ung-han to the Kwantung Army and the Japanese consul general in Mukden.[77] From Major General Kishi of the Kwantung Army, Yü sought not only arms and ammunition but also assurances that in the event of war the security of the Northeast would, in the last resort, be maintained by the Japanese army.[78] To Akatsuka Shōsuke, consul general in Mukden and ardent supporter of Chang,[79] Yü emphasized the threat to Japan as well as to Chang from Wu P'ei-fu, whom he represented as a spearhead of Anglo-American interests in China, and submitted a detailed list of armament requirements, together with helpful suggestions on how the "Embargo on the Sale of Arms to China" might be circumvented.[80]

A favorable response to these requests would seem to have been ruled out by the cabinet decisions of May 1921, already discussed above, but the prospect of an early renewal of the civil war prompted some reconsideration of the stand that should be taken by Japan. Obata, the minister in Peking, was noncommittal and favored "quietly watching the situation,"[81] and Banzai Rihachirō, who functioned as the direct Peking agent of Tokyo Staff Headquarters, counseled caution, warning against possibly disastrous consequences to Japan that might ensue from giving indiscreet support to Chang. His reasoning, however, was that if Chang could be persuaded to adopt a cautious approach, it would be to his own advantage.[82] Akatsuka in Mukden[83] and the Kwantung Army men, however, favored outright granting of Chang's requests. Kishi Yajirō, the army's special service agent in Mukden, recommended arms supply on the grounds that "the need for support of Chang Tso-lin by Japan is not a question of support of a party or a faction, but will have an important bearing on the existence of the [Japanese] empire." [84] His superior, Fukuhara Yoshiya, the Kwantung Army chief of staff, argued that because there was a joint English-American-Chihli effort being made to eliminate Japanese influence in China, Japan must support Chang's efforts to overthrow the Chihli factions. [85] Azuma Otohiko, military attaché in Peking, saw things much the same way. [86]

With the exception of the minister and, to a lesser extent, Banzai Rihachirō, all of these Japanese officials actually in China were thinking, in other words, in terms of supporting in one way or another their "man" in the Chinese civil struggle. Tokyo, however, gave no support to their view, but merely reiterated the principle of nonintervention. The dispatch from Foreign Minister Uchida on January 19 deserves quotation at some length: [87]

1. In Chinese political affairs at present Chang's position is, as a leading warlord, not popular either among the people or with foreign countries, and it seems, in the light of the Washington Conference, that a position such as his will become more and more difficult and it is extremely questionable whether he will be able to maintain it or not.

2. Support of Chang would mean that Japan would have to face great dangers. It is hard to believe that the fact of arms supply could remain undiscovered, and clearly people would not be deceived by the pretext of bandit-punishing. Further, it is possible that Chang might, in self-defense, advertise that he has Japanese support. And whatever else happened, if news of that got out, Japan would attract the criticisms and opposition not just of Chang's political enemies but of the Chinese people and world opinion, compromising our foreign and diplomatic relations. Also English and American support for Wu P'ei fu in retaliation for Japanese support for Chang would lead to an Anglo-Japanese confrontation. Is it necessary to support Chang to the point of risking such dangers?

3. Chang professes to be pro-Japan. Yet we have until now experienced any number of times that his pro-Japaneseness arises from his own calculations, not from any fixed principles or convictions, and once you look to his actual behavior it cannot be depended on. Furthermore, on the other hand, Wu P'ei-fu is not necessarily just anti-Japanese. Whether or not he is made truly anti-Japanese will most likely be determined by what moves Japan makes from now on. Would it not be advisable, considering that he too has power in a certain part of China at present, to avoid at all costs behavior that runs the risk of gravely exciting his hostility by helping Chang?

4. Apart even from the above points, supply of arms to Chang would be an infringement of the agreement between the powers relating to embargo on the supply of arms to China, and would be contrary to the politics of neutrality, impartiality and nonintervention hitherto proclaimed and carefully adhered to by the Japanese government. Therefore, I do not at present see any necessity for Japan to depart from the policies followed till now.

A few days later Uchida followed this up with instructions to Akatsuka to do what he could to ensure that army officers on the spot did not take any steps in contradiction to this line.[88] There were also efforts to make some contact with Wu P'ei-fu, though with little apparent success.[89]

Despite the unambiguous nature of his instructions, Akatsuka submitted a further recommendation on January 25 that Chang's request for aid be met, reiterating the argument that a victory for Wu—meaning a defeat for Chang—would clearly be disadvantageous for Japan, and therefore proposing that Chang be supplied with the arms he needed out of the stocks held by the Japanese army at Harbin.[90] Military opinion too was unchanged. Participants at a conference of senior army officers in China held on about January 20 continued to express strong support for Chang.[91] The persistent discrepancy between the line laid down from Tokyo and that which Japanese diplomats and officers in China continued to proclaim, if not to act on, was a serious embarrassment to the Japanese government. Thus Akatsuka, for example, continued not only to press his government for a change of line but to issue strong public affirmations of support for Chang,[92] while senior army officers not only urged that the arms Chang desired be supplied but also provided indirect aid, as in the affair of the flight of Tuan Ch'i-jui already mentioned (see above, p. 63).

As the war loomed closer and as suspicions in China, sustained by these incidents, persisted that proclamations of neutrality from Tokyo were no more than a screen for large-scale deliberate undercover involvement, the matter was considered further in Tokyo. A paper entitled "On the Imperial Government's Measures in the Chinese Situation Brought on by the Fengtien-Chihli Struggle" was drawn up for cabinet approval on April 21.[93] Though in general it reiterated the principles enunciated in Uchida's January dispatch, it set out one major new step—the withdrawal for the duration of the crisis of Chang's Japanese advisers, Machino Takema, Honjō Shigeru, who had been seconded to his staff in May 1921, and Kishi Yajirō, who was actually not an adviser but the Kwantung Army's special service agent in Mukden (see Table 5, p. 121). This was thought necessary "in the name of respecting the spirit of the nine-power treaty and of demonstrating the line of impartial neutrality and fairness that the imperial government has taken toward China's internal affairs." Two other points in the draft were that further approaches should be made to have Wu P'ei-fu understand Japan's neutrality and impartiality, and that Japanese representatives should consult with the representatives of Britain, America, and the other powers toward taking joint action to deal with the crisis. The draft was, however, relegated from the status of a cabinet decision paper to that of internal reference within the Foreign Ministry,[94] and in the end was used only as the basis of a public statement reaffirming in general terms Japanese neutrality in the dispute.[95] The extreme step of ordering the recall of Chang's advisers was amended to that of simply instructing them to exercise care to avoid involvement in the civil disturbances—a vain hope, as it turned out, for both Machino and Honjō actually served as important staff officers throughout the struggle, though Honjō may have opposed the decision to initiate it, and in the later stages of the fighting Honjō was entrusted by Chang with operational command.[96] (See below, p. 72.)

The Japanese War Ministry too, through its Bureau of Military Affairs (*Rikugun-shō gunmukyoku*), turned its attention to China policy in a paper dated April 23 entitled "The Attitude of the Empire to Chang Tso-lin, Holder of Power in the Three Eastern Provinces."[97] It too rejected the idea that Chang should be supplied with money or arms, and held that the Japanese interest lay in restraining him from any rash moves—although only, apparently, because the time was not then thought ripe for him to move into the central political arena. Given sufficient help in consolidating his hold over the Northeast and gradual growth in his political support, it was suggested that such aid might become appropriate at some future time. This paper, written at a time when most of Chang's forces of about 80,000 men were digging into positions well to the south of Peking and all hope of negotiating the dispute had virtually disappeared, reflects a high degree of detachment from the realities of the situation in China. It should be noted, however, that what was at issue in the policy debates in Tokyo at this time was not the question of support for Chang *as ruler of the Northeast*, the principle established at the Eastern Conference in 1921 and not thereafter questioned, but that of support for his ambition to become ruler of China as a whole, a goal that, as the evidence clearly shows, found scant favor with Japanese policymakers.

The contrast between the friendliness and enthusiasm shown him by the

Japanese he had to deal with in person and the neutrality of official policy must have puzzled Chang. In a speech he delivered at the offices of the South Manchuria Railway Company in Mukden on March 31, after emphasizing that his policy was, as it always had been, "Sino-Japanese cooperation and restraint of Europeans and Americans," he went on to say: [98]

> However, over the past two or three years Japanese government policy has been gradually changing. Unfortunately I am at present unable to figure out what Japanese policy is toward me. If it is that Chang should be helped, then help me. If it is that he should not be helped, then please let that meaning be made clear. There is a proverb: the umbrella that arrives after the rain [is useless].

The War

The sequence of events leading up to the war of April–May can be briefly summarized. The Liang cabinet—and by implication its sponsor, Chang—was under attack by Wu P'ei-fu from as early as January 5, 1922, on grounds of having instructed the Chinese delegates to the Washington Conference to yield ground to Japan on the Shantung question, in return for which Japan was to advance substantial loans to finance the near-bankrupt government. [99] The Shantung question was one well calculated to arouse public opinion, having been at the center of the 1919 disturbances, and Liang found it expedient to plead illness and retreat to Tientsin on prolonged leave, amounting in effect to retirement. While Chang rejected any criticisms of the Liang cabinet and refused to consider backing down, both sides maneuvered, issued telegrams in defense of their respective positions, and prepared for a showdown.

At a "Conference for National Unification," held in Tientsin in March 1922, the anti-Wu forces allied with Chang agreed on their basic strategy. The key principles seem to have been as follows: Sun Yat-sen for president; Liang Shih-i to be retained as prime minister; Wu P'ei-fu to be dismissed from all posts except those of inspector general of Hunan and Hupei (that is, from his subsidiary responsibilities in Chihli, Shantung, and Honan); amnesty for the still unpardoned leaders of the Anfu party; appointment of Chang Hsün to the post of inspector general of Kiangsu, Kiangsi, and Anhwei, and of Tuan Chih-kuei as tuchün of Chihli; revival of the old parliament and establishment of a constitution. [100] The agreement may also have included the commitment to commence joint military action against Wu on April 10 if he refused to cooperate. [101]

The involvement of the Ch'ing restorationist, Chang Hsün, in this strange alliance is further indication of how widely and with what ideological impartiality Chang was prepared to cast his net to bring every conceivable force that might be brought to bear on Wu. Complementary to this strategy were the attempts already discussed to secure Japanese support and weapons, and the attempt to isolate Wu and split the Chihli camp by securing the neutrality of its nominal head, Ts'ao K'un, who was connected to Chang by a marriage alliance.[102] Ts'ao K'un was the leader of a peace party within the Chihli clique, and his representative, a Fengtien man but Chihli militarist and commander of the 23rd Division, Wang Ch'eng-pin, made three goodwill visits to Mukden at this time, in return for which Chang sent Chang Ching-hui to Paoting to discuss possible peaceful settlement of the disputed points.[103] Through February and March, Ts'ao carefully withheld his signature from any of the missives issued by Wu in the early assault on Chang and Liang. Chang meanwhile insisted that his dispute was with Wu alone.

From March 22 Chang believed himself in a position of sufficient strength to disdain negotiations and began to move his troops down below the wall.[104] As he did so, however, his strategy began to fall apart.

In respect to each of its three major points, Chang's plans went awry: the requests for Japanese aid went unanswered; the "united front" of opponents of Wu built up between January and March collapsed in April; and attempts to split the Chihli camp failed completely. Reasons for the withdrawal of the various members of the "united front" were several: Sun Yat-sen's Northern Expedition collapsed as a result of the feuding between Sun and his warlord ally, Ch'en Chiung-ming;[105] Chang Hsün, who was to have commanded a joint force on the Anhwei front, thought better of it as news of his projected involvement caused widespread protest;[106] Tuan Ch'i-jui, when he heard news of these setbacks, decided to remain in Tientsin, and thus played no active role in the ensuing hostilities.[107] Chao T'i, tuchün of Honan, was Chang's one remaining ally who did actually play a part in the war, but he, in command of a poorly trained force of about 25,000 ex-bandits, was checked from any early movement by the quick arrival of Feng Yü-hsiang's troops in his province. When eventually, too late to be of any help to Chang, he did make a move, he was quickly defeated.[108] The hoped-for split between the Wu-led "hawks" and the Ts'ao-led "doves" in the Chihli party also failed to materialize. As

Chang's Mukden forces came down through the passes in force from April 10, a conference of Chihli leaders at Paoting quickly ironed out their differences, so that by the 11th Ts'ao K'un accepted the need for joint military action, put aside all consideration of his family connections with Chang, and added the 10,000 or so men under his command to the unified Chihli forces.[109] The declaration of support for Chihli by the Chinese naval command in Shanghai was a further blow to Chang in that another potential ally, Lu Yung-hsiang, tuchün of Chekiang, was thus rendered too vulnerable to engage in any support action from the Southeast.[110]

The flurry of telegrams and statements, accusations and appeals, issued by both sides in the dispute and by the President and consular body in Peking in the middle and later part of April did little to arrest the momentum toward war.[111] Introduced by several days of skirmishes along the Peking–Mukden and Tientsin–Pukow railways south of the capital area, the principal engagements began April 28. Both armies committed between 70,000 and 80,000 troops to the war, though Wu was reckoned to have the edge in weapons, training, experience, and command.[112] The battle was waged rather evenly until May 4. On that day, however, the entire Fengtien front line suddenly collapsed in disorder, the troops abandoning their positions and fleeing. Accounts differ on the cause of the debacle. According to some, troops of Feng Yü-hsiang's 11th Division simply walked around the right flank of Chang's armies in the middle of the night of May 3, and the resulting encirclement so dismayed the inexperienced Fengtien troops that the lines were quickly broken.[113] According to others, Chang Ching-hui, commander in chief of the Fengtien armies and responsible for the western front, with his subordinate Tsou Fen was in league with the enemy, and it was their deliberate treason that gave the enemy victory.[114] Yet another account has it that responsibility lay partly with President Hsü Shih-ch'ang and partly with Chang Ching-hui. By this version Hsü, who was alarmed at the growth of Fengtien strength, notified Chang Ching-hui at a crucial stage of the fighting that the three supposedly neutral divisions in the capital area were in contact with Wu P'ei-fu and likely to attack the rear of the Northeastern army.[115] He therefore suggested that Chang Ching-hui withdraw his men to the north, to a line between the Great Wall and Peking.[116] Without consulting Chang Tso-lin and not knowing this to be untrue, Chang commenced immediate withdrawal, whereupon the remainder of the front broke in confusion. Whichever of these accounts is true, a good deal of the responsibility for the Northeastern defeat attaches to Chang Ching-hui. Either he allowed his troops to retreat in disarray after defeat, or he was guilty of deliberate treason, or he was taken in by a simple deception and behaved in an irresponsible and incompetent way in ordering precipitate withdrawal of a major part of the army's front line.

Both Chang Ching-hui, who had been overall commander of the Fengtien forces, and Tsou Fen, who was in command of the main section of the Ch'ang-hsin-tien front, were very close to Chang Tso-lin. Already in 1907, when Chang Tso-lin had accepted the post of battalion commander in the reorganized provincial army, the four who accompanied him as company commanders were T'ang Yü-lin, Chang Ching-hui, Chang Tso-hsiang, and Tsou Fen.[117] Chang Ching-hui and Chang Tso-hsiang were actually Chang's earliest known associates from his bandit days.[118] His failure in this war thus involved those longest and most closely tied to him. Tsou Fen, in particular, had been under suspicion for some time before the war.[119] When in Mukden in March to attend Chang Tso-lin's birthday celebrations, he was even briefly under arrest, evidently because it was believed he had established a secret pact with Wu P'ei-fu. Because Chang Ching-hui and Chang Tso-hsiang both interceded on his behalf, he was released, and soon afterward he assumed his critical war command under Chang Ching-hui as commander in chief of the "Pacification Army." Another curious aspect of the affair is that Tsou's 16th Division was actually composed of Chihli troops, formerly Feng Kuo-chang's men, who had been incorporated into the Fengtien Army in 1920 by the simple expedient of appointing Tsou in place of the defeated Chihli commander of the Division, Wang T'ing-chen.[120] For Chang Tso-lin, there was embarrassment over the degree of responsibility for defeat shared by Chang Ching-hui and Tsou Fen. This was compounded by the equally undistinguished role played by Chang Tso-hsiang, who had been "younger brother" to Chang as Chang Ching-hui had been "elder brother"[121] and who had succeeded him as commander of the 27th Division. When news of the collapse of the western front reached him, he too immediately turned tail and his troops fled in total disorder.[122] When Chang Tso-lin and his advisers sat down later to analyze the causes of defeat, two facts were therefore clear: the major responsibility rested with the untrained, ex-bandit associates of Chang, the "old men" of the clique, whereas the "new men," the young and qualified alumni of various military academies, had been either overruled in debates over tactics that preceded the war or given minor roles to play once fighting began. The case for changing the ordering of affairs in the clique was consequently difficult to resist.[123]

A second phase of the war followed further to the north. Chang rallied his fleeing and disordered troops at Luan-chou, about halfway between Tientsin and Shan-hai-kuan on the Peking–Mukden railway. His adviser Machino describes how he and Chang sat on the platform at Luan-chou station as the troops were arriving, with Chang apologizing to them for the trouble they had been through and handing out bundles of 10 *yüan* notes from trunks full of ready cash—three million *yüan* in all that he had rushed to the spot.[124] The 10 *yüan* bonus to each man apparently helped in restoring morale.[*] In the reorganized army, from which Chang Ching-hui and Tsou Fen were conspicuously absent, Chang Tso-lin himself for a time took command of part of the troops.[125] He was also fortunate indeed to enjoy the services of one of the rising stars and greatest military geniuses in the Japanese army, Honjō Shigeru, then on his staff as an adviser and later to become Chief of Staff of the Kwantung Army. Honjō was given considerable authority in organizing the defenses for the Luan-chou battle, and he enjoyed the operational command in the battle itself. A series of engagements was fought, first in the vicinity of Luan-chou and then, after a further withdrawal caused largely by fear of British intervention in defense of its Kailan coal-mining interests,[126] at Shan-hai-kuan. Here, with short supply lines and an assured base area behind them, the Northeastern Army fought well, inflicting heavy casualties on the enemy in fierce engagements in mid-June. All sources seem agreed on the large number of dead and wounded from this fighting,[127] yet its purpose was moral rather than military. For Wu, decisive victory was out of the question unless he was prepared to chase Chang's troops into their home territory, and not only meet there the considerable forces Chang held in reserve but run serious risk of a clash with the Japanese, who were unlikely to allow any operations that would interfere with or damage their interests in the Northeast. Chang, for his part, was fighting to save face after the debacle he had suffered further south. He also had increasing reason to be concerned for the security of his home area, as well as the need to concentrate on meeting the considerable domestic unrest and mounting problems brought on by the defeat in May. (See the discussion in the following chapter.) Eventually, through the

*The monthly salary for a second-class private was 4.2 yüan; *CYB*, 1921–22, p. 527.

mediation of some foreign missionaries from Mukden, a cease-fire was negotiated and his troops withdrew to their home territory. The agreement was signed aboard a British battleship off Ch'in-huang-tao on June 17.[128]

LESSONS OF DEFEAT

The war of 1922 thus marked the first serious reverse Chang had suffered since his arrival in Mukden at the end of 1911. In the sense that he accomplished none of the major objectives that motivated his expedition— vindication of the Liang cabinet, punishment of Wu P'ei-fu, and, above all, national unification—and in that he lost rather than gained considerable territory, lost all influence over Peking, and lost face as well, he was clearly defeated. Yet the consequences of his defeat were very much softened by the fact that his home base in the three provinces remained intact. Thus, when formally dismissed for all his posts and offices by government orders of May 10, Chang simply responded on May 12 with a declaration of independence of the three provinces. How the defeat thereafter affected Chang, the problems to which it gave rise, and the administrative and military reforms carried out in its wake form the subject of the following chapter.

Yet Chang's taste for involvement in the affairs of China as a whole was far from satisfied. Initially it was the product of a desire to gain leverage and support in Peking to allow him to secure and develop his hold in the Northeast. But as Chang became imbued with a consciousness of his strategic strength vis-à-vis North China, and indeed the whole of China, conferred on him by the impregnability, wealth, and growing population of the Northeast, the scale of his ambition greatly widened. In light of this, his defeat could be seen only as a temporary setback. Given the confused state of Chinese military politics and the vacuum of power at the center, no man in Chang's position could be expected to set aside the ambition to follow in the tradition of the great unifiers of China who had emerged in the past on the basis of unified control of the area that he still controlled.[129]

From this perspective, relegation to the Northeast could be seen as an opportunity for Chang to face and rethink some of the problems exposed by the manner of his defeat. These problems were basically three. The first concerned his relationship with Japan. Chang appeared to be unhappy that his requests for Japanese arms and munitions were not met, and that Foreign Minister Uchida was set against intervention on his behalf. Yet how seriously he felt this is a question. Wide-ranging and conspicuous Japanese support would bring long-term political disadvantages likely to more than offset the short-term military advantages. Furthermore, despite the declarations of neutrality in Tokyo, the Japanese officers in his service not only had not been withdrawn but had performed valuable military service for him. He had also established close and amicable relationships with all Japanese agencies in the Northeast, and most important of all, he enjoyed a tacit understanding with the Japanese that support, if necessary intervention, would be forthcoming in the event of threat to the peace and security of the Northeast itself. In China's continuous civil wars this was a considerable strategic advantage. Chang's main problem, therefore, was one of neutralizing Japanese efforts to have him renounce his ambitions toward the rest of China and concentrate on developing the Northeast on the basis of Sino-Japanese "cooperation." His second problem was the need to rethink the question of allies and alliances, and of the principles on which he might best cast his appeal for support, not only from other warlords and their armies, but also from the civil and popular organs such as would be necessary if his ambition were seriously to be set on Peking and unification of the nation. Third was that if he were to rely on his armies to attain his goals, then he had to give serious attention to the problems of proper training, supply, and command.

CHAPTER THREE

Postwar Reorganization, 1922-1924

The leadership and the raison d'être of the Fengtien clique were brought sharply in question by the reverses of May 1922. Clearly reorganization and reform were necessary, and for a time in the crisis atmosphere of the summer of 1922 it seemed that far-reaching change might even be possible. That in the end it was not possible was due to the inability of Chang to allow any significant powers to pass out of his own hands. As the immediate postwar crisis receded, so did his interest in reforms not related directly to military strengthening. But in another, very significant sense, these years were a watershed: relations with Japan, superficially smooth and mutually satisfactory, were modified crucially but imperceptibly as plans for the independent economic development of the Northeast were initiated, and as resistance to exclusively Japanese ties became evident in all sorts of ways—from demands for the abrogation or modification of the unequal treaties to protests at Japanese "cultural" imperialism. Even in the most important military sphere there was a notable switch away from exclusive reliance on Japanese supply of weapons, equipment, and advisers toward a policy of the widest possible diversification.

The first challenge Chang had to meet was that emanating from ambitious or discontented subordinates—a challenge to which his defeat in battle and loss of all claims to formal legitimacy in Peking rendered him vulnerable. Thereafter he faced the longer-term problem of how his newly proclaimed autonomous domain was to be administered. Formal severance of relations with Peking meant little change in itself, for all important decisions concerning the Northeast had long been reserved to Chang alone, but the pressure from below for change within the three provinces was considerable—both from civilian officials who favored rationalization, economic development policies, and permanent or long-term withdrawal from the Chinese civil war, on the one hand, and from the new military men who pressed on Chang the adoption of modern military technique and all-out preparation for renewal of warfare and eventual conquest of China, on the other. For the civilian officials, unification was a distant, expensive, and probably vain dream, and a presently growing, prosperous, and independent Northeast—a "Manchuria" in effect—was much to be preferred; for the military men, the natural advantages of the Northeast in terms of strategic position and comparative wealth needed only to be complemented by efficient, modern military technique in order to create an army so decisively superior to that of all rivals for power in China as to guarantee that Chang would dominate and conquer the country just as Nurhachi had 300 years before.

THE THREAT OF REBELLION

Chang's immediate weakness being obvious, his enemies were quick to attempt to exploit it. While dismissing Chang and his main associates, therefore, Peking, which was by this time under the exclusive sway of the Chihli clique, also announced the names of their designated sucessors, carefully chosen from among those who seemed most independent of Chang or least reconciled to his dominance of the Northeast. The main appointments were as follows:[1] acting tuchün of Fengtien, Wu Chün-sheng; acting tuchün of Heilungkiang, Feng Te-lin; acting civil governor of Fengtien, Yüan Chin-k'ai; and acting civil governor of Heilungkiang, Shih Chi-ch'ang.

Now neither Feng Te-lin, Yüan Chin-k'ai, nor Shih Chi-ch'ang had the kind of independent military base from which to challenge Chang, and, save in the case of Feng Te-lin, who may have nursed old grudges against him, they lacked any obvious motive to engage in such a risky venture. Wu Chün-sheng, however, as tuchün of Heilungkiang and commander of the 29th Division, was somewhat different. He had opposed the war from the outset; his troops played a minimal part in its prosecution; and it was even rumored that there was a pact of sworn brotherhood between him and Wu P'ei-fu, both of whom happened to be of the same provincial origins—Shantung.[2] Under Wu Chün-sheng various schemes had been mooted, particularly by his railway commissioner, Ma Chung-chün, which called for the introduction of American capital into the development of the province, and since the Fengtien-Chihli war was seen, in a sense, as a war between one side backed by Japan (Chang Tso-lin) and one backed by Britain and the United States (Wu P'ei-fu) this fact tended to reinforce doubts about where his loyalties lay.[3] Chang was certainly wary of him, and, although Wu claimed he had no intention of accepting the Fengtien post, Chang moved quickly to force his hand by cabling to that effect in Wu's name anyway.[4]

Chang's fears were not unfounded. On May 19, after the first phase of the war in which Fengtien had been ignominiously defeated, Wu had secretly dispatched a representative to Peking via Dairen to negotiate on his behalf.[5] As the second round of the war opened near the Great Wall, he resolved not to send any reinforcements to relieve the Northeastern armies, and according to his Japanese adviser, he was ready, if pressed, to recruit a force of bandits and send them south instead.[6] He was, however, being watched by Chang Huan-hsiang, who, as commander of the Chinese Eastern Railway, had a force of about mixed-brigade strength based on Harbin, and who prepared to move in to arrest him.[7] A further mixed brigade, the 4th, was also sent to Heilungkiang to reinforce the pressure on Wu, though ostensibly to engage in anti-bandit operations, and Chu Ch'ing-lan, who was actually an ex-tuchün of the province, was appointed an "assistant" to Wu, almost certainly with the idea that he should presently replace him.[8] A little later Chang Tso-lin also attached to Wu's staff no fewer than three of his senior advisers—Yü Ch'ung-han, his chief of staff, Jen Yü-lin, his chief secretary, and T'an Kuo-han, Fengtien Commissioner for Industry.[9] He did not wish to dismiss Wu, however, for fear of the consequences of an open clash in the confused and weakened state of the Northeast.[10] Eventually, even when Wu offered his resignation, Chang refused it. By this time, however, much of the crisis atmosphere of the immediate aftermath of war had passed, and as the tensions were dissipated, the relationship between Chang and Wu gradually improved. Wu in fact retained his post in Heilungkiang until 1928, when he died in the same explosion that killed Chang.

The other major attempt by Peking to instigate upheaval in Chang's domains was through the medium of Kao Shih-pin. Kao, formerly commander of the Kirin 1st Division, has been mentioned above in connection with Meng En-yüan's Kirin-based resistance to Chang in 1918–19. His challenge to Chang in 1922 was short-lived. Having reached an agreement with Wu P'ei-fu, he organized a force made up partly of bandits and partly of regular soldiers who were his ex-subordinates and at the time members of the Chinese Eastern Railway protection force, about 2,000 men in all, and tried to open a second front against Chang in the Sui-fen area in the far north.[11] After Kao issued a manifesto on May 26, 1922, calling for the overthrow of Chang, his forces won some initial successes, taking the township of Sui-fen and making moves to threaten Harbin. However, with the dispatch of regular troops to the area in special trains under Chang Tsung-ch'ang's command, his rebellion was quickly quashed and his army dispersed. By June 6 Sui-fen had been retaken, and Kao, who was reported captured and executed on several occasions after this,[12] did not thereafter present any threat.

CIVILIAN CHALLENGES

The challenge to Chang's autocratic rule that was mounted among civilians and bureaucrats in the Northeast was much more widely based and, though in the long run defeated, left a much deeper impression on the subsequent character of his regime. On May 12 Chang responded to his dismissal by the Peking government by declaring independence: "[President] Hsü-Shih-ch'ang has requested me to give up the Three Eastern Provinces, Jehol and Chahar districts, and Inner and Outer Mongolia. Henceforth these regions shall not be regarded as part of the territory of the Chinese republic." At the same time a similar pronouncement was made from Mukden by the Association of Provincial Assemblies of the Three Eastern Provinces, by the Chambers of Commerce, Educational Associations, and Artisans Associations: "Since the matter of whether Chang [Tso-lin] should be dismissed or not is one that concerns the lives of the 30 million people of the three provinces, we unanimously refuse this illegal order" (i.e. the order for Chang's dismissal).[13] Requests for rescinding the order began also to be submitted by the various organizations in the Northeast to Peking. Then on May 26 over the signatures of Chang Tso-lin, Sun Lieh-ch'en, and Wu Chün-sheng, a circular telegram explaining the severance of relations between the Northeast and Peking was dispatched to those leading political figures still on friendly terms with Chang Tso-lin—Sun Yat-sen, T'ang Shao-i, and the tuchün of Fukien, Chekiang, Anhwei, and Shansi:[14]

Since the establishment of the republic, there has been constant domestic strife and the country has scarcely been one country at all. The root of this evil lies in the warlords who, ignorant of world currents, disregard the rights of the people and set aside the laws. Since there can be no unity and peace without fundamental reform, we cooperated to advance the cause of civil government. As Wu P'ei-fu's arrogant highhandedness grew increasingly intolerable . . . recently the Fengtien armies entered the passes to remonstrate thoroughly with Wu P'ei-fu. However, his tyranny knowing no bounds, Wu P'ei-fu opened war on us, then proceeded all the way to Tientsin to meddle in politics there. For the sake of saving the country, we had no alternative to declaring the independence of the government and politics of the Three Eastern Provinces. Acting in concert with our various fellow generals of the Southwest and the Yangtze, we will protect the law and promote unification. . . . When we see a speedy implementation of legal government, we will at once set aside our arms, return to civil life, and participate no further in politics.

This telegram was issued several days after Chang's return from the front, and it is clear that within Fengtien province, at that time at least, there was little disagreement between civil and military on basic policies that had to be followed in consequence of the outcome of the war: severance of relations with Peking, cooperation with the nationalists in the South against the dominant Chihli clique, and promotion of civil government in the Three Eastern Provinces. It is on the latter point, however, that the civilians seem to have pressed Chang hardest, their demands being aided fortuitously by the accident of Chang's alignment in Chinese politics with the champion of civil government, and by the prevalent mood of federalism within many non-Chihli-dominated parts of China.[15]

These were, at any rate, the principles underlying the discussions that were carried on in Mukden in late May and early June between Chang and leading officials of all three provinces. Wang Yung-chiang played the leading role in these discussions, and their outcome was the appointment of Chang Tso-lin by the Fengtien Provincial Assembly, with delegates present also from the assemblies of Kirin and Heilungkiang, as "commander in chief of the Peace Preservation Army" for the Three Provinces. Sun Lieh-ch'en and Wu Chün-sheng were appointed deputy commanders.[16] The rationale and the principles to govern the new federation were as follows:[17]

By reason of geographical and historical considerations, the Three Eastern Provinces form an autonomous region. . . . For the preservation of the public peace within this autonomous region, we now establish and will jointly follow these principles. Military and civil jurisdiction is to be separate, according to the tendency of the business concerned. The Commander in Chief of Military Affairs will exercise general control to see that the policies of independence develop harmoniously, and the deputy commanders in chief will cooperate with him in this. The commander in chief is to be elected by the joint meeting of the Provincial Assemblies, and he is to appoint his deputies. Civil affairs of the various provinces will be presided over by the governors, and until the promulgation of a constitution, governors are to be elected by the Provincial Assemblies. The system of government of the Three East-ern Provinces will be organized as before, and the joint assembly of Provincial Assemblies will carry on the business of enacting laws.

These terms are very significant. They demonstrate the bid for power that was being made by the civilian interests represented in the Provincial As-semblies.

The Provincial Assemblies had never functioned as representative legis-lative bodies. In the first elections, in 1909, a mere 2 percent of the adult male population enjoyed the vote.[18] After the reforms of 1912 this was expanded to between 20 and 25 percent.[19] Elected representatives served a three-year term, and meetings of the Assembly were to be held once a year for a period of 60 days.[20] Although the powers of the Assemblies were limited, they served nevertheless as avenues of communication between the socioeconomic elite, whom by and large they represented, and the mili-tary authorities, who held real power.

The Fengtien Assembly had shown little previous inclination to assert its prerogatives. For two and a half years from its dismissal in March 1914 till October 1916, it did not meet at all.[21] The considerable grants of military, diplomatic, financial, and judicial power made to Chang Tso-lin in the administrative readjustments that followed 1916 were clearly not contin-gent upon any restraints that might be exercised by elective assemblies; nor were these assemblies ever in fact consulted on any of the major decisions—of war and peace, for example—that had to be taken in sub-sequent years. Thus the joint Provincial Assemblies' statement of principle initiating the new federation was an important attempt at innovation in several respects, above all by the very fact of the Assemblies' involvement in the process of declaration of autonomy, but also by reason of the commit-ment declared to the principle of separation of civil and military powers, the rights claimed by the Assemblies to the appointments of commanders in chief and of governors, and because of the intention stated to establish a constitution. These were the concessions won from Chang Tso-lin in his moment of greatest weakness and in consideration for the conferral on him of a measure of legitimacy for his continued rule of the Northeast when, otherwise, all formal legitimacy had been withdrawn by Peking's orders for his dismissal. The convergence of interest of warlords and As-semblies in the provincial autonomy movement at this time has been de-scribed as follows in a comment on a like situation in the South which may be applied, *mutatis mutandis*, to the Northeast:[22]

The frequency of civil wars made it urgent that local peace and order be preserved. Meanwhile, as various attempts to restore central government failed from 1916, and as the autonomy of local militarists developed, a federal government recognizing local autonomy appeared to be the only way to contain the rampant militarism and to channel political struggles into civil institutions. So the idea of representative government on a provincial level and federal government on a national level took root.

Ironically the theory was welcomed both by local warlords and by civilians. Southern warlords welcomed it as a way to protect their autonomous status from powerful Northern warlords.

For Chang it was a way to protect his autonomous status from the threat of the Chihli-dominated Peking government, whereas for the civilians it seemed a chance to assert policies in the interests of the mercantile and nascent industrial interests of the Northeast.

The process of crystallizing their enhanced relationship vis-à-vis Chang Tso-lin into a formal constitutional document, however, proved too much for the civilians. Through the summer of 1922 various proposals were debated. The Peace Preservation Association of the Three Eastern Provinces, made up of one military and one civil official, five Assembly men, and a representative of the world of commerce, education, agriculture, and industry from each of the provinces—a total of 33—attempted first to define the powers of the commander in chief.[23] He was to be empowered to submit bills to the Interprovincial Assembly; to implement laws passed by it; to convene the army; to commute or increase punishments; to convene the Provincial Assembly and the Interprovincial Assembly every year; to declare martial law; to receive diplomatic representatives; with the consent of the Interprovincial Assembly, to declare war and to negotiate peace and treaties, save in cases of enemy attack on territory under his jurisdiction, in which case he might declare war first; and finally, to have the right to address the Interprovincial Assembly either in person or through a delegate.

Thereafter an Association for the Promotion of Civil Government was formed * with the participation of prominent members of the Assembly,[24] and in August Chang Tso-lin himself opened a meeting of the Peace Preservation Assembly at which principles virtually identical with those enunciated in June and described above were proclaimed.[25] No further progress was made, however, toward drawing up or establishing a constitution for

* One of the originators of this organization was Chao Ch'u-fei, later editor of the *Tun-san-sheng min-pao*, on which see p. 88.

the Three Eastern Provinces. Not only that, but even at the time Chang
appeared to be giving his official blessing to principles such as the election
by Provincial Assemblies of civil governors, or the separation of civil and
military jurisdictions, he was in practice flouting them. The right of the
Assemblies to choose freely their civil governor, something they had certainly never enjoyed before, proved a sufficient test case.

Of greatest importance was the case of Fengtien province itself. Wang
Yung-chiang, combining the post of Acting Governor since May 1921 with
that of Provincial Treasurer, which he had held since May 1917, was a key
figure in Chang's entourage.[26] His role in turning consistent chronic de-
ficits in the provincial finances into substantial surplus earned him the
confidence and gratitude of Chang Tso-lin (see Chapter 1, pp. 30–31). It
was Wang who served as principal architect of the Three Eastern Provinces
Federation and who played a perhaps decisive role in persuading Chang to
avoid any fight to the suicidal finish after his defeat at Ch'ang-hsin-tien in
early May.[27] Yet although he drew up the guidelines of the new federation,
and though he enjoyed wide support in the Assembly, his strength was
more apparent than real. His position was complicated by the attempt of the
new President, Li Yüan-hung, to mobilize the anti-Chang forces behind
Wang by offering him the post of civil governor of Fengtien. Needless to
say, Peking was anxious to have the autonomy of the Northeast rescinded.
Wang, however, was in no position to challenge Chang, and consequently
the "appointment," announced by Peking on June 18, was refused by
Wang on the 20th. On June 26, acting on the principle of separation of
military and civil affairs that had been proclaimed as basic to the new
federation, Wang's supporters in the Provincial Assembly elected him to
the position of governor. Chang was not consulted on the matter, and since
he had overruled similar elections in Kirin and Heilungkiang provinces just
a few days earlier (to be discussed below), the Fengtien Assembly was
attempting in unmistakable fashion to assert itself. However, Wang was in
no position to force a showdown with Chang or to ignore the dominance
that the military in practice enjoyed in Fengtien. Since these successive
indications of Wang's independent strength in Peking and in the Provincial
Assembly could be construed by Chang as a threat, Wang's position became difficult, even dangerous. Pleading illness, he retreated for a time to
the Red Cross hospital in the Japanese-controlled South Manchuria Railway zone, and then fled from Mukden, still under Japanese protection, to

his home town of Chin-chou,* which also happened to lie within the Japanese-controlled Kwantung province.[28]

Wang's illness was genuine, but it was less the reason for his departure from Mukden than the excuse. The real reason lay in the differences between his and Chang's opinions on policies needed for the future. Although the differences cannot be spelled out in detail, it is clear that Wang was holding out for some practical steps in accord with his plans of the Three Eastern Provinces Federation, and using his hold over the provincial finances to put pressure on Chang accordingly. Chang above all needed money; direct expenses of the war amounted to something like 11 million yüan;[29] indirect expenses are impossible to estimate, but Chang demanded 30 million yüan from the treasury to cover the cost of the war.[30] Wang either refused or demanded some unacceptable *quid pro quo*. In his absence the Assembly Speaker, Pai Yung-chen, served as acting governor, but leading political figures strongly disapproved of him as lacking political experience and falling outside any bureaucratic clique,[31] so that Chang had to send a series of delegates to Chin-chou to try to persuade Wang to resume his post.[32] This Wang did, relations with Chang Tso-lin being apparently restored in mid-August on the basis of an understanding that he could administer the civil affairs of the province unhindered while Chang saw to the military.[33] Shortly afterward Chang gave public blessing to the Peace Preservation Principles, discussed above. Yet the victory, if it can be seen as such, was a hollow one for Wang Yung-chiang; his differences with Chang Tso-lin continued, and far from being independent of Chang's military jurisdiction, his work in regularizing and strengthening the finances and the civil government of the province became their essential underpinning. Since every cent spent by the military had to be found somehow by the civil administration, any distinction between them was tenuous.[34]

In Kirin province the issue of civil-military rivalry was greatly compounded by the already long-established spirit of opposition to Fengtien, and by the sentiment that Kirin should be ruled by Kiriners.[35] Kirin representatives were present in Mukden from late May for participation in the

---

*This Chin-chou, on the South Manchuria Railway line not far north of Dairen in the Japanese-run Kwantung province, is not to be confused with the Chin-chou on the Peking–Mukden railway that has been referred to above. These two place names are written with different characters, and the former is now known as "Chin-hsien" or "Kin-hsien."

Joint Assembly meetings relating to the institution of independence and the new autonomous federation. When news of Peking's appointment of Wang Yung-chiang to the Fengtien governorship reached Mukden, Chang Tso-lin, worried that Peking might attempt further interference in the Northeast by making an appointment to the Kirin post also, gave the Kirin representatives to understand that he might not be averse to an election of governor by the Kirin Assembly.[36] However, when these representatives returned to Kirin on June 22 and resolved to conduct an election almost immediately, Chang soon revealed the limits of the latitude he was prepared to allow. At the election held on the 23d, Yü Yüan-p'u, Speaker of the Assembly, was chosen.[37] Chang, however, almost immediately let it be known that his appointment was unacceptable, and that the only acceptable candidate for the post was K'uei Sheng, a man of Kirin origins but currently Fengtien Political Affairs Commissioner.[38] Chang issued a circular telegram stating that the reason for disallowing the election was the technical one that the constitution had not yet been settled, but then proceeded to make nonsense of this by continuing with the appointment of K'uei. Since Yü was a leading exponent of the "Kirin for the Kiriners" idea, opposed to the Autonomous Federation from its inception and apparently intent on reducing Fengtien-Kirin ties to a minimum, Chang went to some length to oust him, working through the Kirin-Changchun police chief and the acting governor of the province to stir up opposition and ensure that Yü and his party would be thoroughly defeated. Yü was neither prepared nor able to resist this attack, so that K'uei, though lacking support in the Provincial Assembly, on a simple nomination from Chang Tso-lin succeeded uneventfully to the governorship.[39] Resentment ran high against him, however, and the rate of resignations he had to deal with made effective government difficult. Eventually, in December, he was forced to resign.[40] Resentment of dictation of the affairs of the province was visible in other ways through this period also: in the insistence by the Kirin Assembly that any constitutional draft should be approved by the individual Assemblies of the Three Eastern Provinces and not simply imposed by fiat from Mukden,[41] and in demands by student groups in Kirin that the institution of the Commander in Chief for Peace Preservation in the Three Eastern Provinces be not recognized since it was opposed to the Autonomous Federation principle, and that military, diplomatic, judicial, financial, and communications powers should be returned to the direct jurisdiction of the central government in Peking.[42]

In Heilungkiang, by contrast with Kirin, the sense of provincial identity was weak, reflecting the relative newness and smallness of the province in population terms—an estimated 2 million as against the 6 million in Kirin and 11 million in Fengtien. According to a study made in 1924, half of the 300 civil and military officials of the province were Fengtien men, 50 were from Chihli, and only 24 or 25, or approximately 10 percent, were natives of the province. Not a single regiment or brigade of the army was under the command of a Heilungkiang native.[43] All important military and political matters, in other words, were reserved for direct decision by Chang Tso-lin or his close associates. Even the telegram by which the decision for independence was announced in the name of the Provincial Assemblies of all three provinces was issued before any such decision had been made in Heilungkiang.[44]

As in Kirin, it appears to have been a suggestion coming from Chang Tso-lin himself that prompted the Assembly on the night of June 21 to elect its Speaker, Liang Sheng-te, governor. Chang may have been influenced, as he was in the case of Kirin, by the Peking announcement of the appointment of Wang Yung-chiang in Fengtien, and also by his suspicion of Wu Chün-sheng, who was then acting as both tuchün and governor. However, Liang's election was unacceptable both to Chang Tso-lin and to Wu Chün-sheng, who hurriedly went to Mukden to discuss it with Chang, with the result that Liang had to stand down in favor of the Commissioner for Education, Yü Ssu-hsing, who thus became governor purely by virtue of the fiat of the commander-in-chief, Chang Tso-lin.[45]

Since the division of civil and military powers and the right of election of governor by the Provincial Assemblies were fundamental to the Autonomous Federation idea, Chang's intervention and disallowance of the elections in Kirin and Heilungkiang was an unmistakable blow to the hopes of the civilians. When Wang Yung-chiang too failed to secure concessions from Chang Tso-lin on control over the affairs of Fengtien, or agreement on rights that might be exercised by the civilian wing of government, the Assemblies quickly relapsed from their brief spell of assertiveness following the declaration of independence into their former supineness. To Chang Tso-lin, representative institutions, whether Provincial or Interprovincial Assemblies, were no more than planks of legitimacy upon which to stand when forced by circumstances *in extremis*, an aid in raising funds, and a channel of communication to other strata of the Northeastern elite. He remained always a military man, who saw government in terms of control

TABLE 2
Major Officials in Kirin Province, December 1923:
Connections and Interrelationships

	Official posts held by:			
Name and principal office	Wives	Relatives	Friends/ colleagues	Total
Sun Lieh-ch'en, Tuchün	3	22	5	27 (incl. 6 magistrates)
K'uei Sheng, Governor	2	13	16	29
Chou Yü-ping, Director of Political Affairs Bureau	1	2	12	14
Ts'ai Yün-sheng, Treasurer	3	8	15	23 (incl. 9 Treasury officials)
Chung-yü, Police Chief	3	6	17	23 (incl. 5 Police Dept. officials)
Ma Chün-ku, Commissioner for Industry	3	8	10	18 (incl. 5 in Dept. of Industry)
Yü Yüan-p'u, Commissioner for Education	1	8	10	18 (incl. 4 in Dept. of Education)

SOURCE: Compiled from information contained in Kwantung Province Police Department Report, Dec. 21, 1923; JFMA 1614 6, pp. 7918–32.

and exploitation, and who was preoccupied, especially after the defeat of 1922, with recovery, revenge against Wu P'ei-fu, and reassertion of his dominance over the central plains and eventually over the whole of China.

However, it is perhaps worth stressing at this point that the reforms demanded by the civilian forces were very limited—a necessary consequence of the narrow and limited base from which they were made. The civilian government they pressed for meant not so much an extension of popular participation and control over the exercise of political power as a shift in the locus of decision making from one section of the existing elite, the military, in favor of another, their own, whose power and interests were based on land and commerce. Thus, for example, it was not part of that challenge to contradict the force of corruption, nepotism, and "cronyism" in determining official appointments. Table 2 gives some indication of how pervasive a force these elements were and suggests that both civilian and military members of the Northeastern elite understood "office" in highly traditional terms. The table applies to official relationships in Kirin province only, but it is the author's impression that the same was true also of the other Northeastern provinces. One example of the "fruits" enjoyed by officeholders is the distribution of "profits" accruing to the provincial treasury and the Yung-heng Bank, the official bank in Kirin, which took place on January 31, 1923. Just over two million yüan was distributed, of which over half was paid to Chang Tso-lin, Sun Lieh-ch'en, the Kirin tuchün, and other senior heads of departments within the province, the other half being paid out in bonuses to minor government officials. Small wonder that protests to Chang Tso-lin by the General Chamber of Commerce calling for an inquiry into corruption in the province brought little response.[46]

ALLIANCES AND IDEOLOGIES

The diplomatic issue that faced Chang's reconstituted administration in the aftermath of the war was two-sided: externally, the position to be taken toward the "powers," especially Japan; and domestically the relationship between the Fengtien and other Chinese political-military groupings contending for dominance over China. In the Fengtien-Chihli war, despite the careful construction of a most unlikely alliance of domestic elements opposed to Wu P'ei-fu, Chang's forces in the end had had to fight alone. Yet the need for, and the logic of, the tie between the two major forces opposed to Wu P'ei-fu—Chang's in the North and Sun Yat-sen's in the South—remained persuasive. In the months following the end of the war, delegates continued to pass to and fro between them.

Whether because of the link with Sun, or because of his own continuing preoccupation with the idea of conquest of all China, Chang began to dabble in the rhetoric of unification, consequently of nation, and therefore of nationalism. At the same time the influx of post–May Fourth nationalist and anti-imperialist ideas from the rest of China in consequence of the May Fourth Movement of 1919 put him under increasing pressure to put his claim to leadership in those terms. Yet Chang himself, fierce opponent in the Northeast of the nationalism of 1911 and 1919, was incorrigible. While he was negotiating with Sun Yat-sen in terms of the interests of the nation, and with Wang Yung-chiang on the principles of the Autonomous Federation of the Northeast, there is no indication that Chang himself took either very seriously. However, as part of his effort to mobilize maximum possible support in his campaign against Wu P'ei-fu, he did give some thought to the question of ideology. He was reported at the time to have taken up the study of Taoism, which in itself is scarcely surprising since it was the conventional retreat of statesmen and generals in defeat or out of office.[47] He also, however, instructed General Hsü Lan-chou to work on the fabrication of an ideology upon which the people of the Northeast might be united. Hsü's brief was somewhat bizarre: he was to work out and propagate a "synthesis of the five religions"—Buddhism, Taoism, Confucianism, Islam, and Christianity.[48] Since there is no subsequent record of how he fulfilled his commission, it must be assumed that it was simply allowed to lapse. Not until 1925, when Chang adopted a stand of virulent anti-communism, did the question of ideology come up again.

Although Chang himself was incorrigible, for those under him the ties maintained with the South after the 1922 war, and the concepts of nationalism, federalism, and representative democracy that were perforce invoked, offered a chance for the formulation and expression of ideas hitherto impossible. Most important was the formation, in October 1922, of the *Tung-san-sheng min-pao*, or Three Eastern Provinces People's Paper.[49] With this paper Kuomintang sentiments were expressed openly in the Northeast for the first time, and under sponsorship from the highest levels. The paper was established partly with a subsidy of 20,000 yüan from Chang Tso-lin's son, Chang Hsüeh-liang, and from Wang Yung-chiang, and it continued to receive a monthly subsidy of 3,000 yüan from provincial government funds. It began as a two-page daily, half of which, because of the subsidy and official tie, functioned as a kind of government gazette, featuring official army and government notices, while the other half represented the views and interests of the founding body—the Society for the Promotion of Civil Government in the Three Eastern Provinces. This organization had been set up in the confusion after the war of 1922 to promote the cause of civil government through the separation of civil and military administration. That cause was quickly lost as Chang reestablished his autocratic control over all aspects of the Northeastern administration, but the organization survived, and indeed was coopted and granted official favor and funds. The consequence of this compromise, however, was that its attention was shifted from the domestic affairs of the Northeast to its foreign relations, and it became the spearhead of the nationalist and anti-imperialist movement in the Northeast.[50]

Chao Ch'u-fei, a 35-year-old Assemblyman who became president of the *Min-pao* in 1924, was chief secretary of the Society for the Promotion of Civil Government in the Three Eastern Provinces, and was reported to have direct Kuomintang ties and to be acting as the liaison man between the civilian faction in the Northeast and the Kuomintang.[51] His previous career included a spell in the South as Director of the Water Transport Bureau in P'ing-nan in Kwangsi,[52] where it may be that he first established links with the Kuomintang. A secret Japanese report on the press in the Three Provinces, completed in 1926, describes the paper as the "organ of the Mukden clique (Kuomintang wing)," and as anti-Japanese in principle.[53] It is important to realize that such a group did exist, with a powerfully sponsored and protected voice, from quite early in the decade, and that when the time came in 1929 for Chang Hsüeh-liang, after his father's death, to carry the Northeast into unity with Chiang Kai-shek's newly established regime, it was actually the climax of quite a long relationship.

THE ECONOMY

Recovery

The resources of the province in 1922, however bled and reduced by war, were by no means exhausted. The principal currency unit of the province, the Fengtien p'iao or paper dollar, though greatly weakened during the war and its aftermath, was able to be restored to relative stability afterward because of this basic strength, and because of the widespread confidence in which Wang Yung-chiang was held. Since this 1922 war is a good illustration of the problem first noted above in relation to Kirin in 1919, and since it is a problem that grew more acute thereafter, it is worth examining briefly here.

Simply stated, the value of the money of the province came to be seen as harnessed directly to the fortunes of the clique in war. War or the threat of war had dramatic consequences for the exchange rate, and as the Fengtien dollar weakened against the Japanese gold yen, which was the fixed unit of transactions on the Dairen Exchange,[54] so the Northeastern economy was increasingly at a disadvantage. From a position of approximate parity in 1917 between the Fengtien silver-based p'iao and the Japanese gold yen, by January 13, 1920, the p'iao reached its greatest strength of 54 to the Japanese 100 yen.[55] To some extent this was a reflection of the worldwide strength and high prices of silver at this time, but it was also a mark of the confidence engendered by the strict monetary policies of Wang Yung-chiang and by the commitment announced at this time to the introduction of a convertible currency tied to strict government guarantees.[56] The considerable weakening of silver on world bullion markets that followed was also a factor in the subsequent weakening of the p'iao, but over and above this the weakening of confidence as a result of the heavy expenditures on adventures south of the Great Wall commencing later in 1920 is clear, and the behavior of the Exchange in 1922 demonstrates it.

From around 116 (yüan to the 100 yen) in January, the rate fell steadily as the prospects of war rose. In mid-April, as Fengtien troops poured through the passes, and substantial amounts of hard currency were reported to have been withdrawn from the treasury and from the main banks in Mukden to support them,[57] the p'iao crashed to 147. For a time, in an attempt to stem its collapse, transactions on the Exchange were limited to 500,000 yüan on any one day and the rate fixed at 138. Despite the restrictions, and the jail penalties that met their infringement, news of the debacle on the front in May produced a slump in the Exchange price to 156. Recovery in the Shan-hai-kuan fighting that followed the regrouping of the armies saw a strengthening to around 130 in July and August. However, in September rumors of a renewal of hostilities were rife, and again, as the rate dropped to 145, Chang Tso-lin found it necessary to step in with an order to the Exchange limiting transactions to 1 million yüan per day at no more than 145 (September 14), and three days later a further reduction to 142.5, backed by a contingent of police to supervise the market proceedings.[58]

Compared with the collapse of the currency that set in later, particularly (for reasons to be discussed below) from 1925,[59] these fluctuations may appear negligible. Yet they are important, in that the causes—the subordination of all affairs in the province to the military, the draining of reserves and the issue of inadequately backed notes to support them, and the frustration of fiscal reform efforts because of the priority attached to military expansion—are all tendencies that continued and that grew more acute subsequently. So too did the consequences: developing antagonism between mercantile and militarist concerns, and growing disbelief on the part of the principal investors in the territory, the Japanese, that the administration was capable of the reforms necessary to attain the kind of stability they desired.

Wang's return to Mukden and the easing of fears from September 1922 of the imminent renewal of the war facilitated rapid recovery of the economy and stabilization of the currency, though its exchange value was never restored to prewar levels. Despite Chang's defeat in the war, his autonomous status afterward gave him access to important new sources of revenue. These were the revenues of the extramural section (Shan-hai-kuan–Mukden) of the Peking–Mukden railway, and of the Northeastern branches of the salt and customs gabelles. When the Fengtien troops withdrew back beyond the Great Wall in accordance with the armistice in July, they carried off with them some 75 percent of the total locomotives and rolling stock of the line.[60] Thereafter Shan-hai-kuan became the junction station between two quite independently administered lines. All revenues collected outside the Wall were remitted directly to Mukden, in defiance of the loan agreement under which the line was constructed, according to which they were to be paid into the Tientsin branch of the Hong Kong and Shanghai Bank, and thence remitted, part in fulfillment of the original British loan, the remainder to the Peking government. From the figures of net surplus declared for the part of the railway remaining under Anglo-Chinese jurisdiction within China proper, it can be calculated that control over Chang's section of the line was worth some 5 million dollars a year to Chang over the next several years.[61] On May 13, 1922, Chang issued instructions that the salt, customs, and postal revenues too were all to be paid directly to him rather than to Peking. The instructions were soon canceled insofar as they applied to the postal administration, but despite strong objections from the foreign officials concerned, appropriation of the Northeastern salt and customs revenues was accomplished without incident. This amounted to just over nine million yüan annually in the case of the salt revenue and 700,000 taels (Haikwan) monthly in the case of the customs.[62]

These amounts were a useful supplement to the normal sources of revenue in Fengtien, and under Wang Yung-chiang's renewed direction of the provincial treasury, it was reported that from these irregular sources, together only with the land tax of regular government income, the ordinary civil and military expenditure of the province should be met, while the 5 million yüan reserves in the treasury should be held for emergency use, and supplemented by all other revenues.[63] The natural wealth of the province, the success of Wang in administering its financial affairs, and the priorities according to which the province's wealth were then employed are illustrated by the estimated figures for 1923, the first full economic year after the Fengtien-Chihli war:[64]

Revenues (regular)	26,787,958 yüan
Expenditures	18,239,221 yüan
Surplus	8,548,737 yüan

Approximately 76 percent of expenditure, or 13,941,158 yüan, was to the military. Clearly this meant that other needs had to be assigned a low priority: only 3 percent, or 637,011 yüan, went to education, for example. Several qualifications are necessary, however, in considering these figures: first, that irregular sources of revenue, such as the Peking–Mukden railway, the salt gabelle, etc., appear to have been excluded; second, that major items of expenditure, especially the arsenal, also appear to have been excluded. Wang himself was later to remark that 20 million had been spent on the arsenal alone in 1923,[65] while a senior English employee of the arsenal also confirms the impression of large amounts being spent on it, although his estimate, 100 million yüan, must be grossly inflated.[66] Also on other details given in this set of figures, other sources differ. One newspaper estimated a provincial surplus for 1923 of as much as 21 million yüan,[67] while the expenditure on education by all three of the Northeastern provinces is elsewhere estimated to have been less even than that reported for Fengtien province in these figures.[68] Nevertheless, although there remain doubts and necessary qualifications, the figures quoted here are probably most reliable, in that they stem from a detailed study of the finances of the province carried out in 1928 by the Research Department of the South Manchuria Railway Company, which was the organization with best access to authoritative sources and responsible for most of the detailed research on Northeastern affairs, especially economic affairs, carried out at this time.

Economic Development and Competition with Japan

The years following the first Fengtien-Chihli war gave plenty of evidence of a new and independent mood at various levels of the Northeastern administration, partly the consequence of being forced by circumstances into alliance with the "progressives" of the South, but also partly the reflection of change in the society itself. The most striking expression of the change was the sharpening of the contradiction between Japanese and Chinese enterprise in the Northeast as a Chinese bourgeoisie became more conscious and more assertive of its interests.

Already in February 1923 the *Min-pao* carried reports of a plan being entertained by the Mukden authorities, worked out by Wang Yung-chiang, for the construction of a railway from Mukden to Kirin and then north to Hai-lin.[69] The problems this plan gave rise to, and the great growth in Chinese railway construction that this announcement presaged, are discussed below. At this time, although the Northeast was relatively well served by railways, less than 1 percent of the network was Chinese.[70] The creation of a distribution and marketing network to rival the monopoly enjoyed by the Japanese South Manchuria Railway–Dairen port network, or else the seizure of control over the latter, was an essential preliminary to the development of an independent Chinese economy. The complement to the planned Chinese railway network, which was to reach deep into the de-

veloping Northeast of Kirin province, was the revival of old plans for the
construction of a harbor at Hu-lu-tao in the northwestern corner of the Gulf
of Liaotung. Work on such a port had been commenced in October 1910,
but suspended a year later for lack of funds and because of the upheavals
attendant upon the revolution. Now an agreement was reached with a Bel-
gian syndicate on construction for a figure of 10 million yüan (approximately 1¼ million pounds),[71] the amount to be secured partly on the port
dues and partly on a second mortgage on the Peking–Mukden railway.[72]
The importance of the port, which was to be linked by a 7½-mile spur railway to Lien-shan on the Peking–Mukden railway, was that it would thus
provide the necessary port outlet for feeder railways from the north such as
the projected Mukden–Kirin–Hai-lin line. It would also constitute a com-
petitive alternative to the Japanese-run South Manchuria Railway–Dairen
port system. Reinforcing this commercial and economic significance for
Chang Tso-lin was the idea that it would serve too as the main home base
of a Northeastern navy. Having been at great disadvantage in the 1922
fighting near Shan-hai-kuan from the lack of naval support, Chang was
anxious to build his own navy in future. (See map on p. 219.)

   Clearly these plans for railway and port construction, and Chang's establishment of a Three Eastern Provinces Communications Committee to
coordinate them,[73] bore the seeds of conflict with Japanese ambition, particularly since the Japanese cabinet too was at the same moment working
on plans for economic expansion into "North Manchuria." By the exercise
of various treaty "rights" gained in the past, it was anxious to expand the
Japanese railway network by the construction of a number of lines feeding
from the same area into the South Manchuria Railway.[74]

   This impression of growing independence and nationalist spirit in the
Northeast is greatly reinforced by a consideration of moves in the fields of
business, law, and education. In March 1923 a South Manchuria Railway
Research Department survey noted that, though almost all cotton in the
Northeast had hitherto been imported from China or abroad, amounting to
an annual sum of 16,300,000 taels, there was still no spinning works there.
The ready availability of cheap labor, low construction costs, low taxes and
rents, the slump in Japanese domestic industry, and proposed import tax
increases that might make the market less accessible in the future were all
factors underlining the desirability of Japanese business moving quickly
into the field.[75] Thus in March 1923, the Manshū Bōseki K.K., or Man-

churia Spinning Company, was established with a capital of 5 million yen, in the South Manchuria Railway zone at Liao-yang.[76] However, almost simultaneously with the establishment of the Japanese works came the news of the establishment of the Feng-t'ien fang-sha-ch'ang, the Mukden Cotton Mill, set up at the instigation of the Mukden authorities.[77] This factory, with capital of 4 1/2 million yüan, was the first of many established with bureaucratic capital and management from this time on. Just over half the shares were held directly by the provincial treasury, the remainder being sold to private capitalists. Capacity of the Chinese mill, however, was only two-thirds that of the Japanese in yarn and one-half that in cloth, and the later establishment of other Japanese mills made things more difficult for the Chinese.[78]

At a conference of leading civil and military figures of the Three Eastern Provinces called by Chang Tso-lin in January 1924, the question of establishment and support for economic enterprises received a good deal of attention. Important decisions taken included the following:[79]

A joint Three Provinces business fund of 20 million yüan to be raised within the next three months; officially run factories to be increased and set up in ten places; the 20 best places of the officially owned mining lands in the Three Eastern Provinces to be opened up within the year; and capitalization to be increased by 2 million yüan and large expansion to be carried out within the year in each of the following: Hu-lan Sugar Manufactory, Mukden Cotton Mill, Yalu River Timber Company, and Pen-ch'i-hu Colliery Company.

In addition to productive industry such as that specified, major expansion was carried out after 1923 in the field of public utilities, of which electric power supply may be taken as representative. In 1916 there were 13 Japanese and five Chinese electric companies in the three provinces. In the following year, five new Japanese companies were set up, and, perhaps stimulated by this, in 1918 five more Chinese companies were established. Then, from 1923 to 1927, 20 new Chinese companies were established, between three and six each year, including both public and private companies. With this rapid expansion, sharp competition developed between Chinese and Japanese businesses in cities like Harbin, Mukden, Changchun, An-tung, Ssu-p'ing-chieh, and Hai-ch'eng, which inevitably enhanced the friction in general political matters also.[80] As the promotion of business became a regular item of discussion at the meetings of civil and military leaders that Chang used to call from time to time,[81] so at the

administrative level various difficulties began to be put in the way of
Japanese enterprises. One of the first moves in this direction was the instruction issued by the Fengtien governor's office to local hsien magistrates
in the province to the effect that leases of land or buildings to Japanese or
Koreans should be granted only after careful official inquiry, never in per-
petuity, and always with residual Chinese sovereignty as a key consideration.[82]

RIGHTS RECOVERY AND FRICTION WITH JAPAN

These preliminary moves on various official fronts to reassert Chinese
economic control over the territory from Japan were fueled and reinforced
during 1923 by demonstrations in various parts of the country protesting
continuance of the lease to Japan of Port Arthur and the Kwantung Peninsula. The original agreements concerning this territory, as for the South
Manchuria Railway and the An-tung–Mukden railway, were for 25 years,
so that they should have reverted to China, or in the case of the railways
become open to purchase by China, in 1923, 1928, and 1933, respectively,
had it not been for the Sino-Japanese treaties of May 1915, adopted in consequence of the infamous "21 Demands." Where public expression of demands for the revocation of these treaties had previously been forbidden, a
Kirin Society for the Support of Diplomacy was formed and began to agi-
tate for the return of Port Arthur and Dairen in February 1923.[83] In March a
meeting was held in Peking sponsored by an organization called the Society of Fellow Provincials of the Three Eastern Provinces Resident in Peking; 1,000 people attended, and a Society for Support of the Return of
Port Arthur and Dairen was formed. Demonstrations took place in Kirin
and Tsitsihar, and the Society for the Support of Diplomacy in Harbin was
reckoned to enjoy the backing of about 80 organizations, or a total of
10,000 people.[84]

In February 1924 the Chinese authorities in the Northeast also laid claim
to criminal jurisdiction over Chinese resident in the Japanese-administered
Kwantung territory or the South Manchuria Railway zone.[85] Little progress was made on this issue either, and since passions were aroused over it,
an editorial in the semiofficial *Min-pao* on August 26 commented as follows:[86]

How can the Japanese police be stopped from running amuck? The Japanese police
treat the people of Manchuria as cows and horses, beating or detaining them as they

see fit. . . . The atrocities once carried out in Taiwan and Korea are now carried out in Manchuria—it is because they see Manchuria as the same as Taiwan or Korea. The Japanese people are surely the world's most cruel and lacking in feeling.

The field of education was of obvious importance. Although, as noted above, it was accorded a comparatively low budgetary priority, the influence of the considerable Japanese-run educational system in the South Manchuria Railway zone inevitably stimulated concern about cultural imperialism, and from this developed both the demand for the development and strengthening of the Chinese system and the movement for the curtailment of the Japanese. The establishment of the Northeastern University is symptomatic of the former. A preparatory committee was set up in the spring of 1922 by Wang Yung-chiang; the university was formally established in April 1923 with Wang as chancellor; and the first group of 310 preparatory students was admitted in mid-July.[87] The land was made available by the provincial government, together with a grant of 2.8 million yüan, and the running costs were to be met nine-tenths by Fengtien province and one-tenth by Heilungkiang. Kirin province decided to go it alone, although its university was not set up until much later, in August 1928.[88] Faculty were recruited on strict academic criteria, and among the early professorial appointees were two foreigners—a German and an American—two Chinese graduates of the Imperial University in Tokyo, and another 13 who had studied in various European and American universities.[89] Initially there were two faculties, one of humanities and law, another of science and engineering, but these were expanded to three in January 1925: humanities and law, in which there were separate departments of English, Russian, law, and politics; science, with separate departments of mathematics and physics; and engineering, with separate departments of mechanics, electricity, and civil engineering. Departments of mining and metallurgy and of textiles were added in July 1926. The university experienced considerable early growing pains, partly because of political and economic uncertainties in the province, but also because of Japanese protest and pressure through the consul general in Mukden, who claimed that the existing tertiary education facilities provided by the South Manchuria Railway Company were adequate. Yet in a period when national universities elsewhere in the country were in a constant state of crisis because of inability to pay their staff or to cover their administrative expenses, the achievement of the provincial authorities in Mukden was con-

TABLE 3
Students from Fengtien Province Studying Abroad, 1925

Country	At official expense	At private expense	Total
Japan	35	146	181
United States	6	27	33
France	1	6	7
Germany	1	7	8
Switzerland	1	1	2
England			1[a]
TOTAL	44	187	232

SOURCE: Manshikai, *Manshū kaihatsu yonjū nen shi* (Tokyo, 1964), vol. 3, p. 94.
[a] Not known whether at official or private expense.

siderable. The Japanese scholar Niijima Atsuyoshi concludes his study of
the university with the judgment: [90]

> Though Northeastern University was provincially run, its laboratory equipment was
> first-class and its professorial salaries were considerably more than those paid in
> national universities. Without a doubt, because of the comprehensiveness and ex-
> cellence of this university, its educational standards were superior to those of the
> Japanese-run higher educational facilities in Manchuria.

Furthermore, complementing the educational commitment represented
by this university went a continuing effort to send students abroad to study.
By 1925 there were 232 students from Fengtien province studying in
foreign countries, as shown in Table 3. Furthermore, in July 1929, Northeastern University took the extraordinary step of dispatching all of its first
graduating class, with the exception of those from the Russian department,
to undertake further study abroad.[91]

The Japanese-run educational system for Chinese students in the South
Manchuria Railway zone was based on a chain of "public schools"
(*kung-hsüeh-t'ang*) in the towns along the railway line. By May of 1925
there were 2,982 Chinese pupils attending ten of these schools. The system
was one of four years elementary and two years higher education. Another
7,907 Chinese students were attending similar institutions in the Japanese-
administered Kwantung province.[92] In 1924 Chinese concern about the
consequences of abdicating educational responsibility to the Japanese became evident. Early in April 1924, Hsieh Yin-ch'ang, Education Commissioner for Fengtien province, in presiding at a banquet for a visiting
Japanese education delegation, attacked the Japanese system of education
as "rooted in Japanese imperialism" and "subversive of the education of

the Chinese people." He continued: [93]

The public schools run by the Japanese along the South Manchuria Railway zone are implementing a monstrous kind of education. I cannot refrain from worrying about the future, since this education not only is unsuitable to Chinese circumstances but serves the function of Japanizing. If they go on in this way, they will destroy the concept of nation among the youth of the Three Eastern Provinces and cultivate instead a lot of pro-Japanese slaves.

On April 11, Hsieh announced that in future foreign-run Christian schools would need permission from him, since "the education of citizens of one country is something that does not admit of interference by another country." [94] In practice, however, Christian missionary schools were treated as much less of a problem than the Japanese schools. On March 22 the first approaches were made to the South Manchuria Railway branch office in Kung-chu-ling by the Chinese magistrate of Huai-te hsien, requesting a site within the zone and permission to construct a Chinese primary school there, to be run by Chinese officials in accordance with Chinese law. [95] This was regarded as a test case, floated with the consent or at the instigation of Governor Wang Yung-chiang, for the general return of educational rights within the area administered by the railway company. [96] While the request was under consideration in the head office of the company, a Society for the Promotion of the Return of Educational Rights within Fengtien Province was formed at a meeting in Mukden, sponsored jointly by the provincial Education Department and the newspaper *Tung-pao*.* The policies decided by this organization included the establishment of Chinese schools as envisaged in the official request, the exclusion of Chinese pupils from Japanese schools, and the general goal of overthrowing "cultural aggression." Hsieh himself, at the annual meeting of the Educational Association of the province, expressed publicly the view that the right to teach should be withdrawn from anyone who was not a Chinese citizen, and urged that Chinese students be forbidden to attend Japanese schools. [97]

In the course of this dispute, a curious exchange of gratuitous Sino-Japanese insults occurred in the pages of two Mukden newspapers that

---

*Dazai, *Manshū gendaishi*, p. 411; *GSS*, 32: 553. This paper, *Tung-pao*, is described in a Japanese Foreign Ministry publication, Gaimushō, *Shina (Fu Hon Kon) ni okeru shinbun oyobi tsūshin ni kansuru chōsa*, p. 9, as the organ of the pro-war party within the Fengtien clique and as having close relations with Chang Hsüeh-liang through its president, Chang Hsüan, who was a former secretary of Chang's. The *Tōsanshō jōhō* (see note 85, p. 283) also stresses that it was the "organ of Chang Hsüeh-liang (cited in Imai, "Tōsanshō," pp. 22–23). Both it and the *Tung-san-sheng min-pao* were founded in October 1922; both were active in gave further evidence of the rising tide of anti-Japanese sentiment in the Northeast and of a stiffening and incomprehending attitude on the part of the Japanese. On April 13 the Japanese *Sheng-ching shih-pao*, the largest-circulation Chinese language newspaper in the province, ran an article under the heading "Mere child's play," which referred in highly sarcastic terms to the modernization program of the Fengtien forces. The point of the article was the allusion to Chang Hsüeh-liang, then only 26 years old but already one of the leading military figures in the Northeast, and one with whom the modernization program was closely identified. The Chinese-run *Tung-pao* at once let fly a riposte under the heading "More than child's play," which referred to Japan as "a country which, although it has many modernists and boasts of liberty and equality, has on the other hand a color-blind boy as generalissimo of its armed forces." This time the unmistakable allusion was to the youthful and mentally unstable Taishō emperor. The Japanese consulate issued strong and continuing protests about what they regarded as a case of *lèse majesté*, and although the Chinese side began by claiming it was no more than a justified reply to the attack launched in *Sheng-ching shih-pao*, eventually a temporary suspension of publication was ordered as of April 23. The anti-Japanese campaign merely shifted to the pages of the *Min-pao*, however, with the publication of a serial article entitled "A history of Japanese aggression in Manchuria," and in the Provincial Assembly a resolution was passed on May 10 calling for an end to foreign encroachment on the rights of Fengtien province.[98]

The educational rights recovery campaign quickly spread from Fengtien to other parts of the country,[99] but in the Northeast itself the movement soon aborted. The immediate goal of the campaign—the recovery from Japan of the right to educate Chinese children along the South Manchuria Railway line—came to nothing. Despite the appeals both through the company and through the consulates and consul general's office in Mukden, the directors of the company decided on May 8 against making any concession.[100] In the summer of 1924 the prospect of renewed civil war led the authorities in Mukden to take steps to suppress the movement as inimical to

---

the rights recovery campaign of 1924, and both seem to have been close to Chang Hsüeh-liang. The *Tung-pao* must have had a brief existence, however, since the exhaustive 1926 study prepared for the South Manchuria Railway Company by Otsuka Reizō (*Manshū ni okeru genron kikan no gensei*) makes no mention of it, although it describes the *Tung-san-sheng min-pao* as being the organ of the Mukden clique, Kuomintang faction, and as being anti-Japanese (pp. 34–35). Neither paper is listed in the standard bibliographies of Chinese newspaper and periodical holdings in European, American, or Japanese libraries.

their efforts to secure Japanese military aid. Hsieh was replaced as Education Commissioner, and anti-Japanese educational propaganda, which had
flourished under him, was ordered rooted out by his successor. "A history
of Japanese aggression in Manchuria" was dropped from the pages of the
Min-pao, and although a serial entitled "A Fundamental Policy for the
Salvation of the Three Eastern Provinces" appeared briefly in September,
this too was suspended for the duration of the war. "A History of Japanese
Aggression" reappeared briefly in the paper in February 1925, but was
quickly stopped after a strong protest from the Japanese consul general.[101]

The years 1923 and 1924 were, therefore, a period in which growing
independence of economic organization and political and cultural mood in
the Northeast were evident, and in which for the first time the demand for
an end to many of the elements that made up Japan's privileged position
was voiced even at an official level. Considerable gains might have been
made had the exigencies of war not brought these moves to a halt, since
open resistance by Japan would have been politically difficult for the
Japanese party cabinets of the mid-1920's, and since military plans for the
conquest of the Northeast had not yet matured. As it was, not only did the
war of the autumn of 1924 produce a distinct shift in the political line of the
Mukden leadership away from confrontation with Japan, but the course of
the war and Japan's involvement in it deepened the proprietorial attitude
toward Chang's regime on the Japanese side, so that the subsequent revival
of independent plans and policies under Chang was seen as intolerable
ingratitude. The war of late 1924 also deepened the contradiction between
the interests of the military and civilian wings of the Fengtien clique, thus
incidentally rendering more difficult the settling of a unified policy on the
crucial question of relation toward Japan. Because of the profound consequences of this war, the development of the Fengtien military and the
nature of the reorganization of forces carried out after May 1922 has to be
examined.

MILITARY REORGANIZATION

The Army

The demoralization and disintegration of the Northeastern armies in the
1922 Fengtien-Chihli war and postwar crisis were of such a degree that
only one benefiting, as Chang was, from virtual strategic impregnability
vis-à-vis the rest of China could have hoped to ride it out. His total military

strength at the onset of the war was five divisions and 26 brigades.[102] Two of the divisions, the 1st and the 16th, surrendered in large numbers during the war, were disarmed and ceased to function; of a third, the 28th, only one brigade escaped intact to the Northeast; Chang Tso-hsiang's 27th Division, the force that had been built up by Chang Tso-lin himself, fled ignominiously from the Ch'ang-hsin-tien front;[103] while the 29th, which played little part in the war anyway, was under the command of Wu Chünsheng, who had opposed the war from its inception and who was suspected of collusion with the enemy. Two mixed brigades, the 6th and 9th, were scattered in defeat in the war, and Pao Te-shan, commander of the 6th, together with the commander of the 2d Cavalry Brigade from Heilungkiang, Chang K'uei-wu, were both executed and many of their men imprisoned in the ensuing purges.[104] Another brigade commander, Chang Ssu of the 4th, was murdered when 1,500 of his troops mutinied in August at Po-k'o-t'u in the Northwest.[105] From other areas—Erh-tao-kou, Ningku-t'a, Tun-hua—the news was the same, of troops mutinying, resorting to banditry, going on the rampage, or just disappearing.[106] The most serious episode, the rebellion of the Kirin 1st Brigade under Kao Shih-pin in collusion with Wu P'ei-fu, has been dealt with above.

After resolution of the immediate problems of independence, Chang Tso-lin on July 18, 1922, formally opened his new headquarters as Peace Preservation Commander in Chief.[107] He had seen in April and May that untrained troops could not face up to battle and inexperienced or ignorant officers were incapable of command. His armies were beset by both problems. The reorganization to which he committed his forces had to be a thorough one.

First of all, the various armies of all three provinces were combined into one, under himself as commander in chief and Sun Lieh-ch'en and Wu Chün-sheng as his two deputies.[108] The basic unit of the army was changed to the brigade. Of the former five divisions, only two, Chang Tso-hsiang's 27th and Wu Chün-sheng's 29th, were retained, while Li Ching-lin, because of his meritorious service in the war, was given command of a reorganized 1st Division. Otherwise all forces were regrouped into 27 mixed brigades and 5 cavalry brigades. In principle a brigade was made up of 3 regiments; a regiment of 3 battalions; a battalion of 3 companies; and a company of 150 men. However, in practice there were a number of irregularities. Chang Hsüeh-liang's 2d Brigade, for example, consisted of 3 regiments of infantry and one each of cavalry and artillery, making it almost equal in strength to a full division. The complete army was thus made up as shown in Table 4.

From the time of this reorganization, frequent reference was made to the existence of "new" and "old" men, or "new" and "old" factions within the Mukden clique, and to the tensions and rivalries between them. The "new" were generally identified as graduates of the Japanese Military Academy, grouped around Yang Yü-t'ing, on the one hand, and another group of graduates of the War College in Peking and the Military School of the Three Eastern Provinces, grouped around Chang Hsüeh-liang and Kuo Sung-ling, on the other. The "old" were the original retinue of Chang Tso-lin, his bandit followers such as Chang Tso-hsiang and T'ang Yü-lin; others such as Sun Lieh-ch'en, who had been with him since 1908; and generally the entire group of ex-subordinates from Chang's original 27th Division. Some of them were in fact graduates of the Military School of the Three Eastern Provinces, but in most cases, since they were seconded to it in their mature years, old ways of thinking seem to have been left little changed.[109] This group always remained highest in Chang's confidence, despite their obvious limitations and failings. Conspicuously absent from its ranks after May 1922 were Chang Ching-hui and Tsou Fen, for reasons already discussed above; and Pao Te-shan, one of those executed after the war, had also served in Chang's original 27th Division. Yet despite these lapses from the group, it still constituted the major strength of the Fengtien military—10 brigades. Sun Lieh-ch'en occupied the nominal position of Director of the Army Reorganization Bureau, but the actual task of reform, military education, and training in the new army was entirely in the hands of the "new" men. Reorganization was based on nine principles: (1) Examinations are to be conducted of candidates for officerhood, and promotion shall be based on this alone. (2) Each unit is to cultivate talent within its military jurisdiction and the incompetent are to be weeded out and replaced. (3) Classes are to commence in each unit on September 1, 1922, and to be conducted two hours daily. (4) Military journals and manuals are to be published in each unit and distributed for the attention of officers and men. (5) It is forbidden for any unit to be below strength; any commander who is found to be drawing pay for such nonexistent troops will be severely punished. (6) Soldiers found to be opium smokers not only will be immediately dismissed but will also be severely punished according

TABLE 4
Army of the Three Eastern Provinces, 1923

Unit number and commander	Location	Unit number and location	Location
DIVISION		16. *Ch'i En-ming*	Fengtien
27. *Chang Tso-hsiang*	Fengtien	17. *Chang Ming-chiu*	Heilungkiang
29. Wu Chün-sheng	Heilungkiang	18. Chang Huan-hsiang (J8)	Kirin
1. Li Ching-lin (PTs)	Fengtien	19. Kao Wei-yo (3P)	Fentien
BRIGADE			(27th Div.)
1. *K'an Chao-hsi*	Fengtien	20. Hu Yung-k'uei	Kirin
2. Chang Hsüeh-liang (3P)	Fengtien	21. Ts'ai Yung-chen	Kirin
3. Chang Tsung-ch'ang	Fengtien	22. Shih Te-shan (3P)	Heilungkiang
4. Chang Tso-t'ao	Fengtien	23. Li Shuang-k'ai (PTs)	Fengtien
5. *Li Chen-sheng*	Fengtien		(1st Div.)
	(27th Div.)	24. Hsing Shih-lien (J8)	Fengtien
6. Kuo Sung-ling	Fengtien	25. *Ts'ai P'ing-pen*	Fengtien
7. *T'ang Yü-lin*	Fengtien	26. *Li Kuei-lin*	Kirin
8. Ch'en Yü-k'un	Kirin	27. P'ei Ch'ün-sheng	Fengtien
9. *Liu Hsiang-chiu*	Kirin		
10. Yü Shen-ch'eng (PTs)	Kirin	**CAVALRY BRIGADE**	
11. Pa Ying-e	Heilungkiang	1. Mu Ch'ün (3P)	Fengtien
12. *Chao En-chen* (3P)	Fengtien	2. P'eng Chin-shan	Heilungkiang
13. Ting Chao (J8)	Kirin	3. Su Hsi-lin	Fengtien
14. Yang Te-sheng	Fengtien	4. Chang K'uei-chiu	Heilungkiang
15. Wan Fu-lin	Heilungkiang	5. Ch'en Fu-sheng	Heilungkiang
	(29th Div.)		(29th Div.)

**OTHERS OF HIGH RANK AND RESPONSIBILITY
BUT WITHOUT SPECIFIC COMMAND**

Sun Lieh-ch'en	Kirin tuchün and Director of the Army Reorganization Bureau
Kuo Sung-ling (3P, P)	Deputy Directors of Army Reorganization Bureau
Chiang Teng-hsüan (J5)	
Yang Yü-t'ing (J7)	Consultant General (Tsung-ts'an-i)
Han Lin-ch'un (J6)	Superintendent of the Arsenal

SOURCE: Sonoda Kazuki, *Tōsanshō no seiji to gaikō* (Mukden, 1925), pp. 335–37; with other biographical detail from Sonoda Kazuki, *Shina shinjin kokki* (Osaka, 1927), and Tanabe Tanejirō, *Tōsanshō kanshinroku* (Dairen, 1924.) For a chart of the 27th Division in 1912, see Sonoda Kazuki, *Kaiketsu Chō Sakurin* (Tokyo, 1922), p. 14 of appendix 1.

NOTE: Names in italics indicate those belonging to Chang Tso-lin's most immediate retinue and in command of a battalion or higher in the original 27th Division formed by Chang in 1912. These men constituted the inner core of the Fengtien clique, and many of them were originally bandits.

Abbreviations:

J: Graduate of the Japanese Military Academy, sometimes called the Cadet Academy (Shikan gakkō), together with the year of graduating class—5th class, etc.

PTs: Graduate of the Short Training School of the Paoting Military Academy (Lu-chün su-ch'eng hsüeh-hsiao).

P: Graduate of the War College (Lu-chün ta-hsüeh).

3P: Graduate of the Military School of the Three Eastern Provinces (Tung-san-sheng lu-chün chiang-wu-t'ang).

to the law. (7) In future, learning shall be valued highly among officers and study will be encouraged. Monthly examinations shall be conducted and those who rate highly will be rewarded. (8) In future, those who have been only through the lower grades of schooling will be ineligible to become officers. No one who has not graduated from primary school or who is not possessed of common sense may become a soldier. (9) In each unit those who are not between the ages of 17 and 40, or whose identity is not clear, or who may have no guarantor, are all to be purged.[110]

From the nature of these principles something of the need for reform may be inferred. Conspicuously absent from them, however, was any prescription for ideological indoctrination, as, for example, in the precepts of Wu P'ei-fu, for whom politics, though of the most traditional, Confucian kind, was the militarist's key concern,[111] or in those of Feng Yü-hsiang, who gave even greater emphasis to the political and religious education of his troops.[112] Within the limits of the principles set out here, however, the changes that took place were not inconsiderable. Rumblings of discontent were reported among the soldiers accustomed to the easygoing regime of opium-smoking, ex-brigand commanders as they began to experience the stiffened discipline imposed by the new, young, college-trained officers,[113] and after a visit to Mukden in August 1922, Lennox Simpson, adviser to the Presidential Office, reported as follows:[114]

The Army Reorganization Committee is sitting under the chairmanship of General Chang's son, General Chang Hsüeh-liang, a popular young officer with a very good command of English. . . . Many officers guilty of cowardice or peculation have been summarily shot, and all men without military education have been summarily dismissed. One hundred military students have been recalled from Europe and offered appointments. A certain number of units in central and northern Manchuria have been given Russian military instructors. Aeroplanes have been bought and an aerodrome is to be established, while the Mukden Arsenal has been improved.

It is a mark of Chang's shrewd leadership in the Fengtien clique that on this, as on several previous occasions already discussed, he understood the need to transcend the limitations of his own experience and background, and to make considerable changes in the organization of his power base in order both to accommodate the newer type of military man emerging within it and to prepare a better-matched force to pit against Wu P'ei-fu in the future. However, the achievements of the reform, though real, were limited. Many units in the army, because of the immunity of their commanders, remained outside the scope of reform. One example, instructive in various ways, is that of Chang Tsung-ch'ang.

Chang Tsung-ch'ang was a native of Shantung, a man of whose wild and uncouth ways many tales have been spun.[115] His connection with Chang Tso-lin dates only from the beginning of 1921, when with Chang's support and encouragement he attempted to overthrow the tupan of Kiangsi province, Ch'en Kuang-yüan, who was identified with the Chihli party. The attempt failed, but Chang Tsung-ch'ang retained close ties thereafter with Chang Tso-lin. In the Fengtien-Chihli war he led a 3,000-man force from Tsingtao in a move designed to attack the Chihli forces in the rear. With the sudden collapse of the front, however, he returned instead to Mukden, and was commissioned to suppress the rebellion of Kao Shih-pin in the North. His record to this point was not only undistinguished but even suspect, since either he or his subordinate was responsible for large-scale misuse of Chang Tso-lin's funds, as described earlier. With his success in the expedition against Kao, however, his star in the Mukden clique rose considerably, and as reward he was appointed commander of the 3d Brigade and Defense Commissioner of the Sui-fen–Ning-ku-t'a area. Though he was quite new to the Mukden clique, his standing was such that he could not be touched by the reformers. From his youth, when he worked on the wharves, in the brothels and gambling dens of Harbin and its environs, he knew that area well, and reportedly spoke Russian fluently. Almost immediately after taking up his appointment he was charged with having permitted 25 gambling dens to open near Pogranichnaya and with being involved himself in the opium business to the point of having already sent 400,000 *chin* of opium to Mukden.[116] Opium was legalized and free for transit if marked with an official stamp at a stamp tax rate of 10 yüan per pound. In August of 1923 no less than 100,000 *mow* of land along the Chinese Eastern Railway in Kirin, under the jurisdiction of Defense Commissioner Chang, was reported to be under opium. During harvest the opium districts were raided by soldiers or brigands, who extorted either taxes or opium, often taking the whole season's product. In the city of Kirin, too, walls and posts in the street were posted with official notices legalizing opium. When, in November 1923, the 3d Brigade returned to Mukden from the defense of the Northwest frontier district, the men carried with them 40,000 pounds of opium for disposal in Harbin, Changchun, and Mukden.

Chang's property in the area, an enormous 20,000 *shang* (approximately 140,000 mow) continued to be farmed for him by the Yu-ning Company after he personally had departed from the area. Each *shang* produced an estimated 20 catty (chin) of opium, making a total of 400,000 chin (approximately 240,000 kilograms). Since a chin was worth 20 yüan, this meant an annual opium income of approximately 8 million yüan.[117] Harbin was credited at this time with 2,000 opium dens and morphia shops. According to the *China Year Book* of 1924–25: "It is almost impossible to accept the Chinese Press reports concerning the extensive use of opium and narcotics in these Three Eastern Provinces, they are so appalling. . . . Through Manchurian towns and ports comes the amazing quantity of morphia, heroin and cocaine which is later smuggled into northern China."[118] This is despite the fact that the International Opium Association in Peking had earlier reckoned that "by 1920 poppy cultivation had practically ceased in Manchuria," whereas conditions in other parts of China "were not so satisfactory."[119]

Despite the reform principles enunciated by the Army Reorganization Bureau, no charges were ever preferred against Chang Tsung-ch'ang, even though he was a relative newcomer to the Northeastern Army. His seizing of this territorial and fiscal base was an important allowance, marking his acceptance by Chang Tso-lin as an important member of the group. It is against a record such as his that the "reform" achievements of the "new" men in the army must be balanced. Despite the apparent confidence that was placed in him, incidentally, Japanese police reports had it that Chang Tsung-ch'ang was working through various agents to expand his forces by encouraging the surrender to him of mounted brigands (*hung-hu-tzu*), Korean rebels, and communists, with a view to assassinating Chang Tso-lin and realigning the Northeastern provinces with Peking under his own rule.[120]

Weapons

Accompanying the army reorganization, with all its limits, went a considerable expansion of the arsenal and a great increase in all sorts of arms imports. Beginning in April 1920, there had been some production in Mukden of rifle bullets and smokeless gunpowder at the military equipment factory, but the arsenal proper was only set up in October 1921, and later called the Three Eastern Provinces Arsenal.[121] Ammunition remained for some time the main priority, other items having to be purchased outside, though considerable expansion was carried out and large funds invested in the works after the war of 1922. From the Englishman Francis ("One-Arm") Sutton, who was employed from about this time to assist in the manufacture of trench mortars, comes the following description of the arsenal as it was upon his arrival: "The arsenal covered an area of about one and a half by about three quarters of a mile: the buildings were placed rather close, and there were many two or three stories high." He was told there were 30,000 employees, and reckoned "there might have been more."

The recently purchased Danish machinery had never even been installed and the little which was unpacked already showed signs of deterioration from neglect. Fantastic sums had been squandered on futile attempts to produce fighter aircraft, heavy artillery and the latest developments in high explosives—all far beyond the capabilities of the arsenal. A group of buildings in one corner, surrounded by a ten foot barbed wire fence and lavishly placarded "Poison Gas Factory DANGER" proved to be not only unused but completely empty. On the other hand supplies of raw and processed materials were surprisingly satisfactory.

Steel and coal, copper mined in the Northeast but refined in Japan, rubber, cement, and lubricating oil were all easily obtainable, while ether and sulfuric acid were in active production and cordite production was actually ahead of requirements and of good quality. For 15,000 pounds sterling down, other terms to be discussed later, Sutton was appointed Master of Ordinance,[122] or, in the Chinese Gazetteer account, director of the trench mortar factory.[123] Ammunition, small arms, and mortars were the items on which the arsenal concentrated.[124] Apart from the Englishman Sutton, the arsenal employed also Japanese, Swedish, Danish, German, and Russian technicians. Equipment and materials were purchased mainly in the first instance from Denmark, but also from Japan, the United States, Germany, and Italy. The avoidance of exclusive dependence on Japan, or on any other single country, in this crucial enterprise is noteworthy.[125] However, although with the Fengtien Cotton Mill the arsenal ranks as the major modern industrial enterprise undertaken in Mukden without outside backing or investment in this period,[126] reliable details of investment in it, and of its organization and output, are not now known.[127]

Arms imports were also necessary for the many items it was not possible to produce locally. Theoretically this should have been difficult, since from May 1919 there was an internationally agreed embargo on the sale of arms to China. However, this was of very limited scope, since many leading arms-producing countries did not sign it, and Mukden, which in 1922 and 1923 seems to have been the leading Chinese arms importer, purchased impartially from countries such as Italy, Denmark, and the United States, which were signatories, to Germany and Sweden, which were not.[128]

To maintain secrecy in some of these transactions a smuggling service was organized by Sutton via ports in Shantung, transport from there being arranged in a fleet of five-masted trading junks.[129] Such covert measures were not always necessary, however, since much important cargo for the arsenal was allowed in through Ying-k'ou customs untaxed and uninspected.[130] Perhaps the largest series of consignments that arrived in the summer of 1923 was one of about 800 tons of Danish equipment. Later in the same year, apparently through channels arranged by Sutton, 12 French light aircraft arrived, which, though disarmed before delivery and "for civilian purposes only," were soon fitted with bomb racks in the arsenal.[131] A total of 40 of these "Bréguet" machines were reportedly purchased.[132] The air force, which was subsequently set up was under the control of a Chang Hsüeh-liang nominee, Chou P'ei-ping, became another important preserve of the "new" element in the Mukden clique.[133]

The mere acquisition of planes, of course, meant little. A highly placed Japanese observer in September 1924, just before the outbreak of the second Fengtien-Chihli war, remarked that the French planes were so bad that out of the materials for five only one flyable plane could be put together. As for the pilots, there were then 15 foreigners (12 of them Russians), and only "about three" Chinese who could fly, though the latter lacked any experience of night flying or bombing.[134]

The Navy

The Northeastern navy was treated with a good deal less priority. Till the 1922 war there were a mere eight boats in an Amur River Defense Command, and no naval force at all in the Gulf of Chihli.[135] After the war, various new steps were taken: a "Navigation Police Office" (Hang-ching-chü) was established at Hu-lu-tao, where the major harbor works were planned, in order to promote naval talent, and plans were laid for regular patrols of the Gulf of Chihli; the River Defense Command was expanded into a Three Eastern Provinces Naval Headquarters, with both maritime and river defense responsibilities; four ships were purchased from the Ying-k'ou Fishing Bureau for an initial maritime force; and at the military conference in Mukden in January 1924, the rather modest sum of 73,000 yüan monthly was set aside for naval expenditure.[136] Despite the embarrassment of having no naval force to back up his armies during the Shan-hai-kuan fighting of 1922, and the virtual certainty that the same area would be of key strategic importance in the future also, Chang appears to have been unwilling to devote much time or attention to the problem of naval development.

EVALUATION OF THE REFORMS AND REORGANIZATION

The question remains, then: did all the changes in the Northeast that followed the war of 1922 amount to much? The promise of representative civil government that had briefly excited the Provincial Assemblies in the heady days of June and July 1922 was soon betrayed. It became clear that civil officials were expected to get on with their task of filling the provincial coffers and that they were not to complain if the funds they raised were then used to finance apparently interminable and inconclusive wars and military preparations. Increasingly the leading civilian, Wang Yung-chiang, evinced frustration at the defeat of his plans for an autonomous Three Eastern Provinces and at the continuing dominance of men he found incompetent, corrupt, and obsessive. In an unusually frank conversation with the Japanese Consul General in Mukden in January 1924,[137] Wang, when asked whether he thought Chang Tso-lin was sufficiently concerned with development, industry, and so on, replied:

Day and night Commander in Chief Chang is concerned only with plans of countermeasures against Chihli and especially Wu P'ei-fu. He is preoccupied only with war and with arms . . . the amount spent on the arsenal last year was 17 million yüan, and the amount left unspent over and above that was 3 million. . . . It must be said that from the point of view of the economy of this province, military preparations are an excessive burden. It is unfortunate that by nature Chang Tso-lin, though sharp as a razor in speech, is extremely vague in his resolve, like *tou-fu* [bean curd]. Though at first appearance of firm character, he is susceptible to favoritism, and lacks decisive will. Also he is deficient in discernment with regard to people. Though there are times when he happens to stumble on the right choice in matters like appointments and dismissals, he still cannot manage to get the right men always in the right posts.

Furthermore, Wang mentioned that he found the situation in Kirin province dangerous because of the "tyranny of the Mukden clique," and the extreme unpopularity of both tuchün Sun Lieh-ch'en and Governor Wang

Shu-han.* A few months later, after the death of Sun Lieh-ch'en and his replacement by Chang Tso-hsiang, Wang described the new tuchün as "impotent, stubborn, and negative," and his chief of staff, Hsi Hsia, though a returned student from Japan and of some ability, as being also very stubborn and negative and worse than Chang Tso-hsiang himself.[138] Wang found Chu Ch'ing-lan, tupan of the Chinese Eastern Railway, "of extremely poor intelligence and bad local reputation," despite his being an imposing figure at first glance.[139] With his antipathy for these "old" members of the Mukden clique, it must have given small comfort to Wang to hear, in August 1923, of moves to reinstate Chang Ching-hui, who, after his disgrace of May 1922, had been residing quietly in Peking.[140]

As for the policy of the "promotion of the talents" in the military, this too was no more than a dictate of necessity, born of the need to put up a better military performance in future if an irredeemable military debacle was not to ensue. The limitations of the policy were considerable. However, the "new" men conspicuous at all levels in the clique—the rationalizers and modernizers—were not themselves united; the new civilians—Wang and his like—wanted peace, and continued autonomy for the promotion of business and prosperity; the new men of the military wanted a chance to show in battle the efficacy of their methods and the superiority of their army to Wu P'ei-fu's. Progressive civilians were thus aligned with the more reactionary of the military—men like Sun Lieh-ch'en and Wu Chün-sheng, who stood opposed to renewal of the war because they were set in comfortable and profitable ways, and could gain little, while they might lose much by it.[141] On top of these new tensions and difficulties arising within the clique, there was also the fear that the growth of anti-imperialist and anti-Japanese sentiment in the Northeast might imperil the relationship with Japan. Thus, although militarily the provinces were stronger than ever before, there were innumerable hidden weaknesses and contradictions.

*On the troubles that developed in Kirin in 1923, see Chapter 4, p. 118.

CHAPTER FOUR

The Second Fengtien-Chihli War

THREE PROVINCES OR ONE NATION?

Wang Yung-chiang was expressing no more than a part of the truth when he complained that after 1922 Chang Tso-lin was obsessed with avenging his 1922 defeat at the hands of Wu P'ei-fu. The fact was that pressures on Chang to overcome his rivals or be overcome by them were as inescapable as his ambition to dominion was unquenchable. In defeat, securing, consolidating, and strengthening his Northeastern base area were paramount considerations, necessary to keep the enemy from encroachment or invasion; once recovery had been effected, Chang Tso-lin was a prey to the same powerful centripetal pressures to assert himself in the central political arena as were his rivals.

The three Northeastern provinces were administered in effect as an independent, or "autonomic," unit from May 1922. It is true that relations with Peking were temporarily severed and differences ran deep, but the Japanese notion of the separateness of the Northeast as a non-Chinese unit, "Manchuria," formed no part of the thinking of the Chang regime. To Chang autonomy was merely a tactical retreat in the course of the drive for absolute power over China as a whole, utterly different in character from the "independence" the region experienced later under the Manchukuo regime. It is this element of constant striving for unification by conquest that must modify the impression of a China in the warlord period as ineluctably rent and divided: thus the apparent contradiction that the period is characterized at once by extreme political and institutional fragmentation and by a high degree of independence of the provinces from Peking, while all the regional military forces were striving for unity of the country. The semiautonomous satrapies that they were able to create never satisfied the militarists who ruled them, least of all Chang Tso-lin, although those of "bourgeois" interests for whom Wang spoke saw peace within limited regional frontiers as preferable by far to the endemic warfare and disruption that accompanied efforts at unification by arms.

DIPLOMATIC PROBLEMS

While pushing rapidly ahead with military reorganization and economic strengthening measures, Chang was also engaged in ceaseless maneuvering with potential allies, supporters, and rivals who were outside his immediate control but whom it seemed either advantageous to court or necessary to neutralize to be ready for a showdown with Wu P'ei-fu. His attention was turned in three major directions: toward the other factions in China proper, toward Japan, and toward the Soviet Union. The latter will be dealt with here first, although necessarily briefly.

The Soviet Union and the Chinese Eastern Railway

The Russian problem centered on the status of the Chinese Eastern Railway.[1] The administration of this Russian-owned and -administered concern was severely disrupted by the Revolution in 1917; in the confused situation prevailing in the first couple of months of 1918, the forces of the Kirin tuchün, Meng En-yüan, succeeded briefly in establishing control over it. This was short-lived, however, since with the Allied anti-Bolshevik intervention that began in April and the Sino-Japanese Joint Defensive Military Agreement of May, overall military control passed to Allied forces or White generals operating under their patronage, and administrative and technical control remained in the hands of General Horvath, general manager of the line from 1902, and an Inter-Allied Technical Board, which was set up in January 1919 to coordinate the transport facilities needed by the allies.[2]

The appointment of Pao Kuei-ch'ing in September 1919 as tuchün of Kirin and president of the railway marked the beginning of a new phase of positive Chinese interest in the line. When Horvath announced his intention to assume "full governmental power as regards the Russian population in the Chinese Eastern Railway territory," Pao protested strongly, and in March 1920, faced also by a Soviet-inspired strike by workers on the railway, Horvath resigned. Pao took the opportunity to further expand Chinese control over the railway, and on October 2, 1920, an agreement was reached between the Ministry of Communications for the Chinese government and the Russo-Asiatic Bank as parent body of the railway, which had the effect of putting it under joint Sino-Russian management.[3] The Russo-Asiatic Bank had evaded Bolshevik control during the Revolution by registering itself as a French company and transferring its head office to Paris. All the Russians appointed under the new agreements, up to the new general manager, B. W. Ostroumov, were therefore Whites. Chinese control, however, was extended from policing to various of the semi-governmental functions formerly performed by the railway administration. In particular, Russian consular jurisdiction was suspended, and Chinese courts were established at Harbin and other cities along the line. However, the "denationalization" of the railway under these arrangements produced a very anomalous situation, since under the terms of the 1896 agreement only Russians and Chinese could be shareholders. No permanent solution to the railway problem could be contemplated till the questions of recognition and diplomatic relationship between China and the Soviet Union were resolved.[4]

The Soviet position on its rights in the railway went through several distinct phases. Briefly in 1918 and 1919 a sweeping and generous policy was adumbrated in which all czarist rights and interests were renounced and the Chinese Eastern Railway offered back to China without compensation. By 1920, however, second thoughts were uppermost. The political fact of cooperation by the Chinese government in making available the Chinese Eastern Railway region as a base for White Russian and foreign (Japanese and American) counterrevolutionary activities, together with a more pragmatic assessment of the economic worth of the line, combined to produce a policy in which Russia's "financial and economic interests" were again asserted. It was on this basis that the question was taken up in the course of prolonged negotiations toward diplomatic recognition. The railway question was eventually dealt with in Article IX of the agreement signed in Peking in May 1924 by Wellington Koo and, for the Soviets, Leo Karakhan. The railway was declared to be a "purely commercial undertaking," with the consequence that,

with the exception of matters pertaining to the business operations which are under the direct control of the Chinese Eastern Railway, all other matters affecting the rights of the national and the local Governments of the Republic of China—such as judicial matters, matters relating to civil administration, police, municipal government, taxation, and landed property (with the exception of lands required by the said railway)—shall be administered by the Chinese Authorities.[5]

It was also agreed (section 5) that "the future of the Chinese Eastern Railway shall be determined by the Republic of China and the Union of Soviet Socialist Republics, to the exclusion of any third party or parties." China's right to redeem and recover the railway was also granted in principle, although the date, amount, and conditions of the reversion were left to be settled by some future conference. Till such conference could be held, an accompanying agreement specified details of provisional management and control of the line.[6] These may be summed up briefly as follows: equal representation of both nations on the directorate, with a Chinese as president and director general; day-to-day management in the hands of a Russian manager and two assistant managers, of whom one had to be Chinese; and application as far as possible of the principle of parity of employment for nationals of both countries.

The flaw in these agreements was that the Peking government, as of May 31, 1924, on which day they were signed, exercised no effective jurisdiction whatever over the territory in which the railway lay: from May 1922, that had been part of the autonomous preserve of Chang Tso-lin. The Soviet side had therefore to reach some accommodation with Chang. Chang too was anxious to settle issues outstanding over the railway in order to secure his rear against any threat on the long border with the Russians, and thus to gain the freedom to concentrate all available forces on the scene of the clash that he was anticipating with Wu P'ei-fu's forces in the South. Evident Russian impatience, and rumors of Russian troop concentrations on his Northern borders,[7] persuaded him to engage in hasty negotiations with the Russians in the autumn, leading to the signature on September 20, 1924, of an agreement between the USSR and the "Government of the Autonomous Three Eastern Provinces of the Republic of China."[8] In this there was no departure in principle from the terms of the earlier Peking agreement, although certain points were gone into in more detail—the conference at which a "final settlement" of the issues connected with the railway was to be reached was to be held within four months, for example, and the term of the Russian concession for the line was reduced from 80 to 60 years. Furthermore, Chang was able to make the actual appointments to the Chinese positions on the new board, putting at its head his old associate and relative, Pao Kuei-ch'ing.[9] Though far from satisfactory and intended to be only provisional arrangements, these remained the basic organizational principles on which the line was run until the "sale" of the Soviet interest in it to the Manchukuo regime in 1935.

Cooperation did not come easily to either party to the agreements. Disagreements between the unlikely partners to the reorganized concern—the nominees of Chang Tso-lin and Moscow—led very quickly to a breakdown of the mechanism of joint control. Reacting against the continuing weight of Russian influence at all levels of the administration, Chinese members of the board simply stayed away. Seven months after the new arrangements became operative, the situation was as follows:[10]

It is now fully four months since there has been a Board meeting and there are some 500 questions awaiting the decision of the Board. Even the 1925 Budget, which was ready at the beginning of the year, has not been passed, so that actually the General Manager is personally responsible for all expenditure incurred during the current year. Undoubtedly the Chinese Directors made a grave mistake not to have been here on the spot when the new Board and new management came into power in October last year, for now the Chinese are likely to pay heavily for this mistake.

General Pao, the President of the Railway, has never been in Harbin since he was elected and there is still speculation as to whether he will ever come. . . . Mr. Yüan Chin-k'ai, the Vice-President, resigned over three months ago and his successor, Mr. Chen Chien, though appointed, is not likely to come to Harbin as he has several other jobs.

The result of this was that the Soviet general manager, Ivanov, was left in almost complete control of railway affairs, and far from there being any approach toward parity of employment, the predominance of Russians actually increased. In the first three months of operation of the reorganized line, the number of Russian employees increased from 10,833 to 11,251, while that of Chinese employees decreased from 5,912 to 5,556.[11]

It is not clear why Chang Tso-lin made such little effort to assert his influence over the railway. In January 1924, it is true that he took the one positive step in the North of forbidding navigation by foreign—in this case almost entirely Russian—shipping on the waters of the Sungari. He persisted in this, despite protests from the representatives of the Chinese Eastern Railway, which operated the largest fleet, and despite appeals from the government in Peking. Eventually—although rather later, in August 1926—he actually seized the Chinese Eastern's Sungari flotilla, much of which had ignored his earlier order.[12] To the end of 1924, however, it must be concluded that Chang pursued a negative policy in the North, following initiatives from the Russians and from Peking. He showed little interest in the possibilities presented by the new situation there, and even tolerated some diminution of his power and influence. Preoccupation with ambitions toward the central plains of China must be reckoned the main cause of this.

It should be recognized, however, that this phase passed with the resolution of the tensions between Fengtien and Chihli, ushering in a stormy period in the relations between Chang and the railway management.

Domestic Alliances

Turning to the question of Chang's maneuverings in the domestic politics of China as a whole, it is apparent that he continued, during the phase of his autonomic administration that followed May 1922, to form alliances according to no other discernible political principle than that of shared hostility to the dominance of Chihli militarists. The failure of his various "allies" to come to his aid in 1922 did not deter him from continuing to think in terms of an alliance that would work in the future to engage Chihli forces on several fronts and destroy them. The question of how such ideological incompatibles as made up the alliance might relate in dividing up the spoils of victory was given little more than passing consideration.

Furthermore, those to whom he looked as prospective allies were virtually the same as those who had failed him in May 1922, in particular Tuan Ch'i-jui and Sun Yat-sen. In the latter part of 1922, delegates hurried to and from the camps of their respective masters, striving to secure the military or political support of the others at smallest cost to his own side and on most advantageous terms generally.[13] Sun Yat-sen was represented by Wang Ching-wei (Wang Chao-ming) and Ch'eng Ch'ien-li, and Chang by various subordinates, but in particular, as his special representative in Canton, by Yang Ta-shih. Yang had been an important revolutionary figure in Mukden during the disturbances of 1911–12, later a member of the first parliament, and from 1922 was employed as an adviser to the Fengtien Governor.[14] From early 1925 the Chekiang militarist Lu Yung-hsiang also became involved in the negotiations, represented in Mukden by his son, Lu Hsiao-chou, who remained there between March and December of 1923.[15] Lu Yung-hsiang was the sole Anhwei clique member left holding power at this time and, since his territory included Shanghai, also controlling considerable wealth. He had been approached by Chang Tso-lin as early as the spring of 1921 with a view to reaching terms on alliance, but apparently decided then to let Chang take on the Chihli forces alone,[16] although one report suggests that both he and Sun Yat-sen were receiving substantial sums of money from Chang prior to the 1922 war.*

---

*Yü Ch'ung-han, speaking to South Manchuria Railway Company officials in Mukden, mentioned that Chang had given Sun and Lu 300,000 and 400,000 yüan, respectively, and

Whether these various negotiations in 1922 and 1923 led eventually to the establishment of formal alliance is open to doubt. Various dates have been suggested,[17] but the better view seems to be that the discussions were never made final.[18] Vague agreements on a Southern parliament, temporary reinstatement of Li Yüan-hung as President, to be followed by either Sun or Tuan or both, as President and Vice-President, and on moves to attract the support of so far uncommitted provinces, proved impossible to translate into any plan for coordinated military action. In November 1923, Chang was persuaded, apparently against his inclination, to reopen the supply of campaign funds to Lu, but he had no great confidence in him, and Lu, for his part, was reluctant to move without cast-iron guarantees of support. Soviet involvement with Sun Yat-sen after the Sun-Joffe agreement of January 1923 made surprisingly little difference to the negotiations, and a letter from Sun to Chang in November 1923 referred with gratitude to the financial aid he had received over the preceding year.[19] This, it should be remembered, was after the arrival of the first Soviet advisers in Canton and the commencement of the Soviet reorganization of the Kuomintang.

In the end, however, the distrust and reserve with which the various parties treated each other made nonsense of any alliance. The initiative was taken by Lu's enemies in August 1924, and Lu was quickly defeated before Chang's move to engage the Chihli forces on a second front in the North could have effect. Sun Yat-sen's forces continued to bide their time. (For discussion of the war itself, see below.)

Domestically, in addition to these negotiations, Chang also engaged (prior to the second Fengtien-Chihli war) in various dealings that he may have felt would present much less difficulty—negotiations aimed at enlisting the support of major Northeastern bandit groups as regular fighting units against Wu P'ei-fu. Partly this was a necessary counter to the efforts of the enemy to use the same forces to stir up trouble in his rear, as in the case of Kao Shih-pin, discussed in the previous chapter. Partly, no doubt, it also reflected the absence of any hard and fast distinction between regular troops and bandits, many commanders in the Fengtien forces having begun their careers at the head of groups of mounted bandits.

The borderline between discontented officials and bandits was perhaps narrower in the Northeast than elsewhere, a fact that Chang could ignore

---

since this act produced no results at all for him, he was loath to do so again. Mukden SMR Office Report, June 16, 1923, GSS, 31: 199.

only at his peril. The sensational exposure of the "Kirin Independence Movement" in July 1923 emphasized this point. This was a movement organized among disaffected members of the local elite of officials, gentry, and merchants who enjoyed strong support among local groups, including coal miners.[20] Estimates of its strength varied greatly, up to 15,000 people by some accounts,[21] including former Governor Hsü Ting-lin and the current heads of the Departments of Foreign Affairs, Education, and Industry in the provincial government.[22] Whether reports that Wu P'ei-fu, or alternatively Ts'ao K'un, was connected with this particular movement were true or not, it was clear that his enemies would be bound to favor such a rebellious movement deep within Chang's territories. Purges alone were no solution. With the prospect of a Southern campaign likely to demand the dispatch of his best troops well below the Great Wall, Chang had to do something about the large groups of armed bandits operating in all the remoter frontier points of his territory. What he did, in the latter part of 1923 and early 1924, constitutes a bizarre episode, worth relating briefly.

Late in 1923 Ch'en Tung-shan, leader of a 3,000-man force operating in the vicinity of Mi-shan, was persuaded to accept official status as colonel in command of his own forces, garrisoning the same area.[23] Also, Chang Hsüeh-liang entertained in Mukden the leaders of the major bandit groupings of Tung-ning, An-ta, Hei-ho, Mi-shan, and Sui-hua, all frontier areas renowned for bandit problems. In a curious gesture he had them stay on the premises of the nationalist newspaper whose foundation he had been partly responsible for—the Three Eastern Provinces *Min-pao*.[24] Discussions on this occasion seem to have been inconclusive. However, another plan, conceived about the same time, was carried much further. It involved working through the defeated allies of 1922—former Honan tuchün Chao T'i and his brother, Chao Chieh, a well-known bandit in the So-lun area of Inner Mongolia—to recruit the main bandit forces around So-lun into Chang's service.[25] This plan was to meet several objectives. The most immediate was to deny these forces to the enemy, since Wu P'ei-fu was believed to have agents working on them. Another was to make active use of them, transformed into a regular cavalry unit and equipped with the best that could be supplied from the Mukden arsenal, to collaborate with Mongolian Prince Darkhan in a thrust deep into Outer Mongolia aimed at the seizure of Urga.[26] Darkhan was linked to Chang by a marriage alliance from the days of Chang's rise to power in the same Mongolian frontier region.* From early 1924 Yang Yü-t'ing, Chang's top strategist, was entrusted with planning the operation.[27] Lu Chan-k'uei, the ex-brigand who played the central role in these plans, built up his force—originally some 1,500 to 2,000 men—till it was 7,000 strong.[28] The Urga plan was reckoned to need three brigades in all, so a considerable detachment of "regular" troops would have had to be used to back him up.[29] There was Japanese involvement in the operation also, in the person of a missionary adventurer called Deguchi Onisaburō. Deguchi had founded a bizarre new religious cult, *Omotokyō* (Great Beginning Teaching), and, since he was also an avid proponent of Japanese imperialist expansion, was pursuing both religious and secular goals by attaching himself to Lu's camp as a first step in the promotion of his teachings in Mongolia. In Mongolia, he hoped to work in alliance with native Mongolian Lamaism and with the Chinese Fyflot (Red Swastika) Association.[30]

However, the whole scheme backfired as Lu's men took advantage of their official patronage and their new weapons to go on the rampage throughout the area between T'ao-nan, Pai-yin-t'ai-lai, and So-lun. Their effectiveness as a military unit was obviously open to serious question, and it may also be that the official favor shown them by Chang was resented by the other "regular" forces in the area. In early June, Lu and 38 of his guards and henchmen went to discuss with K'an Chao-hsi (Defense Commissioner for the T'ao-nan area) the problems that had arisen between his men and various "regular" detachments. All were seized and shot, apparently on Chang Tso-lin's express orders. Deguchi escaped and thereafter abandoned his Mongolian plans, and those of Lu's followers that survived simply resumed their previous outlaw activities. As in 1921, Chang's plans for an expedition against Urga were shelved.[31]

Japan: The Role of "Advisers" in China

With the political situation in China effectively deadlocked, the Soviet Union absolutely distasteful to Chang ideologically, and the Chinese Eastern Railway a substantial source of potential friction, Japan represented to Chang the one force that might conceivably tip the scales in his favor in the struggle for power in China. It is not surprising, then, that the major theme in his maneuverings and negotiations prior to the renewal of hostilities with

*Chang's second daughter (by his first wife, Chao) was married to Darkhan's son. Sonoda, *Kaiketsu Chō Sakurin*, p. 20.

Wu P'ei-fu in the autumn of 1924 was the effort to maintain the best possible relations with Japan, and to secure reassurances of every possible support. This process was complicated by the extremely diffuse nature of Japanese operations in Northeastern China—where power and initiatives might be exercised at any one time by Japanese consuls, under the Ministry of Foreign Affairs, by the semigovernmental South Manchuria Railway, by the Kwantung Army, or by the group of officers seconded to Chang's staff as advisers or *ku-wen*. The offices of Korean Governor-General and Administrator of Kwantung province were also occasionally involved. Coordination of the line being pursued by all these offices and their staffs was often far from perfect.

As perhaps might be expected, those Japanese in closest touch with Chang—his advisers—tended to be most enthusiastic in his support. They functioned as intimate members of his command post, in effect as senior staff officers, and those who spent a long time in Mukden were especially prone to identify their own professional advancement with Chang's and to commit themselves wholeheartedly to his cause. The system of secondment of Japanese officers as military advisers to the staff of Chinese armies dates from as early as 1901, when Major Tachibana Shōichirō was sent to Paoting at the invitation of Yüan Shih-k'ai to help in the training of his "new" army. Already by the time of the Russo-Japanese War there were more than 20 Japanese officers, pigtailed and dressed as Chinese, serving as instructors and advisers under Yüan Shih-k'ai, while others were attached to the staffs of regional military commands in Hupei, in Central China, and as far inland as Szechwan.[32] As military historian Ralph Powell comments, "one of the major shifts in military policy during the period 1901–1903 was the growing tendency throughout the empire to employ Japanese officers instead of Germans as instructors."[33] By 1912 there were 25 foreign advisers attached to the central government in Peking, six of whom were Japanese, and of that six, two were senior military men.[34] The practice continued, and although there has never been a comprehensive study devoted to it, there can be little doubt that, in the case of the Northeast in particular, the role they played was considerable. According to one Japanese estimate, though it is given in passing and not specifically directed at this problem, there were in July 1928, one month after Chang Tso-lin's death, no fewer than 50 Japanese advisers with the Fengtien Armies.[35] Table 5 is therefore obviously very incomplete and is intended to list only the most senior and influential Japanese officers serving Chang.

TABLE 5

Principal Japanese Military Advisers, Instructors, and Liaison Officers
in the Three Eastern Provinces under Chang Tso-lin

Subject	Rank	Period served
FENGTIEN PROVINCE		
Advisers:		
Kikuchi Takeō[a]	Lt. Col.; Col. (Aug. 1917)	1916–1919
Machino Takema[a]	Major; Lt. Col. (July 1918); Col. (Aug. 1922)	1916–1928
Honjō Shigeru	Col.; Major Gen. (Aug. 1922)	May 1921–Aug. 1924
Matsui Nanao	Col.	Aug. 1924–1928
Giga Masaya	Major	1924–1928
Bando Matsuzō[b]		1922–1926
Instructor:		
Araki Gorō[c]	Lt. (Major Gen. Huang Mu of the Fengtien Army)	1922–1926
Liaison officers (Kwantung Army, Mukden special service agents):		
Kishi Yajirō	Major Gen.	May 1920–Aug. 1924
Kikuchi Takeo	Major Gen.	Aug. 1924–March 1926
KIRIN PROVINCE		
Advisers:		
Saitō Tsune	Col.	March 1918–Aug. 1920
Suzuki Yoshiyuki	Lt. Col. (period of secondment uncertain)	1921 (active)
Hayashi	Lt. Col. (period of secondment uncertain)	1925 (active)
HEILUNGKIANG PROVINCE		
Advisers:		
Saitō Minoru	Lt. Col.	Feb. 1918–June 1922
Korenaga Shigeo	Lt. Col. (period of secondment uncertain)	1924–1925 (active)

SOURCE: For biographies of Honjō, Machino, Matsui, Kishi, and Kikuchi, see Tōa dōbunkai, *Zoku taishi kaikoroku*, vol. 2, pp. 849–57, 871–88, 888–906, 937–43, 944–54. Other sources are as follows: Inaba Masao, "Shingai kakumei yori . . . ," in Doihara Kenji Kankōkai, pp. 163, 168, 527, 529; Araki Gorō, "Uridasareta Manshūkoku," *Bungei shunjū*, April 1964, p. 263; Machino Takema, "Chō Sakurin bakushi no zengo," *Chūo kōron* (Tokyo, Sept. 1949), p. 74; Kokuryūkai, *Tōa senkaku shishi kiden* (Tokyo, 1936, 1966), vol. 3, p. 85; Kuo Ting-yee and James W. Morley, *Sino-Japanese Relations, 1862–1927* (New York, 1965), pp. 166–68.

[a] Machino was an instructor at the Police College and an adviser to the Ministry for the Interior in Peking between 1906 and 1913. He first met Chang Tso-lin early in 1912, when he was dispatched to Mukden to help in the suppression of the revolutionary forces. According to "Aizu shikon fūunroku" (Tokyo, 1961), pp. 91–95, and to Machino's own account in *Chūo kōron* (Tokyo, Sept. 1949), p. 75, he stayed at Chang's house advising Chang during the course of the purges and counterrevolutionary terror.

Both Machino and Kikuchi were advisers to previous military governors of Fengtien also, commencing in November 1914. Machino resigned his active commission early in 1923 and thereafter, as a reserve colonel, served Chang as a "private" adviser.

[b] Bando probably functioned more as interpreter than adviser. He was a graduate of the renowned Japanese language institute in Shanghai, the Tōa Dōbun Shoin.

[c] Araki (on whom see especially Chapter 5, for his role during the Kuo Sung-ling rebellion), though a graduate of Japan's prestigious Officer Cadet School (Shikan Gakkō), was by his own account a *tairiku rōnin* (continental adventurer), and though he rose to high rank in Chang Tso-lin's service and also retained close contact with the Japanese military, he did not rise above his graduating rank, second lieutenant, in the Japanese Army.

Kwantung Army special service agents (*tokumu kikan*) who were responsible for liaison with the Chinese authorities in Mukden are also listed in the table, since the role they played was similar to that of advisers, and indeed they were often mistakenly referred to as such.

There were, of course, also nationals of other countries on Chang's staff—the Englishman Captain Sutton in the arsenal from 1922 to 1925; an American commercial adviser, Carleton Baker, from the autumn of 1920 until June 1923; French instructors and aviators attached to the air force from 1922; White Russian officers and contingents serving in the army as mercenaries, particularly under the command of Chang Tsung-ch'ang; and no doubt various foreign adventurers such as the Italian fascist Amleto Vespa, who claimed to have been a secret agent of Chang from 1920 to 1928.[36] However, none of these was as influential as the Japanese; nor does it appear that any of the others was in the Japanese position of serving and reporting not only to Chang Tso-lin but also to his own military headquarters and superiors in Tokyo. Despite the introduction in Japan in the 1920's of a new, cooperative multilateral foreign policy toward China—of which the Washington Conference decisions and treaties were the principal embodiment—the Japanese advisers in China continued to function as if nothing had changed.

In 1922 the dangers to which this might give rise were realized in Tokyo, but the plan to withdraw all advisers in the crisis of that year was nevertheless shelved and they played an important role in the Fengtien-Chihli war of May. After the war, in July, the cabinet took another look at the problem.[37] The direct participation of Japanese officers in Chinese military affairs led inevitably to their involvement—or at least to allegations of their involvement, which was just as injurious—in China's political affairs. Political change in China at this time was after all largely a reflection of changes in the military balance of power between the armed camps of various warlords. The Japanese government was therefore bound to be, and in this case it was agreed had been, seriously embarrassed in carrying out its post–Washington Conference diplomacy by the actions and involvement of these officers. The embarrassment arising from the apparent contradiction between the neutrality proclaimed by the Ministry of Foreign Affairs and the necessary partiality of the ku-wen group of advisers in China was compounded when various Chinese leaders tried to suggest their own invincibility by spreading the word that they had Japanese backing, whether they had or not. It was also recognized that as the partisan sentiments of these officers were transferred into the ranks of the China Station Army, the Kwantung Army, and even staff headquarters and the Army Ministry in Tokyo, the independence and flexibility of the armed forces were seriously impaired. After a comprehensive survey of the problem, the cabinet noted:

In this situation, with the Imperial Government constantly being put into a disadvantageous position in its diplomatic relations and having always to be making explanations, the harm that Japan suffers is probably incalculable. The recent behavior of Chang Tso-lin's Japanese ku-wen military attachés in the Fengtien-Chihli war is certainly an apposite example.

However, a long recital of the evils of the system led to the lamest of conclusions:[38]

No blame should be attributed to the efforts of the diplomatic authorities, who have striven to change quickly with the times, and who, whenever the occasion has arisen, have pressed the military to reconsider and to change. And so it is absolutely essential that the heads of our various offices in China too should realize the importance of the situation outlined here whenever any problem arises over the question of employment or reemployment of ku-wen, and that before opening negotiations with the Chinese side they should first ask for instructions and then should act in accordance with the intentions of the Ministry.

This meant, in effect, that the system continued unchanged. From 1922 until 1924, when the second Fengtien-Chihli war broke out, Chang was served by Colonel Honjō Shigeru, who was later to become commander of the Kwantung Army; by Machino Takema, who actually joined him much earlier and stayed with him right until his death; and by Kishi Yajirō, not exactly a ku-wen yet nevertheless in very close relationship with him as the Kwantung Army's special service agent in Mukden (see Table 5). In August and September of 1924 Kishi was replaced by Major General Kikuchi Takeo, and Honjō by Colonel Matsui Nanao. The instructions Matsui carried with him as he took up his post provide the most concise and authoritative statement of the role these ku-wen were expected to play:[39]

1. During the period of your secondment you are to facilitate the mutual cooperation of Japanese and Chinese armies in the event of emergency by influencing the military-related installations of Fengtien province to be modeled on those of the [Japanese] Empire.
2. To fulfill your duties you will need to act as liaison with the Headquarters of the Kwantung and Korean armies, and with the Imperial [Japanese] military officials in Mukden, Harbin, etc., and of course to maintain close contact with officers serving in the Three Eastern Provinces.

3. You must strive to provide intelligence information to this Department as far as is possible and without obstruction about military matters, internal affairs, communications, financial and economic matters, geographical resources, and the influence of the powers in Fengtien province.

The role of the ku-wen, by promoting the integration of the armed forces of the country to which he was seconded with his own country and, by proving his worth as a military specialist and thus gaining the confidence of the highest levels of military and civilian planning, gaining access to a wide range of intelligence information, was evidently of considerable value to his home country in extending its influence and control. It is clear that the Japanese government was aware that its publicly proclaimed policies of neutrality and nonintervention in Chinese internal affairs were compromised by the close involvement of these officers in Chinese affairs, and the fact that no steps were taken to end the anomaly indicates that the advantages of the system were so great that its abolition could not be seriously contemplated.

Other nonofficial but nevertheless important channels of communication between Chang and the Japanese were the representatives of the major Japanese business interests in the Northeast. Far outweighing any in importance was, of course, the South Manchuria Railway Company. Kamata Yasuke, who headed the Mukden branch office of the company continuously from 1915 to 1929, was intimately associated with Chang,[40] and Matsuoka Yōsuke, who served on the directorate between 1921 and 1926, was also involved in negotiations with Chang over very substantial matters. So too was Etō Toyoji, a Mitsui factor who became acquainted with Chang when he went to Mukden to take over the Mitsui branch office there in 1913, and who, because of his long friendship with Chang, together with his familiarity with business and political leaders of Mitsui/Seiyūkai circles in Tokyo,* became a key go-between in the negotiations between Chang and the Seiyūkai party and government in 1927 and 1928[41] (On this see below, Chapter 6, p. 241.)

Two-Faced Diplomacy

Whatever the channel, however, the problem Chang faced in making his appeals for aid from Japanese agencies was that he had always to offer

---

*The Seiyūkai party (Rikken seiyūkai, or society of friends of constitutional government) was established in 1900 and formed the government under General Tanaka Giichi between April 20, 1927, and July 2, 1929.

some quid pro quo. Chang's strength lay in his ability to persuade the Japanese that he was doing the best he could do to advance their interests but was held back all the time by the political fact of mounting anti-Japanese feeling and rights-recovery fever, which could not be completely curbed. At the same time he had to persuade Chinese opinion that he was doing the best he could to advance Chinese national interests—resisting determinedly every pressure from Japan that it was at all possible to resist. This Janus pose was at best difficult to maintain; at worst it was calculated to draw fierce attack from both sides. Through the remaining and mature years of his power, Chinese nationalism and Japanese imperialism developed into raging currents through which the ideologically rudderless Chang, however adroit in his maneuvering, was increasingly hard put to steer.

The issues on which Chang came under pressure from the Japanese side arose mainly from the Japanese demand for the full implementation of various treaties and agreements, notably the 1915 ("21 Demands") Treaties, but also various other agreements granting rights of railway construction to Japan. On these and similar issues Chang's room for maneuver was strictly limited. Following the Washington Conference and Japan's withdrawal in 1922 from Siberia, North "Manchuria," and Shantung, a powerful and widely based movement grew up in China to demand also the return of Dairen and Port Arthur—the key towns in the Japanese-leased territories in the Kwantung Peninsula.[42] Under the 1915 Treaties the lease governing these territories was extended from its original term of 25 years, terminating in 1923, to one of 99 years, thus valid until 1997. The Chinese delegation in Washington raised serious objections to the validity of these 1915 Treaties, but they were rejected out of hand by Japan.[43] Thereafter the Chinese movement for the recovery of the Kwantung Peninsula spread to the Northeast.

Chang adopted a carefully ambiguous position on the issue: in January 1923 he gave assurances to the South Manchuria Railway president that he would use force to suppress any demonstrations calling for the return of the leased territory and he would inform Peking that he considered the "circumstances and the time" not right for such a movement.[44] But at a policy-making conference of his top aides in April, he ruled that whereas care should be taken to avoid arousing Japanese resentment, it was equally important not to oppose too strongly the nationalist rights-recovery movement since this would excite the suspicions of the Chinese people.[45]

On railway construction too, Chang was compelled to attempt to placate two increasingly irreconcilable constituencies. While he was assuring the Japanese that he was sympathetic to their plans for the expansion of the network of Japanese-controlled or -financed lines, his administration was working at the same time on plans for developing a purely Chinese network with Chinese capital only—and thus was diametrically opposed to any extension of Japanese influence (see discussion in Chapter 3). Thus, although Chang could give assurances and hold out hopes to the Japanese of realizing various plans to expand into the far north of "Manchuria" and into Eastern Inner Mongolia, he was also, for example, sending instructions to the Governor of Kirin province to delay and fob off the Japanese in negotiations over the line that they were most anxious of all to see built—the line linking Kirin and therefore North "Manchuria" to Japan by the most direct route, across Korea. Such a line would have the effect of tightening the economic incorporation of the area into the Japanese sphere, and incidentally of providing Japan with fast direct military connections into the North.[46] Chang's position was unenviable, but his policies were not calculated to please any party for very long.

PREPARATIONS FOR WAR AND OVERTURES TO JAPAN

In August 1923, Chang renewed his request for Japanese arms to strengthen his preparations against Chihli, first through a representative of the Kwantung province Governor,[47] and then later through his adviser Honjō.[48] Honjō took the liberty of giving in reply what he described as a "private opinion in order to prevent any misunderstanding by Chang." The important parts of Honjō's opinion paper were as follows:[49]

2. Though the [Japanese] Empire has always been especially generous toward the Eastern Provinces, it cannot possibly meet a desire for a complete arms transfer, since this would be a breach of international trust. So it will be necessary for you, as Commander in Chief, to make various plans. . . .

3. In the event of any disturbance being created in the Eastern Provinces by armed force from outside, even though there is no deliberate aggressive action by the Eastern Provinces, the [Japanese] Empire is determined always resolutely to put a stop to it regardless of who the adversary is, whenever the occasion, and whatever the circumstances.

4. As for the military activity by you [Commander in Chief] within the passes, the [Japanese] Empire always demands that you exercise circumspection so that order may be maintained in the Eastern Provinces. However, we would not be

inclined to hold to such expectation in the event that the power of the Southern anti-Chihli armies were to reach to the north of the Yangtze.

5. . . . In order to deal with the situation in future, you must exert the greatest effort to perfecting your own military preparedness. This perfection depends on the training and readiness of your armies as well as on the preparation of weapons and ammunition. I find it regrettable that there are many respects in which the training and equipment of armies outside the capital [Mukden] are inadequate.

Such sentiments were judged in Tokyo to indicate too great partiality for Chang and to be inconsistent with the officially proclaimed line of "absolute neutrality." It was feared that they might give rise to misunderstandings among other factions in China to the effect that Chang enjoyed Japanese guarantees of the security of his house and person. Clauses 4 and 5 ran the risk of inviting misunderstandings about how the expansion of the power of the anti-Chihli forces might lead to opposition from Chang and to his moving into the central area. The Southern anti-Chihli forces were those of the armies allied with Sun Yat-sen in Kwangtung, still a motley force, although the Kuomintang was reorganized along Bolshevik lines at the Second Congress in January 1924, and the development of a party army was given high priority from that time. Clause 2 seemed to suggest that, whereas complete arms supply to Chang was out of the question, perhaps partial supply might be considered, and since Chang's arsenal was operating with increasing efficiency, he could have no need of more than that. Honjō was therefore rebuked and cautioned.[50] Yet the trend of thinking in the Kwantung Army at large was almost as distant from the official line of neutrality and noninterference as was that of men, like Honjō, who were actually members of Chang's immediate entourage. A Kwantung Army Staff paper of October 1923, directed primarily to the problem of preventing China's falling under international control, expressed the view that it was necessary "to deal with the highhandedness of Chihli, which is the greatest evil in the present confusion." It therefore criticized the policy of "so called nonintervention in internal affairs" as leading to China's becoming dependent on other powers, thus serving "to make weaker and weaker the links between China and Japan."[51]

There seem to have been no special or extraordinary steps taken to aid Chang Tso-lin during 1923 or the early part of 1924, since the autumn of 1924, with the prospect of hostilities again imminent, found Chang again issuing an urgent appeal.[52] The gist of it, as communicated through his advisers Honjō and Matsui to Foreign Minister Shidehara and Kwantung province Governor Kodama, was that the attempted national unification by the Chihli forces, with English and American backing, threatened Japanese interests in the Northeast. Chang affirmed that he himself was for unification "through the pro-Japanese elements," and asked therefore whether Japan was prepared to aid him, and if so by what concrete measures. To reinforce his claim, he pointed also to the fact that the Peking government had recently drawn closer to the Soviet Union—a reference to the conclusion of the negotiations in May—and added that, since Sun Yat-sen was "already more than half red," he himself was under pressure from both front and rear by Chihli and the Soviets.[53]

This appeal for aid on the grounds of determined anticommunism was one that Chang used frequently from this time on, however hollow it may have rung on this occasion, since Chang was loosely allied with Sun Yat-sen, who in turn had entered on the path of commitment to alliance with the Soviet Union through his agreement with Adolf Joffe in January of the same year, and since Chang himself was about to sign an agreement with the Soviet Union. Tokyo, however, adopted an apparently unsympathetic stance.[54] Its response to the crisis as it developed in September and October is discussed in detail below.

THE COMING OF THE WAR

The 1922 Fengtien-Chihli war was the outcome of an acute disequilibrium in the relationship between various warlord factions, which its inconclusive outcome did little to resolve. By the spring of 1923, renewed outbreak of fighting was widely anticipated. However, in April a bandit attack on a train at Lin-ch'eng in Shantung province—when many passengers, including foreigners, were kidnapped—aroused strong foreign calls for intervention in China; and the likelihood that renewal of the civil war might provide a pretext for intervention, and even possibly partition of China by the powers, operated as a deterrent to immediate hostilities. The fact that postwar reorganization and reform programs were still not complete reinforced the need for disengagement,[55] and a "Peace Agreement" was signed between Fengtien and Chihli representatives in June 1923. Though none of the matters of substance dividing the two sides were resolved by the agreement, it did lead to a real relaxation of tensions.[56] Its principal advantage for the Fengtien side was that it allowed the reorganization under way in both civil and military spheres to continue, and for the Chihli side that it allowed the undiverted attention of Ts'ao K'un's followers to be devoted to the business of securing him the presidency. However, while the "new" men in Fengtien continued with their reforms, the Chihli grip on China south of the Wall gradually tightened. Military offensives by Wu P'ei-fu followed the apparent political triumphs of Ts'ao K'un in Peking. By mid-1924, as Sheridan had pointed out, Wu controlled most of China proper, the uproar over the Lin-ch'eng train affair had subsided, and an incident was all that was needed to spark the delayed civil war.[57]

Chihli dominance was contested by three main forces: those of Chang Tso-lin in the Northeast, the Nationalists in the South, and Lu Yung-hsiang in Chekiang. The ideal battle plan might have been to dispose of such enemies one by one, but since the alliance between them, however loose, made this difficult, the next best thing was to tackle first the weakest: Lu Yung-hsiang. Lu's jurisdiction was one of major importance, since—although technically limited to Chekiang province—it also included by an anomaly the city of Shanghai and thus control over two key supports of warlord power: money, much of it in the form of revenues from the opium trade, and weapons, from the Shanghai Arsenal.[58] These two factors meant there was implacable rivalry between Lu and neighboring Kiangsu tuchün Ch'i Hsieh-yüan. In September 1924, war finally broke out between Ch'i, backed by a coalition of neighboring Chihli-aligned armies, and Lu, who appealed immediately for aid from both Chang Tso-lin and Sun Yat-sen.[59] Sun Yat-sen, although he announced on September 13 his intention to launch his projected Northern Expedition, was prevented by events in Kwangtung from making much headway.[60] It was the involvement of Wu P'ei-fu and Chang, backing their respective protégé in this relatively minor, short, and local war, that brought on the reopening of hostilities between Fengtien and Chihli. Chang was reluctant to commit himself fully or at once to Lu's support, and his eventual involvement, though nominally on Lu's behalf, was too late to save him. The military conference in Mukden in late August called for cessation of hostilities but was unable to determine what positive steps were necessary beyond agreeing to subsidize Lu's armies with a four-month salary advance for his troops.[61] It was only when it became apparent that Chihli armies were mobilizing against him in the North that Chang organized his forces into an "army of suppression" (*chen-wei-chün*), divided into six route armies, and made clear his intention to fight.[62] The early reluctance on Chang's part to take full-scale action in Lu's support was matched on the Chihli side by the refusal of Feng

Yu-hsiang to leave the capital area with his forces to reinforce Ch'i Hsieh-yüan.[63] However, the brief stalemate in the Yangtze fighting was broken soon enough, as much because of "treachery and insubordination" in the ranks of Lu's army as of any other factor.[64] On October 13 Lu fled to Japan, and at the end of the month he took refuge in Mukden.[65]

VICTORY AND ITS PRICE

Fengtien-Chihli hostilities opened in mid-September and were marked in the early stages by a series of Fengtien victories on the Jehol front. In October, however, the focus shifted to Shan-hai-kuan, which became the scene of prolonged and indecisive though costly fighting, with no major breakthrough occurring until the coup d'état of Feng Yü-hsiang on October 22 completely altered the complexion of the war. This was an event of pivotal importance, not only in its impact on the fates of the contending North China warlords, but also in the new height of Japanese plotting and interference that accompanied and partly caused it—totally belying the continued official protestations of absolute neutrality. The military detail of the war will therefore be dealt with here summarily;[66] the coup that served as its climax in rather more detail.

Feng Yü-hsiang was known to be a frustrated and dissatisfied follower of Wu P'ei-fu.[67] Having refused to deploy his troops southward to aid in the Kiangsu-Chekiang war, he then obeyed only with bad grace the order of September 23, 1924, to proceed to the Jehol front in the war against Chang Tso-lin. As Pye relates it:[68]

Feng's position was that of a military commander who had little to gain from the campaign against Fengtien and possibly a great deal to lose. The success of the Chihli forces would mean that Wu P'ei-fu would have extended his military domination over most of North China and that Feng would be deprived of his control of the capital, being left instead in charge of the less desirable area of Jehol. On the other hand, a resounding victory by Chang, who appeared to have great advantages in terms of preparation, equipment and unified command, would have spelled the end of Feng's ability to maintain his independent military power.

As the fighting at Shan-hai-kuan bogged down and Wu was obliged to take personal command of the front (on October 11), Feng Yü-hsiang and Wang Huai-ch'ing, commanders of the 3d and 2d Armies, both refused orders to back him up by moving in to attack the flanks of Chang's main force.[69] Wu realized he was in serious trouble as a result and cabled President Ts'ao K'un for permission to withdraw from the front to deal with the insubordination of his commanders.[70] Since this was not granted, he was still locked in position on the stalemated Shan-hai-kuan front when, on October 23, Feng arrived in Peking after a forced march from Jehol to carry out his coup d'état. Wu was then promptly dismissed. Ts'ao K'un was deposed and orders issued for his arrest, and an immediate halt was ordered to hostilities in the war. It is necessary to look carefully at the web of intrigue that lay behind these events, since the character and relationships of the protagonists for power in China thereby can be made to stand in significant relief.

The crux of the affair was a substantial bribe to Feng. The money for it was loaned to Chang Tso-lin by Japanese sources and transmitted to Feng through Japanese intermediaries. Shortage of funds had long been a grievance of Feng's, first against the Peking government and then against Wu.[71] This was no doubt known in Mukden, through Japanese intelligence sources if no other; and since Feng entered into some communication with Mukden even before departing for the Jehol front in late September,[72] there was ample time and opportunity for him to turn the situation to good advantage.

Before the outbreak of hostilities in September—indeed for several months before—it had been rumored in North China that plotting was afoot: Chang Tso-lin, Tuan Ch'i-jui, Lu Yung-hsiang, and Sun Yat-sen were thought to have secured some agreement from Feng Yü-hsiang that he would betray Wu P'ei-fu in September.[73] Whatever agreement there may have been, however, was of the most tentative kind, since after the war began intensive negotiations became necessary before the deal could be concluded. In Tokyo, Teranishi Hidetake, reserve army colonel and a supernumerary retainer of Sumitomo Joint Stock Company, upon hearing of the outbreak at once cabled Tuan Ch'i-jui urging him to join in the anti-Chihli war. He then set out first for Mukden, where he met with Chang to discuss the question of cooperation between Tuan and Chang in more detail, and then for Tientsin to work on the plan of bringing Feng Yü-hsiang to the point of changing sides in the war.[74] At about the same time, one of Chang's advisers, Machino, was also dispatched to Tientsin to represent him in negotiations there, while another, Matsui, handled the Mukden end of the affair.[75] While Teranishi and Machino established communications with Tuan, Tuan in turn negotiated with Feng, employing as his principal go-between Huang Fu, a returned student from Japan who "spoke Japanese, and had many Japanese connections" and who was an ex-Foreign Minister and Minister of Education.[76] Huang advanced all possible arguments to persuade Feng to betray Wu, including the clinching one: the cash payment. He also put into Feng's hands copies of documents detailing moves of the President to promote ties with the United States. These were obligingly provided for him by Doihara Kenji, who in turn was given them by the Japanese adviser in the President's office, Banzai Rihachirō, who presumably made use of his position to filch them in the first place.[77] Details of the precise U.S. connection described in these papers are not known, but worth noting in this connection is the contemporary Chinese Communist Party characterization of the war as one between rival Japanese and American imperialisms, fought by their respective puppet forces in China. The third "Declaration on the Present State of Affairs," issued by the Party Central Committee in September 1924 pointed to various evidence of Anglo-American backing for Chihli: a loan of one and a half million pounds by a British corporation for the construction of the Taokow–Tsinan railway; substantial arms supply deals between the U.S. Minister in Peking and Wu; U.S. involvement in the organization and training of Wu's air force; and the promise of a U.S. radio station in Shanghai, which was given by Ch'i Hsieh-yüan at the outset of the Chekiang-Kiangsu war. Turning to Fengtien, the declaration referred to various arms supply dealings, plus a reported agreement between Chang and the Japanese for Japanese military and financial aid in exchange for the right to hold 30-year leases in "Manchuria" as evidence of Japanese backing for Chang Tso-lin (and also French backing, since French influence was considerable in the Northeastern air force).[78]

There appears to have been no special reason why Feng should have been surprised or angered by any revelations of Anglo-U.S. collusion with Wu and Ts'ao, and he must have been well aware, for example, of the details mentioned above in the CCP Declaration. Any reaction on patriotic, nationalist grounds would at any rate be hard to square with his own readiness to go along with the Japanese.

The decisive factor, over and above his strategic considerations, was undoubtedly the cash.[79] One million Japanese yen is the lowest of various figures put on the bribe, and two and a half million the highest.[80] Though victory might seem to have been cheap at either price, Chang was reported to have agreed to put up the money only with the utmost reluctance when the urgent request from Tuan Ch'i-jui was put to him by Matsui and Yang Yü-t'ing.[81] Once the decision was made, the money was quickly loaned to

Chang by the South Manchuria Railway Company, which accepted as security from Chang the deeds relating to a large tract of his personal property in Mongolia. Thereafter it passed through various hands. Chang believed it safest to entrust it to Japanese channels and thus called on his adviser, Matsui, to see to the business of dispatch. Matsui sent it through the Mitsui Bank Mukden Branch to the commander of the Japanese Army garrisoned at Tientsin, Yoshioka Kensaku, who in turn passed it on to Tuan Ch'i-jui.[82] From there, evidently in the form of a check drawn on the Yokohama Specie Bank, it passed through various hands before reaching Feng, among those involved being Major Matsumuro Takayoshi, an acquaintance of Feng's who was recalled from his other duties and seconded to Feng's staff as an adviser just before the coup d'état took place.[83] Upon arriving in Feng's camp, Matsumuro also became deeply involved in planning the military details of the coup or, on his own account, its direction. He remained thereafter in Feng's service until August 1929.[84]

JAPANESE RESPONSIBILITY: COMPLICITY IN HIGH PLACES?

The degree of complicity and responsibility borne by Japanese officials, businessmen, and army officers in China for the crucial events of October 1924 is clear from the above account. There is, however, a further dimension. The plotting seems to have been known in advance and approved at the highest levels of the army serving not only in China but also in Tokyo. The relevant entry made by General Ugaki, Army Minister, in his diary is suggestive:[85]

Before the balance between the two sides should be completely broken, [we] mobilized politicians, businessmen, political parties, etc., with the idea that we would have to afford considerable support to the present power holder, Chang, through both visible and invisible channels, in order to make Japan's position in Manchuria much stronger (the feeling at the time when the confrontation of the two armies at Shan-hai-kuan began); and just on the eve of the decisive battle, the subsequent situation developed as a result of our secretly providing considerable support.

Furthermore, according to the biography of the Army chief of staff, Field Marshal Uehara Yūsaku, it is "in no small measure due to the Field Marshal's stratagems behind the scenes that Chang Tso-lin was barely able to maintain his position, and that Wu P'ei-fu, who boasted of his ever-victorious army, met with overwhelming defeat."[86] It was Uehara who had been responsible for the appointment as military attaché in Peking of a

certain Hayashi Yasakichi, whom he thereafter used frequently as a channel for the issue of secret instructions and directives on China operations. It
was this Hayashi who, shortly before the coup, dispatched Matsumuro to
the camp of Feng Yü-hsiang to participate in the military planning of the
operation.[87] According to the same biography of Uehara, it was also
Hayashi who played the major role in persuading Feng to reach agreement
with Fengtien.[88]

Nor did these machinations, concerned in the main with promotion of
the split between the forces of Feng Yü-hsiang and the main Chihli armies,
exhaust Japanese involvement in the war. What actions were taken on a
smaller scale to aid Chang Tso-lin's armies operationally cannot be fully
known but seem to have been considerable. The Japanese intelligence system in China did what it could to damage Wu P'ei-fu's cause by broadcast-
ing propaganda and false information about his situation throughout South
China, as a result of which the Yangtze tuchün were dissuaded from coming to Wu's aid,[89] and by setting up liaison with Chang Tso-lin's armies so
that, among other things, Chang would have adequate warning of any
naval operations on his seaward flank during the Shan-hai-kuan battle.[90]
Direct Japanese participation in the Fengtien war effort was coordinated by
Colonel Matsui, who had just joined Chang as adviser. He assigned the
Japanese officers serving under secondment as advisers in the Northeast
to various sections of the army. These included Lieutenant Colonel
Korenaga, Major Giga, Major Hamamoto, and Lieutenant Araki (General
Huang Mu). Matsui himself participated directly in staff headquarters
planning, engaged flying officers from Japan, and worked on making ready
the Fengtien air force.[91] Later Wu Chün-sheng, who commanded the 5th
Army in the war, remarked, "In this war it was entirely with the help of the
Japanese government and people that the present result has come about."
He added that he was "simply astounded" at the activities of Colonel
Korenaga on the battlefield, and by his abilities.[92]

It is clear from all of this that the Japanese military at all levels did what
could be done to aid Chang Tso-lin and to see Wu defeated, paying scant
regard to the official Japanese line on the war.

The basic principles of policy toward Northeast China and Chang Tso-
lin as enunciated and practiced under the Hara ministry (1918–21) have
been discussed on pp. 50, 57, 59. No major restatement of policy was undertaken from then until May of 1924, when a "General Outline of Policy
Toward China" was agreed jointly between the Foreign, War, Navy, and

Tientsin Conference of December 1924. *Left to right*, Feng Yü-hsiang, Chang Tso-lin, Tuan Ch'i-jui, Lu Yung-hsiang; *at rear*, Wu Kuang-hsin.

Chang Tso-lin with retinue of Japanese advisers and their wives, probably mid-1924. *Front row, from right*, Machino Takema, Kishi Yajiro, Chang Tso-lin, Honjo Shigeru.

Chang Tso-lin's armies on parade, prior to the second Fengtien-Chihli war, about September 1924.

Part of the Fengtien air force, about September 1924.

Chang Hsüeh-liang inspecting the Fengtien air force, about September 1924.

Chang's armies relaxing on a frozen river during progress south through Shantung in late 1924 or early 1925.

Chang Tsung-ch'ang about to board a troop train during a southern advance along the Tientsin-Pukow railway, probably early 1925.

Part of the Fengtien Army's artillery, late 1924.

Finance ministries in the Kiyoura cabinet.[93] Clause 3 of that Outline specified the need to have good relations with powerful regional leaders in China as well as with the central government. Clause 8 dealt with "Manchuria," sections 1 and 2 reading as follows:

1. In line with our established policy toward Chang Tso-lin as actual ruler at present of the Three Eastern Provinces, we should continue to give him friendly assistance and to support his position. However, we must be careful that this does not create any difficulties for Imperial [Japanese] interests in China as a whole. Always giving the appropriate lead to Chang, we must have him realize that his having real power is after all because of the backing of Japanese strength in Manchuria and Mongolia, and have him always respond with a friendly attitude to our country.

2. Since we look on the maintenance of order in Manchuria and Mongolia as particularly important because of the considerable interests the [Japanese] Empire has in that area and because of its relation to control of Korea, we must always exercise the utmost care, and take appropriate steps where we recognize it to be necessary in the interests of self-defense.

Shidehara Kijūrō, who assumed the Foreign Minister's portfolio for the *Kenseikai* in the three-party ministry set up in June 1924, at once announced in general terms a policy of nonintervention in the internal affairs of China,[94] but he made no attempt to deal with the problems inherent in the crucial cluster of Japan's special rights and interests in the Northeast.[95] The crisis of the autumn thus provided an early test of the compatibility of general principle with established special interests. Shidehara has won general acclaim for resisting calls for intervention during this crisis, and consequently the record deserves careful attention.[96] It should be noted at the outset, of course, that decisive *Japanese* intervention is not at issue, given the evidence already discussed, and that defense of Shidehara must rest on the claim that he was either ignorant of what was done by Japanese agents to bring on the coup d'état or, if not ignorant, at least unable to assert his authority to stop it.

Since the Kiangsu-Chekiang war began on September 1 and showed every sign of leading quickly to reopening of hostilities between Fengtien and Chihli, the consul general in Mukden, Funatsu Tatsuichirō, in a dispatch on September 5 to the head of the Asian Bureau of the Ministry of Foreign Affairs, was first to suggest that some Japanese initiatives might become desirable, or even necessary, as the situation developed.[97] A victory by Chang Tso-lin, he argued, would provide the occasion to promote again the rise of Tuan Ch'i-jui to the presidency, with Chang's backing.

Tuan's ambition to unify the country on the basis of intimate Sino-Japanese cooperation in 1917–18 was, it will be remembered, favored with immense Japanese aid, and Funatsu was thus hearkening back to an old dream. But, he went on, if England and America were to incline toward mediation to prevent a defeat for Wu P'ei-fu, then Japan should seize the initiative and mediate in such a way as to prevent the extinction of Chihli, while leaving itself room to exercise restraint over both the Tuan clique and the Fengtien clique. If Chang were not to win outright, he seemed to be saying here, then Japan should at least ensure that, however indecisive the outcome between the Chinese factions, the Japanese interest would be maintained. If, on the other hand, Chang were to suffer defeat, the Japanese government should, he recommended, take steps to make clear the importance of its interests in "Manchuria" and, under the pretext of preventing any disturbance of order, prevent invasion by Chihli armies into the area east of the Liao River. Implicit here is Funatsu's assumption of a fundamental distinction between China south and north of the passes—for even a hypothetical "defeat" for Chang meant only forced withdrawal to the north, where Japan's rights and interests were of such consequence that no disturbance could be tolerated and no anti-Fengtien army bent on Chang's overthrow could be admitted. The final argument advanced by Funatsu was that even if Chang were to be defeated, i.e. forced to withdraw to the east of the Liao, that would not necessarily be disadvantageous for Japan, since the rights recovery movement, which had been gaining strength in the Northeast, would thereafter be more easily restrained. This, in other words, would be the price expected of Chang for the sealing of the defenses of the Three Eastern Provinces against invasion.

Funatsu did not refer specifically to military intervention, but clearly that had to be envisaged as a possible last resort once the commitment to prevent Chihli armies marching into the Northeast was accepted. Shidehara took no notice of what thus on the face of it appeared to represent a complete reversal of his "nonintervention" policy, which instead he simply restated.[98] As the center of fighting shifted from Jehol to the vicinity of Shan-hai-kuan at the beginning of October, however, the possibility of a sudden breakthrough by the Chihli armies, after which Mukden itself would quickly come under attack, had to be seriously entertained.

From the semigovernmental South Manchuria Railway Company, which with its enormous interests in the area had much at stake, came a plea for decisive action. Matsuoka Yōsuke, the most active and influential member of the directorate, saw the basic weakness of China policy in the past as stemming from "the failure to establish any far-reaching interventionist policy." He was particularly critical of the embarrassment caused by "trifling interventions" that tended to arise through the presence of Japanese army offiers as advisers in the camps of virtually all Chinese leaders: "At present our army men employed by Wu P'ei-fu and the Chihli side and those employed on the Fengtien side are contending vigorously against each other, and in Tokyo too the Fengtien and Chihli cases are being promoted by both sides, which makes the situation worse than it was before." The solution, as he saw it, was to withdraw all these advisers, or ku-wen, from China and to adopt the course that he said he had been re-commending for years: "Trifling interventions should be completely stopped. We should establish the principle of large interventions (while it goes without saying that on the surface we proclaim the principle of abso-lute nonintervention in Chinese internal affairs). We favor those who are pro-Japanese, and we spurn those who are anti-Japanese." [99] Matsuoka's recommendation had the virtue of simplicity and forthrightness, and in-sofar as it called for combining the moralistic rhetoric of nonintervention, at which Shidehara was so accomplished and persuasive, with large-scale undercover intervention, it did actually spell out the approach that was adopted.

Protestations of neutrality and nonintervention were issued on Sep-tember 10 and 11th by Foreign Minister Shidehara and on September 22 through a Foreign Ministry spokesman. [100] Similarly Shidehara issued gen-eral admonitions to nonintervention to the consul general in Mukden and to the governor of Kwantung province, Kodama Hideo, on September 8 and 16. [101] Furthermore, Shidehara declined, in the first instance at any rate, the suggestion from the two officials closest to the scene, Minister Yoshizawa in Peking and Consul General Funatsu in Mukden, that both belligerent parties should be warned about the consequences of expanding the fighting in the Northeast. Such action, he believed, might lead to intervention in Chinese affairs. [102] However, the cabinet meeting on September 12, which endorsed the line of nonintervention, also made a specific reservation on the course of action that might become appropriate should the disturbances spread to the Northeast. [103] On October 4, as the Shan-hai-kuan fighting got under way, Yoshizawa pressed for reconsideration of "appropriate plans" to meet any of the contingencies that might possibly arise out of this fighting. In addition to continuing to favor the issue of warning both combatants, he suggested that the outlay of "a total sum of three to four million, or five or six million yen" on both Fengtien and Chihli at the existing crucial juncture of the war would be sufficient to achieve Japanese objectives. He expressed the hope that Shidehara would give the matter rapid consideration and reply as a matter of urgency. Shidehara, however, decided that it was not necessary to reply at all.[104]

As the deadlock at Shan-hai-kuan continued, and fear deepened that a Chihli breakthrough might suddenly jeopardize Japan's position in the Northeast, Shidehara modified his position to the extent of authorizing the issue of a caution, on October 13, to both sides in the war.[105] On October 23, the day of Feng Yü-hsiang's coup but before news of it reached Tokyo, the Japanese cabinet met again to reconsider the situation. Shidehara continued to resist extremist demands within the cabinet for a dispatch of troops to relieve Chang Tso-lin's armies, and, since he threatened to resign rather than yield to this pressure, this has often been taken as proof positive of his determination to refrain from intervention. What is most interesting and little noted about this meeting, however, is the fact that Shidehara put the case *against* intervention in such a way as allow Wu P'ei-fu's armies to be blocked by Japanese forces from reaching Mukden—although by "railway guards" rather than regular troops:*

1. The government has previously decided in cabinet on a policy of noninterference in China's internal disputes, and announced this both at home and abroad. Since it would be a clear interference to aid one side and would mean going back on a prior strict declaration, whether or not international confidence is kept is a grave matter affecting the fate of the nation.

2. Even if Wu P'ei-fu were to follow up his victories by invading the Three Eastern Provinces, he must cross the South Manchuria Railroad to move his forces into Fengtien. Since Japan has by treaty the right to station troops in the railway area, *he can only cross it after doing battle with and defeating our railway guards*. And in the case of the Chihli army approaching Fengtien after a long march, I doubt if they would have the strength left to meet our crack forces in the fire of battle. And even if Wu P'ei-fu were to rule Manchuria, it is by no means impossible that we could bring him to respect our established rights, in the same way as Chang Tso-lin [italics added].

*Ikei, "Dai niji," pp. 213–14; Shidehara Kijūrō, pp. 100–101. Shidehara's third point was that relations between Wu P'ei-fu and Feng Yü-hsiang were so sour that the Chihli campaign was likely to collapse internally anyway, and no special expedition in aid of Chang was necessary. Since that is precisely what happened later the same day, some doubt arises about whether Shidehara was stating a presentiment or whether he had actual foreknowledge of the affair.

Shidehara's determination to preserve Japan's rights and interests in the Northeast free of disturbance from China's civil wars thus led to a commitment, in effect, to the preservation of Chang Tso-lin, since, because of it, he was afforded the privilege of a Japanese-defended Northeastern sanctuary. This constituted the greatest and longest continuing interference in China's internal affairs through the whole of the Shidehara term of office.

It is a mark of the blindness of successive Japanese administrations on the "Manchurian" question that the contradictory nature of the non-intervention proclaimed in paragraph 1, and the intervention contemplated in paragraph 2, of Shidehara's argument on this occasion was not appreciated. Shidehara, in short, had as little respect for Chinese sovereignty *in the Northeast* as the military had. The intervention that took place under his tenure at the Ministry of Foreign Affairs in late 1924 may not have been specifically authorized by him but it was designed to achieve policy objectives he fully endorsed. He refused to consider the question of implementation of those objectives until the last moment, and when he did, the intervention he foreshadowed was of a kind no less drastic than that recommended by his Minister in Peking and implemented in fact by the Japanese military.

CONSEQUENCES OF THE WAR

The domestic consequences in China of this war—however attenuated its "civil" quality must be judged in view of the degree of Japanese intervention—were important in a number of ways. It remains here to recount briefly the course of events set in motion by Feng's coup, and then the implications of the new situation for Japan-China relations, for the internal power balance between rival forces in China as a whole, and within the successful Mukden clique itself. At Shan-hai-kuan, news of the coup in Peking produced no immediate breakthrough for Fengtien, but since, as a result, Wu's forces were left exposed to the rear as well as embattled in the costly war of attrition on their front, and since they no longer had secure supply lines or possibilities of reinforcements, a general retreat was ordered on October 30.[106] Many surrendered, the main force fleeing by sea to Tangku and Tientsin. From there, as the enemy closed in, Wu and his main force again fled, this time south to the Yangtze and thence back to their old Loyang headquarters.[107] Feng Yü-hsiang, having oc-

cupied Peking, went on November 5 to occupy the Forbidden City, sending
the young emperor into exile in Tientsin, and reorganized his forces as the
first Kuominchün, or National People's Army, a second and third Kuominchün being organized by his allies and co-conspirators, Hu Ching-i and Sun
Yo.[108] His position was progressively weakened, however, as the Fengtien
Armies moved south in strength following the collapse of the Chihli lines,
advancing rapidly down the Tientsin-Pukow line to effect an unprecedented
expansion of Chang's power right to the Yangtze.[109] A six-day conference
in Tientsin, November 11–16, with the participation of Feng, Chang, and
Tuan Ch'i-jui, saw the appointment of Tuan as provisional chief executive,
and from Canton came the announcement that Sun Yat-sen had accepted
the invitation to come north to Peking to discuss the question of the future
unification of the country.[110]

The following year, 1925, the military situation gradually stabilized as
follows: Feng Yü-hsiang and Chang Tso-lin both renounced their titles as
inspecting generals and accepted appointments as defense commissioners
of the Northwest and Northeast, respectively; Feng retired to Kalgan,
where, *faute de mieux*, he became increasingly the recipient of Soviet aid;
and Chang moved steadily to increase his hold over the vital coastal provinces of China from the Amur to the Yangtze. On December 11, 1924, Li
Ching-lin was appointed tupan of Chihli province and K'an Chao-hsi
tutung of Jehol, though in the former case Li's authority was challenged
from the start by the continued existence and power exercised by Kuominchün troops in the western part of the province. Chang Tsung-ch'ang was
appointed tupan of Shantung in April 1925. In Kiangsu, Lu Yung-hsiang
remained at least nominally an outpost of Anfu power from his appointment as tupan in January 1925, but he was in fact totally dependent on
Fengtien military power. Recognizing this, he resigned in August, and was
replaced by Yang Yü-t'ing, one of Chang Tso-lin's right-hand men.
Another Fengtien man, Chiang Teng-hsüan, was at the same time appointed to Anhwei province.[111] By August 1925, in other words, Chang
had succeeded in establishing his power, through direct protégés and subordinates, over a vast stretch of rich, populous, and strategically vital territory, comprising the provinces and special administrative areas of Fengtien, Kirin, Heilungkiang, Shantung, Anhwei, Kiangsu, Chihli, and Jehol.
Feng and his allies meanwhile consolidated their strength in a great Northwestern bloc, comprising the provinces and administrative areas of Suiyan,

Chahar, Kansu, Honan, and Shensi, an impressive bloc in terms of geographical extent but most of it poor and backward, with no access to the sea or to any port.

This military ascendancy of Chang, and the political sway of the ex-Anfuite leader Tuan Ch'i-jui, which were thus achieved in 1925, represent a high point in the penetration of Japanese influence in China,[11] since both in their different ways had been groomed as Japanese protégés. The extension of Chang's power southward beyond the passes, however, was a development favored only at some of the lower levels of Japanese policy thinking, and was certainly not positively encouraged, since his primary role in Japanese policy terms was to preserve the Northeast free of the disturbances of civil war and to facilitate the exploitation of the interests already acquired there. The dangers of embroilment in the wars south of the Wall leading to damaging upheavals in the Northeast were reckoned to outweigh the long-term advantages that might be won, were he eventually to be able to impose his yoke on China as a whole. The fact that Chang was presently all but toppled by a combination of renewed interfaction warfare arising from the challenge to his control over his newly acquired Southeastern territories, and rebellion arising from within the core of his own Mukden clique, indicates the force of this analysis.

CHAPTER FIVE

The Kuo Sung-ling Affair

CHANG AND THE PROBLEMS OF 1925

By August of 1925 Chang's power was dramatically extended, but by asserting his authority in areas far beyond his Northeastern base he became increasingly vulnerable. Very quickly his enemies came to hope, and his allies to fear, that he had overreached himself.

In his newly established domains he was especially dependent on two things: first, on the continued existence of the Tuan government and of the balance of power between Chang and Feng that sustained that government; second, on his ability to retain the loyalty of subordinates, many of whom now came to wield considerable power in territories remote from Chang's Mukden headquarters. His retinue was swollen in the wake of his triumphant advance, so that the faithful comrades of his bandit days were outnumbered by newly trained professional military men, or by carpetbaggers. Neither had any reason to become permanently devoted to Chang. Furthermore, the enormous geographical spread of his power brought acute political and administrative problems. For one thing, the support of vast armies in continuing, far-flung campaigns was extremely expensive. Given a spell of stability in which these new territories might be exploited, there were obviously great potential gains, but in the short run, and in a situation of continuing instability, the burden on Fengtien province was considerable. Spiraling inflation and an end to hopes of fiscal and economic reform were among the consequences.

Chang's ambition to be the unifier of modern China was betrayed not least by his inability to establish any organizational principle or unifying ideology to match the efforts at conquest of his reorganized armies. In terms of organization he could not transcend the clique, whereas in terms of ideology he moved slowly from the confused gropings of his early career to the sterility of a simple anticommunism. As mass anti-imperialist and worker movements began in 1925 to sweep through the cities of the east coast, which were under the control of Chang and his nominees, the ruthless and indiscriminate repression they meted out and their unfailing deference to and preference for foreign interests earned them the unremitting hostility of the progressive, urban population.

Yet despite all these failings, such as might otherwise have put an end to his career, Chang was saved by the fact that he remained a better instrument of Japanese imperialist purposes than any rival. It was for this reason that he survived.

In this Chapter we examine the situation of the Mukden clique in the time of its ascendancy in Eastern China in 1925, looking first at the structure of the clique itself, and continuing the analysis, begun in Chapter 3, of its constituent elements and what united them. After considering the quality of rule that it brought to the territories it was newly administering, we look at the relationship of the Mukden clique with other warlord factions in China as a whole, the breakdown of equilibrium between them, and the renewal of war. Kuo Sung-ling's rebellion, which altered the course of the war, is treated at length, as an illustration both of the innate weakness of the Mukden clique and of its dependence in the last resort on the support of Japanese imperialism. That the intervention described here was decisive, and that it occurred at the height of what is still often thought of as the peaceful, "negative," economically oriented diplomacy of Shidehara's Foreign Ministry, points to the need for some reevaluation of the terms within which Japanese policy in the 1920's is often discussed. This problem will be considered again in the final chapter.

THE MUKDEN CLIQUE

Civilians and Militarists

Within the Mukden party itself there remained, despite the steady expansion of 1925, considerable differences over policy between civilian bureaucrat and militarist wings. Some, best represented by Wang Yung-chiang, were opposed in principle to any expansion of the power of the group outside the confines of the basic "Three Eastern Provinces." Wang was worried by the expense of maintaining a huge army (350.000 in September 1925, or nearly double what it had been before the war of 1924— and that not including the Jehol and Shantung units[1]), and by continuing massive expenditures on the arsenal and air force, these being the major factors in the decline in value of the main currency unit, the *ta-yang-p'iao*, and steady inflation. He argued strongly for detachment from the civil wars of the South and concentration on the policy of "defense of the borders, pacification of the people" (*pao-ching an-min*)—the policy proclaimed, but not followed, since 1922. Even in the heady days immediately following the triumphant conclusion to the Fengtien-Chihli war in 1924, Wang was opposed to any southward moves and several times made known that he was considering permanent retirement.[2] In threatening to retire, he clearly hoped to exercise some leverage over policy formation, knowing that his financial and administrative talents were crucial to the success of the militarists, and knowing too that the militarists knew this. The deal he had tried to strike with Chang Tso-lin after the first Fengtien-Chihli war, the separation of military and civil administration in a separate and self-governing Three Eastern Provinces, had been an impossible one, certainly never honored on the side of the militarists (see Chapter 3). The second Fengtien-Chihli war alone cost some 70 million yüan, and Wang was the main person expected to find and to keep finding such money.[3] The revenues of Fengtien province had risen from about 10 million yüan, when he was first given responsibility for the provincial finances in May 1917, to approximately 34 million by 1925, but, apart from the special expenses of the war itself, the ordinary military expenses of the province rose after 1922 to between 17 and 18 million, while the arsenal was taking a further 22 to 23 million yearly.[4] The situation could clearly not be allowed to continue long without inviting bankruptcy. Yet, when Wang argued his case at an important military conference in Mukden in late April 1925, he was overruled, and the only apparent concessions made to his position were the orders that other provinces in the Chang bloc should also foot their share of the bill, for the war of 1924 at least.[5] But even if the amounts prescribed were paid—of which we have no record—they would have amounted to a small part of the actual expense involved. The amounts demanded of Kirin, Heilungkiang, Chihli, and Jehol were 8, 5, 5, and 4 million yüan respectively, a period of two years' grace being allowed in every case.[6] Wang's plea for increased civil expenditure—in the budget for education, for example, to cover especially an increase in teachers' salaries—was countered by Yang Yü-t'ing's insistence on a continuing high military expenditure, to allow for the expansion of the arsenal and unification of the weapons system. This difference over fiscal priorities was a simple but important one. Chang Tso-lin himself complained at the time about the troublesomeness of the opposition between these two wings of his follow-ers.[7] The decisive emphasis on military priorities from this time meant also that Wang's plans for independent economic growth, especially railway construction, had to be abandoned in some cases, drastically reduced in others.[8] Furthermore, the extremely high military demands, well above the actual revenues of Fengtien province, forced on the authorities the expe-dient of issuing paper money, unbacked by specie. In April alone the note issue amounted to 10 million yüan.[9]

"New" Militarists and "Old"

On top of the differences over priorities between the leading civilian official and the militarists of the clique generally, differences between dif-ferent wings within the military also intensified in the wake of victory and expansion from the end of 1924. The distribution of the spoils of victory presented obvious problems, since there were only a handful of provinces to be bestowed by Chang on his retainers, and they were far away from Mukden itself, so that military coordination and supply, as well as surveil-lance (to prevent betrayal or independence) were also difficult. These were problems that Chang showed no greater capacity to resolve in 1924–25 than he had in 1921–22.

The general differences of "old" and "new" elements within the clique have already been referred to (p. 102). A look at the appointments that it fell to Chang to make during late 1924 and 1925 in the light of this dif-ferentiation underlines the difficulty he experienced in trying to keep equilibrium between them. Also, because the richest pickings were limited by the number of these new provinces, Chang reinstituted the division sys-tem in his armies so that jealousies and discontents could be eased by a policy of generous promotions.[10] The principal appointments, however, were to the four provinces and one special administrative area won during the course of the war and its aftermath. To Jehol he appointed an old com-rade, K'an Chao-hsi, very much one of the "old" members of the clique, interested more in the profits to be made from the opium trade than in any questions of development or reform, a man who had made no contribution whatever to the success of the clique in the second Fengtien-Chihli war, yet who was promoted at one leap from brigade commander to tutung. To Shantung he appointed Chang Tsung-ch'ang, a latecomer and associate rather than a direct member of the clique, but nevertheless unmistakably associated with the "old" rather than the "new" elements. Li Ching-lin was appointed to Chihli, Li being a representative of the "new" group but associated with that part of it led by Chang Hsüeh-liang and Kuo Sung-ling sometimes referred to as the "*ta-hsüeh*" group, in reference to the fact that its leading figures were graduates of the Lu-chün ta-hsüeh or War College in Peking, in contradistinction to the other part of the "new" group, led by Yang Yü-t'ing, the "*shih-kuan*" or "*shikan*" group, graduates of the Shikan Gakkō, Military Academy or Cadet Academy, in Tokyo.[11] Two of the latter, Yang himself and Chiang Teng-hsüan, were appointed tupan of Kiangsu and Anhwei, respectively. Rivalry between these two wings of the "new" group in the clique was fierce, and most aggrieved at not gaining a provincial command in the expansion of 1925 was Kuo Sung-ling. According to various reports he had been promised either Kiangsu or Jehol, but in the end gained neither, owing largely to the strength of Yang and the opposition between them.[12]

Kuo was the leading senior member of the Chinese-trained "new" men in the Fengtien clique, and for an understanding of his neglect in the apportionment of new provinces after the second Fengtien-Chihli war, a brief sketch of his background and position within the clique is necessary.[13]

Kuo Sung-ling: A Profile

Born in Shen-yang hsien in 1883 (i.e. in Fengtien province), Kuo entered the army early and was for much of his career a protégé of Chu Ch'ing-lan, under whom he served first as company and then as battalion commander in the 33d Mixed Brigade in Szechwan from 1908 to 1911. (Chiang Teng-hsüan, later to be put to death by Kuo, also served Chu as a staff officer at this time.) With the upheavals of the Revolution of 1911, Kuo went north, where he entered the Army Officer Institute (Lu-chün chiang-hsiao yen-chiu-so) in late 1911 or early 1912, and in 1913 was appointed a staff major under General Chang Hsi-luan, the Fengtien commanding general. He then spent some time studying in the Staff College in Peking, and upon graduating in 1916 was sent to Kwangtung, where he served as a staff officer under Chu Ch'ing-lan in the Kwangtung-Kwangsi-Kiangsi-Hunan border defense command. Upon Chu's resignation from the Kwangtung governorship, Kuo became a teacher on the staff of the Military School in Mukden, and in this capacity first established his links with the Mukden clique through being a teacher of the young Chang Hsüeh-liang. In 1920, as Chang Hsüeh-liang became a brigade commander, Kuo won the appointment as chief of staff and commander of the second regiment under him. In May 1921, he became commander of a newly formed 8th Mixed Brigade, and his troops fought with distinction in the war of the spring of 1922. In May 1924, as Chang Hsüeh-liang became commander of the 27th Division, Kuo was appointed concurrently commander of the 2d Brigade under Chang, principal of the Military School of the Three Eastern Provinces, and also chief of staff of the Army Reorganization Bureau. In the second Fengtien-Chihli war, as deputy commander of the 3d Army, he led the crack troops of the 3d and 6th brigades in the main offensives at Shan-hai-kuan, remaining camped after the war near Tientsin. In April 1925, he became commander of the Northeastern Army's 6th Division, in which the former 2d and 6th brigades were merged, and in the crisis of the autumn, as the Northeastern troops were reorganized for deployment against both the Kuominchün armies and the Southeastern alliances led by Sun Ch'uan-fang, Kuo became, first, deputy commander, and then, in the absence of Chang Hsüeh-liang, who was called back to Mukden by his father for consultations, acting commander of the main strength of all the Fengtien armies, a total of some 70,000 men. From this position, on November 23, he launched his bid to overthrow Chang Tso-lin.

Several points stand out about Kuo's career. He was only introduced into the Fengtien clique in 1920 by Chang Hsüeh-liang on the basis of a teacher-student relationship. He was already at this time 37 years of age, and had accumulated a good deal of experience under his former patron, Chu Ch'ing-lan, in Szechwan, Kwangtung, and the South. Some sources suggest that he actually became a Kuomintang member during his sojourn in the South, and there may be some significance in the fact that he owed his rise in Mukden to the recommendation of Chang Hsüeh-liang, the man who, perhaps more than anyone else in the clique, had had connections with the Kuomintang. Kuo's indignation and resentment at the way the affairs of the clique were being run emerge in detail in the statement that he published to attempt to justify his mutiny, but even before that it was clear that he felt frozen out of any territorial base as well as any place in the policymaking circles of the clique, and that he attributed this largely to the hostility between Yang Yü-t'ing and himself, seeing Yang as the evil genius behind Chang Tso-lin.

With a look at these 1924–25 appointments as a whole, therefore, several points are clear: when it came to distributing rewards within the clique,

the "old," untrained, ex-bandit comrades of Chang were not forgotten,
despite their repeated failures in battle (it should be remembered that the
other two tupan responsible, under Chang, for the Northeast were also of
this category—Chang Tso-hsiang and Wu Chün-sheng); the Japanese-
trained wing of the "new" officer group was favored, though its contribution to the clique had been confined to staff work, planning, and equipment; whereas the Chinese-trained wing, which proved itself in command
during the Shan-hai-kuan battle of late 1924, as well as being responsible
for much of the new training program within the army, was passed over,
with the exception of that somewhat peripheral figure, Li Ching-lin,
Chang Hsüeh-liang of course is a special case. He was still very young, and
was evidently being groomed as his father's successor, so it is not surprising that he retained an active troop command, where he could be readily
available for consultations with Chang Tso-lin. When one considers the
problem of how the clique went about apportioning rewards and appointments, its structural weakness becomes apparent. What united it was no
more than a combination of personal ties to Chang or his associates, plus
the opportunistic conviction that attachment to Chang's bandwagon offered
better prospects of advancement than other alternatives. That Chang was
relatively more successful in building and maintaining his Fengtien clique
than were warlords elsewhere in China was due not to superiority in organization or to any unifying ideological commitment, but rather to his
wealth, his favorable geographical location, and Japanese backing.

NEWLY CONQUERED TERRITORIES AND
THE QUALITY OF MUKDEN RULE

Shantung

In the aftermath of the second Fengtien-Chihli war, Chang's power was
extended for the first time to the heavily populated provinces of North
China—Shantung and Chihli. Since he saw these as stepping-stones to
control over the whole country, it is worth considering what impact he had
on them.

Chang's authority over such areas was, of course, limited: having nomi-
nated one of his subordinates to hold office, he himself had little interest
and almost no means of interfering with how such office was executed.
Subordinate members of the clique who won these appointments raised
their own revenues, maintained their own armies, and maintained order in

whatever way they saw fit. Ultimately they depended on Chang for weapons, usually from the Mukden arsenal, occasionally for extra funds,* and for aid against aggression from outside. Their main obligation was to coordinate their forces with those of the clique as a whole, under the overall command of Chang Tso-lin, when large-scale joint military action was concerned. These arrangements are analogous to the system of autonomous "garrison areas" described for the province of Szechwan by Robert Kapp,[14] but they are on a much larger, provincial rather than subprovincial scale, and were not formalized but simply contained within the loose overall structure of the Fengtien clique. Even in his "home territories" in the Northeast, where Chang did attempt to impose a degree of administrative centralization over and above mere military coordination, he did so in a purely personalized way, never attempting to create a formal bureaucratic structure. However, although his actual involvement in the internal affairs of Shantung and Chihli was minimal, Chang Tsung-ch'ang and Li Ching-lin were seen as representatives of the Fengtien clique, and it was judged accordingly.

When Chang Tsung-ch'ang took office as military governor of Shantung, on April 24, 1925, the situation in Tsingtao was already very tense. Shortly after his appointment, the city was hit by a wave of strikes and labor militancy directed particularly against the extensive Japanese cotton interests concentrated there. Japanese pressure was immediately brought to bear, to put an end to the strikes, on the Peking government through Minister Yoshizawa Kenkichi in Peking, on Chang Tso-lin through Consul General Yoshida Shigeru in Mukden, and on Chang Tsung-ch'ang through Consul General Horiuchi in Tsingtao. To supplement these overtures two Japanese gunboats were dispatched to stand by offshore.[15] On a purely private basis, the cotton industrialists of the Kansai region had Machino Takema, then briefly in Japan on a visit, cable Chang Tsung-ch'ang on their behalf, as his friend as well as adviser to Chang Tso-lin, urging him to act.[16] Before dawn on the morning of May 29, Chang acted; 1,700 of his troops were sent in to "kick the workers out of the mills, arrest the leaders, and put an end to further trouble by prohibiting the formation of secret labor unions."[17] No precise figures on the resulting casualties are known, but in one encounter alone one worker was killed and 16 others wounded or

---

*In mid-1925, at least, Chang Tsung-ch'ang was being subsidized by Chang Tso-lin to the extent of 400,000 yüan monthly; MCG, Oct. 1925, p. 29.

injured.[18] The following day, Consul General Horiuchi secured the agreement of Chinese officials that, in addition to the 80 arrested and imprisoned on the 29th, a further 200 likely troublemakers from the three Japanese factories affected should be arrested and another 500 sent back to their village, where they should be made to find suitable guarantors and given into the jurisdiction of their local magistrates. Lists of those to be arrested were prepared by the factories and passed through the consulate to the Chinese authorities for execution. Chang Tsung-ch'ang's intention was to have all those arrested shot, but he was persuaded by the Japanese authorities that this might only make matters worse.[19] What happened to the men thereafter, however, is not clear. They may have eventually been released;[20] but it is more likely that they were sent off to their villages, and it is quite possible that summary punishment was administered once they were moved away from Tsingtao.[21] Japanese gunboats steamed away on June 3 and the factories reopened shortly afterward.

Workers thereafter were reduced to the level of virtual slave labor: jointly with some guarantor they were compelled to sign a pledge to strive wholeheartedly in their work to obey the instructions of superiors and to abide strictly by all regulations and orders, neither to organize nor to join any assembly or society not recognized by Chinese officials or the factory, and in the event of breach of such pledge to agree that such breach should be met by instant dismissal, appropriate punishment by the factory, or being turned over to Chinese officials for punishment.[22] By the time the events of May 30 had convulsed the cities of South China into general strike, Tsingtao was quiet. Strikes and campaigns in protest against the Shanghai Incident organized in late July were quickly broken, again by the use of the army; this time the leader of the strikers, Li Wei-nung, and the editor of a newspaper supporting the nationalist movement, Hu Hsin, were both executed.[23] Chang Tsung-ch'ang was reported to have received 300,000 yüan from the Japanese for carrying out this operation.[24]

Although it cannot be denied that the problems of Shantung province—particularly overpopulation, recurrent famine, endemic banditry, and a most intense form of exploitation of the peasantry—made things difficult for Chang, nevertheless the policies he adopted greatly exacerbated the situation. To increase his revenues, Chang Tsung-ch'ang not only ordered great increases in the basic rate of land tax, but also tacked to it a series of surtaxes, and devised numerous new taxes as well. Thus, in one county, Po-shan, the tax per mow on cultivated land in Chang's time increased sevenfold, from .22 yüan to 1.47 yüan.[25] This may have been an exceptionally large increase, since the Japanese scholar Amano Motonosuke has estimated for the province as a whole that "the average land tax per mow rose from an index base of 100 in 1902 to 268 in 1925 and to 468 in1927."[26] In addition, however, it appears that the land tax may have been levied more than once in a year, and perhaps as much as four times in places,[27] whereas surtaxes—if the county of Chi-tung slightly after Chang's time, in 1930, may be taken as indicative of the general trend at least—could be as much as eight times as high again as the basic tax rate.[28] Miscellaneous new taxes under Chang included a poll tax and taxes on cattle, dogs, cats, and on all sorts of human activity.[29]

The increased revenues obtained in this way were employed overwhelmingly on military purposes. Thus, where 50 percent of the provincial budget (of approximately 12 million yüan) was expended on the military up until 1925, between 1925 and 1928 under Chang, that figure increased to 89 percent (50 million in a 56 million budget). Expenditure on civilian administration was correspondingly cut, to a 9 percent share, and the remaining 2 percent, approximately 1.4 million yüan was devoted to educational and industrial development.[30] The worsening economic situation of the province was reflected in sharp devaluation of the currency, steep rises in commodity prices—the 1928 prices of kao-liang (sorghum), millet, wheat, and beans were on the average 2.23 times higher than the previous year—and, not surprisingly, a phenomenal rise in emigration to the lands being newly opened in the Northeast. Both in 1927 and 1929 the number of immigrants to the Northeastern provinces, overwhelmingly from Shantung and Chihli provinces, was over one million, a dramatic increase over the 572,000 of 1927, or the fewer than 400,000 of 1923 and 1924.[31] Of course, not only the economic policies of Chang Tsung-ch'ang were to blame for this, but increasingly the war itself, as the railways bisecting the province became important foci of the fighting. Ramon Myers quotes a study by the Research Department of the South Manchuria Railway Company to the effect that, "between 1925 and 1927 areas around Chining in Shantung were devastated by fighting, and peasants lost an estimated 213,000 head of cattle and labor animals totalling 120,000 mules and 440,000 donkeys. Nearly five million people in thirteen countries were affected by this conflict, and emigration from this region was great."[32]

Three things stand out, however, from this brief account of Chang Tsung-ch'ang's regime in Shantung: it was at once servile toward imperi-

alism, particularly Japanese imperialism, brutally repressive toward
Chinese nationalist and labor movements, and rapacious and parasitic toward the economy and polity of the province as a whole. Insofar as he is
remembered as simply the "Three Don't Knows"—"He didn't know how
many soldiers he had, how much money he had, how many concubines he
had. It was, however, conceded that Chang had concubines of 26 different
nationalities; each had a washbowl marked with her flag"[33]—history has
dealt with him rather more kindly than he deserved.

Chihli

Li Ching-lin, as Chang Tso-lin's man in Chihli, was a less flamboyant
figure, but just as ruthless in his suppression of mass movements and defense of foreign interests. Li was by origin a Chihli man, but because his
military career from the late Ch'ing had been entirely in the Northeast, first
in Heilungkiang and then in Fengtien from 1917, he had become recognized as a member of the Fengtien clique. As a graduate of the Paoting
Military Academy he was considered one of the clique's "new," professional, military men.

In August 1925, not long after Li took up office in Chihli, the province
was affected by waves of unrest set in motion by the events of May 30 in
Shanghai, where the action of a British police detachment in firing on a
group of Chinese demonstrators, killing nine, had sparked a widespread
anti-imperialist movement of protest. In Tientsin there were strikes first in
the British shipping firms, then in the Japanese cotton mills. The Yü-ta
silk-reeling works were wrecked by workers, joined by local peasants. As a
result, Li ordered a siege of the works, and in the ensuing battle 20 workers
were killed and 300 injured.[34] Union organization in Tientsin was forbidden, and Li's regime, like that of Chang Tsung-ch'ang, was distinguished
by the imposition of varied new and "illegal" taxes, confiscations, and the
like, possibly in both cases with some idea of establishing an economic
base powerful enough to allow breaking away from allegiance to Chang
Tso-lin.[35]

The other Chang appointees to provincial control south of the Great Wall
(in Kiangsu and Anhwei) actually exercised authority for such a brief
period following their appointments at the end of August 1925 as not to
merit discussion here. Shanghai, however, though a slightly special case,
should not be overlooked.

Shanghai

The ideal of a demilitarized Shanghai had been put forward several times during 1925, a Shanghai in which no regular troops would be stationed (only police and militia), and in which the arsenal would be closed down. The idea was attractive, not least to the citizens of Shanghai, precisely because of the evident danger of a clash between rival warlord armies for control of the city. It also had some attraction for warlords and politicians alike, since a clash in Shanghai would be likely to draw the foreign powers into military intervention in defense of their interests. In January 1925, a demilitarization order was issued by Tuan Ch'i-jui in response to an urgent petition from the Merchants' Association of the city, and a clause to that effect was written into the truce agreement arrived at between Sun Ch'uan-fang and Chang Tsung-ch'ang at Shanghai on February 3.[36] The agreement was honored only briefly. On June 13, some 2,000 Fengtien troops were led into the city by Chang Hsüeh-liang, protesting the need to restore order in the wake of the May 30 disturbances. His forces quickly set about suppression of worker and student organizations, giving welcome assurance to the Japanese authorities that order would be restored.[37] Though Chang Hsüeh-liang returned to Mukden after only a brief stay in Shanghai, he was succeeded on June 22 by a larger force of some 8,000 Northeastern troops under Brigade Commander Hsing Shih-lien. By June 26 business life was back to normal, and on July 23 these troops dealt the movement a major blow by sealing the headquarters of the three main radical labor unions.[38]

Leading British business interests were delighted at the vigorous stand adopted by the Mukden authorities and strongly urged their government to give its backing to Chang Tso-lin's efforts "to restore peace in China." The Foreign Office, however, was too cautious to take steps openly to this end, on the grounds that all warlords were equally corrupt and unreliable, and that backing for one of them would in any case be self-defeating, since it would be bound to alienate Chinese support for such a leader.[39] Another two tumultuous years passed in China before the British government took the halfhearted step of deciding that aid to Chang in the form of private loans "should not be discouraged."[40] By then, however, Chang's star was falling, and aid, however copious, was incapable of reversing the trend.

In 1925, however, whether in Chihli (Tientsin), Shantung (Tsingtao) or Shanghai, or indeed wherever the authority of Chang Tso-lin's nominees was felt, the same uncompromising resistance was evident to the new tides then rising in China, and the same anxiety to appease the major foreign interests, whether Japanese, British, or American. That the kind of aid he wanted was not forthcoming in the case of Britain was not Chang's fault. As the tempo of class struggle quickened, the reactionary nature of the Mukden regime became necessarily more explicit, and its prospects for imposing any form of unity over China as a whole more attenuated.

WARLORD POWER BLOCS AND RIVALRIES

The broader context within which the situation on the eve of Kuo's rebellion has to be understood is that of the relations between the Fengtien faction and other centers of power in China. The southern extension of Chang Tso-lin's power down to the Yangtze naturally provoked fierce opposition and resentments that tended to unite his rivals against him and to blur the distinction between rival and ally. As we have said earlier, by August 29, 1925, the alliance of Kuominchün and Fengtien that sustained the Peking government was divided into two great blocs: that of the Kuominchün, nominally under Feng Yü-hsiang's control in the Northwest and West, comprising the provinces and special administrative areas of Suiyan, Chahar, Kansu, Honan, and Shensi; and Chang's in the Northeast and East, comprising the Three Eastern Provinces proper, together with Shantung, Chihli, Jehol, Kiangsu, and Anhwei.[41] Between the two the line dividing their respective spheres of jurisdiction was always a source of potential discord, and no point was more openly contested than control over the capital, Peking, and its environs. In addition to the rivalry between these two great Northern blocs, Fengtien faced one great Southeastern rival—Sun Ch'uan-fang, the sole Chihli clique representative to survive the war of 1924, retaining control directly over Chekiang province, and indirectly over Fukien. In this case too, the central point at issue was that of control over a major city—Shanghai. With control of these cities went prestige, sources of revenue, and, in the case of Shanghai at least, weapons, since control of Shanghai meant control also of an important arsenal.

In October 1925, the commencement of the Kuomintang's Northern Expedition, which was designed to eliminate the warlords and to unify the country on the basis of nationalism, anti-imperialism, and antifeudalism, was only eight months away. The balance between the three major warlord forces, which Kuomintang military planners saw as constituting the main opposition to their advance—Chang Tso-lin's in the North and Northeast, Feng Yu-hsiang's in the Northwest, and Sun Ch'uan-fang's Chihli forces on the Yangtze—was then at its most fragile. Each of the three was as suspicious of his ally as of his enemy, and seeking to neutralize the possibility of a hostile combination against him. Between Chang and Feng full-scale hostilities were predicted from time to time during 1925, being actually promised by Chang himself during March of that year.[42] They seemed imminent in May, when Chang Tso-lin dispatched troops to the capital area, which till then had been the preserve of Feng's Kuominchün, but were averted by Feng's strategic withdrawal and by the desire on the part of both to avoid further provoking the powers during the tense days of the May 30 incidents.[43] In the autumn, rivalry for control of Peking was further fueled by the realization that with such control went control over central revenues, insignificant at the moment but expected to be augmented by the sum of approximately 20 million yüan annually as a result of the "Special Tariff Conference" scheduled to convene in Peking on October 26.[44] The Washington Conference powers were expected there to move toward gradual restoration of tariff autonomy to China by approving various interim surtaxes. Not only could such a windfall be expected to give a decisive advantage to the militarist controlling Peking as against his rivals, but the rivals themselves were to be impoverished, if the proposals on the conference agenda went through, by the abolition of the likin taxes, a major source of revenue to all provincial militarists as of late 1925.[45] Consequently Chang and Feng, although vying with one another for control of Peking, nevertheless both supported the convening of the tariff conference; whereas others, especially Sun Yat-sen and Wu P'ei-fu, who stood only to lose greatly by the achievement of tariff autonomy or agreement on an interim surtax so long as they were excluded from any voice at Peking, stoutly opposed it.[46]

WAR AND REBELLION

The tariff conference was actually under way in the autumn of 1925 before war broke out between Chang and Feng, and when it did it was occasioned initially by the struggle for control of Shanghai—between the Fengtien Armies trying to establish themselves on the Yangtze, and Sun Ch'uan-fang in Chekiang. The nascent political forces of the May 30 period were only dimly understood by the militarists, and the struggle that broke between them in October 1925 over Shanghai had remarkably little to do with the great issues that had shaken the city only a few months before. It was the move by Fengtien military men into Shanghai in the summer of 1925, described above, followed shortly afterward by the appointments of Fengtien men to control of Kiangsu and Anhwei provinces, and the steps to reopen the arsenal in Shanghai to supply Fengtien's Southern armies, that provoked Sun Ch'uan-fang into action, with the hope of stemming the Fengtien expansion before the new territories it had swallowed up on the Yangtze could be properly assimilated and defended.[47] On October 11 he began troop maneuvers so obviously threatening to the Fengtien garrison in Shanghai that its commander, Hsing Shih-lien, ordered withdrawal just three days later. On the 15th Sun assumed overall command of a five-province army made up of forces from Chekiang, Fukien, Anhwei, Kiangsu, and Kiangsi, and ordered a five-pronged attack on Fengtien positions. Sun was acting in accordance with a plan conceived in conjunction with Feng Yü-hsiang and the Kuominchün.[48] The plan seems to have been that an initial attack from the south would draw Fengtien forces into southern Shantung and northern Kiangsu, whereupon Yüeh Wei-chün's Kuominchün forces would launch an attack on them from the west, and when further troops had been dispatched from the Northeast, Feng Yu-hsiang would attack Tientsin, with the hope of cutting Fengtien communications and supply lines. In this way, as the *China Year Book* noted, "It was hoped that the whole Fengtien force would be induced to spread out on a very long and vulnerable line so they could be annihilated piecemeal."[49]

Things did not work out like this, however; Fengtien took a very passive line toward its interests in the Southeast, abandoning most of Kiangsu and Anhwei provinces with no attempt to defend them, and falling back upon the important railway junction town of Hsü-chou in northern Kiangsu, close to the borders of Shantung, Anhwei, and Honan, to regroup there under the command of Chang Tsung-ch'ang. The apparent ease with which they were evicted encouraged their enemies and led to the formation of a wider anti-Fengtien alliance, including militarists from as far as Szechwan and Kweichow. On October 21 Wu P'ei-fu emerged from retirement to assume overall command of an allied force to attack the retreating Fengtien armies at Hsü-chou. Yet despite the agreements on coordinated action

against Mukden's forces, both within this newly forged alliance and between it and the Kuominchün, cooperation was in practice little evident.
Feng Yü-hsiang felt an understandable reluctance to allow the chance of
recovery to Wu P'ei-fu (since he had no reason to think that Wu would
easily forgive and forget the betrayal of 1924). Thus the Kuominchün remained inactive, watching the situation. Sun Ch'uan-fang also remained
suspicious of Wu, in effect vetoing his initial plan to dispatch troops via
Honan province to aid in attacking the Fengtien positions at Hsü-chou.[50]

Faced with the threat of hostilities on two fronts, the Fengtien leadership
gathered to discuss how best to deal with the situation. The hard-liners at
this conference saw that, in the event of such a two-front battle, many of
the Southern positions currently held would become untenable, the whole
army would have to be pulled back to the Tientsin area, and conceivably
the base area of the Three Provinces itself might become threatened. Thus,
it was argued: better to abandon the most exposed positions—particularly
those along the Peking—Hankow railway line—and to concentrate troops
in the capital area in an attempt to drive back the Kuominchün first, and
proceeding later to deal with Sun and Wu. Those advocating a softer line
tended to downplay interests in the Southeast, even to the point of favoring
an accommodation with Sun Ch'uan-fang, withdrawal from Shantung, and
concession of Feng Yü-hsiang's demands on the Peking–Hankow line.
They believed in trying to work for cooperation with both Wu and Feng in
joint support of the Tuan cabinet, the tariff conference, and the convening
of a National Assembly.[51] Wang Yung-chiang, the leading Fengtien civilian official, seems to have been the main person associated with the latter
view.[52] At any rate, Chang Tsung-ch'ang's Shantung armies joined with
the retreating armies from the South under Chiang Teng-hsüan to attempt
to hold the line at Hsü-chou, while Chang Hsüeh-liang led substantial reinforcements south of the Great Wall to Luan-chou to join the Chihli army of
Li Ching-lin and the Jehol army of K'an Chao-hsi in opposing the Kuominchün forces in the capital area and the Northwest. By early November there
were 70,000 men under Chang Hsüeh-liang in the area between Shan-hai-
kuan and Tientsin, a further two divisions and seven cavalry brigades—
perhaps another 50,000 men—advancing on Jehol, and a reserve force of
another 40,000 men camped just beyond the Great Wall at Chin-chou.[53]
These movements effectively dissuaded Feng Yü-hsiang from thought of
more active cooperation with the plans of Sun, Wu, and the Yangtze al-

liance. Under the sponsorship of Tuan Ch'i-jui, peace delegates from the Kuominchün and Fengtien met several times at the beginning of November to attempt to iron out the main obstacle to resurrecting their alliance: the Kuominchün demand that Fengtien troops be withdrawn from the Peking–Hankow railway positions they were occupying, and that Tientsin harbor be opened to them. Fengtien held out on these issues until November 7, when the fall of Hsü-chou to Sun, and the withdrawal of Fengtien armies from their last positions in Kiangsu province, prompted a fresh look at the situation. The threat of resignation by Tuan in the event of full-scale fighting in the capital area, added to uncertainty about the response that should be expected from the foreign powers in case of such an outbreak, lent extra persuasiveness to the idea of détente, and on November 12 Fengtien agreed to the two points mentioned above. An agreement was thus signed incorporating these points and providing for the establishment of a joint action bureau in Peking to coordinate an attack by the Kuominchün on the Peking-Hankow railway against Wu P'ei-fu's positions, and an attack by Fengtien forces on the Tientsin–Pukow line against the forces of Sun Ch'uan-fang.[54] Actually, this plan did not materialize either, and by mid-November the situation in the Southeast also quieted down, as Sun Ch'uan-fang rested apparently satisfied with his conquest of Kiangsu and Anhwei, leaving him in effect the master of a coalition of five Southeastern provinces—Kiangsu, Anhwei, Kiangsi, Fukien, and Chekiang—and the most powerful figure in the Chihli clique.

The situation in the Southeast froze, for the time being, along these lines; in the North, however, the Tientsin agreement between Fengtien and Feng's Kuominchün won but the briefest of interludes, time for Feng to put the finishing touches to a plot designed to destroy Chang Tso-lin's power from within, using Kuo Sung-ling as his Trojan horse. With the apparent easing of the situation after the signing of the agreement, Chang Hsüeh-liang was recalled on November 20, for consultations with his father in Mukden. His deputy, Kuo, stepped into command of the main Fengtien forces, the 3d Route Army. This was made up of six divisions (the 4th, 5th, 6th, 7th, 10th, and 12th), two artillery brigades (1st and 2d), and five battalions of engineers—a force formidable not only because of its numbers (approximately 70,000) but because it included the best trained and equipped units in the Northeastern armies, specially put together as the strongest possible force with a view to battle against Feng's Kuominchün.[55] Kuo's decision to rebel followed agreement reached with Feng on the following points:[56]

1. Kuo is to issue a circular telegram calling for the resignation of Chang Tso-lin.

2. If Kuo is attacked from the rear by the Tientsin-based forces of Li Ching-lin while in the process of moving to compel such resignation, Feng is to send troops to his aid.

3. If Li Ching-lin remains neutral, he is afterward to be appointed tutung of Jehol.

4. Chihli province and the whole of the Peking–Hankow railway line are to form the sphere of influence of Feng.

5. The disposition of the Three Eastern Provinces is to be left completely to Kuo Sung-ling.

This agreement seems to have been signed by Feng on November 20 and by Kuo on November 23 or 24, although it may have been agreed to in principle as early as the Tientsin negotiations leading to the agreement of November 12.[57] At a question-and-answer session held the following year at Sun Yat-sen University in Moscow, Feng described five other conditions put to him by Kuo, to which he said he had also agreed: (1) overthrow of the warlords, who were a curse on the country and a disaster for the people; (2) establishment of a young government; (3) implementation of a common people's government; (4) compulsory education, and (5) protection of workers.[58] However, there is no other record of the existence of such terms, and it is not inconceivable that they were thought up on this occasion with the idea of impressing his Soviet hosts.

With the understanding with Feng settled, Kuo summoned the commanders of the units under his command for a meeting on November 22. Having explained his grievances against Chang Tso-lin and Yang Yü-t'ing, Kuo drew up a circular telegram calling for Chang's resignation. He indicted him specifically for allowing Japan's influence over himself and over the territory as a whole:[59]

The Three Eastern Provinces, being long under the influence of a powerful neighbor who is based in a part of those territories, has been unable to withstand the restraints imposed in terms of railways, manufacture, education, and administration. Thus, in the near future the Three Eastern Provinces seem likely to become part of that [neighbor's] territory. Yet you take no steps to deal with the group of 28 or so wicked and crafty concilors who surround you. And further, as the currency, which is the basis of the economy, becomes a foreign currency, the native currency of the Three Eastern Provinces is no more than waste paper.

Consequently, Kuo called upon Chang Tso-lin to resign and to hand over authority to his son, Chang Hsüeh-liang, who was of course Kuo's patron within the clique. There was little likelihood of this happening, but the formula was a more discreet one that that of outright rebellion in his own name.

It was a far from auspicious beginning for his campaign when no fewer than three divisional commanders (P'ei Ch'ün-sheng of the 12th, Chao En-chen of the 5th, and Ch'i En-ming of the 10th) had to be locked up, together with Chiang Teng-hsüan, the retreating Anhwei tupan, and 28 lesser commanders who withheld their support. Chiang Teng-hsüan, who seems to have expressed strong opposition and who, with Yang Yü-t'ing, was a leader of the main rival faction within the Mukden military, was shot. The other detainees were sent to Tientsin, to be held there by Li Ching-lin, thus raising a strong presumption of Li's complicity in the whole operation.[60] Indeed, it is most unlikely that Kuo would have shown his hand in this way unless he were sure of Li's support, since without it he could quickly become cut off from Peking and Tientsin and his only possible supply route would be threatened.[61] The failure of Kuo's first plan, for a quick coup d'état and arrest and deposition of Chang Tso-lin, left him vulnerable, the 2,000 troops he dispatched secretly to Mukden on the night of November 23 being stopped and disarmed at Shan-hai-kuan.[62] With this he had no alternative but to march openly on Mukden, and, dividing his forces into four armies renamed the 4th Kuominchün to underline unity with Feng Yü-hsiang's forces, he began to move.[63]

Both Feng Yü-hsiang and Li Ching-lin issued circular telegrams on November 25 calling for Chang Tso-lin's resignation, and two days later Feng joined in a formal declaration of war on Chang.[64] However, Kuominchün involvement was less than Kuo might have expected: the 2d and 3d Kuominchün moved from Honan and Shensi against the Fengtien forces led by Chang Tsung-ch'ang in Shantung but made little headway, and from late November were actually retreating in defeat; units of the 1st Kuominchün waited until December 3 before moving, and then only against the weakest and least defended sector of Chang's domains—K'an Chao-hsi's Jehol.[65]

But if Kuominchün support was disappointingly halfhearted, news that Li Ching-lin was to throw in his lot with Chang was a grievous setback. Li did not announce this until Kuo's forces had advanced beyond the Great

Wall and thus out of his territory, and it meant, in effect, that the Kuomin-chün's main force would be tied down by the joint opposition of the Chihli-Shantung armies of Li and Chang Tsung-ch'ang, and thus unable to give greater support to Kuo for some time.[66] The reasons for Li so deciding seem to have been various. Fear for the welfare of his mother in Mukden may have been one.[67] More important, though, was simple distrust of Feng. Though he resented the fact that the Tientsin agreement between Feng and Chang had been reached through Chang's concession of Chihli territory along the Peking–Hankow line within his jurisdiction, yet he knew that Feng's record of betrayals gave little reason to expect harmonious cooperation to last long, especially since Feng's desire to expand his control to include the port of Tientsin had been made clear. Though he added his name on November 25 to the demand for Chang Tso-lin's resignation, he later explained he had had to do this, and his freedom of action had only begun once Kuo's forces were out of his territory and directly engaged with those of Chang Tso-lin. The prisoners entrusted to him by Kuo were then all released.[68]

Despite these blows, the Kuo campaign in its early weeks won a series of rapid victories. The Fengtien Armies, led by "old" comrades of Chang none of whom had ever won a single battle, withdrew steadily along the Peking–Mukden railway to the town of Lien-shan, 200 miles east of Shan-hai-kuan, where on December 5 the combined forces of Chang Tso-hsiang, Chi Chin-ch'ün, and Chang Chiu-ch'ing suffered the most serious defeat.[69] As reports of collapse of the Lien-shan front came in, Chang made plans to flee to the safety of the Japanese-controlled South Manchuria Railway zone.[70] The several days that followed December 5, 1925, marked the absolute nadir of his fortunes. For a time he lapsed into a "semidemented state."[71]

Had he been fully aware of the disarray, the incompetence, and the thoughts of treachery entertained by the "loyal" commanders he was depending on, he might well have collapsed altogether—either fleeing or committing suicide as other reports held him to be contemplating.[72] At Lien-shan, Chang Tso-hsiang's troops broke ranks and fled, many of them abandoning their weapons, as soon as Kuo's artillery opened up.[73] The collapse of Chang Tso-hsiang's positions in 1925 bears a striking similarity to that of 1922. As these forces retreated all the way back to Kirin, leaving the remaining Northeastern armies in an apparently hopeless position,

Chang Tso-hsiang explained to Chang Tso-lin that he had received reports
from the civil governor of Kirin of some kind of plotting, presumably by
Kirin independence supporters, which necessitated his immediate return.[74]
What seems in fact more likely is that, since Chang Tso-lin seemed bound
to be overthrown, Chang Tso-hsiang and others in authority in Kirin were
themselves giving serious thought to the idea of declaring independence, or
of working out some kind of understanding with Kuo. The civil governor
of Kirin had been all along opposed to the involvement of the Northeastern
armies in the wars south of the passes and could be expected to have had
some sympathy for Kuo's demands.[75] Furthermore, when news of the
Lien-shan defeat reached Harbin, Chang Huan-hsiang, who was then governor of the Tung-sheng Special District controlling the whole of the
Chinese Eastern Railway zone, summoned the director general of the
railway and the *Taoyin* (circuit intendent) of Pin-chiang (Harbin and its
environs) to a midnight conference at his residence to propose that for the
time being they declare neutrality in the war between Kuo and Chang, later
shifting their allegiance to Kuo. The *Taoyin*, Ts'ai Yün-sheng, was reluctant to agree to this, so a further, enlarged meeting of the leading figures of
Harbin was convened the following day. At this Chang Huan-hsiang announced, and the gathering acquiesced, that since Chang Tso-lin was
bound to be overthrown, a delegation should be sent to Mukden to welcome Kuo Sung-ling. A circular telegram was also issued to the country at
large (though not to Chang Tso-lin) announcing his approval of the rising
and urging Kuo's entry into Mukden.[76] Papers later confiscated from the
headquarters of the Kuo campaign revealed that there had been secret contacts between Chang Huan-hsiang and Kuo.[77]

K'an Chao-hsi also established secret contact with Kuo.[78] In his case a
principal objective throughout the disturbance seems to have been to guard
the year's opium profits and crop. From November 26 or 27 he commenced
a leizurely withdrawal from Jehol, taking with him some 20 million yüan
worth of opium, which had been exacted as tax, and dispatching his chief
of staff, Ch'iu T'ien-p'ei, to propose some settlement to Kuo. Ch'iu remained with Kuo till just before the final collapse of his campaign.
Everyone down to the lowest private soldier in K'an's army was reckoned
to be carrying opium, and, being "completely an opium army," it is not
surprising that its main interest in the war was how to avoid any part in it.[79]
With the collapse of Kuo's resistance on December 24, K'an actually

briefly raised the flag of rebellion against Chang himself. He was, however, persuaded by Wu Chün-sheng to desist, and the matter was quietly forgotten.[80] After the war K'an was somewhat nervous about showing his face in Mukden and announced instead that he was leaving for extended studies abroad.[81] He was, however, soon reinstated owing to the intercession of Wu Chün-sheng, who was a kinsman of both K'an and Chang Tso-lin.[82]

To complete this record of indecision, betrayal, and unconcern about Chang Tso-lin's fate among the "old" members of the Fengtien clique supposedly closest to him, it should be noted that Wu Chün-sheng was also highly reluctant to send troops from Heilungkiang. Wu appears to have planned to leave for the front on December 3, delayed till the 5th, and then canceled his departure on receiving news of Lien-shan, and at a military conference that he convened on December 6 to have seriously considered declaring neutrality.[83] It was not until much later that Wu decided to commit his men to the final battle against Kuo.

REBELLION THWARTED

Some Internal Weaknesses

How was it that the disintegration of the forces under Chang was arrested and their morale stiffened and restored to the point that they could suddenly turn the tables on Kuo in late December? One factor is simply that Kuo's strength was much more apparent—by contrast with Chang's—than real. His army was not equipped for a long campaign, much less for a winter campaign, and Kuo made no effort to inculcate the belief that the men were fighting for a cause worth the effort. When Li Ching-lin turned against him at the beginning of December, thus cutting Kuo off from any hope of supplies or aid from his rear, he was reckoned to have food supplies to last only another four days, a mere 400,000 yüan in cash, and no equipment to keep out the cold.[84] On December 2 or 3 the weather became especially unfavorable. A foot or so of snow fell, and the temperature dropped to 20 degrees below before the Lien-shan battle. Kuo's forces were still in summer dress and many suffered frostbite. Another 6,000 were reported to have surrendered at Lien-shan. As the army approached closer to Mukden, many more either deserted, since their homes were nearby, or surrendered. After the capture of Chin-chou around December 7, Kuo's army stopped to plunder the city, its practice thus demonstrating, contrary to Kuo's vague promises, that it remained a conventional, warlord force, offering little prospect of any revolutionary alternative to the Chang regime.[85]

Intervention: What Price Shidehara Diplomacy?

The second, and more important, reason for Kuo's defeat is that Chang's side in the war had the benefit of strong, probably decisive Japanese support. The record of past cooperation of various Japanese agencies with Chang has already been described. From it at least two salient characteristics emerge: first, that Japanese agencies on the spot in the Three Eastern Provinces, both civil and military, were much more fully committed to supporting him than were their home authorities in Tokyo; second, that subject to this qualification the Foreign Ministry, and Minister Shidehara, were adamant that civil disturbances in China should not be allowed to disturb the order of those areas in which Japan was heavily interested, so that in effect Chang's enemies could not hope to overthrow him by laying siege to Mukden unless they were prepared to take on the Japanese forces as well. Regular protestations of "absolute noninterference in the internal affairs of China" thus meant no more than interference only when absolutely necessary in the defense of those inviolate Japanese interests. Commitment to the defense of Chang, in the last resort by quelling "disorders" that threatened him (since they were bound to threaten Japanese interests too), was combined with an ambiguous attitude to Chang's attempts at expansion of his territory or conquest of China as a whole—enthusiasm on the one hand, since he represented a bulwark against communism, rights recovery fever, and its attendant "disorders," but also concern, since his involvement in civil wars south of the Great Wall carried with it the risk of extension of such disturbance to the Northeast, the bleeding of the Northeast to finance and sustain such war effort being also inimical to Japanese investment.

It was within the context of such general feelings toward Chang Tso-lin that news of Kuo's sudden rising against him broke, apparently quite unexpectedly, among the Japanese. Kuo was personally not unknown in Japan, since he attended the annual military maneuvers held at Sendai in Northern Japan only a matter of three weeks before turning against Chang. Those who met him there seemed to form a highly favorable impression of him, and it is likely that Kuo's misunderstanding of some remarks made to him in conversation on that occasion influenced his decision. Army Minister Ugaki confided to his diary after conversation with Kuo that he found him

"that rarity among Chinese—the embodiment of the military type." [86]
When he heard news of Fengtien's withdrawal from the Southeast under
pressure from Sun Ch'uan-fang, Kuo decided to cut short his stay in Japan
and return at once. In the course of a 1½-hour conversation, Ugaki took
the opportunity to offer him some advice, evidently in the hope that it
might reach the ear of Chang Tso-lin on his return. The lesson of Yang
Yü-t'ing's retreat from Kiangsu, he suggested, was that the power of the
clique was overextended. For the time being, Chang should preserve his
strength and wait for another day. Perhaps withdrawal from Chihli should
even be considered. He made it clear that he was not altogether happy with
Chang, saying that it would not do for him to engage in rash and foolish
actions with no regard to the situation in the country as whole.[87] Kuo, for
his part, was much impressed with what he saw in Japan, expressing the
wish to return in future to study military science there;[88] and he must have
hoped for sympathetic response to his anti-Chang campaign, especially
since several of his objectives had been suggested by the Japanese Army
minister. He reckoned without two things, however: the strength of pro-
Chang feeling among all the Japanese agencies working closely with him
on the spot in China and the influence they could wield, and the horror of
any encroachment of Bolshevik or Soviet ideas in the Northeast, something
that became a very powerful force working against Kuo once his alliance
with Feng Yü-hsiang was known.

When news of Kuo's move broke in Mukden, the Kwantung Army's
garrisons in the Northeast as a whole were considerably below strength.
The Kwantung Army command, it should be understood, covered both
those units stationed in the Kwantung leased territory, which were subject
to no limitation by treaty, and the "railway guards" responsible for the
protection of the South Manchuria Railway, whose numbers were subject
to limitation.[89] However, although Japan might claim justification by
treaty for a force of approximately 15,000 of these "railway guards," the
actual strength was always below this, was considerably reduced after the
Washington Conference, and seems to have amounted to no more than
7,800 men in mid-November 1925.[90] This was further reduced, however,
as Staff Headquarters in Tokyo decided on November 16 that the easing of
tensions in the North of China following the Chang-Feng agreement made
it unnecessary to extend the term of service of the 2,240 two-year enlisted
men. These therefore began their leave on the 19th, less than a week before
Kuo began to move, leaving only 5,560 Japanese troops to defend Japanese

interests throughout the Northeast exclusive of the Kwantung leased territory.[91] Startled by the sudden change of circumstances, the first thing the Kwantung Army commander did was to cable the Army Ministry and Staff Headquarters for instructions on what steps should be taken "if it is the policy of the central authorities that the Kuo army should not be allowed to proceed as far as the left bank of the Liao River."[92] The reply from Staff Headquarters made no reference to the Liao River's representing any kind of defense line. It maintained the desirability for the time being of pursuing the policy of nonintervention in China's internal affairs but suggested that various steps, including the dispatch of reinforcements, might be appropriate in the event of disturbances spreading and damaging Japanese interests in the South Manchuria Railway zone. The following day the Kwantung Army began concentrating its forces in Mukden (though not yet reinforcing them),[93] and at the same time dispatched Lieutenant Colonel Ura Sumie to see Kuo and ascertain his intentions.[94] He went, however, as a personal representative of the Kwantung Army's commander in chief, General Shirakawa Yoshinori, and not at government orders. Yet Kuo's failure, during his two-hour interview with Ura, to persuade him—and through him, Shirakawa—of the reason and point of his cause, was ultimately fatal.

Kuo began by advancing seven general reasons for his action, ranging from the fear that Russian and Japanese involvement with Feng and Chang might eventually bring on world war, through opposition to the policy of unification by force, desire to respond to the feelings of the people for peace, and the deleterious effects of war on the economy of the provinces, to the weakness and poor morale of the army, and general "strategic considerations."[95] He also drew Ura's attention to the telegram he had sent on November 25 to the ministers of the various powers in Peking, pledging continued respect for the established treaties, asking for their strict neutrality, and promising to protect the lives and property of foreigners in the war zone. Ura's reply was brief and restricted to three points. First, since Kuo professed to stand for peace, why was it that he now initiated this campaign by arms, especially since a compromise agreement, however limited, had just been reached between Chang and Feng's Kuominchün? Second, in view of the reports of plundering and burning by Kuo's troops as they took Hai-yang chen and Ch'in-huang-tao, how did Kuo expect the Kwantung Army to react if this continued once his forces crossed to the north of the Great Wall? Third, since Kuo and the Changs were like members of one family, and since Yang Yü-t'ing had left Mukden and Chang Hsüeh-liang had come to Ch'in-huang-tao to see Kuo as soon as he heard of the rising, could not a peaceful settlement be worked out? Yang had indeed fled to Port Arthur as soon as he heard of Kuo's demands, and since hostility between him and Kuo was believed to be the main cause of Kuo's discontent, Ura appears to be suggesting here that Yang's permanent "retirement" might open the way to settlement between Kuo and the two Changs. Kuo, however, did not respond to the suggestion. He claimed that it was only after Chang Tso-lin had given orders to advance troops against the Kuominchün, in breach of the Tientsin agreement, that he had acted, and that therefore there was no contradiction with his stand for peace. He also argued that he had had no intention of attacking Mukden, only of "returning the soldiers" there, but was forced to fight when they were attacked.

Ura was left far from satisfied on the major points. Though he conceded the Tientsin agreement to have been fragile, yet he said: "It is not an indisputable fact that it was actually you who broke through the thin ice?" Furthermore, for Kuo to say he was merely "returning" his troops, with no aggressive purpose, was totally disingenuous; and Ura warned him that, in the event of the South "Manchurian" area becoming the scene of battle, "the Kwantung Army must of course take appropriate measures." He concluded that Kuo was "totally lacking in sincerity." The impressions that Ura then conveyed to Shirakawa upon return to Port Arthur were as follows:

1. Kuo Sung-ling is absolutely determined to suppress Chang Tso-lin.
2. There is no hope of a peaceful solution.
3. Kuo looks likely in future to adopt the principles and policies of the Kuomintang for his political platform.
4. Surrounding Kuo are mostly Kuomintang politicians.
5. Kuo has definite contact with Feng Yü-hsiang.
6. There is as yet no complete fusion between the politicians and the military commanders in Kuo's entourage.
7. Even among the high-ranking officers in Kuo's army there are those who are not happy with the present rising.
8. There is a common feeling of unease among the officers concerning their families in Mukden.
9. Among the ordinary soldiers too there are those who feel the present rising is immoral and that its outcome is still in doubt.

These negative findings were accepted by Shirakawa and became the basis of subsequent Kwantung Army action. Concluding from what Ura reported that Kuo's campaign was likely to turn the Three Provinces into an area of

172

THE KUO SUNG-LING AFFAIR

armed conflict and that Kuo was set on introducing Soviet influence there, the Kwantung Army commander began drawing up plans for keeping the peace within the railway zone, and even, where necessary, in Mukden itself and other centers.[96] At the same time, Shirakawa must have judged Tokyo to be unaware of just how serious the situation was,* and so dispatched Ura to report his impressions directly. While on his way to Tokyo, Ura met the press at Shimonoseki and spoke of the threat that was developing to the lives and property of Japanese in the area, announcing also that "our army headquarters" would refuse to admit belligerents of either side to the Japanese sphere of influence, and making the real point of his mission plain by suggesting that present troop strengths were scarcely adequate to carry out this policy that had been decided upon.[97]

Other voices were readily added to the chorus calling for stronger measures in the defense of Japanese interests. Chang Tso-lin's adviser Major General Matsui Nanao cabled the Vice-Minister of Foreign Affairs on November 30 to inform him that "Kuo is a pure extremist. If he was to enter Mukden, he would at once announce rejection of all treaties, and Japan's so-called special rights would come to nothing. . . . The argument is no longer effective that it makes no difference whether it is Chang or Feng who takes control in the Three Eastern Provinces."[98] Yoshida Shigeru, consul general in Mukden, cabled the Foreign Minister on December 1: "To protect our position in Manchuria, and furthermore to break out of the present situation in which the development of our influence is completely stalemated, I am sure it would not be to our disadvantage if we were now to help Chang Tso-lin in his extremity and make it easy for him to rise again."[99] Since this suggestion for the time being went unheeded, Yoshida became most concerned at the way the situation was developing. On December 5, just before the Lien-shan battle, he suggested that mediation between the two warring factions should be attempted by Japan, with the conditions for such mediation being understood as the surrender of the Mukden forces and unconditional retirement of Chang on the one hand, and agreement by Kuo on preservation of existing Japanese interests on the other.[100] When Shidehara replied that mediation might be undertaken only if requested by the parties to the dispute and if it was in accordance with the noninterference policy,[101] Consul Uchiyama was sent to talk with Kuo, but because of a break in railway communications, he did not even make con-

* Judging by the reply received from Tokyo in response to his earlier request for instructions. See above, p. 170.

tact with him.[102] After the one failed effort, he did not try again, mainly because of the changed situation in the Chang camp at that time, the stiffening of the will to fight, and the certainty that Chang would no longer be interested in such mediation. This proposal by Yoshida has to be seen as a desperate last-minute effort to save a situation in which Chang seemed certain to be defeated, when he was indeed completing his plans to flee, and when Yoshida, having despaired of Kuo's being overthrown, was anxious at least to establish some influence over him to offset the links with Feng, and through him with Moscow.

Yoshida's fears were shared within the South Manchuria Railway Company also. From the president and director of the South Manchuria Railway Company came similar appeals. The president, Yasuhiro Tomoichirō, cabled Shidehara on December 2:

I am afraid that the rebel general Kuo Sung-ling . . . may succeed in the Three Provinces, and that in accordance with the slogan of him and his ilk—cancellation of the unequal treaties—the Three Provinces may fall and be taken over by an exclusively Red movement, and that this place may develop into a free zone, with no Mantetsu and no Kwantung government.

He called for Japanese intervention both visible and invisible to see that such an outcome was avoided.[103] Matsuoka Yōsuke, a director of the company, was of the same view. Because of the importance of the area to Japan, he thought that, whereas in principle there should be no interference with the free exercise of power by the authorities of the Three Eastern Provinces, yet "where there is a move to overthrow someone advantageous to us and replace him with someone not to our advantage, we should prevent it." The preservation of order in the area over the past ten years, so that Europeans and Americans were able to invest with an easy mind only there, in the whole of China, he held to be obviously due in the main to the might of Japan. But, he went on,

The power of Chang Tso-lin, who has, generally speaking, maintained the peace of the Three Eastern Provinces until now by either basing himself on this foundation or cleverly using it, must also be recognized. And, except on minor or abstract issues, it is well known that Chang Tso-lin has in recent years come in the main to back our institutions.

Matsuoka emphasized strongly the dangers of Communist encroachment on the Three Provinces, and noted that it had been decided in the time of the Hara cabinet to support Chang Tso-lin as actual power holder in the area and thought it would be a "stab in the back" to change that policy now.[104]

A further consideration, though it is one to which Matsuoka made no direct reference, was the considerable financial losses Japanese business interests stood to suffer if Chang Tso-lin was defeated, and of course the South Manchuria Railway's economic stake in the Three Provinces was considerably greater than that of any other Japanese organization. Figures are not available on the precise holdings of the railway and debts owing to it in Fengtien p'iao, the local currency unit, but they must have been considerable. One estimate puts them at around 60 million,[105] though its basis is unclear. What is certain is that there was widespead fear that the fall of Chang might also mean the collapse of the currency.[106] Its value was always a barometer of his fortunes, and sank catastrophically after the battle reverses of December 5, from the pre-rebellion exchange rate of between 160 and 170 to the Japanese 100 gold yen to between 230 and 240 just before the war's end.[107] The panic was further fueled by the announcement from Kuo that after entry into Mukden he would halt all dealings in the p'iao until it had been "reorganized," which was taken to mean either heavy devaluation or renunciation in favor of a completely new currency.[108] The railway company could not afford to ignore the threat this posed to its interests. It is necessary to remember that these interests were substantially greater in sheer economic terms than those, for example, of Chang's government. Although the revenues of the latter in 1925 amounted to approximately 34 million yüan (see above, p. 148), the profits reaped by the South Manchuria Railway in 1925 from its railway operations alone amounted to 58.6 million yen.[109]

Since the average rate of exchange over the whole of 1925 was 168 Fengtien yüan to the 100 Japanese (gold) yen notes, this means that Fengtien revenues were no more than 35 percent of the South Manchuria Railway's profits, the converted figures being either 34 and 98.4 million in yüan, or 20 and 58.6 million in yen.[110]

Thus the Kwantung Army, senior consular officials, the South Manchuria Railway Company, and incidentally also the Kwantung government[111] and organizations of Japanese residents in the Northeast,[112] were all agreed on the importance to Japan of preventing a Kuo victory, and the need therefore for Japan to aid Chang to prevent his being defeated. In the deliberations in Tokyo on the policy to be adopted toward the crisis precipitated by Kuo, the priorities were seen somewhat differently from the way

they were seen by the men on the spot, and greater attention had to be paid
to the exigencies of Japanese foreign policy as a whole, and especially
China policy as a whole. Army Minister Ugaki, for a start, had shown
considerable enthusiasm toward Kuo following their meeting shortly before the outbreak of the rebellion (see above, p. 168). He also felt a strong
distaste for Chang and for his methods of rule. Yet these personal feelings
were set aside when he came in early December to reflect on how the crisis
affected Japanese interests. That he gave considerable thought to the problems is clear from his diary, which is worth quoting at some length: [113]

Not only my feelings but also those of most Japanese toward Chang Tso-lin have
changed greatly since last autumn. His brigandish character, the way he is always
looking for opportunities to extend his fame and fortune, paying no attention even
to treachery in order to do so, increases in me the feeling of a kind of disgust, to the
point where now I wonder whether it might not be to the advantage of Japan if he
were to come to some kind of setback. [There is a feeling] at large, and especially in
diplomatic quarters, that it would make not the slightest difference if Chang was
overthrown as ruler of Manchuria and replaced by Kuo or Feng.

Ugaki felt, however, that whether or not Japan's rights and interests in
south "Manchuria" were established to the point that no successor to
Chang could infringe upon them, Japan's plans for future expansion into
north "Manchuria" made it imperative that Chang not be overthrown.

However, Chang's power over North Manchuria was not gained in the space of a
day and a night, but is the crystallization of more than ten years of effort. Whoever
replaced him, even though he entered Mukden, it must be reckoned that it would
take at least several years before his power extended into North Manchuria. I am
now attempting to expand into North Manchuria, steadily, and through the power
of Chang. If Chang was to go, I would lose this convenience. Also, the leaders of
Kirin and Heilungkiang, being in a naturally antagonistic position to the new center
in Mukden, would become rivals. If this happened, then just as Feng Yü-hsiang,
for the sake of his own survival, now depends on Red Russia, using it and being
used by it, so it is clear that our development would be arrested through the penetration of the power of Red Russia into North Manchuria with the emergence of a
second and a third Feng. Consequently, the complete destruction and collapse of
Chang would be disadvantageous to our country in its Manchuria-Mongolia policy.
I believe that the existence of Chang Tso-lin, holding power in North Manchuria
even if that power sould be reduced from what it is today, is necessary to our
Manchurian policy, and especially to our North Manchurian policy. Yet this does
not mean that we should aid Chang to the point of ignoring the overall
disadvantages—for example, in incurring the resentment of the whole of China.
Even among the measures for aiding Chang short of incurring these overall disadvantages, there are various stages. In short, I believe it wise, for the sake of the

empire, to make great efforts to maintain the existence of Chang, so long as we do not incur these overall disadvantages.

The two fundamental questions, therefore, were the Communist threat and the Japanese efforts to effect a stronger economic penetration of North "Manchuria," on which negotiations were at the time under way at various levels with Chang Tso-lin's administration. For both of these reasons the existence of Chang was necessary to Japan, though the steps to ensure his continued existence had to be taken with care, since active and visible support for Chang would rebound in a way detrimental to Japan's China policy as a whole. In the same vein, at a cabinet meeting on the eve of the Lien-shan battle, Ugaki stressed the point that "to aid Chang positively would be very dangerous." [114] Reflecting this extremely cautious attitude, the instructions sent by the Army Vice-Minister to the Kwantung Army chief of staff before the Lien-shan battle fell far short of what had been requested. Troop reinforcements were ruled out, except as a possible future option; steps were suggested to try to cast Kuo in the light of the ambitious aggressor; and Chang's advisers were to apply pressure on him to have him "be patient and prudent, preserving his strength in order to permanently secure the boundaries and pacify the people of the Three Eastern Provinces." [115] With Chang facing a desperate battle, to be followed by probable defeat and collapse, such instructions have a curiously unreal air. The impression is strengthened when one realizes that not long before this Staff Headquarters in Tokyo had decided that preservation of peace in the area was "an absolute demand of the empire, always, regardless of the circumstances." [116] Refusal by the Army Ministry and Headquarters to countenance conspicuous intervention at this stage was matched by Shidehara as Foreign Minister, who emphasized at the cabinet meeting of December 4 that Japanese policy had to be determined by looking at the situation in China as a whole, and since Japanese interests in Peking and in the Yangtze area were considerable, absolute neutrality in the current dispute was the only possible course. [117]

After Lien-shan, however, the situation immediately became much more pressing. Yoshida cabled from Mukden, repeating his request for reinforcements "because of the failure of the Mukden army," and a similar request was sent in from the Kwantung government office by Kodama Hideo. The Kwantung Army set about the second stage in its "troop concentration," mustering all available men at Mukden and other strong points along the South Manchuria Railway line, and also deploying ordinary troops on important roads to a distance of one kilometer outside the railway zone, and mounted patrols to a distance of four kilometers. The call for extra troops was reiterated by Yasuhiro for the South Manchuria Railway also.[118]

Consultations in Tokyo between the Foreign Minister, Premier, and War Minister on December 7 resulted in the first positive action authorized from Tokyo.[119] This step, ratified by a cabinet council meeting the following day, consisted of issuing a warning through the Kwantung Army commander to both Chang and Kuo about the need to respect Japanese rights and interests in the area over which they were likely to be fighting. While stressing the Japanese policy of strict "non-interference in internal affairs," the warning continued:[120]

It must not be forgotten, however, that there are in Manchuria hundreds of thousands of Japanese subjects engaged in peaceful pursuits as well as an immense amount of Japanese invested capital. Therefore, should a situation develop as a result of hostilities or disturbances, whether in the railway zone or in the adjacent districts, calculated to jeopardize or seriously menace these important interests of Japan, the Japanese forces would be constrained to act as duty demands. I have no doubt that both contending forces will pay due regard to this special position of my country with regard to China, but I feel in duty bound to declare that, if an emergency such as that indicated above should arise, recourse must be had to such steps as may be required by the circumstances.

Shidehara seems to have considered such a warning, delivered impartially to the commanders of both armies, all that was necessary in defense of Japanese interests at that time, and to be perfectly consistent with his "noninterference" line. The military, however, clearly did not accept it as enough, and paid scant regard to the spirit of neutrality either in the issuance of the warning or in application of the line designated. Staff Headquarters in Tokyo cabled the Kwantung Army command on December 7 top secret orders to be ready to get reinforcements from Korea, the following day ordering the Kurume Division to be ready to dispatch troops. For his part, the Kwantung Army commander cabled both the general chief of staff and the Army Minister and repeated his view that a show of military force would be necessary to attain Japanese goals but that existing forces were inadequate to the purpose and he would therefore need reinforcements. He also at the same time increased the concentration of troops in Mukden and moved divisional headquarters for the whole of "Manchuria"

to Mukden.[121] Reports of these stepped-up defensive moves by the
Japanese were most unsettling to Kuo as he continued to advance through
the southern part of Fengtien province, for how could he overthrow Chang,
who was also based in Mukden, without thereby creating the kind of disturbances that would trigger military intervention by these Japanese forces?

When Kuo tried to clarify the precise circumstances that would precipitate such intervention, in the course of several meetings with Colonel Ura,
who delivered the warning note to him at Chin-chou on December 10, he
found good reason for concern.[122] Ura was unmoved by Kuo's desperate
attempt to persuade him of his absolute commitment to the defense of
Japanese interests, and by his resolute denial of any Communist connection. The crux of their interview came with Kuo's attempt to elicit a definition from Ura of the limits of the term "in the railway zone or in the
adjacent districts." Kuo was asking, in effect, where it would be permissi-
ble to fight and where not, where the Japanese defense perimeter began and
ended. He specifically asked about the then encampment position of
Chang's armies at Chu-liu-ho near Hsin-min, but could get no satisfactory
reply from Ura. He was told only that since his army was conversant with
the situation in the Three Eastern Provinces, the areas in which there were
Japanese rights and interests should be known to it. Because Kuo insisted
that his queries on the extent of the Japanese defense perimeter and the
precise treaty terms on which such authority was claimed be referred to
General Shirakawa, the tone of the interview became noticeably chilly.
The Kwantung Army position was most clearly put by Ura when he stated:
"I would like you to know that our imperial government has measures
completely prepared to deal with whatever action you may take."[123]

Chang Tso-lin accepted the Japanese warning without hesitation or question, and with very good reason, since it clearly gave him the advantage, as
power holder, against Kuo, who would obviously have to disturb the peace
to usurp that power from him. Kuo's troublesome, querulous manner
turned Shirakawa further against him.[124] As an advance guard of some
2,000 of his troops, diverging south from the main army toward the mouth
of the Liao River at Ying-k'ou, camped across the river from the city on
December 12, Shirakawa stepped in to prevent their taking it, giving Kuo
the answers for which he had pressed in his discussions with Colonel
Ura.[125] Chang's small garrison (about 350 men) had actually fled, leaving
the city wide open to Kuo's advance,[126] and some of Kuo's men had
crossed the river, when the local Japanese commander, on instructions

from Shirakawa, moved in to Ying-k'ou and forbade the crossing of the river. The command, handed to the representative of the Kuo forces at 4:30 P.M. on December 13, was in three parts: no entry into Ying-k'ou; retreat to beyond a 30-kilometer radius from the South Manchuria Railway line; and no crossing of the Liao.[127] Japanese reinforcements were brought into Ying-k'ou to reinforce the command, and Kuo's forces retreated. With Kuo's Ying-k'ou route of advance ruled out by Japanese intervention, the position was as described by Putnam Weale: "So the rebel army was thus limited to advancing along an immense, sandy waste through which the Chinese railway runs on a causeway, where no army can find food and shelter, knowing that even if their action was successful it would be useless, as the prize—Mukden—was locked up behind dense lines of Japanese troops."[128] Kuo's strategy of a two-pronged advance on Mukden had to be scrapped, and his forces joined up again at Kou-pang-tzu to prepare for an assault on the positions that Chang was preparing by the Liao River further north, at Hsin-min.

The steps that Shirakawa had taken were on his own initiative, however, and were considerably revised in the instructions he received from Ugaki the following day. While endorsing the general principle that not only direct combat operations but also military activities threatening to disturb the peace of the railway zone should be forbidden, Ugaki reduced the extent of this zone from the 30 kilometers set by Shirakawa (approximately a day's march) to 20 Chinese li (approximately 12 kilometers, or the distance a shell might travel), on either side of the railway line.[129] Separate instructions from Shidehara to Yoshida in Mukden elaborated by pointing out that the ban on the entry of Kuo's forces into Ying-k'ou was thereby lifted, since the existence in or passage across this defensive zone by either army could be tolerated so long as there was no action contravening the terms of this warning.[130] However, when Shirakawa commmunicated the warning to both armies on December 15th, he not only made no reference to the fact that the crossing of the Liao or entry into Ying-k'ou was no longer forbidden, but, by sending an extra company of troops from Liao-yang to reinforce the defenses of Ying-k'ou created the strong impression that his original orders stood, amended only in respect to the distance involved.[131] Kuo could only protest weakly, asking again what justification there was in the treaties for such measures by Japan.[132] In this instance, therefore, the initiative and the independent authority of the Kwantung Army were decisive in calling a first halt to what had seemed the unstoppable advance of Kuo's army, although other branches of the Japanese administration in the North-east clearly connived at the army's actions—Yoshida's failure to publish Shidehara's interpretation of the revised instructions being a clear example.

The second major act of intervention was one that was cleared at all levels up to Shidehara, Ugaki, and the cabinet. That was the decision of December 15 to authorize the dispatch of reinforcements to strengthen the Japanese defenses in the area. The repeated requests for such a step from all Japanese officers, officials, and private organizations on the spot have been mentioned already. Toward mid-December the tempo of such calls increased and their content came to focus more directly on the Red threat represented by Kuo. Major General Matsui Iwane, military attaché at Pe-king, deliberately played on this fear by remarking in a press interview, "it is obvious that the downfall of Marshal Chang may mean China's going Bolshevik quickly."[133] The Kwantung Army chief of staff likewise put the issues starkly in a dispatch of December 12. Speaking of the Three Eastern Provinces, he wrote:[134]

Overall he [Chang] has striven to prevent their going Communist and has taken steps in accordance with Japanese interests. If Kuo Sung-ling were to replace him, and of course if Heilungkiang and Kirin were to become independent, there is no doubt that the fiendish hand of Red Russia would reach directly into this area. Especially one shudders at the thought of how Chang Tso-lin and the officers and troops under him might act after Chang's downfall. And it is hard to calculate the harm that would result in economic circles from large-scale confusion.

The public clamor in Japan itself for stronger measures in the defense of Japanese interests was also a major factor behind the decision of December 15.[135] That decision may be seen as a logical consequence of those that had preceded it, in that warnings to the belligerents could not be expected to have much effect unless supported by a show of strength. Without such reinforcements the Kwantung Army's chief of staff argued that "perhaps the troops will all be killed."[136] It was an argument none the less compel-ling for being patently absurd, given the strong reasons on the part of both armies for avoidance of offense to Japan. Shidehara, who resisted this con-clusion up until the Ying-k'ou incident, as a result of that incident came to accept the need for reinforcements.* Approval by the cabinet on the morn-ing of December 15 was followed by the dispatch of some 2,500 troops,

* Shidehara, in his foreign policy speech to the 51st Diet in January 1926, emphasizes his change in views on the need for reinforcements following the Ying-k'ou incident, when it "became clear" that the forces available were so few that they "would have difficulty in fulfilling their duty" (Eguchi, p. 86). Falconeri's speculation (pp. 234–36), on the basis of

mostly from the Kurume 12th Division. In the first instance, the numbers were to be about 3,500, but 1,000 men were to be from Korean units able to be on the scene almost immediately and due to leave again once the mainland reinforcements arrived, which was expected to be around December 21.[137] Technically, the troops were replacements, to fill the ranks of forces depleted in mid-November. Yet, despite Shidehara's earnest efforts to represent them as such and to deny that they amounted to a departure from his nonintervention policy, their dispatch was an unmistakable boost to Chang. The context of the action was important—following as it did immediately after the conspicuously partisan actions of the Kwantung Army at Ying-k'ou and after issuance of warnings whose constrictive force, nominally directed at both sides, was actually felt by one side only.

However, even while the decisive steps for the salvation of the Chang cause were authorized in Tokyo, military authorities there were still careful to hedge their bets. Colonel Sasaki Tōichi, a specialist in affairs relating to the Kuomintang, was dispatched by the General Staff to make an effort to contact Kuo. Sasaki says that he was sent because it was thought that Kuo was going to take Mukden, in which case his presence would be necessary "to adjust relations with the Japanese army that would arise with his entry into Mukden." The fear evidently persisted, in other words, that, despite all the steps that had been taken, Chang's defenses would collapse, in which case Sasaki, if present in Kuo's camp, would prove a useful medium for the application of Japanese pressure. Sasaki left Tokyo on December 19, arrived at Mukden on the 22nd, but when he requested a locomotive and passenger car from the Kwantung Army special service agent in order to go to Kuo's territory, he was told that no aid would be given to "behavior designed to support the rebel." While in the course of making a long detour to reach his objective, the war ended. His story suggests, at best, a high degree of lack of coordination between General Staff in Tokyo and Kwantung Army command.[138]

The Fengtien Clique Revived

Immediately before the issuance of the first Japanese warning, Chang was in the depths of despair, making preparations for sudden flight into the

---

Shidehara's consistent opposition to such reinforcements up to the day before the cabinet decision—that he also argued against Ugaki at the cabinet meeting when the decision was taken—is not supported by evidence and seems unnecessary in view of Shidehara's own perfectly reasonable explanation. Foreign Ministry objections to troop reinforcements up to this date are referred to scathingly by Ugaki, p. 48–49.

Japanese-occupied zone; after it, he quickly gained confidence, and determined to gamble everything on a battle at the Liao River. The site for this
battle, which did not begin until two weeks later, had been chosen by the
evening of December 8.[139] Though there is no evidence on the point, it was
probably chosen at the suggestion of Chang's Japanese advisers, since the
Liao River site, at Chu-liu-ho just near Hsin-min, was conveniently distant
from the main concentrations of Japanese interests along the South Manchuria Railway line, and was also far enough removed from Kuo's positions for Chang to be able, by ordering the destruction of the Peking–
Mukden line in front of Kuo, to slow his advance greatly and win valuable
time to organize and concentrate his own forces. While Kuo's problems of
lack of supplies, money, and winter equipment could be expected to intensify, Chang was preparing to fight only 30 miles from Mukden, his troops
well fed, clothed, and supplied, and fully paid. There were many pointers
to a strengthening Japanese commitment to see Kuo defeated: the warning
itself, the reports of Japanese dissatisfaction with Kuo after the interview
with Colonel Ura, the Kwantung Army troop movements, the active participation of Japanese officers as advisers in various units of Chang's army,
and even the provision of a 15-inch heavy artillery unit manned by 14
Japanese reservists under Lieutenant Araki Gorō.[140] All of these actions,
capped by the intervention at Ying-k'ou and the second warning, served
not only to restore confidence to Chang but to convince his subordinate
generals to begin moving their troops toward the appointed position by the
Liao.[141] Japanese troop concentrations in Mukden and other major centers
also allowed Chang to reduce his garrisons there to an absolute minimum.

Kuo's Last Battle

The climactic battle of the war opened on December 21 as Kuo's Northeastern Kuominchün entered Hsin-min, capturing it after a short struggle.
For two days the outcome remained in doubt, fortunes alternating about
evenly until the morning of the 23d, when Kuo's forces, being first pinned
down by heavy and accurate artillery fire that hindered advance, were suddenly attacked in the rear by a large force of Heilungkiang cavalry, which
had circled behind them undetected during the night.[142] By one account,
the cavalry was led by a Japanese officer, Lieutenant Colonel Korenaga,
and the Kirin artillery units were commanded by a Major Hayashi, the
former serving as "adviser" to Wu Chün-sheng in Heilungkiang and the

latter to Chang Tso-hsiang in Kirin.[143] The surprise cavalry assault led quickly to a rout, many of Kuo's senior officers surrendering, a few seeking refuge in the Japanese consulate in Hsin-min, and only a small force retaining its identity as Kuominchün and escaping, to link up later with Feng Yü-hsiang.[144] Kuo himself, with his wife, attempted to flee incognito, but was found hiding in a pile of radishes in a farmhouse cellar in the village of Su-chia-t'un, about 12 miles from Hsin-min, taken to local army headquarters, and shot.[145] On Christmas Day the bodies were exposed in the marketplace in Mukden. Li Ching-lin's prolonged resistance to the Kuominchün forces around Tientsin, where he held out until December 24, prevented aid reaching Kuo from his Kuominchün allies until too late. Li finally fled to Shantung, where he set up a joint military command with Chang Tsung-ch'ang, Chang Tsung-ch'ang being thus the sole Chang Tso-lin nominee to provincial control within the Wall to retain his power into the beginning of 1926.

CONCLUSIONS

From this attempt to piece together in some detail the complex fabric of events and relationships as they developed during the episode of Kuo's rebellion, a number of conclusions may be advanced.

1. Kuo's rebellion was ill-conceived, inadequately prepared, and hastily executed. From the start it gave little promise of developing into a radical alternative to Chang Tso-lin's administration. Though evidently influenced by Kuomintang ideology and by the atmosphere of antimilitarism prevalent among the people at large, Kuo was extremely vague about what he intended to do once he replaced Chang, and made little effort to fan the flames of popular resentment against Chang, concentrating instead on the most narrowly orthodox, military approach. The fact that he chose to unfurl his banner of revolt at a time of détente and disengagement between the Fengtien and Kuominchün forces made him seem the militant transgressor of the peace rather than its champion, as he wanted to be seen. Personal considerations, jealousy and hatred of Yang Yü-t'ing, and resentment against Chang Tso-lin for not having rewarded him with provincial command after the second Fengtien-Chihli war were at least as important as any political objections he had against Chang. Two sets of miscalculations were fatal to him: first in relation to the support he expected from Feng Yü-hsiang's Kuominchün and from Li Ching-lin and dissident comman-

ders under Chang; and second in relation to Japan, from which he obviously expected benevolent neutrality at least, after his conversations there in the autumn immediately preceding the decision to rebel.

2. The episode reveals unmistakably the innate weakness of the internal organization of the Mukden military clique. It had never been subjected to such pressure before and was brought to within an ace of total collapse in a matter of two weeks. Many of those in top positions of authority were shown to be either incompetent or disloyal, though loyalty had been the prime consideration in deciding on their appointment. Under pressure it became clear that their commitment to Chang was subordinate to their private interests of wealth, power, and patronage. They were thus perfectly willing to abandon Chang, and either to make a deal with Kuo or to attempt to establish their territory on an independent basis, until they saw what they took to be decisive evidence that Japan was stepping in to preserve Chang. Only then did the Kirin and Heilungkiang units, for example, leave for the front.

3. Japanese intervention was decisive in preventing Chang Tso-lin's defeat. It consisted in the following: (a) Invocation of the (by then) well-established principle that fighting should not be permitted in the vicinity of Japanese interests—thus effectively ruling out attack on Chang's Mukden stronghold, or on other major cities and towns under his jurisdiction. (b) Denial to Kuo's army of access to Ying-k'ou, even when it had been abandoned by Chang Tso-lin's army; refusal of permission to cross the Liao River, and imposition of a cordon 30 kilometers wide along either side of the South Manchuria Railway line, within which Kuo's army was forbidden to enter at a crucial time in the fighting. (c) Concentration of troops in Mukden and strategic points in the railway zone, followed by their reinforcement from Japan and Korea. Whereas the reinforcements were few in number and did no more than restore Japanese forces to roughly their pre-crisis strength, the context and timing of their dispatch were such as to give a great psychological boost to Chang Tso-lin's forces, and to convince his subordinate commanders that their cause would prevail, while at the same time plunging the Kuo camp into gloom and disarray. (d) The active participation of Japanese officers in planning and prosecuting the defense campaign of Chang, whether by the advisers in the service of Chang and his subordinates in Kirin and Heilungkiang, or by the secondment of the artillery unit under Lieutenant Araki.

4. The responsibility for Japanese involvement rests in differing degrees at different levels of the administrative hierarchy. Within China all Japanese agencies of which any record exists—military, civil, and semigovernmental (such as the South Manchuria Railway Company)—favored support to prevent the overthrow of Chang Tso-lin. Their thinking was determined by three main considerations: desire to maintain the existing framework of government in Northeast China, in which Japanese interests were protected and advanced through the symbiotic relationship with Chang Tso-lin; fear of communism, with which Kuo, through his relationship with Feng Yü-hsiang, was associated; and opposition to any civil disorders likely to damage Japanese interests (China's civil wars had always hitherto been kept from crossing the Great Wall into the Northeast).

In Tokyo, the positions of the army and foreign ministries have generally been distinguished, but the difference, we would suggest, relates not so much to principle as to the degree of reluctance with which the decision to support certain measures was agreed upon, or to the insistence on maintaining the rhetoric of nonintervention while authorizing the intervention. Army Minister Ugaki and the General Staff were as much persuaded of the three points just mentioned as were their agents in China. But they were much more chary of stirring up a hornet's nest of anti-Japanese feeling by being seen to aid Chang "positively." Their instructions were initially clear on the end but vague on the means, implicitly allowing a degree of discretion in interpretation to the officers concerned with their execution. Central army policy and Ugaki's thinking were clear: preservation of order in the Northeast was an "absolute demand" of the empire, and Chang, for all the dissatisfaction felt about him, was nevertheless "necessary" to Japan. Notwithstanding the urgent appeals from Kwantung Army command, the degree of intervention necessary to attain these ends was authorized only gradually, beginning with advice and persuasion, ranging through the first warning and the concentration of existing forces in Mukden and other cities in the zone, and working up to the issue of the second warning and the dispatch of troop reinforcements. The readiness to turn a blind eye to the extremely partial initiatives of Kwantung Army command, and even to the blatant overstepping of instructions, points to the fact that the men on the spot were expected to exercise wide discretion in carrying out their commissions. This abdication of authority at the center greatly facilitated the taking of more and more independent initiatives on the part of the Kwantung Army from the time of this affair through the 1930's.

On the part of the foreign ministry, Shidehara was as implacable as anyone in insisting on the inviolability of Japanese rights and interests in "Manchuria."[146] Yet, looking at China policy as a whole, and, like Ugaki, seeing the dangers of repercussions against Japan's crucial trading interests on the Yangtze that open intervention in defense of those interests might stimulate, he preferred to procrastinate, hoping intervention would be proved unnecessary, and only actually agreeing to it when he seemed to have no alternative. Like Ugaki, he too could be defied with impunity by his agents on the spot in China. The failure of Yoshida Shigeru to publicize Shidehara's important December 15 directive lifting many of the restrictions that had been imposed on the Kuo Sung-ling forces has been mentioned above (p. 179). On the following day, December 16, Shidehara sent instructions that the senior Japanese advisers attached to Chang, Matsui Nanao and the Mukden Special Service Agent of the Kwantung Army, Kikuchi Takeo, should both be recalled—obviously hoping thereby to avoid the kind of embarrassment that had arisen in the past from the appearance of involvement by Japanese officers in China's civil wars—but this instruction too was ignored.[147]

The following episode is further evidence of Shidehara's poor control over his subordinates. On December 16 or 17 Shidehara dispatched Consul Uchiyama to explain to Kuo that the Japanese government, despite the troop reinforcements then on their way to China, was maintaining a strictly neutral attitude. Uchiyama planned to meet Kuo's foreign affairs spokesman, Yin Ju-keng, in Dairen, but while Uchiyama was en route to Dairen, Yin was ordered by Kwantung Governor Kodama to leave the territory. Shidehara had therefore to ask Yoshida to smooth over the bad feeling between Kodama and Kuo's representative, and Uchiyama had to be sent to look for Yin in Chin-chou, which was bound to cause considerable delay.[148] As in the case of General Staff agent Sasaki (see above, p. 181), it appears that Uchiyama failed to make contact, the former having been impeded from doing so by the actions of the Kwantung Army, the latter by the actions of the Kwantung government, which was nominally under Shidehara's jurisdiction.

The failure on the part of both Ugaki and Shidehara to concern themselves with these infractions, plus their predilection for the issuance of loose instructions to their subordinates in China, suggests that absolute insistence on Japan's rights and interests, coupled with the readiness on occasion to turn a blind eye toward some of the ways in which these rights and interests were advanced, was also part of Shidehara diplomacy. "Absolute noninterference in the internal affairs of China" was the formal diplomatic posture; the reality was quite different.

CHAPTER SIX

Chang's Last Years

INTRODUCTION: THE PROBLEMS

The course of Chang Tso-lin's career, from the beginning of 1926 to the time of his death in June 1928, is infinitely complex, yet at the same time the easiest phase of his career to interpret, since the forces working through him and the military group around him had by this time crystallized in an unmistakable form. In the Three Eastern Provinces the Mukden clique became fiercely repressive, exploitative, and parasitical; in China as a whole, more rabidly and blindly anti-Communist; and in relation to Japan, truculent but, under pressure, compliant. This compliance was more and more obviously reluctant the more demanding Japan became. Clearly Chang Tso-lin had tried to use the Japanese as much as he was used by them, but it was an uneven and in this period a hopeless struggle. The only hope of successful resistance Chang might have had was to mobilize the nationalist and anti-imperialist sentiments of the masses, but that very possibility was foreclosed by the nature of his past compromises. Thus, rather than open the floodgates to mass anti-Japanese sentiment for fear that he too might be swept away, Chang continued to serve Japanese imperialist interests, however painfully and adroitly he temporized before yielding.

However, in Chang's final years, his magic deserted him: in the Three Eastern Provinces repression led to widespread disorders and virtual collapse; in China as a whole Chang's simple anticommunism was decisively rejected; and pressures from Japan developed so inexorably that eventually he was swept away by them.

THREE PROVINCES: ACCUMULATED CONTRADICTIONS

Civilian Versus Military: Wang's Last Stand

All of this was foreshadowed in the immediate aftermath of the Kuo Sung-ling rebellion, as in January 1926 Chang and his advisers sat down to rethink their basic objectives. There was little that was new about the debate and the positions taken in it; indeed it was virtually the same as had taken place following the great trauma the clique had previously experienced—in the defeat of May 1922. When they totted up the costs of the previous year's sporadic but continuous warfare, and noted that in the end it had brought absolutely no benefits to be weighed against costs, the argument for withdrawal from the struggle for control of China and concentration of development of the Northeast was difficult to resist. Initially Chang himself indicated tacit admission of the point by announcing in late December of 1925 that he intended to reduce his armies, economize, develop the frontiers, regularize the finances, and turn his attention to economic development, adopting as his principle "pacification of the people, defense of the borders" (an-min pao-ching).[1] Yet as the bargaining developed in January on the details of the changes, it became clear that Chang was determined to resist pressure toward the changes that were most widely hoped for.

On January 6 Chang proffered his resignation,[2] only to withdraw it several weeks later, on January 22, when, as expected, representatives of the three Provincial Assemblies and of the principal Associations of the Northeast called on him to plead for reconsideration. In inviting him to assume the post of Commander in Chief of Peace Preservation, however, they also suggested, by inserting careful reference to a constitution to be drawn up to regulate the new autonomous region, that the comander in chief was not to be an absolute ruler.[3] When Chang, the following day, replied accepting the new post, he was notably vague on the conditions that were to govern it. He did, however, call for advice on how military expenditure might be cut and the funds thus saved be used for the promotion of business and industry, communications and education.[4] When the advice came, drafted by Wang Yung-chiang, it proved too much for Chang to accept. Differences over basic policy led presently to Wang's resignation, which was perhaps a more serious blow to the clique as a whole than the rebellion of Kuo Sung-ling that precipitated it.

Wang's argument was a simple one. The income of the province (Fengtien) for 1925 had been 23 million yüan; yet military expenditure alone was 51 million yüan. Since no conceivable tax increase could cover such a deficit, military retrenchment was necessary. The major single item of military expenditure—the arsenal—he proposed to reduce from its then top priority at 23 million a year to four-tenths of that size; the army proper he thought should be cut to three of four divisions, and Chang Tso-lin's secret military expenditures, running at 10 million in 1925, should be eliminated altogether. Wang's program was blunt and simple: "From now on, setting aside the old idea of excessive reliance on arms, we must plan to make good the impoverishment of years of continuous war by striving to maintain the security of the Three Eastern Provinces and reviving industry, hereafter not concerning ourselves with the affairs of the rest of China."[5]

This was too much for Chang. In mid-February Wang left Mukden for his native Chin-chou,* and presently, as Chang gave no sign of yielding, submitted his resignation, setting out his reasons and his criticisms in two letters that were given considerable publicity.[6] In the first of these, after describing the parlous state of the finances upon his assumption of responsibility for the treasury in 1917, and the efforts he had devoted to restoring them to order and developing the affairs of the province, he went on:

> However, affairs became unsettled and frequently we were involved in battle. But we knew only how to advance and not how to retreat. Now, because of military affairs, the finances of the province are again reduced to confusion. Military expenditure is being increased over and over again and without limit, and it is impossible to implement any fixed policies. Life gets daily harder for the people. In such conditions, to plan for future prosperity would be like climbing a tree to look for fish.

Appeals from Mukden to persuade him to return to his post were ignored, and a second letter from Wang, dated March 5, reiterated his demands for fundamental reorganization and retrenchment, particularly in the military program. Unlike the 1922 situation, however, Chang refused to make concessions. Wang was in fact never seen in Mukden again, since he died in Chin-chou the following year.

At this point it is worth noting that Wang's voice within the Mukden clique was always the voice of rationalized, bureaucratic capitalism, as distinct from Chang's blatantly militaristic and crudely exploitative semifeudalism; and it is worth asking what significance may be attached to the fact that the two principal influences trying to dissuade Chang from involvements in the civil wars of China as a whole were, from as early as 1918, the Japanese, and from at least 1922 but possibly earlier, Wang Yung-chiang. The explanation seems to lie in the fact that Wang, the bureaucrat, opposed to the irrationalism and risks of war, was the spokesman for a "capitalism in three provinces," and thus for a "Manchuria" if

---

*I.e. Chin-chou on the South Manchuria Railway line within the Japanese-administered Kwantung province north of Dairen.

not a "Manchukuo," whereas Chang, the militarist, remained obsessed
with the idea of China as a whole, and with the ambition to rule over it. The
independent Northeast line for which Wang stood, under the slogan *"pao-
ching an-min"* (protect the borders, pacify the people), is the line the
Japanese military, and on occasion civil and business leaders too, had been
intermittently working and plotting toward as early as 1911. Significantly,
in November 1927, just before his death, from the political wilderness of
Chin-chou Wang dispatched to Japan his long-time friend and adviser
Iwama Tokuya, to carry to authoritative sources there his vision of "realizing in Manchuria an anti-Communist state based on the ideals of Japan-
Manchuria cooperation and defense of the borders, pacification of the people." Iwama was also to make arrangements for a visit by Wang himself.[7]
Thus it appears that Wang had come full circle from identification with the
anti-Japanese and nationalist sentiments he was associated with in 1923–24
to positive quest for Japanese patronage. He was believed by the Japanese
to be the leading proponent among Chang's advisers of a more conciliatory
line toward Japan, and had he survived it seems safe to assume that he
would have emerged from retirement to contribute actively to the cause of
Sino-Japanese cooperation in the new state of Manchukuo. Chang Tso-lin,
on the other hand, as military leader of the Northeast, could not in practice
abandon his interest and involvement in affairs south of the Great Wall,
even in terms of pure self-interest and defense, although he did at times
practice autonomy of administration as part of the maneuvering necessary
in the struggle between himself and his contenders for control over the
whole of China. Wang, the bureaucrat, was thus in the long run a man
more congenial to Japanese imperialist interests than Chang, the militarist.[8]

Economic Dislocation: Moneymaking and Inflation

After Wang's retirement in early 1926, he was replaced as governor by
Mo Te-hui, a 44-year-old native of Kirin province, graduate of Peking
University, and former holder of various offices in Fengtien and Peking.[9]
Mo's job, however, remained much what it had been under Wang—that of
raising money to sustain the military campaigns of Chang and his armies.
As Wang had rightly emphasized, there were limits to the extent that this
was possible without causing economic chaos, and therefore social and
political disruption. Wang resigned after seeing the Three Eastern Provinces brought to the brink of such disintegration. Mo presided over a phase

of rapid acceleration of the process, and under Liu Shang-ch'ing, who succeeded him in the autumn of 1927, the process reached a certain climax.[10] Since this process was a continuous one, very much conditioning the kind of diplomatic and military responses that Chang could make to the events of these years, we propose to consider it first, only then turning to the military and diplomatic developments.

The question of decline in the value of the currency of the Northeast has already been discussed briefly as a by-product of extensive military commitments undertaken south of the Great Wall in 1922 and again in 1924–25. The exchange value of the silver-backed Fengtien dollar, the *ta-yang-p'iao*, was of course affected by world trends in the silver market, and through most of the 1920's prices on the New York silver bullion market tended to slide downward. The Fengtien currency was also affected by conditions in Japan, since its exchange was measured in terms of either the Bank of Chōsen's gold-backed yen or the Yokohama Specie Bank's silver-backed yen. Neither of these factors, however, can be invoked to explain those sudden fluctuations in value of the p'iao that closely paralleled the military fortunes of Chang's armies. For these the only explanation is that confidence in the currency evaporated as Chang's armies were threatened, since it was assumed that those armies were its main support. It was known that vast sums were being spent on war expenses, that much of such money had to be shipped out of the treasury in specie form to cover the cost of war in areas outside of Chang's jurisdiction where the p'iao was valueless. It was believed that the amounts being spent amounted to more than the revenue of the province, and it was understood that the deficit was met simply by the issue of nonconvertible paper currency unbacked by specie.

The fluctuations in the value of the p'iao during the autumn and winter of 1925–26, shown in Table 6, provide an excellent example of the way in which the fate of the currency was linked with that of Chang's armies. After the resolution of the Kuo affair in military terms, the p'iao still did not recover as it might have been expected to. The main reasons for this were the continuing general unease about depletion of the reserves and overissue of notes, rumors of a new issue of another 30 million, or even 50 million yüan in notes (February 1926),[11] the resignation of Wang Yung-chiang and the publication of his reasons for resigning, and the renewal of positive interest in campaigns by Chang's armies south of the Great Wall. By the end of April the value of the p'iao had sunk to the level of 280–90

TABLE 6
Japanese Gold 100-Yen Exchange Value in Fengtien P'iao
on the Mukden Exchange

Date	Event	P'iao per 100 yen
Oct. 16, 1925	Prior to Sun Ch'uan-fang's rising	158.60
19	Sun Ch'uan-fang's rising	176.00
Nov. 10	Rumors of crisis between Chang and Feng	201.00
21	Rumors of compromise between Chang and Feng	186.50
24	Kuo Sung-ling rebellion	190.50
29	Kuo army enters Shan-hai-kuan	199.00
Dec. 12	Liao River battle approaching	215.00
16	Crisis deepens in Chang's army	234.50
19	Japan dispatches troops	222.00
24	Kuo's army completely defeated	196.00
Jan. 11, 1926		206.70
21		221.20

SOURCE: Nishimura Shigeo, "1920 nendai Tōsanshō chihō kenryoku no hōkai katei," *Osaka gaikokugo daigaku gakuhō*, no. 25, July 1971, p. 144.

on the Exchange; by May 24 it was 380, and then, as the situation in China as a whole and the urgent military conferences in Mukden suggested that a new war was imminent, it dropped to 430 on the following day—that is to say, nearly double what it had been at the height of the Kuo Sung-ling crisis less than six months before. At the beginning of June widely promulgated rumors of the arrival at Ying-k'ou of a shipment of some 100 cases of new notes from an American note-printing company sent the Exchange plummeting again, to reach 490 by June 7.[12] Thus, although the Fengtien p'iao may be described as having weakened or declined through the fluctuations of 1920–25, the Kuo Sung-ling rebellion marks a watershed, after which it can only be described as collapsing, somewhat in the manner of the French and German currencies after World War I. Early in 1927 it broke the 1,000 mark. By early January 1928, it had sunk to 2,000, and in February it plummeted to 4,000.[13]

To mid-1926, despite understandable alarm at the process, the Mukden authorities did little to arrest the trend save to announce the issue of a 50 million yüan bond "for support of the currency," and issue assurances to the effect that rumors were false, lack of confidence ill-founded, and the reserves intact. The blame was placed on currency speculators. Both Governor Mo and Yang Yü-t'ing, Chang Tso-lin's senior civil and military advisers, denounced the "wicked merchants" in the Japanese-administered railway zone as the prime culprits.[14] Having adopted this explanation they spelled out the consequences in ensuing months. Attempts were made to fix the exchange rate by administrative fiat, an expedient that had been adopted occasionally before without much success, and increasingly the use of terror was adopted as a method to deal with the problem. On August 8, 1926, five leading dealers from the various exchanges were arrested, their goods were confiscated, and, on the 19th, after one of them had been arraigned personally before Chang Tso-lin, all were ordered shot.[15]

But these draconian methods could do no more than temporarily stop the rot that had set in. No such methods could restore the confidence that people had lost in their money. Furthermore, as it happened, the fears that the people entertained were well founded. Paper notes were being issued in increasingly reckless and extravagant amounts as Fengtien became progressively more deeply involved in the affairs of China as a whole from 1924 on, as Table 7 indicates. Clearly, from 1926 on, bank notes were being issued in a veritable flood, and this was the prime reason for their decline in value. The total volume of Fengtien notes in circulation at a given time is extremely difficult to determine. One estimate by a Japanese bank suggests the figure of 2,800 million by the end of 1927,[16] which would be considerably more than the total of the issues listed in Table 7. That table is based largely on the report of the Currency Reorganization Committee of the Three Eastern Provinces (Tung-san-sheng chin-yung cheng-li wei-yüan-hui), a Chinese body established in October 1929, which submitted its report in May 1931. It is possible that this committee might have been inclined to underestimate the total, and thus the scale of the problem it faced, whereas the Japanese banking source might have tended to exaggerate it. Another Japanese estimate of the total at the end of 1929 gives the figure of 3,000 million.[17]

Fengtien notes were not the only notes in circulation in the Three Eastern Provinces, but they did constitute, as of December 1927, 72 percent of the total.[18] The rest were the issue of the provincial banks of Kirin and Heilungkiang, or of Chang Tso-lin's privately run Frontier Bank. The other provincial banks, however, displayed the same tendency as that described for the Official Bank of the Three Eastern Provinces.[19] Limiting our attention here, therefore, to the Official Bank, we find it impossible to know for certain against what reserves in specie these notes were issued. According to Wang Yung-chiang, who listed what was in the provincial treasury at the end of 1925, the reserves then amounted to approximately 68 million yüan in various forms of specie.[20] These could certainly not have increased la-

TABLE 7

Fengtien Paper Dollars and Loans Issued by the Official Bank
of the Three Eastern Provinces

Date	Nonconvertible notes (million dollars)	Index	Loans to official agencies (million dollars)
July 1918	6	20	
1921	30	100	
July 1924	60	200	
January 1925	130.4	447	117.5
March 1926	208	693	274.0
January 1927	325	1,083	422.5
January 1928	470	1,567	1,110.2
April 1929	1,867	6,223	1,538.7

SOURCE: Nishimura Shigeo, "1920 nendai Tōsanshō chihō kenryoku no hōkai katei," *Osaka gaikokugo daigaku gakuhō*, no. 25, July 1971, p. 139.

ter, and indeed were almost certainly depleted. In March 1927, Governor Mo had to concede that the direct disbursement of military funds from the Official Bank as well as from the treasury had been a major cause of the decline of the p'iao—something attributed up to that time only to the wickedness of merchant speculators. He promised that in future such funds would be issued only from the treasury, though clearly he had no way to enforce such a promise.[21]

Efforts at Recovery

The general lack of confidence in the regime, which developed strongly especially after 1926, was reinforced by the devices adopted in the effort to shore up the currency and to raise more funds for the province's war chest. The case of the 50 million yüan in "currency regularization" bonds, mentioned briefly above, is a typical one. Details of the bond issue were published in May 1926. From these it was clear that a forced levy of funds was projected rather than voluntary subscription. The amounts to be secured from the various sectors were fixed by regulation—9 million yüan from the officials of the three provinces, 8 million from the banks, 21 million from agriculture, and 12 million from commercial circles. With the idea of restoring parity between the face value of the currency and the silver specie, the bonds were denoted in terms of hsien ta-yang (real ta-yang) yüan, as distinct from the depreciated ta-yang yüan actually in circulation. They were issued at a discount rate of 2 to 1—that is, two of the existing paper yüan dollars were calculated as being equal to one of the new hsien ta-yang, this being of course rather better than the going rate on the exchange at the time. The bonds were to be interest-bearing from the date of issue (at 6 percent), but not redeemable until three years later. The plan was a dismal failure, however. Despite the announcement of punishments for officials responsible in the case of quotas not being filled, the period for subscription had first to be extended from six to nine months, but even then only one-fifth of the projected amount could be raised. In late September 1927, as Mo Te-hui was replaced as governor by Liu Shang-ch'ing, the scheme was abandoned. From December of 1927 the subscribed amounts were returned, first to the officials, but in returning them the value of the bonds was calculated in the proportion of one hsien ta-yang bond being worth three of the then current paper ta-yang dollars. Since the exchange value then current for an actual specie dollar was between 12 and 20, the losses suffered were considerable.[22] In the end, therefore, far from helping to regularize the currency, the bond scheme greatly weakened public confidence.

The squeeze on the people was made more acute by the operation of a highly inequitable taxation system: 70 percent of the revenues of Fengtien province (in 1926) were derived from indirect taxes, the burden of which was heaviest on the masses of poor and working people. The May 1931 report of the Three Eastern Provinces Currency Reorganization Committee was bitterly critical of the way in which companies, banks, large-scale merchants, and prominent officials were all exempt from taxation while rickshaw pullers and small shopkeepers, for example, were subject to heavy levies.[23] A sweeping set of increases, made necessary to support large armies in continuing warfare, was introduced in November 1926, designed to boost the regular tax revenue of the province by 22 million yüan. This was a 75 percent increase over the 1924 figures. Similar increases were also imposed in Kirin province, applicable from 1927.[24] In Fengtien all taxes were raised again by 20 percent in January 1928, and again by varying amounts in May.[25] The major form of direct taxation, the land tax, was in the process subject to so many additional levies— nominally for local administration, schools, police, etc., but actually almost exclusively for military purposes—that the overall figure of approximately 8 yüan per *shang** increased gradually after 1922, and rapidly after 1926, to approximately 100 yüan per shang by 1928. Reckoned in terms of

*The size of a shang varies in the Northeast, according to locality, between 6 and 10 mou. One acre equals about 6.6 mou (Lee, p. 193, note 50).

percentages of crops, this represented an increase from between 3 and 4 percent to between 25 and 28 percent. The land tax proper accounted for only 3.7 yüan of this figure.[26] Furthermore, in certain regions the burden was considerably heightened by reason of special compulsory acquisition orders for war supplies. The large armies, 100,000 and more, which especially from 1925 on had to be sustained often in distant places, presented formidable problems of supply. These could be eased by the expedient of "living off the land," or simply grabbing everything possible from the local peasants, as in the Liao River campaign against Kuo Sung-ling in late 1925, or by forced levies on banks, chambers of commerce, or farmers. A single example of the latter is that of T'ieh-ling hsien, a comparatively rich district slightly north of Mukden, which, in the period from July to October 1927, was ordered to send to Mukden 10,000 *shih* (picul) of kao-liang, 100 carts, and 200 laborers. Such orders became increasingly typical through 1927 and 1928.[27]

Many devices were adopted in the effort to raise extra funds and supplies. The establishment of an "Opium Suppression Bureau" (Chin-yen-chü), which promptly opened a chain of opium shops throughout Fengtien province after January 1927, is another example. Through the sale of licenses for the production, sale, or consumption of opium, a sum of 10 million yüan was raised in that year. The bureau was headed by an old friend of Chang Tso-lin, and it operated independently of the regular civil government authorities, who for that reason developed a strong antipathy toward it. After his appointment to the governorship in September 1927, Liu Shang-ch'ing appears to have incurred the wrath of Chang Tso-lin for dispatching agents throughout the province to investigate the bureau's activities. After the death of Chang in June 1928, the shops run by the bureau were closed and the bureau itself reorganized in an effort to live down the bad reputation they were winning for the province. In neighboring Kirin the military governor, Chang Tso-hsiang, was strong enough to resist the idea, and consequently this particular experiment was confined to Fengtien alone.[28]

At the beginning of January 1928, as the Kuomintang's Northern Expedition was recommencing and military funds were urgently needed, Chang conferred with his advisers and decided the sum immediately required was 50 million yüan, of which 30 million should come from Fengtien and 10 million each from Kirin and Heilungkiang. A special train under armed guard was dispatched to Mukden on January 8 to bring in the cash. Since

the tax increases mentioned above could not cover such an amount, the
authorities concerned had to resort to various devices—for example, the
levy of 10 percent of the salaries of officials of the Peking–Mukden railway
line for the months of December and January.[29] The fact that the Fengtien
p'iao declined by 500 points to 2,000 in January, that the "Big Sword"
rebellion broke out in Eastern Fengtien, that strikes and bankruptcies mul-
tiplied may be attributed to the kind of fiscal violence typified by this
episode.

Public Wealth, Private Wealth

Moreover, not all moneymaking was directed to "public" or military
ends, for Chang Tso-lin and his associates took advantage of their official
status in the Three Provinces to engage in speculative ventures on a large
scale, purely in pursuit of private profit. The destructive consequences of
these manipulations of the economy, particularly in the 1926–28 period,
were enormous. In the case of Chang Tso-lin, a taste for commodity speculation seems to have been whetted early and then encouraged by Japanese
businessmen, who found it greatly to their advantage to trade advice to
Chang on when to buy and sell commodities, in return for trading and
business concessions and privileges.[30] The principal commodity concerned
was the soybean, which through most of the 1920's was the principal export item of the Three Provinces, and which in turn made the Three Provinces one of China's major export areas. The operations were carried out
either directly by the banks, in which Chang and other leading officials
invested, or by grain companies (liang-ch'ien) directly affiliated with the
banks and sometimes directly owned by generals or officials. The banks,
incidentally, far from being mere fiscal organs, were involved in virtually
any business from which profit might be extracted—pawnshops, brew-
eries, oil storage depots, flour mills, woolen mills, exchange shops, electric light companies, printing works, and gold mines, and in dealings in
coal, lumber, hides, shipping, and of course grains.[31] So far as the soybean
was concerned, the crop was harvested in the autumn, though in many
cases a deal relating to the future crop (the "green field") was concluded in
the spring or early summer, when many peasants were compelled to sell,
however cheaply, in order to buy daily necessities.[32] Once the crops were
harvested, they were purchased by the grain companies or bank agents (or
delivery taken, in the case of already pledged crops), and either sent in

bean form or processed in local mills into oil and cake for transportation south to the export market outlet in Dairen. Since the profits from transportation and exports were monopolized by the large Japanese trading companies, Chinese entrepreneurs perforce directed their attention to the phases of production and initial marketing or processing of the beans.[33]

Especially from 1926 observers noted systematic efforts being made by what might be called pure "warlord capital" to corner the market in that year's crop. The process is well described in the following:[34]

The two months of November and December are the time when the demand for Fengtien notes is at its greatest and when the gold and silver notes sold on the market reach large amounts, since the farmers in the interior have to be paid in Fengtien notes. So it is usual for the Fengtien notes to be at their strongest then. At the same time the activities of the Official Bank of the Three Eastern Provinces are also really astounding. At the height of the commodity season it issues extra Fengtien notes, with which its affiliated grain companies make forced purchases of the commodities from the local farmers; it then sells them in Dairen and deposits the silver and gold notes obtained in this way in foreign banks. Choosing the time around Autumn Harvest festival, when the current price of the Fengtien notes is at its lowest, it then sells these and again lays in Fengtien notes. In this process it takes a double profit.

The same account goes on to note that the most active grain-dealing businesses included the San-yü and the Tung-feng, the former owned by Chang Tso-lin and the latter by Chang Hsüeh-liang and some associates.[35] The volume purchased on behalf of the Official Bank is estimated to have been 22,000 cartloads, of value approximately 64.68 million in Japanese silver yen in the 1926–27 season.[36] In 1928 the bank was reported to have bought up to 11,000 cartloads of soybeans, 6,000 of wheat, and 1,000 of miscellaneous grains in "North Manchuria" alone.[37] The Official Bank was not the only one engaged in such speculative activities.

The provincial banks of Kirin and Heilungkiang provinces performed much the same role for the military elites of these provinces as did the Official Bank for Fengtien, with similarly inflationary consequences. The Kirin provincial bank developed into a large-scale entrepreneurial organization especially after 1918, all of the businesses it established including the name of the bank, Yung-heng, in their names. It too was especially involved in grain dealing.[38] A Japanese estimate made in 1932, possibly exaggerated but not necessarily by much, was that "two-thirds" of the most remunerative undertakings in Kirin province "were operated (classed as his personal property) by General Chang Tso-chang [*sic*, for Chang Tso-hsiang] or by members of his numerous family."[39] Likewise in Heilungkiang the Kuang-hsin company, as the provincial bank was known, operated a similar range of businesses. Though earlier figures are not available, it appears to have bought up 18,000 cartloads of soybeans and 2,000 of wheat in 1929, making a profit of 8 million yüan.[40]

Clearly the potential for friction between the dominant Fengtien and the subordinate Kirin and Heilungkiang groups within the faction led by Chang Tso-lin was considerable, once these banks moved into large-scale operations aimed at cornering the grain market. Through control and manipulation of the currencies in which the produce was bought, through control of the issue of credit,[41] and gradually through sheer intimidation,[42] potential rivals outside these groups could be and were frozen out, allowing them to establish dominance not only of the grain trade but of virtually all lucrative enterprises.[43] Since the friction between the separate groups within the Fengtien clique does not appear to have led to open clashes, it must be presumed that it was contained within the overall hierarchical structuring of the clique under Chang's dominance. Non-warlord concerns, however, did undoubtedly suffer from being gradually frozen out of the many profitable enterprises, among which the grain trade was foremost. Merchants affiliated with Japanese trading concerns were affected by the process as much as any and were resentful of it.[44] Thus it seems that the picture drawn by some writers about the Japanese dominance of the grain trade may be oversimplified. The proposition that "Japanese merchants underwrote Chinese grain brokers, turned them into compradores,"[45] serves to conceal a sharp contradiction that developed between warlord and Japanese-dominated financial interests in the late 1920's as the latter were frozen out at least from all lower levels of the trade. The establishment of a Chinese (albeit warlord) controlled railway network to transport this warlord-monopolized trade, and the fear that through its diversion from Dairen Japanese profits from the trade would be eliminated altogether, reinforced this contradiction in the Japanese-warlord relationship in the late 1920's.

As the pure warlord capital that was concentrated in these banking concerns developed increasingly monopolistic tendencies, the distinction between the public interests of the Fengtien clique, as represented especially by the continuing war, and the private interests of those who constituted it, became very tenuous. It is indicative of the blurring of lines between public and private concern that from 1925 the managing director of the Official

Bank of the Three Eastern Provinces (Tung-san-sheng yin-hao) was an old personal retainer of Chang Tso-lin, P'eng Hsien. From the time when Chang was mere commander of the 27th Division, P'eng had been entrusted with care of his very considerable private wealth as well as those resources controlled by him in official capacity. P'eng's relations with Chang were reported to be so close that he was regarded as one of the family. Since P'eng became in the process the reputedly wealthiest man in Liao-yang hsien, the relationship seems to have been a mutually satisfactory one.[46]

The private wealth of the major Northeastern warlords is difficult to assess. Chang Tso-lin, Chang Hsüeh-liang, Wu Chün-sheng, and Chang Tso-hsiang are thought to have amassed the largest estates, however. Chang Tso-lin was estimated to be worth about 50 million yüan, exclusive of deposits in his name in the Official Bank.[47] He owned large tracts of land in the Lien-shan Bay area and in Pei-chen and Hei-shan hsien in the North, and his business and financial interests were wide-ranging, control of the Official Bank of the Three Eastern Provinces and ownership of the Frontier Bank being central. He also either owned or had substantial investments in enterprises ranging from pawnshops and grain companies (owning those under the name "San-yü" in Mukden and Hsin-min) through coal mines, oil and flour-milling businesses, and such large-scale joint official/private concerns as the Mukden Cotton Spinning Mill, the Mukden–Hailung Railway Company, and the Northeastern Aviation Company.[48] His wealth was both cause and consequence of his power: cause in that regular payment and occasional cash handouts to his men, plus good uniforms and supply, ensured their loyalty, and consequence in that his power as dictator gave Chang license to make the rules by which the economy and politics of the Northeast should be run. For all his wealth, however, Chang was no great consumer: a simple man, he was satisfied with the services of his five wives, regular gambling and mah-jongg sessions with his cronies, an occasional opium pipe, and a few conspicuous items such as the large bulletproof Packard twin-six with its specially mounted machine guns, in which he traveled locally around Mukden.[49]

Public Poverty: The Exploited and Their Response

The cumulative effects of war and the various abuses here outlined—encouragement of opium, increased taxes and numerous other forced levies in cash or kind, and currency manipulation—were inevitably traumatic. Whereas the ruling group prudently shifted its wealth to foreign banks[50]—as safeguard against inflation or sudden reverse in the fortunes of war—the masses were caught in a vicious spiral of rising prices and worsening conditions, to which they responded with increasingly militant political activity, from strikes and demonstrations to outright rebellion in certain areas. A brief account of this general worsening of conditions serves to complement the picture of parasitical profiteering and exploitation by the ruling clique.

Table 8 illustrates the rapidity of the decline in living conditions that followed the second Fengtien-Chihli war. Taking a longer time scale and looking at prices in Mukden between 1912 and 1927, one finds a phenomenal average increase of 982 percent.[51] Wages, on the other hand, despite steep rises during the period of 1918–20, began to register a real decline in the mid-1920's.[52] It was at precisely this time that the currency began to collapse and prices soared. Some idea of the absolute decline in conditions may be gained by considering the following figures comparing the situation in February 1927 with that of 12 months later. Taking 100 as the 1927 index in all cases, by the following year labor wages had increased to an index of 339, official salaries to 358, while prices, averaging out nine daily commodities, had increased to 437.[53] The incidence of strikes, therefore, shows a marked upward swing, especially from March 1926, the graph of such incidents following closely the graph of fluctuations in the value of the Fengtien notes.[54] From the autumn of 1927, arrest and summary execution became the lot of radical labor organizers in the key sectors in the Northeast.[55] Small businesses were also reduced to dire straits by the same conditions, and this was reflected in the number of bankruptcies—400 in the city of Mukden in the first three months of 1927, for example.[56]

Conditions in the sphere of agriculture were similar—the main tendency being the accelerating class differentiation and polarization between large-scale landowners, on the one hand, and a peasantry that either was landless or possessed only minute pockets of land, on the other. A 1925 survey of 806 farm households in Shen-yang and Liao-yang hsien—that is to say, the areas adjacent to the most urbanized parts of Fengtien province—showed that 63 percent of the households were landless, while even among those possessing land 74 percent had fewer than three chōbu (approximately 7.35 acres).[57] The burden of increased taxation fell heavily on the agricultural population, and additional levies over and above the officially stipulated

TABLE 8

Price Rises in the City of Mukden, August 1924 to June 10, 1926

(August 1924 = 100)

Commodity	August 1924	December 1925	May 1926	June 1926
White rice	100	133	200	258
Glutinous rice	100	130	206	259
Kao-liang	100	115	240	240
Wheat	100	146	242	269
Barley	100	124	172	193
Millet	100	125	238	250
Soybean	100	155	255	295
Flour	100	164	300	309
Sugar	100	98	133	158
Oil	100	135	259	270
Salt	100	187	300	325
Beef	100	138	225	275
Lamb	100	150	233	275
Pork	100	156	271	291
Eggs	100	175	150	188

SOURCE: Nangō Tatsune, *Hōten-hyō to Tōsanshō no kin-yū* (Dairen, 1926), pp. 236–37.

land tax came to represent 88.7 percent of the burden of actual payment. Many of these additional taxes were simply disguised levies for war purposes.[58] Furthermore, poor and middle-income peasants suffered from the crippling rates of interest at which they had to contract loans to tide them over the summer period until crops could be harvested and sold, ranging in the villages from 40–50 percent up to 100 per cent per month.[59] Pawnshop rates were similar, and, as mentioned above, the alternative faced by the farmer in need of short-term capital in the summer was the advance sale of his crop, at between 50 and 60 percent of its actual worth, to the agents of the banks and warlord/bureaucratic/landlord cliques that bought it.[60]

The Beginnings of Resistance

While the workers' response to the deterioration in their conditions issued in a series of strikes, peasant resentment flared into open rebellion in the winter of 1927–28. With most of Chang Tso-lin's best forces tied up south of the Great Wall and local defenses much depleted, rebellion broke out in three Eastern hsien of Fengtien province—T'ung-hua, Chi-an, and Lin-chiang. Adherents of the Big Sword Society (Ta-tao-hui), declaring themselves allies of the peasants and demanding the overthrow of the tyrant Chang Tso-lin, began attacking police stations, banks, and government buildings in early January. They were quickly successful in capturing the county town of T'ung-hua and several other important towns in the area. The success of the movement was explained by the Mantetsu Research Department as follows: [61]

But while the Big Swords resisted only the Officials, they neither harmed nor plundered the common people. Yet the Army of Suppression was the epitome of oppressiveness wherever it went, so that the peasants came to respect the Big Swords and to be imbued with their spirit of resistance to the Officials, from whose exactions they had been suffering for many years. Spontaneously they made common cause with the Big Swords and the Big Swords day by day grew in strength.

When Ch'i En-ming, who was dispatched at the head of a force to deal with the Big Swords, tried the traditional tactic of simply enrolling them as government militia, whole areas began to come under their exclusive sway. When Wu Chün-sheng was ordered to take over from Ch'i in February, he therefore switched tactics and adopted a campaign of ferocious and often indiscriminate slaughter, which was gradually successful, at least in forcing the movement underground again. [62] Survivors of the rebellion later formed an important component in the partisan forces organized after 1931 to resist the Japanese invasion. [63] The Big Sword rebellion did much to heighten the atmosphere of unease and crisis in Mukden, coming at a time of raging inflation, strikes, and bankruptcies, with grave uncertainty about the war front, amid reports of strikes and resignations from the police and of whole companies of troops deserting with their weapons—presumably either to take up banditry or to throw in their lot with the Big Swords. [64]

The years 1926–28 were therefore fateful ones for the Three Eastern Provinces, years in which Chang Tso-lin's hitherto secure rear began to disintegrate under the pressure of accumulated contradictions within it, which the strains of long, expensive, and distant campaigns helped to intensify. For an understanding of these developments, it is necessary now to look at some of these campaigns and at Chang's overall China policy, since the one serves as counterpoint to the other.

MILITARY DEFEAT: IMPERIAL DREAMS EXPLODED

Chang-Wu Reconciliation and Conquest of North China

In January 1926, even as he was negotiating within the Northeast on the basis of restraint from further involvement in the affairs of China south of the Great Wall, Chang was a party also to other negotiations toward effecting a reconciliation between Wu P'ei-fu and himself as a basis for a renewed bid for national power. Despite the long enmity between them and the two wars they had fought against each other, there was no difference on fundamental principles, and there was considerable weight of circumstantial factors on both sides favoring cooperation.

In the turmoil brought on by Kuo Sung-ling's revolt, Chang had lost control over much of Chihli province (Li Ching-lin being forced to take refuge in Shantung late in December of 1925), and also over Jehol (K'an Chao-hsi being replaced there by Feng's nominee, Sung Che-yüan). But the greatly strengthened Feng was as much abhorred and as much a threat to Wu P'ei-fu as he was to Chang. Wu was nominal head of the Bandit Suppression Armies with his headquarters at Hankow, intent upon extending his power north into Honan and east into Anhwei. Both, furthermore, saw themselves as victims of Feng's double cross and were reluctant to trust him again. The feasibility of an alliance between them was first explored by subordinates in late 1925, and a general agreement was then reached the following January, according to which it was reported that "Fengtien recognized Wu's territorial base along the Yangtze valley while Wu in return pledged his support to Chang in the struggle to eliminate the Kuominchün influence from north China." [65]

The alliance is significant in that it marks the beginnings of the final coalition that was to dominate North China until mid-1928, in which individual warlords merged their differences and sought increasingly to find their ideological justification in terms of anticommunism. The immediate enemy in the North was Feng Yü-hsiang, who had after all been receiving arms from the Soviet Union, while in the South the Kuomintang also appeared deeply committed to its Soviet alliance. Feng himself, interpreting the reconciliation between Chang and Wu as well as the defeat of Kuo Sung-ling to mean a shift in the balance of forces against him, resigned all his offices in January 1926 and, after watching the course of the various campaigns the Kuominchün was involved in, left China for an extended stay in the Soviet Union, which rendered him even more liable to attack as a Red by Chang and Wu.

The advantage, as Feng appreciated, did indeed lie with Chang and Wu, although they pressed it slowly. To the south, Wu's forces succeeded in rolling back the 2d Kuominchün from Honan after a short campaign in

February and March 1926, and Wu also succeeded in establishing firm control over Hupei after the death in February of Hsiao Yao-nan. Meanwhile, to the north, the remnants of Kuo Sung-ling's rebel forces, a 10,000-man force under Wei Yi-san, the so-called "4th Kuominchün," was pushed back beyond Shan-hai-kuan by mid-January, and Sung Che-yuan's brief control over Jehol was cut short by T'ang Yü-lin after a brief but bloody campaign in February, in which one report suggests that Sung lost "about half of his men."[66]

Until late February Chang Tso-lin was involved in the fighting mainly by proxy, through his subordinates Li Ching-lin and Chang Tsung-ch'ang on the Tientsin–Pukow railway line, and through his new ally, Wu P'ei-fu, on the Peking–Hankow line. Chang was so pleased by the course of events, however, that on February 24 he summoned his top advisers to a meeting in Mukden, at which he determined upon a plan of positive involvement in the ensuing melee, and decided to entrust overall command of the armies to be dispatched to his son, Hsüeh-liang.[67] At this point Wang Yung-chiang decided to resign, believing Chang to be in breach of the understanding arrived at only a short time before not to countenance such operations south of the Great Wall again; also from this point the Fengtien currency began to decline steeply.[68]

These domestic reverses may of course have seemed inevitable temporary setbacks to Chang in the light of the advance of the allied anti-Kuominchün campaign. A general offensive, opened in the Tientsin area on March 17, soon forced the Kuominchün to withdraw to Huang-ts'un, only 40 li from Peking. At several conferences at Tientsin and Ch'in-huang-tao in late March, the allies agreed to press their campaign to Peking. They also reached rough agreement on distribution of territory in the event they accomplished their goal of dislodgement of the Kuominchün.[69] Chang Tso-lin apparently found the agreement to his satisfaction, since he is said to have stopped at Chin-chou and several other stations on his way back from Ch'in-huang-tao to Mukden in order to distribute some 200,000 yüan in cash among the officers and men of his army to encourage them in the coming struggle.[70]

The outlook for Feng Yü-hsiang, whose troops began a strategic retreat from Peking on March 28, seemed not at all bright. When Yen Hsi-shan, long proudly neutral tuchün of Shansi province, decided to throw in his lot with Chang and Wu by cutting off the retreat of Feng's forces along the Peking–Suiyuan railroad at Ta-t'ung, the Kuominchün's prospects seemed even more dismal.[71] On April 2 the bombing of Peking began. The Feng-tien air force, Chang Hsüeh-liang's special pride and responsibility, proved itself not only inaccurate but positively ineffective, and soon drew a protest from the diplomatic corps.[72] On April 7 a concerted attack was mounted by a force of 105,000 men, made up of detachments from the armies of Chang Tso-lin, Li Ching-lin, and Chang Tsung-ch'ang. Under this pressure the Kuominchün again retreated, this time to the pass at Nan-k'ou, some 30 miles to the northwest of Peking, abandoning the capital completely by April 16. As Chang and his allies prepared to move troops into the city, Chang issued this justification for the campaign: "Along with Wu [P'ei-fu] I cannot bear to sit idly watching as Feng stirs up the students, promotes communization, and plunges the people of our country into danger."[73]

Anticommunism is the most constant theme running through all the public pronouncements issued by Chang from this time on, and it was evidently the main plank of his alliance with Wu. This became apparent as their representatives met to discuss what form the new government should take, once Peking had fallen to them. Since Tuan Ch'i-jui fled after a coup against him in the last days of the Kuominchün control, and most of the cabinet also prudently disappeared at the same time, something had to be done about a government. Chang Tso-lin, no doubt with one eye on the deteriorating situation in his own territory in the Northeast, and possibly still with some hope of attracting Wang Yung-chiang out of retirement, announced first that he intended to hand over all political affairs at the center to Wu P'ei-fu, withdraw all his armies back beyond the pass at Shan-hai-kuan, and concentrate on implementing the policy of "*pao-ching an-min*" (defense of the borders, pacification of the people). Whether he did actually entertain such a plan must be doubted. But even if he did, he was bound to have strong suspicions that, if he were to implement it, Wu would simply regain the dominance in central affairs that the Chihli clique had enjoyed in 1923 and 1924 and that had been the underlying cause of the war in the autumn of 1924. Wu's attempts to have Dr. W. W. Yen (Yen Hui-ch'ing) reassume the premiership must have strengthened Chang's doubts, since it was Yen who had signed the order for the punitive expedition against Chang in 1924. Chang's reluctance to abandon a voice in central affairs must also have been conditioned by the thought of possible financial gains that might accrue as a result of tariff revision, as well as the entitlement to foreign loans that a legitimate Peking government might claim. Consequently, it took two months of protracted negotiations between representatives of the two sides before a compromise agreement could be reached. The more difficult constitutional issues, and the question of the presidency, were simply shelved. Both Wu and Chang saved face by agreeing to recognize the establishment of a Yen cabinet, which would, however, at once resign, to be replaced by a cabinet under Tu Hsi-kuei, a politically neutral admiral from Fukien, whose administration it was understood would be provisional anyway. The main point of the agreement was that the joint anti-Kuominchün campaign should continue to be pushed against the new positions at Nan-k'ou, and that other questions, including that of distribution of territory, should be set aside for the time being.[74] The agreement settled, Chang and Wu both came from their respective headquarters at Tientsin and Paoting to exchange greetings at several formal meetings on June 28. Having done so, they parted, never to meet again.[75]

Even before this agreement, hostilities against Nan-k'ou had begun, though they made little initial headway against the well-constructed fortifications prepared by the Kuominchün. On August 1, however, a second general offensive began, into which the allied forces threw something like 450,000 men, including 80,000 directly from Fengtien, plus Wu Chünsheng's cavalry, and other indirectly subordinated forces like Chang Tsung-ch'ang's Shantung Army.[76] Wu P'ei-fu's contribution, however, was plagued by instability and insubordination in his armies, and by deepening concern over the events on the Yangtze, where in the absence of Wu's main forces the Kuomintang's Northern Expedition was making dramatic advances.[77] Still, the prolonged siege inevitably wore down the Nan-k'ou defenders, and on August 14 the surviving 100,000 soldiers of the Kuominchün were given orders to retreat again, abandoning Chahar and Suiyuan and pulling back to the hinterland of Kansu and Shensi.[78]

This resolution of the Nan-k'ou struggle meant in effect that Chang Tsolin was left in sole control of North China, and stood, in a sense, at the zenith of his career. His two principal rivals had been Feng and Wu. Feng's forces, however, were beaten and exhausted, though intact, and Feng's return to China and his announcement of commitment to the Three Principles of Sun Yat-sen could do nothing in the short run to revive them. For Wu P'ei-fu, Chang's other great rival, the victory at Nan-k'ou was a particularly hollow one, since victory over Feng at the Great Wall could not compensate for the loss he sustained at the same time in his territory of Hunan, to which he had then to return. Apart from Feng and Wu, the only

other figure of consequence in North China was Sun Ch'uan-fang, overlord
of the five Southeastern provinces of Chekiang, Fukien, Kiangsu, Anhwei,
and Kiangsi, but Sun's highly ambiguous role in the North-South confrontation left him extremely vulnerable to attack and at the same time hard
pressed to find allies to help him resist it when it came. Consequently he
fought alone when the Kuomintang Armies moved against him and, after a
resounding defeat at Kiukiang on November 4, was reduced to fleeing
alone and in disguise to Tientsin to plead for aid from Chang Tso-lin.[79]

Despite the Nan-k'ou success and the eclipse of his main Northern rivals, Chang moved slowly to consolidate his position in the North, at the
same time vacillating on what to do about the threat presented by the rapid
expansion of Kuomintang power in the South. Wu and Sun fought their
decisive battles against the Kuomintang on the Yangtze alone, being either
unable because of mutual fear, suspicion, and rivalry to call for aid, from
Chang or each other, or unwilling, for the same reasons, to offer it.[80] After
several months of inactivity, the defeat of Sun Ch'uan-fang suddenly
roused the Mukden leadership to action. Summoning his main advisers and
subordinates to a conference in Mukden on November 8, 1926, Chang
decided to return again to Tientsin. Once there, the decision was soon
taken to dispatch an army south against the Kuomintang, and Chang
Tsung-ch'ang actually gathered a force of 150,000, which began to move
south on November 26. No sooner had it done so, however, than Chang
Tso-lin countermanded the order, making clear that it was not for the time
being to cross the Yangtze.

Ankuochün: Peking Policies and Government

The only positive step immediately taken was the purely formal one of
reorganizing the various Northern personal and provincial armies under a
unified central command and with a name more appropriate to national
ambitions—the Ankuochün, or "Pacify the Country Army." With the
backing of 13 provinces and three special administrative areas, Chang on
December 1 accepted the seals of office as commander in chief, and on
December 27 made his ceremonial entry into Peking, over roads sprinkled
with yellow earth in the manner of the Ch'ing emperors. Chang Tsung-
ch'ang, Sun Ch'uan-fang, Wu P'ei-fu, and Yen Hsi-shan were named deputy commanders, although Wu and Yen were not consulted and played no
significant role thereafter. Furthermore, since Wu was in no position to
exercise a voice in the Peking administration, Chang reorganized the

cabinet to remove those Wu nominees who were seen to favor Chihli too
overtly in orientation. The new cabinet set up under Wellington Koo on
January 12 included a number of "Research clique" members,* however,
thus avoiding an excessively Mukden or militarist appearance. As commander in chief of the Ankuochün (in effect military dictator), Chang based
his claim for support by the powers primarily on the fact that he was
fighting "the red peril," which was the "world's enemy" too. Chang's
headquarters were festooned with slogans such as "Overthrow Soviet
communism," "Absolutely destroy communism." [81] Apart from this opposition to communism, Chang's "policy"—gradualism in foreign affairs,
respect for the treaties, recognition of foreign loan obligations, prohibition
of anti-imperialist movements and of strike propaganda—betrayed both the
blind conservatism of the unregenerate warlord he was and the readiness to
perform the traditional "strongman" or "watchdog" role that foreign governments and interests in China expected of its ruler. [82]

Chang's views changed little during the 18 months he ruled North China
as the head of the Ankuochün coalition. This was a period of extraordinar-
ily complex fighting, intrigue, and negotiation, in the course of which the
Ankuochün displayed a growing sense of incompetence and lethargy, and a
mood of *fin de siècle* descended on Peking. In the autumn of 1927 one
observer noted that members of the governing board in Peking were spending their time in feasting and revelry, so that government offices did not
open until two or three in the afternoon, that Chang himself was engrossed
in mah-jongg, and his son, Hsüeh-liang, had become "pallid and lifeless"
from overindulgence in opium. [83] Another observer reports: "At the time
when he was threatened by formidable enemies from all directions, Marshal Chang ordered his ministers to draft regulations for weddings and fu-
nerals. Like the emperors of former dynasties, he offered sacrifices to Con-
fucius and Kuan Yü in person." [84]

The military campaign began in February 1927, as Chang decided to
send a Southern expedition through Honan province, notwithstanding the
opposition of Wu P'ei-fu. The division among Wu's subordinates between
one faction favoring cooperation with Chang Tso-lin and another advocating reconciliation with Feng Yü-hsiang allowed the Mukden forces, under
Yü Chen, to cross the Yellow River and fight their way fairly easily to

---

*The Research clique was a small, conservative, republican group, originally followers of
Liang Ch'i-ch'ao, which chose to support the Northern, warlord-backed regimes in Peking
rather than the Canton-based Kuomintang regimes after the death of Yüan Shih-k'ai in 1916.

Kaifeng and Cheng-chou (by March 15). Thereafter the Fengtien Army main units, under Chang Hsüeh-liang and Yang Yü-ting, deployed slowly south along the Peking–Hankow railway until the real battle for the province began with the Wuhan armies advancing north under T'ang Sheng-chih, while Feng Yü-hsiang approached from the West via Loyang. After heavy fighting in May, the Northerners were forced to withdraw back across the Yellow River at the beginning of June.[85] At roughly the same time another Southern army under Li Tsung-jen and Pai Ch'ung-hsi was pushing back the Chihli-Shantung forces of Li Ching-lin and Chang Tsung-ch'ang along the Tientsin–Pukow line in the East with such speed that on May 25 the newly formed Tanaka administration in Tokyo decided on the first dispatch of troops to Shantung province in defense of "Japanese lives and property."[86]

Southern Policy: Conquest or Compromise?

Paralleling this first phase of the campaign was a debate within the An-kuochün on the objectives that should be sought, and corresponding negotiations with opposing forces in search of a possible basis of settlement. In early 1927 Yang Yü-t'ing was commissioned to carry on negotiations for the Northern coalition, Li Shih-tseng for the South. Yang himself at this stage was one of the moderates in the Ankuochün, interested in exploring the possibilities of some sort of agreement between the two sides based on the Three Principles of Sun Yat-sen, or, failing actual agreement on principle, then agreement on a provisional division of the country into relatively autonomous Northern and Southern spheres. On March 10, a statement appeared over Chang Tso-lin's name proclaiming approval "in general" of the Three Principles of the People, and of the Kuomintang proposal for settlement of major questions through convening of a "national conference."[87] In April the search of the Soviet embassy in Peking by Chang's police, followed shortly by the execution of leading Communists, including Li Ta-chao, preceded by a matter of days Chiang Kai-shek's coup against the Communists in Shanghai. Yet, despite the unanimity of view that became evident in both North and South on the need to combat communism and suppress strikes and labor activity and to seek modification of the unequal treaties only through negotiation, no compromise was reached.[88] It remains somewhat of a puzzle why the coalition of Kuomintang politicians and warlords that the Northern Expedition became in the process of conquering South China was not able to reach a compromise with the Ankuochün warlords in the North. Since no real issue of principle was at stake in the fighting, one must conclude that what was at issue was consideration of face and power. After Yen Hsi-shan made his peace with the Kuomintang on June 3, 1927, thereafter accepting the position of commander in chief of the Northern Route Revolutionary Army, Yen too strove to effect a reconciliation between Chiang and Chang. As Gillin notes, the reason was "chiefly in order to forestall an invasion of Shansi by Chang's powerful armies, but also because the complete defeat of either side would leave Shansi at the mercy of the victor." The conditions put forward by Chiang, however—retirement of Chang Tso-lin, reorganization of the Ankuochün, adherence to the Three Principles of the People, and the raising of the Kuomintang flag—were too much for Chang to accept.[89]

As the prospect of compromise faded, preparations for the ultimate trial of strength went forward. On June 18, 1927, Chang assumed the office of generalissimo (ta-yüan-shuai), and the government in Peking was reorganized in the interests of much greater Northeastern and personal Chang control. Abandoning any pretence at constitutional forms, Chang became in effect dictator. His prime minister was a Shantung man, P'an Fu, who from the late Ch'ing had combined an entrepreneurial career with various governmental and semigovernmental posts. He had been finance minister from 1926, when Chang and Wu P'ei-fu jointly established their authority over Peking, and then communications minister under Wellington Koo from early in 1927. Nearly all members of the cabinet were known as followers of one or other leader of the Mukden clique.[90]

While the Northern regime thus strengthened itself by narrowing down and reducing the Ankuochün constituency to its original Northeastern core, the South, by persuading Yen Hsi-shan to raise the Kuomintang flag (June 3), by winning Feng Yü-hsiang to the Nanking cause (June 21), and then resolving the differences between Wuhan and Nanking (September), was doing the opposite.[91] As the idea of a North-South compromise began to fade in the early summer of 1927, fighting was resumed in mid-July. Again Sun Ch'uan-fang's army made its way south, capturing Hsü-chou on July 24, part of the force then moving on to attack Feng Yü-hsiang's army in Eastern Honan at Kuei-teh. While that front bogged down, however, Sun Ch'uan-fang pressed on to take Pukow and Yang-chou and to open an all-out attack across the Yangtze on Nanking. On August 26, under a heavy protective bombardment, Sun's men crossed the river. A fierce and bloody battle ensued over the following days, but Sun's force was the end of too long a supply line, with inadequate support, and consequently became sandwiched between the Nanking defenders and relief Southern armies that were quickly sent to their aid. Its communications were quickly broken, its ammunition was exhausted, and on the 31st it was forced to make a disastrous retreat across the Yangtze again. No proper shipping was available, and in the ensuing melee Sun's army was virtually destroyed, with 6,000 killed or wounded, over 10,000 captured, and another 1,500 disarmed. It was a severe blow to the Ankuochün, not only in pure military terms but in psychological terms as well,[92] sapping its confidence in its ability to operate effectively in the unfamiliar conditions of the South.

Though the *Ankuochün* thrust into Northeastern Honan province took longer to repel, since Feng was troubled by rebellions among his subordinates at the same time, it was nevertheless repelled in the autumn of 1927. Feng's forces then captured Hsü-chou on December 16, and met up with other Kuomintang forces which had fought their way directly along the Tientsin–Pukow line. The Ankuochün in the East was reduced, therefore, to concentrating on the defense of Shantung. Further Southern offensives were not seriously contemplated from this time on.[93]

In the West all attention focused on the problem of Yen Hsi-shan. As the prospects of Yen engineering a compromise between Chang Tso-lin and Chiang Kai-shek disappeared, it became necessary for the Ankuochün to set about dislodging Yen, who was commander in chief of the Kuomintang's Northern Route Army, from his Shansi base. Furthermore, before an offensive could be carried out south along the Peking–Hankow line, the Shansi problem had to be faced, since part of the line actually lay in Shansi. After several skirmishes along the borders of the province in late September, the Ankuochün-Shansi war, sometimes called the Fengtien-Shansi war, began in earnest in early October. The Shansi Army, which Gillin describes as "ill-trained and outnumbered" in this conflict, suffered a series of defeats, and made repeated overtures to the Northern Expedition to bring it relief.[94] The fall of Hsü-chou and the withdrawal of the Ankuochün on the Eastern front in mid-December greatly encouraged Yen's resistance. Since he knew that his men could hold out for a relatively long time defending their home territory and using all their familiarity with its difficult terrain, he could afford to wait for the Ankuochün; and from December 1927, he did precisely this, ignoring all Ankuochün overtures for settlement.[95]

Mukden's Collapse and Withdrawal

The final phase in the struggle, although something more than one million men were involved, over a front that stretched across much of Central China, was brief and anticlimactic. Most of the hostilities were concentrated on the three main radial lines leading to and from Peking—the Peking–Suiyuan, Peking–Hankow, and Tientsin–Pukow railway lines. On March 19 Chang Tso-lin summoned his leading advisers—Chang Tsung-ch'ang, Sun Ch'uan-fang, Chang Tso-hsiang, Yang Yü-t'ing, Chang Hsüeh-liang, and Ch'u Yü-p'u, and Prime Minister P'an Fu—and drew up plans of attack. As the orders to advance went out a few days later, Chang called together 100 of the officials working in Peking to proclaim to them the policy of "blood and iron" and resistance to the end against communism, since, as he put it, the two characters *kung-ch'an* (communism) "express all the crimes of rape, robbery, murder, and arson." Even though circumstances made it difficult for officials to be regularly paid, he therefore urged them to persevere for the sake of the country.*

When the fighting began, however, it was this very spirit of perseverance that proved to be missing in Chang's armies. War weariness, poor morale, and even outright cowardice were evident from the start. A month's fighting in Honan against units of Feng Yu-hsiang's army on the Peking–Hankow railway drained all will to fight even from the main Fengtien Armies under Chang Hsüeh-liang and Yang Yü-t'ing. Early in May the campaign was abandoned and these armies withdrawn to defensive positions in the Paoting–Te-chou area. Their collapse was no doubt influenced by news of the crumbling of the campaign on the Tientsin–Pukow line and in Western Shantung province also. After one abortive attempted offensive in the Hsü-chou direction by Sun Ch'uan-fang in mid-April, the armies in this sector fell back so quickly that by April 22 or 23 both Chang Tsung-ch'ang and Sun Ch'uan-fang were in Tsinan, and a week later in Sang-yüan on the borders of Shantung and Chihli, leaving Tsinan wide open for the triumphant entry of Chiang Kai-shek on May 2.[96] Recognizing the inevitable, Chang Tso-lin on May 9 ordered his armies to take up purely defensive

---

*Chang's continuing preoccupation with communism is curious in the light of the unequivocal position Chiang Kai-shek had taken on this matter from April 1927. It should be remembered, however, that Chang saw Feng Yü-hsiang as the main source of the Communist threat, which is partly explicable in terms of the aid that Feng received from the Soviet Union and that helped him to sustain the Kuominchün, perhaps tiding it over from what might have meant extinction at the hands of Chang's armies in 1926.

positions in the Te-chou area (1st, 2d and 7th armies under Sun Ch'uan-fang, Chang Tsung ch'ang, and Ch'u Yü-p'u), Paoting (3d and 4th armies under Chang Hsüeh-liang and Yang Yü-t'ing), and Kalgan (5th Army under Chang Tso-hsiang).[97] Finally, at a conference in Peking on May 31 the decision was made to withdraw completely to the Northeast. At 1:15 A.M. on June 3 Chang Tso-lin, together with P'an Fu and a considerable retinue of leading military and civil officials, boarded a special train bound for Mukden. The following morning at around 5:30, just outside Mukden, at the point where the Peking–Mukden tracks pass under those of the South Manchuria Railway, the train was rocked by a severe explosion.[98] Chang died soon afterward, as did Wu Chün-sheng, but since their deaths were the product not of the civil war but rather of imperialist aggression, discussion of the event is postponed until the following section.

CHANG AND THE POWERS

The West: Appeals Rejected

The earliest appeals by Chang for support and aid from the Western powers were made in the summer of 1925, and have been briefly dealt with above. Beginning in late 1926, however, he renewed his appeal on so many occasions and in terms so insistent as to seem almost obsessed by it. The economic problems of this period, in particular the need to explore every possible source of funds, are clear from the earlier section of this chapter. What is different about Chang's orientation from approximately mid-1925 is that he turned increasingly to the West, and away from Japan, as hoped-for benefactor. The realization that he could not expect greater Japanese aid than he had enjoyed in the past, when it had been of crucial importance although of limited scale, and the desire in any case to avoid too great dependence on Japan were factors lying behind these overtures. From late 1926 British diplomatic dispatches are filled with appeals from Chang, and occasionally with threats of what might happen if aid were withheld. The British management of the Kailan Mining Company was summoned before Chang in December 1926 and told that the company would be put out of business unless it came up with 20 million (Chinese) dollars to support Chang's war chest.[99] At roughly the same time Chang began to stress his case for official aid to Miles Lampson, the British Minister in Peking, suggesting that perhaps Boxer indemnity funds might be applied to his benefit, and intimating that unless he were given a sum of, say, £20 million sterling, he would have to leave Peking and return to

Mukden—implying that extremist and antiforeign campaigns could then be expected to spread quickly to the North. He also indicated that he was considering dismissing the Inspector General of Customs, which was taken to mean that he wanted funds from that source too. Since he represented himself as the last bulwark against the advance of communism in China, he became particularly aggrieved at Britain in early 1927, as signs of a modus vivendi between the British government and the nationalists began to become apparent.[100] In March 1927, he actually proposed a joint campaign by Britain, France, Poland, and his own regime against the Soviet Union, whereupon Miles Lampson reported to London: "I threw the coldest cold water on such inanity, but it does not do to tell Chang Tso-lin that he is an ass; he is apt to resent it."[101]

Yet the constant appeals for aid and cooperation that Chang made at this time appear in the end to have been fruitless. Certainly they were so far as the British government was concerned; probably likewise for the other governments concerned too. The French government made overtures to the British Foreign Office in August 1925 to have the embargo on the sale of arms to China lifted in order to meet Chang's orders for artillery, but seems not to have pressed the idea when the British opposed it.[102] British official opinion ran increasingly hostile to Chang in his last years. Sir John Pratt noted rather typically in the Foreign Office in January 29, 1927:[103]

Chang Tso-lin has been angling for British support for some time now and blandishments having failed he has now resorted to threats. We need not take either too seriously. It has long been our declared policy not to support any faction or any militarist in China. This policy is based on the principle that if a faction cannot command enough support among the Chinese themselves to establish its power in China it is very improbable that it will be able to do so—for any length of time—by means of foreign gold or foreign bayonets.

A few days later Pratt wrote: "Marshal Chang began life as a brigand, and has not changed very much. He may prove worse than the nationalists."[104]

British official policy toward Chang apparently did not change, and, though he made some favorable impression on British representatives in Peking who had to deal directly with him, such sympathies were so unorthodox that they were expressed only in private correspondence or after Chang's death.[105] Opinion in private business circles, however, remained much what it was in 1925, tending to favor Chang as an anti-Communist who would protect foreign interests and be easy to do business with. Since the Foreign Office adopted a discouraging but neutral attitude toward the

question of the activities of British commercial interests, it is difficult to
know for sure the outcome of the various projects floated in these circles
for aiding Chang, but there is no evidence to suggest that substantial aid
was ever forthcoming from private business circles.[106]

The Soviet Union: The Struggle for the Chinese Eastern Railway

Having followed the Peking government in reaching agreement with the
Soviet Union for joint control of the Chinese Eastern Railway in September
1924, Chang was slow thereafter to push his claims further. Actual control
of the railway remained in Russian hands, although several of Chang's
nominees sat on the board and the line was guarded by his troops. However, from early 1925 there were several factors predisposing Chang to
take a more positive interest in the railway and in his whole Northern frontier. As the feud with Wu P'ei-fu was resolved, Chang's political and military influence spread rapidly south toward the Yangtze, and the ideological
justification for his regime was cast increasingly in terms of militant anticommunism.[107] Furthermore, as relations between Chang and Feng Yü-
hsiang, the two nominal backers of the Peking government, deteriorated,
and as their strength was consolidated into discrete and hostile blocs of
provinces in the Northeast and Northwest, respectively, Feng's Kuominchün became the recipient of Soviet aid, arms, and advisers, and Chang
was enraged at what he saw as Soviet interference to bolster his one remaining powerful North Chinese rival.

From 1925, therefore, Chang began to apply pressure to the Russians.
For one thing, he decided to push ahead, with Japanese aid, on the construction of a railway between T'ao-nan and Ang-ang-ch'i.* T'ao-nan was
from October 1923 the terminus of a 194-mile spur leading into the Northwest from Ssu-p'ing-chieh on the South Manchuria Railway.[108] The extension was to take the line another 140 miles up to Ang-ang-ch'i, just
south of the tracks of the Chinese Eastern Railway. It would thus compete
with the Chinese Eastern for transport of freight from the developing
grainlands of the North. It was also a potential Japanese military threat in
that it would provide easy potential access to the North over standard-
gauge tracks for Japanese troop trains.[109] The Russians were very conscious of the threat, and even the London *Times* described the line as "a
challenge to the Russian position in North Manchuria, politically as well as

*On the railway matters discussed here and subsequently, see the railway map on p. 219.

economically."[110] Chang actually agreed on the construction of the line
with Matsuoka Yōsuke for the South Manchuria Railway Company on
September 3, 1924, but further developments were delayed by the war and
the greatly changed political situation that developed from it. Preliminary
construction work was begun in March 1925, and all Russian expressions
of concern, through the Foreign Ministry in Moscow, the Ambassador in
Tokyo, and Ambassador Leo Karakhan in Peking, were ignored. The line
was completed in April 1926, and began regular operations in October.
The question of its extension across the Chinese Eastern to the capital of
Heilungkiang province, Tsitsihar, then arose, and the Russians, whose
consent was necessary, at first refused it. However, when Wu Chün-sheng,
tuchün of the province, insisted the line would be built anyway, the
Russians eventually, in August 1927, relented, agreeing to the connection
to Tsitsihar by means of a viaduct over the Chinese Eastern Railway.
Though from the Russian perspective this line, built with Japanese funds,
was a Japanese commercial and potentially military threat, it must be said
that it developed in fact into a major segment of the Chinese network,
feeding, via Chinese-built connections, not to the South Manchuria Railway, but to the Peking–Mukden line at Ta-hu-shan, and thus not strengthening but rivaling the Japanese South Manchuria Railway system (see
below).[111] Although there is no direct evidence that the Chinese authorities
consciously planned to use the Japanese to their own ends in this way, a
strong inference to that effect may be drawn from the general thrust of railway planning from around 1923.

The significance of the pattern of railway linkages that ensued was thus
different according to the perspective of the viewer: to the Japanese, the
important thing was the development of the link from Ssu-p'ing-chieh to
Tsitsihar via T'ao-nan and Ang-ang-ch'i; to the Chinese, on the other hand,
it was the link from Ta-hu-shan to Tsitsihar via Cheng-chia-t'un, T'ao-nan,
and Ang-ang-ch'i; and to the Russians what was important was the weakening of the Chinese Eastern Railway monopoly on freight from the Northern
districts, whether the goods were carried south on Japanese or Chinese
railways being of little concern. When it began to appear that Chang was
moving toward complete recovery of the Chinese Eastern Railway, Russian concern understandably deepened further. Evidence that he was doing
so gradually accumulated.

In May 1925, the Soviet manager of the railroad, Ivanov, attempted to

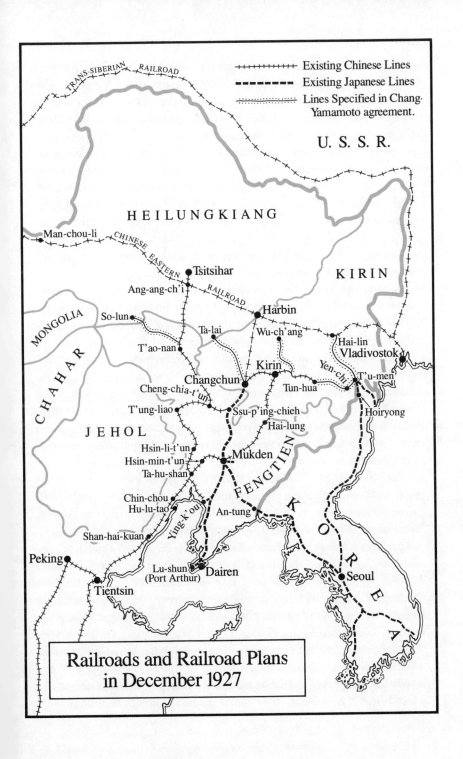

++++++++++	Existing Chinese Lines
- - - - - - -	Existing Japanese Lines
:::::::::::::	Lines Specified in Chang-Yamamoto agreement.

TRANS-SIBERIAN RAILROAD

U. S. S. R.

HEILUNGKIANG

Man-chou-li

CHINESE EASTERN

KIRIN

Tsitsihar

Ang-ang-ch'i

RAILROAD

So-lun

Harbin

Ta-lai

Wu-ch'ang

Hai-lin
Vladivostok

T'ao-nan

MONGOLIA

Kirin

Yen-chi

T'u-men

CHAHAR

Changchun

Tun-hua

Cheng-chia-t'un

Hoiryong

T'ung-liao

Ssu-p'ing-chieh

JEHOL

Hai-lung

Hsin-li-t'un
Hsin-min-t'un
Ta-hu-shan

Mukden

FENGTIEN

Chin-chou
Hu-lu-tao

An-tung

K
O
R
E
A

Shan-hai-kuan

Ying-k'ou

Peking

Lu-shun
(Port Arthur) Dairen

Seoul

Tientsin

**Railroads and Railroad Plans
in December 1927**

interpret the provision of the 1924 agreements that only Chinese and Russians were to be employed on the line to exclude White Russians, who were citizens of neither country. Chang protested strongly, sent troops to Harbin to back up his protest, and Ivanov was forced to back down.[112] The issue was left to be settled by the conference, which, according to the 1924 agreement, should have met within six months in order to make final disposition of all railway matters. However, when this conference met eventually in Peking on August 16, 1925, it disbanded again almost immediately without actually resolving anything.[113] Shortly afterward, when Chang was under severe pressure from the collapse of his positions in the Southeast and from the rebellion of Kuo Sung-ling, which occurred on November 23, the Soviet manager began to apply counterpressure against his Chinese partners in the railway.

On November 10, before the Kuo rebellion but at a time when Chang was hard pressed by Feng Yü-hsiang's Kuominchün and attempting to retreat in orderly fashion from positions in Anhwei and Kiangsu, Ivanov gave notice that from December 1 advance payment would be required for Chinese troops or railway guards requiring transport on the railway.[114] At a Harbin meeting of the board of directors on November 30, the Chinese members protested and Ivanov temporarily stayed his hand. He made no further move while the crisis over Kuo lasted, an important restraint, since Kuo's action was based on an agreement with the Soviet-sided Kuominchün.[115] On January 16, however, rather than transport 3,000 Chinese railway guards, who declined to pay in advance, he suspended all traffic on the Harbin–Changchun section of the line. On January 22 he and three of his Russian colleagues on the directorate were arrested on orders from Chang. The line was placed under complete Chinese military control, with the co-opted assistance of White Russian technical experts.

The Soviet response was immediate. Ambassador Leo Karakhan protested and, on the day after Ivanov's arrest, issued a three-day ultimatum demanding his release and the restoration of normal service on the railway. On January 25, just before the ultimatum expired, Chang capitulated.[116] Having done so, however, he continued to show no interest in a comprehensive negotiated settlement of the railway question. The underlying difficulty was in fact as much financial as political: the Soviet side insisted that its interest in the line was economic and financial, a legacy of the investment in money and labor by the Russian people under the czars, which it would not relinquish without due consideration; Chang, however, was loath to provide any such consideration, particularly at a time when he was squeezing every possible source of revenue to raise funds for military purposes. A Sino-Russian conference to discuss the railway issue met a second time in December 1925, but again disbanded fruitlessly. After being forced to back down in the course of the Ivanov affair in January 1926, Chang set about piecemeal recovery of the railway on his own terms.

In February and March of 1926, through Chang Huan-hsiang, who was military governor of the Chinese Eastern Railway zone and commander of the railway guards, he ordered all municipal assemblies along the railway, including the Harbin municipal assembly, which had been entirely Russian, to adopt Chinese as the official language. When they were slow to comply, he dissolved them and set up new and exclusively Chinese councils in their stead. He also closed the land department of the railway, and instituted new proceedings for the registration of real estate and real estate dealing, which had the effect of weakening the Chinese Eastern's claims to its extensive land holdings. In August he commandeered the Sungari and Amur River fleets belonging to the railway, together with wharves and warehouses, to a total value of 14 million (Chinese) dollars. The education system was also taken over, on the grounds that it had been used for the dissemination of Communist propaganda.[117]

This amounted in sum to a wide-ranging attack on the Soviet stake in the North. Coupled with the reverses suffered by the Soviet-aided Kuominchün early in 1926, it gave rise to fears on the Soviet side that Chang as a Japanese cats-paw was softening their position preparatory to some kind of renewed Japanese offensive. In the early months of 1926 both the Comintern[118] and the Politburo were deeply concerned. A special commission of Far Eastern affairs, set up under Trotsky to report to the Politburo, presented a special resolution, which was accordingly adopted on March 25. Its keynote was appeasement in order to prevent the formation of an imperialist united front. E. H. Carr summarizes the resolution as follows: "Japan must be conciliated by recognizing *de facto* Japanese control over South Manchuria *'for the immediate future.'* The autonomy of Manchuria under Chang Tso-lin, though it could not be recognized in theory, must be accepted in practice in return for an agreement by him not to move against the south." (Carr's italics.)[119]

Ivanov, the Soviet manager who had so offended the Chinese in January, was withdrawn from his post and replaced in April 1926; Karakhan, despite the demand for his withdrawal, remained until the following year but maintained a low profile; and a special mission under the Deputy People's Commissar for Communications, L. Serebryakov, was sent to placate Chang. After discussion with Chang in Mukden late in April, Serebryakov went on to Tokyo in May, and it was later announced that "a satisfactory agreement" had been reached on "the principles to be maintained by both governments in the question of the economic development of Manchuria" as well as on technical railway matters.[120]

Despite the efforts at appeasement by the Soviets, which were extended in 1927 to accommodation on the question of the profits of the Chinese Eastern—a sharing arrangement that meant in its first year a considerable 8.5 million yüan each[121]—the problems implicit in its unresolved status remained, and were exacerbated by Chang's ideological stance of militant anticommunism. The Soviet Union in fact maintained a conciliatory policy in the Northeast despite the constant erosion of its position, until 1929, when Chang Hsüeh-liang attempted once again to effect complete recovery of the line. Only then, beyond the time span now under consideration, did the long-simmering differences erupt in to a full-scale diplomatic crisis.

One last point that should be noted about the Chinese campaign over the Chinese Eastern Railway from 1925 is that, although the Japanese could not but be sympathetic to its antibolshevism, and attempted to play on it to gain consent to their plans for expansion into the North and the CER sphere, satisfaction on that score was combined with unease that from the Chinese perspective the resolution of the Chinese Eastern question would open the way to a full-scale reconsideration of the status of the South Manchuria Railway.

Chang and the Japanese Connection: Account Rendered

Chang's ambition versus the Japanese interest. By 1926 the Japanese stake in the Northeast was considerable, and expectations for the future were correspondingly great. In the industrial sector, the amount of Japanese capital invested was probably already dominant (see Introduction). The largest Japanese enterprise, the South Manchuria Railway Company, wielded enormous power, its profits amounting in the mid-1920's to more than three times the entire government revenues of Fengtien province (see above, p. 174). As the p'iao began to weaken steadily against the Japanese yen thereafter, the company grew even stronger. Increasingly Chang was seen as Japan's man, a "clerk in the branch office," and as owing a considerable debt of gratitude to Japan for the many times he had been bailed out of trouble largely by Japanese aid and intervention.[122] Yet there were many ways in which the Japanese government and business were dissatisfied with the slowness of their expansion and penetration, and there was also a constant nagging fear that Japan's "special position" was highly vulnerable, precisely because it had become inextricably linked with the fate of Chang himself. This sense of insecurity reflected doubts that the 1915 treaties, on which technically much of the Japanese position in the Northeast rested, would be unenforceable because of the duress under which they were negotiated, against a Chinese administration more powerful and more nationalistically inclined, or with less reason to favor Japan's requests than Chang's.

As Chang began to move, in early 1926, toward reinvolvement in the affairs of China south of the Great Wall, there was therefore Japanese concern on two grounds: that the strains of war would prove damaging to the economy of the Three Provinces, a fear well enough grounded, as the first section of this chapter demonstrates; and that war would lead to Chang's defeat and the installation of an administration that might be hostile to the continuation of Japan's special interests there, a fear equally reasonable, in view of the policies proclaimed by the Kuomintang and the rapid expansion of the area under its control from mid-1926. It was in late August 1926, after the successes of the Fengtien Armies at Nan-k'ou and after the first triumphs of the Northern Expeditionary Armies, seriously jeopardizing Wu P'ei-fu's Central China base, that the Japanese authorities began once again to put pressure on Chang to withdraw to the Northeast. Through Japanese military channels Chang was strongly advised to adopt Wang Yung-chiang's "*pao-ching an-min*" policy, while at the same time being given clear intimation that he might expect generous Japanese assistance in carrying out urgently needed reforms in finances and internal affairs and in pursuing a development program if he agreed.[123] Chang not only did not comply with the suggestion but proceeded gradually to tighten his hold over the administration in Peking, resorting meanwhile to draconian methods to arrest the collapse of the Fengtien currency. In mid-September, as a result, the chief Japanese officials, concerned at the deteriorating economic situation in the Northeast, held an emergency meeting in Dairen to discuss what should be done. The Kwantung governor, the president of the South Manchuria Railway Company, the commander in chief of the Kwantung Army, and the Mukden consul general took part. After a protest by Yoshida Shigeru, then consul general in Mukden, against Mukden re-

strictions on the exchanges and the attempted imposition of an artificially
fixed exchange rate, which proved unavailing, further Japanese consultations were conducted in October in an attempt to unify the line followed by
all Japanese agencies concerned with developments in the Northeast.
Thereafter, at successive meetings with Chang, Yoshida continued to press
him to revert to the theme of the "Greater Three Eastern Provinces," for
which again Japanese aid and support were promised.

But the increased Japanese pressure was counterproductive. A greatly
irritated Chang refused any concessions to Yoshida, and negotiations between the two were cut short when Chang, on November 8, made the
fateful decision to shift his headquarters to Tientsin, whence he soon
moved to Peking.[124] He neither returned to Mukden nor met with Yoshida
again.

Needless to say, these altercations in Mukden were the reflection of the
deep and continuing search for a satisfactory Northeastern policy conducted not only in China itself but at the highest civil and military levels in
Tokyo. Although the War Office was responsible for issuing the warning to
Chang, already mentioned, the Foreign Ministry was working on a detailed
plan for the reform of the Northeast that might be put to Chang, at the same
time approaching Japanese financiers to see what loan funds might be made
available to him should he accept it. In many respects this plan was identical to the one that Wang Yung-chiang had represented in the debate with
Chang six months earlier: a constitution for the Three Eastern Provinces,
division of civil and military affairs, establishment of a systematic budget
and a central bank, and the setting up of Japanese commercial ports along
the railways.[125] Only the final point distinguishes this plan from Wang's.

It was not only that Chang spurned these overtures for disengagement
and return to the Northeast, with the continuing deterioration in the
economy of the region that resulted, that upset the Japanese. Their patience
was also growing short at the lack of progress in talks on long-standing
differences with Chang over Japanese treaty rights and railway ambitions.
There was a strong feeling in Japanese quarters that he had a debt of
gratitude to Japan that he should repay by adopting a more cooperative
stand on these matters. When the outlook for Chang had been bleakest in
early December 1925, Yang Yü-t'ing had gone to Port Arthur and Dairen
to appeal for Japanese aid, promising as quid pro quo precisely the concessions Japan most wanted, including recognition of the Japanese right to
reside in, and presumably also to do business in, the interior, and also to

construct the railways it had been pressing for.[126] Whether any such agreement was formally reached as a condition for Japanese intervention on Chang's behalf is not clear; but it is clear that the belief on the Japanese side that Chang Tso-lin was "insincere" in his dealings with them was greatly strengthened from this time, as were the voices favoring adoption of a stronger line in dealing with him.

Anatomy of a special relationship: greed and seduction. As this mutual hardening of attitudes developed in late 1926, the Japanese found it no longer possible to get things done in their accustomed way. These ways had been many and varied, broadly typical of the kind of semicolonial relationship that existed between Japan and Northeast China, and as such worthy of a brief digression. By their very nature many of these channels of communication were secret or semisecret, and must therefore be pieced together from partial and sometimes indirect evidence. They included, however, the use of spies and informers, bribery, cajolery, and threat. Furthermore, since the execution of Japanese policy was in the hands of a cumbersome four-part administration (consuls, South Manchuria Railway, Kwantung government, and Kwantung Army)/ Each of which had developed different traditions, different procedures, and to some extent different ideas about the goals of Japanese policy, the possibilities of confusion were considerable. Some examples of the kind of unofficial diplomacy paralleling the official may illustrate the point.

The case of the Chi-Hui railway (from Kirin to Hoiryong),* which Japan wanted to build as a link between its Korean network at Hoiryong and Kirin city, there connecting with lines running to Changchun and up into Heilungkiang province, is instructive. The railway had a double importance for Japan, as opening a route of major significance both economically and militarily from the Japanese mainland across Korea, its colony, and direct into the region it saw as "North Manchuria." Such a line, it was anticipated, would play as great a role in integrating the economy of that region with Japan's as had the South Manchuria Railway in the South, while at the same time its strategic value was highly appreciated by both the Japanese Army and Navy, the former seeing it as opening a route ideal for a military thrust against the Soviet Union and hoping for its continuation eventually right to Inner Mongolia, and the latter seeing it as facilitating the rapid supply of grain to Japan that would be necessary in the event of a clash with the United States.[127] The line was one of those for which

---

Hoiryong in Chinese is read *Hui-ning* and in Japanese *Kainei*.

unsecured loans were advanced through the Japanese financier Nishihara Kamezō in 1918—10 million yen in this case—but it developed into a major bone of contention between the two countries, since the Chinese side consistently refused to agree to its construction; and it was not in fact completed until Japan eliminated the opposition and established the puppet state of Manchukuo. The line passed through many vicissitudes in the meantime.

In 1920, after the Japanese had persuaded Chang Tso-lin to dismiss from the governorship of Kirin a man they suspected of being pro-American (see p. 41), they succeeded in installing as Commissioner of Foreign Affairs for the province a man who acted, in effect, as a secret Japanese agent. He was Hsieh Chieh-shih, a Taiwanese who had studied and taught in Japan for a number of years in the late Ch'ing, and who later had worked as an associate of the reactionary monarchist Chang Hsün. His services as a proponent of Japanese interests, and as a source of inside information on Chinese official thinking, were so great that the then Japanese consul general in Kirin intimated he would be rewarded from funds made available by joint Sino-Japanese enterprises. He was, in short, bought.[128] By 1924, however, Chinese opposition to the line still remained strong, especially in the Kirin Provincial Assembly. Consequently, representatives of the South Manchuria Railway, working through local Japanese businessmen, tried to influence the Assembly in their favor.[129] The methods employed in this case were left unstated, but the presumption that bribery was again employed is strong. In 1925, Matsuoka Yōsuke, as a Mantetsu director, met with Chang Tso-lin in May to press him strongly on the issue, but Chang would not yield. However, in October, a loan agreement for 18 million yen relating to the section of the line between Kirin and Tun-hua, halfway to the Korean border, was signed in Peking by Matsuoka and Chinese Communications Minister Yeh Kung-ch'o upon the express instructions of Chang.[130] At the time, Chang's freshly established control over the Southeastern provinces of Kiangsu and Anhwei was under threat from Sun Ch'uan-fang, while relations with Feng Yü-hsiang in the Northwest were also close to rupture. Above all, Chang wanted funds for his war chest, and this agreement seems to have been effected by the payment of a substantial bribe to Chang from Mantetsu.[131] The agreement itself was kept secret and only divulged when the papers relating to it were found in the offices of the Communications Ministry by Yeh's successor in the next cabinet.[132] Subsequently the construction contract for this section of the line was given to a joint Sino-Japanese company, the Tung-ya t'u-mu (Tōa Dobuku, or East Asia Engineering Company), in which the majority of shares were held by Mantetsu, the remainder by Chinese officials, and the president of the company was none other than Chang's friend and adviser, Machino Takema.[133] The possibilities for continued graft in such an arrangement were obvious.

When the question of completion of the line by its extension across the border to Hoiryong came to be considered again early in 1927, the consul general at Chien-tao advised Tokyo that substantial bribes to Chang Tso-lin and Chang Tso-hsiang (military governor of Kirin province) would be necessary again, but was mildly critical of the way Mantetsu had gone about distributing its largesse in the past, spending "enormous sums in bribes" in Mukden, while not paying out enough in Kirin. He went on to make the significant observation, "Since for many years Mantetsu has been paying substantial bribes to Mukden officials . . . it would be very difficult for any organ other than Mantetsu to try afresh to make any progress on the railway question in Manchuria."[134] The same point was made in a paper prepared in May 1927 for presentation to the Eastern Conference in Tokyo the following month. Amau Eiji was the newly appointed first secretary of the Japanese Ministry in Peking and familiar at first hand with conditions in the Northeast from his service as consul general at Harbin. In discussing the various outstanding issues between Japan and China, Amau said:[135]

There is no prospect of solving these difficulties by ordinary diplomatic means. Either we use our power to coerce the other side, or we use its greed to seduce it. There is no other way. Looking at negotiations up until now in various parts of China, we see that the solution of crucial issues has always been accompanied by the use of force or the exercise of bribery in one form or another. Examples of this are especially numerous in the Three Eastern Provinces. In negotiations carried on by Mantetsu over the past 20 years, bribery has been especially effective.

Mantetsu's role in arranging the crucial bribe to Feng Yü-hsiang in late 1924 is another example (see above, p. 132). A further example that occurs in negotiations between Chang and Mantetsu President Yamamoto in late 1927 is dealt with below.

By their very nature, however, most of these shady deals have left no record. To ignore this aspect of the relationship would be, nevertheless, to convey a very misleading, one-dimensional impression of foreign relations. The high-handed use of corruption by the Japanese to suit their own imperialist ends, together with the cynical and contemptuous attitude toward Chinese officials that it engendered, were important factors in the development of the Sino-Japanese conflict. The contempt was heightened from 1926 by the fact that the established methods described here no longer seemed to be working, in turn a product of several main factors: a decline in the economy and the developing crisis that threatened Chang's rule—and therefore the basis of Japan's position in the Northeast—internally; Chang's deepening involvement in civil wars that threatened Japan exter-nally; and the rise of a powerful Chinese nationalism which Chang and the Chinese authorities in the Northeast could certainly not afford to ignore, even though, as the Japanese suspected, they may have used it often to their own, not necessarily nationalistic ends. Matsuoka Yōsuke, the main person responsible for top-level Mantetsu negotiations in China from the time of his appointment to the directorate in 1921 until his resignation in 1926, spoke frankly at a meeting in the Ministry of Foreign Affairs on November 19, 1926, of a breakdown in the channels of communication with the Mukden leadership. Though making no direct reference to the use of bribery, he described the approach to Chang Tso-lin as the alternating of a severe Japanese line, mediated through the consul general in Mukden, then Yoshida Shigeru, and a conciliatory line, either through the Mantetsu Mukden office chief, Kamata Yasuke, or through Chang's Japanese adviser and personal favorite, Machino Takema. But when he came to consider why this established two-track approach to Chang should no longer be working, Matsuoka was able to suggest only that some personal antipathy between Machino and Okura Kimmochi, also a Mantetsu direc-tor, might be responsible.* The underlying causes were beyond his com-prehension.

Efforts to break the logjam of unsettled issues with Chang were inten-sified through 1927, but while the hard line was pushed more and more aggressively through Yoshida Shigeru, the soft line was neglected, and Machino, in particular, came under suspicion among the Japanese au-

---

*"Mantetsu kanbu to Hōten kanken to no kankei" (Relations between Mantetsu manage-ment and Fengtien officials), conversation between Matsuoka Yōsuke and Kimura Eiichi, head of the Asian Bureau of the Foreign Ministry, November 19, 1926, JFMA PVM 23, pp. 4–15. Matsuoka's high evaluation, on this occasion, of Machino's relationship with Chang Tso-lin is notable. He was of the impression that Chang discussed all important matters with Machino, trusted him completely, and was on such intimate terms with him that Machino could, on occasion, yell at Chang, berating him for his misdeeds. Since otherwise Chang seemed to open his heart only in the company of long-established comrades who had been with him from his bandit days, this special relationship with Machino, which Matsuoka en-deavored to use when negotiating with Chang, was remarkable.

thorities because he was thought to have gone too far in identifying himself with Chang, and indeed to have become more Chinese than Japanese. Yoshida, on the other hand, developed an arrogance and contempt for the Chinese he was dealing with that drastically reduced his effectiveness as a negotiator, and that inclined him toward more high-handed and unilateralist military actions by Japan in pursuit of its goals.[136] Yang Yü-t'ing described Yoshida as behaving as though China were a "vassal state."[137]

Matters in dispute. Before we consider the course of Japan's effort to get its way, it is necessary to set out briefly the issues it was pressing. Withdrawal from the civil war in China, administrative and fiscal reform, recognition of Japan's rights under the Sino-Japanese ("21 Demands") Treaties of 1915 to reside, do business, lease land, etc., in the interior of the Northeast have already been mentioned. The other, more specific and immediate issues may be grouped under those concerning railways, taxes, and miscellaneous matters.

Matters of dispute concerning railways fell into two categories: cases of Japanese protest against Chinese construction or projected construction of lines, on the one hand, and cases where the Japanese side claimed entitlement to construct lines, based on treaties, prior agreements, or loans already advanced, on the other.* In this railway issue, particularly in cases of the former kind, the clash between Japan's ambition to retain Northeast China as an economically subjugated region, with the economic arteries— the railways—under its exclusive control, clashed most frontally with the Chinese ambition to establish a transport network under Chinese control.

No independently financed and controlled Chinese railroad (from 1905 this meant no non-Japanese-financed railroad) was built in the Northeast until 1922. In the winter of that year work was begun under the auspices of the provincial government on a 253-kilometer line stretching from Ta-hu-shan on the Peking–Mukden line northwest to T'ung-liao, a town on the Inner Mongolian frontier of Fengtien also known by its Mongolian name, Pai-yin-t'ai-lai. The section to Hsin-li-tun was completed in 1925, and the entire line in October 1927.[138] Its construction aroused grave concern among the Japanese. There already existed a railway built with Japanese loan funds from Ssu-p'ing-chieh on the South Manchuria line via T'ao-nan northwest to Ang-ang-ch'i on the Nonni River just south of the Chinese Eastern Railway, with a branch line also connecting T'ung-liao direct to

*For railway details, consult map on p. 219.

Ssu-p'ing-chieh. These had been designed as feeder lines to attract freight from this developing area to the South Manchuria Railway, and thence to export outlets via completely Japanese-controlled facilities at Dairen. The completion of the new Chinese line, however, made it possible that, contrary to all expectation, the Japanese feeder lines might become feeder lines into a Chinese network, since such a network now existed from Ang-ang-ch'i in the Northwest right to Peking or to the projected Chinese port on the Gulf of Chihli at Hu-lu-tao.[139] The construction of the line itself, and then the connection at T'ung-liao, was therefore protested vigorously and on every possible occasion by Japan from August 1926, but despite some delay on the Chinese side, through traffic was operating by December 1928, making what a Japanese writer described as "a perfect western trunk line system parallel to the South Manchuria Railway."[140] The Japanese protest was based on a protocol alleged to have been attached to the 1915 Sino-Japanese treaties in which China recognized the transfer to Japan of former Russian railway rights in the Northeast. This protocol was said to have precluded the Chinese from constructing railways "in the neighbourhood of or parallel to" the South Manchuria Railway or "any branch line which might be detrimental to the interests of it."[141]

To the east of the South Manchuria Railway, as to the west, a new, purely Chinese network was developed from the mid-1920's. Construction was begun in July 1925 on a 319-kilometer line from Mukden to Hai-lung and, with its completion in the summer of 1927, on a 183-kilometer extension from Hai-lung to Kirin city. When this was completed late in 1928, it established the link between the two provincial capitals that had been the goal of civilian officials in the area from at least 1923.[142] From November 1926, repeated Japanese protests to the construction of this line were based also on the "no parallel lines" protocol, as well as on the terms of various railway agreements between China and Japan in 1913 and 1918.[143] In pressing ahead with the construction, however, the Chinese side chose to ignore such protests.

Into the second disputed category—in which the Japanese claimed entitlement to construct lines in accordance with existing treaties, agreements, or loans—fell first and foremost the Kirin–Tun-hua–Hoiryong route linking Kirin province direct to Korea, a line that has already been discussed above. Second, and as a westward extension of the same line, was the Changchun–T'ao-nan route, since Changchun and Kirin were already linked. This was one of the five lines the Chinese government in 1913 agreed that Japan should be entitled to build, and it was also one of four lines for which a preliminary agreement was signed in September 1918 and a Japanese advance of 20 million yen handed over as part of the Nishihara loans. In practice, as Japanese pressure for some resolution of disputed railway and other issues intensified in 1927 and 1928, the Japanese side concentrated on the section of the line between Changchun and Ta-lai.[144] It is significant that these two lines, together with almost all the others pressed by Japan at this time, cut a swathe across Kirin province from the Korean border to Inner Mongolia through some of the richest lands in the entire Northeast, and it is no coincidence that Kirin became the center of the fiercest and most widespread anti-Japanese movement as a result.

As for matters of dispute concerning taxes, after the breakup of the Tariff Conference in Peking in the summer of 1926, the Canton government of the Kuomintang unilaterally began collecting the 2.5 percent import surtax that the conference had been unable to agree on. Chang's administration in the North, after calling in October 1926 for the extensive revision of its relationship with Japan under the 1896 commercial treaty, implying that that treaty might be renounced if it could not be renegotiated on better terms,[145] went on to follow the Southern example by beginning to collect the import surtaxes in March 1927. Japanese officials in the Northeast protested repeatedly at what they saw as a violation of the treaties, but they had little alternative but to pay the sums demanded while continuing to protest strongly against them.[146]

Miscellaneous matters of dispute were many and varied. One relatively important one was the banning of the *Sheng-ching shih-pao*. This was a Japanese-owned, Chinese-language paper published in Mukden. It was also the largest-circulation Chinese-language newspaper in the province, and it had already demonstrated once before its antipathy to the Chinese authorities in Mukden (see above, p. 99). An order banning it was suddenly issued by the Chinese authorities on June 10, 1927, on grounds of its having slandered the Fengtien military.[147] Since the paper was believed to be an organ for the expression of the views of Japanese Consul General Yoshida,[148] the episode may be seen as part of a many-sided confrontation between Yoshida and the Mukden authorities. It developed into a prolonged and extremely bitter dispute.

Another important dispute was the problem of the establishment of a Japanese subconsulate at Mao-erh-shan. Mao-erh-shan, also known as Lin-chiang, was a town on the Chinese side of the Yalu River with a population at this time of some 30,000 Koreans in the area. In March 1927, Japan proposed that a subbranch of its An-tung consulate be established there, and in mid-April the vice-consul-designate arrived at the town on the Korean side of the river and sought a meeting with the magistrate of Lin-chiang hsien to discuss arrangements. The request for an interview was several times refused and eventually, on May 29, the assistant consul and his retinue crossed the river anyway. Very quickly a storm of opposition developed against the Japanese in which the buildings designated as the Japanese office were destroyed and the assistant consul and his party driven from the town and forced to flee back across the river. Although it was clear that local police and officials were party to these happenings, if not actually instigators of it, Japanese protests went unheeded in Mukden and Peking.[149]

Developing through the course of all of these issues and the negotiations over them is the element that surfaces most starkly in the Mao-erh-shan affair—that of anti-Japanese, nationalist sentiment, fueled and fanned by the resentment of Japanese power and dominance of the Northeast and of the evident Japanese ambition to extend that power, and above all aroused by the belief that the much trumpeted "positive" diplomacy of the new Japanese Premier, Tanaka Giichi (from April 1927), constituted an acute threat to China. The growth of this movement in the latter part of 1927, with the Japanese complaint that it was officially sponsored and demand that it be absolutely suppressed, came in itself to constitute a major issue between the two countries.

The Tanaka cabinet: a fresh look at the problems. In April 1927 the government of Wakatsuki Reijirō fell, and with it ended Shidehara's three years at the Ministry of Foreign Affairs. The China issue was not the immediate cause of the government's downfall, but heavy criticism of the "negativeness" of Japanese policy in the face of the rising nationalist and anti-imperialist movement in China contributed substantially to the climate in which the changes occurred. The formation of a new government was entrusted to Tanaka Giichi, who, though an army general and leading figure in the Chōshū clique with which the Japanese army had been identified since the time of the Meiji Restoration in 1868, was also president of the Seiyūkai. As such, from 1925, he had been most vocal in denunciation of Shidehara's China policy. With the establishment of his government there was, therefore an increasing backlog of vexing issues on which there was a diminishing inclination to compromise, together with an assumption on the Japanese side that failure to progress in the negotiations with China was due in large measure to the spineless and vacillating way in which the previous administration had conducted them.

Yoshida Shigeru in Mukden offered the first specific advice to the new cabinet on how the many outstanding issues should be dealt with. As soon as the new cabinet had been installed, he wrote a letter to the chief of the Asian Bureau of the Foreign Ministry, stressing the following points:[150]

1. It is desirable that the preservation of the peace in Manchuria, whether inside the railway zone or not, should be entrusted to our forces wherever they can be deployed.

2. It is desirable that any strikes instigated by the Southern army or by the Soviets taking advantage of the unease in economic circles and the collapse of the Fengtien p'iao should be strictly suppressed by our authorities.

3. It is desirable that our Manchurian administration should be implemented through the strength of the empire, in whatever circumstances and setting aside all petty stratagems. We should not have to rely on Chang or Yang or Wang to get things done.

4. The important points in our Manchurian administration should be railway and fiscal policy for the Three Eastern Provinces. In this area we should attempt to implement the following two measures: to work out a substantial plan for the currency system and to think out a system whereby the Japanese, Russian, and Chinese railways in the Three Eastern Provinces might be linked up as one unit.

This appears to have been the first serious recommendation from a senior Japanese official, civil or military, for an effective takeover of Northeast China—for there is no doubt that Japan's assumption of responsibility for preserving the peace, suppressing strikes, compelling various "reforms," and coordinating all railways was a formula for such a takeover.[151] The implementing of such a plan clearly called for the use of Japanese military force, though Yoshida no doubt believed the threat alone would be sufficient. Yoshida, though he had been long in office under Shidehara, was well attuned to the positive mood of the new cabinet. His prescription was actually a good deal in advance of the thinking of Tanaka and his immediate associates, as Tanaka's first instructions on China policy, issued on May 20 to Minister Yoshizawa in Peking, indicate. There, Tanaka was content to issue the very general prescription that Chang Tso-lin should be "made to abandon his outdated ideas" and to concentrate on the Three Eastern Provinces and on the suppression of communism there.[152] Tanaka refrained from making any decisions about the means of realizing such a goal pending the gathering in Tokyo of all the senior officials concerned with China policy, the gathering known as the Eastern Conference, which did not meet until June 26. In other words, for three months after his accession, he made no major departures from the policy of his predecessor so far as the Northeastern question was concerned.

After the collapse of Chang Tso-lin's attempt in May 1927 to push south on two fronts against Feng Yü-hsiang and the Kuomintang, however, Tanaka had to give serious consideration to the options open to him in the event of continued failure by the Ankuochün and the continued advance of its enemies. His detailed inquiries of Yoshizawa and Yoshida on this count have been discussed at length elsewhere and need only be summarized here. Yoshizawa believed that Japan had to continue to work through Chang Tso-lin, even if he had to withdraw in defeat to the Northeast. Provided he withdrew without fighting and concentrated on reform, however, Yoshizawa recommended that Japan persuade the Kuomintang to desist from attacking him there. Yoshida, whose personal antipathy to Chang has already been discussed, was less committed to seeing Japan's interests served through him. He thought any government that would protect and guarantee Japan's interests would be acceptable. Furthermore, lest those interests be prejudiced by the prosecution of a North-South war into the area, he recommended certain preventive steps: denial of the use of the Peking–Mukden railway to the Chinese military; exclusion of Chinese soldiers from an area within 20 li of Tientsin; and even temporary Japanese occupation of main points along the Chinese railways in the Northeast. As Iriye points out, the dilemma that arose for Japan at this point was "whether Japanese rights should be considered genuine economic rights, without political implications, or whether they should be linked with China's civil war so as to induce Chang Tso-lin to accept them in return for certain favours." [153]

The Eastern Conference met in Tokyo from June 26 to July 7. [154] Before that, however, there were some signs of stabilization within Chang's regime. On June 18 Chang became Ta-yüan-shuai or Generalissimo, sometimes known as Grand Marshal, and the P'an Fu cabinet was installed. Thereafter Chang was in effect in dictatorial control of North China. June was also a month in which there were various overtures toward a peaceful compromise settlement between North and South, and the possibility of a clash between the Nanking, Wuhan, and Feng Yü-hsiang forces disrupting the Southern advance seemed quite real. Consequently, the rather wild proposals that had been coming from Yoshida and some of the military were moderated when the actual conference met. Though Yoshida continued to insist that the goodwill of Chang's administration should be irrelevant to the prosecution of the Japanese case—since that case rested on treaty rights enforceable against any Chinese regime in power in the Three Eastern Provinces, whether Chang or not—he conceded that the area concerned was, after all, Chinese territory, and that Chinese sovereignty should be preserved and force avoided in bringing the Chinese to see the propriety of the Japanese position.[155] The principal document before the conference relating to the problem of the Northeast was one prepared by the Asian Bureau of the Foreign Ministry entitled "On Solving the Problem of Political Stabilization in Manchuria and Mongolia."[156] It too was a rather modest document, and its proposals were further cut down in the course of the conference, so that in the end it was decided to set aside all other issues for the time being in order to concentrate on solving the various questions connected with railways. Other Japanese treaty rights, matters of economic and fiscal reform, were shelved.

However, apart from its specific decisions, there were several themes running through the Eastern Conference, and some decisions on principle that emerged from it were of considerable moment in determining the subsequent course of events. Above all, it was unanimously assumed by all, and clearly stated by several including Tanaka himself, that Northeast China ("Manchuria") was to be treated differently from the rest of the country, whether because of the special rights and interests accruing specifically to Japan under the treaties, or because of the more intangible factor of the sacrifices Japan had made in the region during the war with Russia, or because of its importance to Japan's defense. The assumption was not new, and indeed it was shared by Shidehara as the justification for the various interventions in China's affairs that have been discussed in earlier chapters. However, the political developments in China were reaching a point where such interventions were less and less likely to be accomplished with the discretion and the immunity that Shidehara enjoyed. Tanaka's direct approach, his determination to get quick results, and his abhorrence of compromise on matters of principle greatly enhanced the possibilities of clash and the likelihood that the Japanese case could in the end only be made by force of arms. In the statement that he issued at the close of the conference, and that was then published with the exception of one clause, the following sections dealing with "Manchuria and Mongolia" are a pungent expression of the sentiments that guided Tanaka:[157]

6. Manchuria and Mongolia, especially the Three Eastern Provinces, have vital relations with Japan from the viewpoint of our national defense and national existence. Our country not only must be especially concerned with the area but also has a *duty and a responsibility*, as a neighbouring country, to make the area a happy tranquil land for foreigners and natives alike by maintaining peace and developing the economy.

7. If an influential leader of the Three Eastern Provinces respects our *special position* in Manchuria and Mongolia and sincerely makes efforts to stabilise the same area, our government should support him with appropriate means. (This section not to be made public.)

8. If it is anticipated that the upheaval will spread to Manchuria and Mongolia, public peace and order will be disturbed, and our *special position* as well as our rights and interests will be violated, we must be prepared to take immediate and appropriate means to protect the area and to maintain it as a peaceful land for development by both natives and foreigners.

It is not surprising that widespread reports of this conference and of Tanaka's views, not to mention the rumored presentation by Tanaka to the emperor of a "Memorial" on July 25, advocating Japanese occupation of Northeast China and gradual invasion of the rest of the country,[158] aroused widespread attention in China and fanned the flames of anti-Japanese sentiment into an increasingly active campaign.

Several weeks after the conference ended, Yoshida received definite instructions from Tokyo on how negotiations with Governor Mo in Mukden (in the absence of Chang Tso-lin in Peking) should be conducted.[159] To induce Chang to be amenable to the Japanese demands, Yoshida was told he might offer provisional acceptance of the 2.5 percent import duty surcharge, which was already being levied anyway, as a carrot, while hinting also at a big stick, in the form of possible refusal of transport of military goods on the South Manchuria Railway, refusal of the supply of coal and other raw materials to the arsenal, refusal of passage of military trains along the Peking–Mukden railway across the point where its lines intersected with those of the South Manchuria, and finally withdrawal of cooperation by all Japanese organs in the area. The specific railway construction demands that he put to Mo were for the Kirin–Hoiryong and Changchun–Ta-lai lines, a line to the Hsin-ch'iu coalfields, which Japan had high hopes of opening, and others that, however, might be withdrawn depending on the overall progress of the negotiations.

On July 23, 1927, Yoshida called on Governor Mo to press the Japanese demands and hint at the sanctions if they were not met. By August 2 no satisfactory response was forthcoming, so Yoshida sought authority from Tokyo to go ahead with the closure of the Peking–Mukden line to military trains at the crossing with the South Manchuria line. Two days later he warned Mo that this closure might take effect on August 7. Quite on his own initiative he also began planning, with a high-ranking Kwantung Army staff officer, Colonel Kōmoto Daisaku, and with the army's special service agent in Mukden, the steps necessary to provide military backing to the threat. His taking of such drastic steps was beyond his authority, though it is true he was told on July 20 that he might hint at them. His going beyond the hint to the reality was something that clearly Tanaka had not bargained for, and though Yoshida had already issued the order on August 4, he was much embarrassed to receive word on August 5 that, whereas the hint was acceptable, the threat was not to be carried out. The execution of Yoshida's threat was not only vetoed in Tokyo but also strongly opposed on practical grounds as well as on those of principle, by senior officials of the Kwantung Army, Kwantung government, and South Manchuria Railway, as well as by the acting ambassador and military attaché in Peking. However, as on the earlier occasion (see above, p. 179), Yoshida's plain excess of his authority in a matter that might have had serious consequences indeed went once again unremarked.[160] Tanaka was as little concerned with such infractions as was Shidehara.

However, at this time Chang's Ankuochün was heavily involved in crucial battles with the Kuomintang in Central China and could not afford to ignore the threat of a major Sino-Japanese incident arising in Mukden. Further intensive diplomatic exchanges produced a *démarche* on August 10, with Yang Yü-t'ing indicating in Peking acceptance of the Japanese position on the railway questions, plus a readiness to discuss the other disputed questions, including that of the Mao-erh-shan consulate.[161] He did so, however, not to a Japanese official but merely to the representative in Peking of the Okura *zaibatsu*. Chang personally confirmed the concession, though attaching to it the condition of a 10 million yen loan on the security of his own personal property, which presumably he wanted Okura to negotiate for him. The Okura representative was urged to proceed at once to Mukden and win Yoshida over to Chang's new position.[162]

At this time, of course, Chang was investigating every conceivable source of funds to sustain his war effort. It is notable that such an indirect approach was adopted by the Chinese side on this occasion, a reflection of

the distaste felt for Yoshida and of the hostility that had built up between
Yoshida and Governor Mo, the two negotiating principals in Mukden to
this point. Henceforth both sides decided the negotiations should be shifted
to Peking. In view of subsequent events, it is also likely that the Chinese
were temporizing to gain relief from the pressure on them rather than indicating actual readiness to submit to the Japanese terms. Thus, although the
negotiations were shifted to Peking, they were greatly complicated by the
anti-Japanese movement that began to develop at the same time, with such
speed and, initially at least, such freedom from restraint that the implication of official backing seemed inescapable. Tanaka's "positive" diplomacy, as mediated through Yoshida, turned out to be merely tough pos-
turing, and the stimulus it gave to the development of this nationalist
movement proved to be its greatest lasting consequence.

The new anti-Japanese movement: sponsorship in high places? Anti-
Japanese sentiments had been strong in the Northeast before, but, save for
a brief period in the spring and summer of 1924, repression had always
kept them from developing into an organized movement. The wide publicity given the Eastern Conference, and the particular importance attached
there to the achievement of Japan's demands in the Northeast, greatly excited this fear and antipathy toward Japan, but with the difference that,
from August of 1927, a well-organized movement developed, openly
backed by the highest levels of business and by important political
figures—something quite unprecedented in Japan's experience there. Less
than a month after the conference disbanded, and while the Mukden
negotiations were approaching a climax—two days before Yoshida's ultimatum to the governor—an "Association for Backing Diplomacy" was
formed within the Fengtien Provincial Assembly, and within a few days
similar associations were also formed within the Educational Association
and the General Chamber of Commerce.[163] When the new organization
within the Provincial Assembly declared its objective to be "to resist violent oppression by foreigners," there was not much doubt about which
foreigners were meant.[164] On September 4 this association sponsored a
kuo-min ta-hui or mass assembly of citizens, which took the form of a
demonstration with a march from the Provincial Assembly buildings
through the city to the governor's offices. Japanese estimates of participants ranged from 6,900 to 20,000. The demonstrators shouted anti-
Japanese sentiments and carried banners and flags inscribed with slogans
such as "Down with imperialism," "Down with the Tanaka cabinet,"

"Down with Manchuria-Mongolia-ism," and "Resist the Japanese construction of a consulate at Lin-chiang." After dispersing, they broke up into groups to carry on lecturing and propaganda activity throughout the city.[165] From the Chamber of Commerce it was reported that notices were being sent out to Chinese firms advising that Japanese goods should be boycotted.[166]

Naturally the Japanese suspected promotion at the highest levels, i.e. by Chang Tso-lin himself. Since Chang had suppressed all anti-Japanese movements to this time—in 1919, 1923, 1925, for example—this suspicion would seem to have been well-founded. Furthermore, the authorities of the Provincial Assembly, Chamber of Commerce, etc., that sponsored the demonstration were men highly unlikely to take such drastic action unless they had a clear understanding that Chang was unlikely to oppose it. On September 7, therefore, Yoshizawa told Chang that it was clear his officials were behind the outburst, blaming Governor Mo especially, and demanded that it be suppressed.[167] To appease Japan, Chang then ordered that a second round of demonstrations planned for September 10 and 11 be forbidden under penalty of the firing squad.[168] The Japanese remained far from satisfied that this was sufficient, however. In T'ao-nan on September 14 another large-scale demonstration took place outside the offices of the South Manchuria Railway Company, participants variously estimated at 4,500 to 12,000.[169] Thereafter such large-scale, open demonstrations were not repeated, but anti-Japanese feeling was reported to be intensifying in Fu-shun, T'ieh-ling, An-shan, Changchun, Harbin, and Pen-ch'i-hu, and it was believed that officials in the Northeast had been secretly instructed from Peking that, whereas the large demonstration was to be suppressed, the movement itself should be sustained. Because of it, Chang's bargaining hand would be strengthened, since the nonimplementation of key Japanese demands could be excused as impossible, however desirable because of the strength of public feeling, even though Chang was doing all in his power to suppress that feeling.[170]

It was a dangerous game for Chang Tso-lin, if in fact he did play it like this. Since he had allowed no political freedoms before, it was not to be expected that the freedom to be anti-Japanese could be suddenly allowed and yet restrained from developing into other political demands. The possible hornet's nest that was being stirred up became clear when, on the eve of the second planned Mukden demonstration, handbills were found calling for the overthrow of Chang and an end to warlordism.[171] Second, of course, he ran the risk that the Japanese would see through his ploy—if it was such—and that his position, if once he came to be believed anti-Japanese, would be difficult indeed. For the time being, Chang satisfied the Japanese authorities sufficiently by his order forbidding demonstrations, by his dispatch of Yang Yü-t'ing to Mukden on September 20, 1927, to remonstrate with business and local political leaders, and by ordering the replacement of Mo Te-hui, by then not only the principal object of Japanese resentment but also much out of favor with Chang himself, by Liu Shang ch'ing, whose reputation with the Japanese was thus far unsullied. Mo became Minister of Agriculture and Industry in Peking.[172] A characteristically extreme appeal from Yoshida that Japanese troops be used to put down the movement was rejected in Tokyo, and Tanaka determined to push ahead with negotiations with Chang in Peking.[173]

That the problem had not been solved, however, became clear in November 1927, when a controversy arose over a proposed 30 million dollar loan from the National City Bank of New York and J. P. Morgan and Company to the South Manchuria Railway Company. Negotiations had progressed close to the point of signature when they were made public. Much of the proposed loan was to be used for the purpose of buying more rolling stock and heavier rails and for the development of the company's collieries and other installations.[174] On November 23 a group of Chinese financiers and business leaders cabled to Washington their opposition to the loan on the grounds that the company was an "imperialistic Japanese political and economic instrument."[175] The Nanking government also opposed the loan.[176] So, too, however, did Yang Yü-t'ing, who was one of Chang Tso-lin's closest advisers. In an interview with the press on November 29, he declared that "the Japanese exploitation of Manchuria had gone far enough, and if the United States countenanced an extension of the process by providing financial assistance the hostility of the Chinese would be aroused against the American people. American capital would be welcomed in Manchuria, but not American capital invested so as to strengthen Japan's hold over Manchuria."[177] Soon afterward the Provincial Assemblies of the Three Eastern Provinces joined in sending a cable to President Coolidge asking him to use his influence to prevent floating of the loan.[178] The negotiations were halted and the loan was not floated. That Chang was engaged in a complicated game in which the role of Japanese puppet was less and less palatable to him was clear from a statement by Chang himself in October 1927, in which he went so far as to say that "there [is] no possibility of an extension of Japanese railroad interests, via the Chinese Eastern Railroad, from Changchun to Harbin or any other extension of Japanese railroad interests in Manchuria . . . you may read in the papers some morning that the Japanese control Manchuria, but I control Manchuria."[179]

The expression of sentiments such as these by Chang and Yang seemed to indicate a hardening of position on their part and added strength to the suspicion that the anti-Japanese movement was indeed being secretly promoted by them to suit their own ends. The alternative theory—that they were merely protecting themselves against attack as Japanese puppets, and remained, despite such public statements, strongly pro-Japanese—became more difficult to sustain. On the day following Yang's widely reported remarks, Yoshizawa wrote him a private letter asking him what he meant by them, and Honjō Shigeru, then military attaché in Peking, called on Chang to discuss the situation. The replies were far from reassuring to the Japanese. Chang complained that it was Japan's responsibility he was being frustrated by attacks from the South in his ambition to become "emperor with Japan's support," while Yang explained that, since the position of the Mukden clique was weakening in Peking, the railway questions could only be dealt with by secret and irregular methods—neither of which replies actually met the question. Yang resisted later Japanese pressure to correct press accounts of his remarks.[180]

The first Chang-Yamamoto agreement. Talks with Chang were resumed in Peking in late August by Minister Yoshizawa, but suspended again on September 9 on instructions from Tanaka as a protest against the anti-Japanese outbursts.[181] However, a second, secret channel of negotiations, which had also been set in motion in August, was not suspended. This was between the newly appointed president of the South Manchuria Railway Company, Yamamoto Jōtarō, a close associate of Tanaka and former chief secretary of the Seiyūkai, and Chang.[182] The negotiations had been opened in August on Yamamoto's behalf by Etō Toyoji, then resident in Peking as a director of the Sino-Japanese Corporation. They were carried on in such secrecy that even Yoshizawa did not know of them until afterward. Recalling his part in the negotiations 43 years later, Etō was emphatic about the attitude of determined opposition to the Japanese plans on the part not only of Chang Tso-lin himself but of all his closest aides, and of Yang Yü-t'ing in particular. The use of veiled threat eventually induced Chang to soften his position: the threat that if Chang did not cooperate, the Japanese military would aid his enemy, Chiang Kai-shek.[183] Japanese hostility—even, as Chang well knew, the withdrawal of the kind of support he had enjoyed in the past from Japan—would make his position absolutely untenable. Thus, when Yamamoto arrived in Peking on October 8, he found a surprisingly complaisant Chang and soon drew up for his signature a set of remarkably comprehensive documents purporting to constitute not only a resolution of the railway issues but also a general political agreement covering the future of the Northeast.[184] In this Chang was to accept Japan's rights to maintain order in the Three Provinces and to agree to open the entire Northeast, including Mongolia, to foreign residents, with rights to own land, engage in business, and freely export whatever was manufactured or produced. Japanese rights were to remain intact within the South Manchuria Railway zone, but otherwise the provisions of the 1915 ("21 Demands") treaties concerning the area were to lapse, though all other relevant Sino-Japanese treaties were to continue in operation. The railways that the agreement stipulated should be built by the Japanese under loan agreements were T'ao-nan to So-lun, Tun-hua to T'u-men, Changchun to Ta-lai, Kirin to Wu-ch'ang, and Yen-chi to Hai-lin.* As Iriye comments:[185]

The second of these was a section of the Kirin–Kainei [Hoiryong] line which the Foreign Ministry had most wanted built. The third had also been on Tokyo's priority list. The fourth and the fifth had not been contemplated either by the Foreign Ministry or at the Eastern Conference, and the first was the very line the Foreign Ministry had strongly opposed as unduly irritating to the Soviet Union because of its proximity to the Siberian border. Yamamoto had thus caused Chang Tso-lin to make a contract which was out of accord with the policies and directives carefully framed by officials of the Tokyo government.

But was it actually a settlement, a "contract" as Iriye describes it? Chang appears not even to have signed it, despite being repeatedly urged to do so by Etō and Machino, the two Japanese closest to him.[186] It appears that Chang initially gave Yamamoto the impression that he was agreeable to all its terms, but after doing so he was confronted by fierce opposition from Yang Yü-t'ing, and after considerable discussion with him decided simply to write the character yüeh (read) on the draft, giving as excuse for not signing the opposition both among the people at large and among members of the government.[187] He had been given a 5 million yen bribe to

*For the location of these projected lines in relation to existing Chinese and Japanese lines, see map, p. 219. Why Yen-chi–Hai-lin and not T'u-men–Hai-lin is not clear.

help buy the opposition within his government, but that appears not to have been sufficient.[188] He had also asked for liquidation of his debt of 2.4 million yen to the South Manchuria Railway Company, money the company had advanced him in 1924 at a time when he needed ready cash urgently during the second Fengtien-Chihli war in order to bribe Feng Yü-hsiang.[189] The record is not clear on how this request was received. Yet for all the money that he had his company advance in the effort to buy consent to Japanese ambitions, Yamamoto got no more than an agreement of very ambiguous status, certainly much less than a treaty or even a contract. Furthermore, though the terms were more sweeping and decisive than anything contemplated at the Eastern Conference in June–July, several major issues were not touched upon—the Mao-erh-shan consulate and the 2.5 percent import duty surcharge, for example. But even if these qualifications on the status or the content of the agreement could be overcome, there still remained grave doubt on what value it represented to Japan. Publication or attempted execution of it would be likely to have provoked crises at several levels. In the first place, Chang would have faced possible rebellion in the Northeast and greatly stepped up anti-Japanese activity there. Machino had advised Tanaka he thought this a likely outcome even when he heard only of the railway proposals on talking to Tanaka before the Eastern Conference.[190] Second, Chiang Kai-shek could scarcely have ignored an agreement whose effect was to reduce Northeast China to effective colonial status. Thus there was a strong possibility it would have sparked a new crisis in Japan's relations with him were it known. The reported American loan to the South Manchuria Railway Company pales in significance beside this agreement, and yet it drew a sharp protest from Nanking.

These considerations, which seemed likely to restrain Japan from publication or implementation of the agreement, may therefore have weighed with Chang in persuading him to give it his agreement, in however attenuated a form. The threats that the Japanese negotiators used were also something he could ill afford to ignore at a time when the renewal of hostilities against the South was expected at any time.[191] Chang may also have hoped that quick settlement of these issues might open the way for Japanese aid in his Southern campaign. It is also possible, however, that Chang could see the writing on the wall about the future of his Southern campaign and preferred the role of a Japanese-sponsored quisling in the Northeast to absolute defeat.

That the Chang-Yamamoto agreement was not implemented was due in the end not to any initiative on Chang's part but to the fierce opposition it aroused among Foreign Ministry bureaucrats jealous of their privileges and highly indignant at being totally by-passed in the negotiations.[192] Tanaka himself was surprised at the scope of the agreement, and on October 18, just three days after it had been signed, he ordered Yoshizawa to take the documents back from Chang. However, there was widespread concern at this action in the South Manchuria Railway Company, in military circles in China, and in the Foreign Ministry as well. By October 20 Yoshizawa too was having second thoughts about his protest against the procedure employed in the negotiations and thought better of sacrificing the tremendous gains the agreement represented. Tanaka, on receipt of this opinion from Yoshizawa, instructed him to try to get Chang to put the agreement on a formal basis by having him write to him (Yoshizawa) expressing his intention to regard the agreement as the basis for a formal settlement of the railway issues. Chang, possibly relishing the evidence of confusion in Japan, took his time in replying, and when he did so wrote to Tanaka rather than Yoshizawa. However, since all the railways concerned lay in Kirin province, he told Yoshizawa that the negotiations should be carried on henceforth with the authorities there, particularly Chang Tso-hsiang.[193] This was evidently a device to further prolong the negotiations, since Kirin was known to be the locus of the strongest anti-Japanese feeling.[194] It was, in sum, a poor conclusion to the six months of intensive diplomatic activity on the part of the Tanaka cabinet: suspicion and hostility toward Japan were gradually magnified, Chang and other leading officials were antagonized, and confusion and division in the Japanese chain of command were exposed, while from Chang nothing was conceded in the end beyond a willingness to continue negotiating.

Japanese approaches to Chiang Kai-shek. The resumption of the Northern Expedition in December and the early indications that it might proceed quickly to a decisive victory made this inconclusive situation all the more vexing to Japan. Negotiations were resumed on January 8, 1928, mainly in Peking, but were soon stalemated as Yang, Chang Yin-huai, heading the Communications Committee of the Three Eastern Provinces, and Chang Tso-hsiang conceded nothing, pleading as their reason the opposition of government, Provincial Assemblies, and commercial circles.[195]

However, as the eventual outlook for Chang in the civil war became gloomier, Japan began to turn its attention to Chiang Kai-shek to see what sort of understanding could be reached with him about Japan's rights and interests in the Northeast. Since the assumption that the Three Eastern Provinces ("Manchuria") being quite distinct from "China proper" had long been a basic component of Japanese thinking, both civilian and military, under Shidehara as under Tanaka, negotiations with Chiang focused not on substantive issues there but on persuading him to adopt a similar view, excluding the Northeast from the projected unification. Tanaka met in Tokyo on November 5 with Chiang, who promised to give consideration to Japan's special position there, and in early January he received the agreement of Chiang's aide, Chang Ch'ün, not to pursue Chang Tso-lin into the Northeast if Japan could persuade him to withdraw there.[196] It had always been an object of Japanese policy to dissuade Chang from involvement in affairs south of the Great Wall, but since advice to this effect was being ignored by Chang, in late March of 1928 Yoshizawa wrote to Tanaka advising that the time had come to decide whether to take strict measures with Chang at once or else wait until the power of the Mukden clique was shaken.[197]

Yoshida Shigeru, who by this time was back in the Foreign Ministry in Tokyo, having been succeeded in Mukden by Hayashi Kyūjirō, was again an advocate of strict measures at once. In line with his proposals, the Ministry began to work on the text of the message that should be sent to Chang. On March 10, Arita, the new head of the Asian Bureau, produced a draft, in which Japan's demands were to be backed by sanctions ranging from withdrawal of advisers and instructors, through withdrawal of the Ministry from Peking, to build-up of troops in the railway zone, occupation of the Fengtien arsenal, and the halting of military trains on the Peking–Mukden line at the crossing point with the South Manchuria line.[198] The warning—perhaps ultimatum better describes it—was stayed for the time being, however, and attention was diverted to Shantung, to which a second Japanese troop dispatch was authorized by the cabinet on April 18, leading to the Tsinan Incident shortly afterward, on May 3.[199] Japanese actions in Shantung, while ostensibly in defense of Japanese residents there, also had the objective of blocking the spread of "disturbances" to Peking and the Northeast. Tanaka's authorizing these troops movements, and in effect backing the arrogant and autonomous behavior of his field commanders, was not inconsistent with the understanding he had arrived at with Chiang

Kai-shek and Chang Ch'ün, since he saw his support for the Kuomintang as predicated on the exclusion of the Northeast from its jurisdiction.[200] Since the Southern Armies simply deflected their advance on Peking around Shantung province in order to avoid further altercations with the Japanese, the question of compelling Chang's withdrawal to the Northeast became urgent.

Chang Tso-lin's withdrawal: Tanaka and the uses of ambiguity. Chang, however, had taken heart at the Japanese involvement in Shantung, interpreting it as a sign of readiness to back him. On May 7 he finally reached agreement with Yamamoto on the various disputed railway matters that had been in abeyance since the previous November, and over the following week he signed contracts relating to four of them: Yen-chi to Hai-lin, T'ao-nan to So-lun, Tun-hua to T'u-men, and Changchun to Ta-lai, work to be commenced within three months.

It was a bitter surprise for Chang, having concluded these agreements, to be told by Yoshizawa, who called to see him in the middle of the night of May 17–18, that he must either retreat to the Northeast at once or face the prospect of his forces being disarmed at Shan-hai-kuan by the Japanese Army if he left later.[201] The Japanese cabinet the previous day had decided that both Chang and Chiang Kai-shek should be warned that, in the event of the war spreading into the Peking-Tientsin district and threatening the peace and order of the Northeast, the Japanese government might be constrained to take "appropriate and effective steps" to maintain peace and order in "Manchuria."[202] Spelling out just what this meant in his instructions to Yoshizawa, Tanaka wrote that, should the fighting spread to the Peking-Tientsin area, Japanese forces would prevent soldiers of either side crossing through Shan-hai-kuan with their weapons. Yoshizawa was to do his utmost to persuade Chang to withdraw immediately, on the understanding that he might take his armies with him intact if he were to do so. Consul General Yada in Shanghai, in communicating the same warning to the nationalist authorities in Shanghai, was to stress that, once the Northern Armies withdrew beyond Shan-hai-kuan, there would be no question of their returning.[203] Furthermore, despite the appearance of neutrality about Japanese concern for the peace and order of the Northeast, the cabinet made it clear on May 18 that, because of the disturbed conditions prevailing in the Northeast and the widespread opposition to Chang Tso-lin, it was desirable that the Northern Armies return intact and with strength sufficient to cope with any disorders that might ensue. Japanese commanders in the field were therefore to use their discretion about how such a result was to be achieved.[204]

Chang had many times been advised to abandon his ambitions toward China south of the Wall and had always hitherto been able to ignore such advice.[205] This time, however, he pleaded in vain that he was the last bastion against China's going Red, and within a matter of days of his second meeting with Yoshizawa, on May 19 he decided he had no alternative but to accept the Japanese advice.[206] He had, in fact, no alternative, since, apart from the Japanese ultimatum, the will to fight had gone out of his armies and his senior commanders all favored retreat. By May 23 his decision to comply with the Japanese advice was made clear to the Japanese, and it was ratified a week later by a conference of the principal commanders of the Ankuochün.[207]

The final question to be resolved was whether he should be allowed to withdraw with his armies in good order and intact or not. The Japanese government position seemed clear from both the published warning and the instructions dispatched to its principal representatives in China: so long as disturbances had not spread to the Peking-Tientsin area by the time Chang made his retreat to the Northeast, he should be allowed to do so with his armies intact; if he waited until the war spread to North China, Japan would have to disarm his forces before allowing them to cross Shan-hai-kuan. Yet on this important question Tanaka allowed a distinct ambiguity. Kwantung army commanders were strongly in favor of disarming Chang's forces at Shan-hai-kuan regardless of the state of the war at the time. Suzuki Sōroku, general chief of staff, accepted their position and, in discussion with Tanaka on May 20, seems to have succeeded in extracting the promise from him that an order to that effect would be transmitted the following day, once authorization was received from the emperor.[208]

Not surprisingly, this caused considerable excitement in the Kwantung Army, since execution of such an order could be expected to lead to a crisis whose only conceivable outcome was Japanese military conquest of the Northeast, not to speak of what it might mean for relations with the Kuomintang government. Kwantung Army command, which by May 18 had already moved its headquarters to Mukden and begun concentrating its troops there ready for dispatch along the Peking–Mukden railway to Shan-hai-kuan, was thus expecting orders to move south on May 21. Such orders did not materialize. Kwantung Army authorities realized there was a discrepancy between their understanding of Tanaka's position and the

Foreign Ministry representative's understanding of it when they compared notes with consular officials on the night of the 20th. As Tanaka continued to procrastinate, insisting up to May 31 that the time had not yet come to move the Japanese troops south to Shan-hai-kuan, the Kwantung Army, seeing that Chang's retreat was imminent, took the initiative independently.[209]

Muraoka Chōtarō, commander-in-chief of the Kwantung Army, made secret approaches to the commander of Japan's North China garrison army to have Chang Tso-lin assassinated before his return. When Muraoka's staff officer, Colonel Kōmoto Daisaku, learned of this, he thought he could do better by arranging the murder in the Northeast in such a way as to foment the immediate crisis that, it was hoped would allow a Japanese military takeover as a result.[210] The plotting and execution of the deed were relatively simple matters and involved only a small number of officers, plus a regiment of engineers recently arrived from Korea who helped in supplying, placing, and detonating the explosives. Chang made no secret of his departure from Peking, and the conspirators had no difficulty in identifying the train's single luxury compartment, in which Chang, together with Wu Chün-sheng and a Japanese adviser, Major Giga, were traveling. The explosion occurred at 5:30 A.M. as the train passed beneath the South Manchuria Railway lines just outside Mukden. Chang died a few hours later, Wu outliving him only by a matter of days. The Japanese, Giga, escaped with only minor injuries.[211]

Kōmoto's initiative failed to achieve its main purpose—that had to wait upon another explosion, on the South Manchuria Railway line more than three years later, on September 18, 1931. Indeed, under all the circumstances, Kōmoto's action was singularly counterproductive, since not only did it not lead to the resolution of any of the issues disputed between China and Japan, on which Chang Tso-lin just before his death appeared to have made major concessions, but it led very soon to the establishment of the Chang Hsüeh-liang regime, which, by making its peace with Chiang Kai-shek's nationalist government at Nanking, realized the worst dreams of both Kōmoto and Japanese Premier Tanaka. It was an action, therefore, rich in ironies: concerning Chang, whose life had been spared by Tanaka 23 years previously, that it should be taken now as the culminating incident in the era of "positive diplomacy" toward China inaugurated by the same Tanaka; for the South Manchuria Railway Company, whose railway development plans had just been agreed on with Chang after prolonged negotiations, that the plans should now be shattered as a result of Kōmoto's initiative, since the agreement with Chang was a purely personal one of highly dubious legality and would have to be broached again afresh with his successors; and for Tanaka himself, since Kōmoto committed the most decisive positive act of his ministry, although Tanaka did not actually take the initiative save in a negative and ambiguous way.

Conclusions

For most of the second and third decades of this century Chang Tso-lin dominated Northeast China, and was a figure of major importance to China as a whole. Yet he has been little studied, and even after perusing all the known available evidence in the effort to reconstruct his life and career, it has to be admitted that he remains a shadowy and enigmatic figure. He was a self-made, unlettered man, and Confucian influences on his formation were minimal, both because of his family and class background and because of the frontier society into which he was born. Yet, ensconced in his last years in the imperial palace in Peking, he allowed or encouraged the growth of an imperial cult around his person, and while his armies were collapsing, he occupied himself with empty rituals. He was certainly a stranger to the currents of modernity flowing from the West—science, democracy, and nationalism—and he was fiercely hostile to communism; yet nationalism and anti-imperialism at least were sentiments frequently voiced by spokesmen for the Fengtien clique, and its economic and especially its railway policies were seen by the Japanese as an acute threat to their position. He was not a charismatic leader, but a man of shrewdness, adaptability, ambition, and on occasion ruthlessness. By what passions he was moved it is difficult to know, since, unlike some other warlords of his time, he wrote nothing himself, and since those who have written about him tell us little about the man himself except that he had five wives, eight sons, and six daughters, that he frequently smoked opium, and that he had a passion for gambling, especially at mah-jongg but also at poker.[1] As his biographer, Sonoda, described him in 1922, he was "a thin, yellow-faced little man, five feet two in height. Despite his fame, he is meek-looking and there is nothing distinctive about him. At a glance he is a complete rustic . . . completely ordinary."[2]

Yet Chang was also the greatest of the warlords, dominating in the Northeast one of the richest, largest, and strategically most vital areas of China from 1912 until his death in 1928, and periodically controlling also the major cities and much of the eastern coastline of China down to the Yangtze. His success in doing so may be attributed to a number of factors.

First was that the Northeast was a vast, rich, underpopulated, and developing region. Its wealth was such that Chang's armies were the most regularly paid, the best fed, clothed, and equipped in China; money was lavished on the arsenal; the air force was one of the earliest in China; the services of foreign experts and advisers could readily be secured.

Second, among all the warlords Chang was uniquely favored by his geographical position. While strategically well positioned for any advance he chose to make into the central plains of China, he was also virtually impregnable against attack by armies from the South. This natural advantage was also reinforced by the working of Japanese policy.

The other major factor in Chang's successful rise and power in the Northeast was his creation of the Mukden clique. Personal loyalty to Chang was the major force in its establishment and coherent functioning; yet the administration mediated through it was much more complex than the personality of Chang appears to have been. Because all the Northeastern elites were consulted in determining clique policy, Chang's rule was, on the whole, readily accepted by them. For obvious reasons the military element was dominant, and with the single exception of Kuo Sung-ling, senior officers remained loyal to Chang throughout his career, whether they were old bandit comrades from his pre-Russo-Japanese war days or graduates of various modern officer-training academies in China or Japan. No less important, however, was his ability to retain the loyalties of the civilian elite of the Northeast, particularly of powerful gentry figures such as Wang Yung-chiang. He depended on this element for the administration and policing of his territories, the collection of revenues, and the management of profitable enterprises. Within these limitations he allowed it considerable autonomy, and in the heyday of civilian influence in the councils of the clique (1922–24), it promoted various productive enterprises and development schemes, fiscal and administrative reforms, and even injected an ideological element of nationalism and anti-Japanese imperialism into the policies and programs adopted. Its interests, however, though inextricably intertwined with those of Chang and the Northeastern military, were inevitably subordinate to them. A strong military was necessary to maintain order in the Northeast—to suppress bandits and social unrest internally, and to resist the incursion of outside forces, either foreign or domestic (from elsewhere in China). The bourgeoisie in the Northeast could only develop, therefore, either as an appendage of foreign, particularly Japanese, concerns based in the Japanese-controlled zone, or by currying favor with the military. Wang Yung-chiang's relationship with Chang is sufficient illustration of the dependence and weakness of the merchant gentry of the Northeast, a weakness that was greatly accentuated after Wang's resignation. The futile efforts on several occasions by Provisional Assemblies in all three of the Northeastern provinces to assert the principle of separation of civilian and military government further reinforce the point. *

Bureaucratic reform, anticorruption drives, and rationalization in the administration were all encouraged by the military, since they offered promise of expanded military budgets and therefore of victory in the civil war. But the war was in turn strongly resented by the gentry officials, since it vitiated their reforms, produced rampant inflation and unrest, and imperiled the social order. Thus they preferred military-dominated bureaucratic capitalism in three provinces, or four, or five, to national unification if it could only be bought at such a price. Consequently the irony, several times noted already, that although Chang and the militarists remained obsessed with the goal of unification of the nation, Wang and the civilians, though giving lip service to the idea, were actually committed to progressive severance of the ties between the Northeast and the rest of China and to the building up of a prosperous, peaceful, and independent "Manchuria." It is true that from 1922 leading civilians gave some support to nationalist ideology, to the rights-recovery and anti-Japanese movement, and to economic competition with Japan, but this has to be understood in the context of their "Mandarin" hostility toward involvement of the masses in campaigning toward such ends (it is significant that Wang Yung-chiang first rose to prominence when he threw his support to Chang Tso-lin in his efforts to preserve Mukden from the revolutionaries in 1911–12). The program of economic nationalism that was born under Wang's patronage from 1922 bore the seeds of ultimate conflict with Japan, but as the conflict approached, the bureaucrats who had been associated with it soon lost heart and then accepted with apparent equanimity the change of status of the Northeastern provinces into a Japanese-sponsored Manchukuo.

It would, however, be quite misleading to suggest that by contrast with the civilian officials Chang and his leading military advisers, for all their

*See above, especially Chapters 3 and 6, *passim.*

preoccupation with the exigencies of war and the attempt to unite the country, thought of the "nation" in modern terms. Rather should he be seen as standing in the tradition of Chinese unifiers of the past—developing his strength in a virtually impregnable sanctuary on the fringes of the empire in a time of disintegration and collapse. He is the type of man who in another age might have ascended the dragon throne. In the Republic of China in the 1920's he was an anachronism.

If his strengths were in terms of wealth, strategic position, and ability to create and sustain in the Mukden clique a viable and widely accepted instrument of government as well as a formidable war machine, his limitations were also obvious. For much of his career there is no discernable political or ideological principle behind his actions. It is true that in later years, especially after 1925, he became a fervent, even violent anti-Communist. There were several reasons behind this: a security concern about his Russian frontier; a desire to win the backing of the Western powers by pandering to what he thought they most wanted of a prospective Chinese ruler; a natural antipathy for any movement committed to the overthrow of the order he had imposed. But reinforcing all these considerations was his awareness that some ideology would be necessary to sustain his claim for national leadership. He appears to have had some understanding of this deficiency from at least 1922, when he actually commissioned Hsü Lan-chou to see if he could not manufacture such an ideology (see Chapter 3, p. 87). As Chang appears at crucial times in his career (Tientsin in late 1924, Peking in 1927–28) to have withdrawn into seclusion, where with his closest cronies he devoted himself to mah-jongg, opium, and singing girls, ideological motivation seems not to have worked very strongly on him. The catholicity with which he made alliances in the ongoing Chinese civil war throughout his career points to the same conclusion: Chang was a premodern figure, himself unmoved by modern ideological considerations, however much he strove to utilize them to advance his cause.

Although this ideological weakness meant that Chang attracted little following outside the Northeast and exercised never more than military control over other regions, his second weakness—his misunderstanding of Japan—proved ultimately fatal. Other warlord studies may be or have been completed without particular attention being directed to the problem of the relationship between warlordism and imperialism. In the case of Chang Tso-lin it is impossible to sidestep the issue; yet it is also most difficult to answer it categorically. Certainly Chang was no Japanese puppet; yet neither was he in any sense a nationalist or an anti-imperialist. Japanese power in the Northeast was a factor he had to contend with one way or another, either by placating or resisting it. Resistance was out of the question unless Chang was first able to do one of two things: either to widen and popularize such a move by involving the masses in it—a dangerous move, since it would be likely also to threaten his own autocratic rule at the same time—or, by first successfully resolving the perennial civil war in China in his own favor, to have the resources of the whole nation to back him. Chang ruled out the former course, and his ill fortune at war deprived him of any chance to try the latter. The course he in fact followed was to try first to secure Japan's benevolent neutrality as he built and consolidated his power in the Northeast, then to gain positive support, whether military, political, or diplomatic, as he strove to extend his power over the country as a whole. He aimed, in other words, to use Japan; Japan, in turn, aimed to use him, and in a contest so unequal the outcome was never in doubt. What Chang was prepared to offer the Japanese in return for their support was too little. While continually suggesting he was pro-Japanese, Chang conceded less and less of what Japan actually wanted, and under his auspices the Northeastern administration adopted a developmental program in increasingly sharp opposition to Japan's plans.[3] It is scarcely surprising that Japanese support for him dwindled and hostility and suspicion grew. Thus, although he stood at one of the focal points of tension between Chinese nationalism and Japanese imperialism, Chang was as unable to relate to the one as he was to the other, and he was incapable of generating any alternative.

Insofar as he tried to use Japan to strengthen his own position, while at the same time resisting being used as a tool to further Japanese penetration into China, Chang may have been naïve, but it seems clear from the record that he stood firmly for the unity and integrity of China and was prepared only for the most unavoidable tactical compromises with the Japanese or with the Chinese proponents of an independent Northeast. To this extent, therefore, he merits a more positive assessment by the historian than he has commonly received.

Japanese policy, on the other hand, devious and sometimes apparently contradictory, was at all times inimical to the possibility of a united or independent China. The basic principles of China policy as set out in the Hara cabinet of 1918–21 remained unchanged throughout the successive

party cabinets of the 1920's.* The fundamental premise was that Japan's
accumulated rights and interests should be maintained regardless of
changes in the Chinese political situation, and in pursuit of that end Hara
distinguished clearly between the "neutral and impartial attitude" that
should be proclaimed publicly and the support that should be covertly provided for the "pro-Japanese elements." Chang was identified as one of the
latter, but, unlike Tuan Ch'i-jui, he was classified as a regional leader only,
whose ambitions toward power over China as a whole Japan consistently
frowned upon—at the highest levels at any rate, though among Japanese
officials and officers actually stationed in China, Chang frequently enjoyed
enthusiastic cooperation even in his most ambitious plans.

The principle of limited and conditional support for Chang was
reaffirmed in May 1924 by the Kiyoura ministry (see pp. 134–39); and
when Shidehara became Foreign Minister in June 1924, he made no attempt to review the underlying principles of the China policy he inherited.
True, his commitment to nonintervention and neutrality was proclaimed
more fervently and more rhetorically than ever before, but the rhetoric
must be carefully distinguished from the political substance. The crisis of
the autumn of 1924 revealed its hollowness. The nonintervention principle
had its equally crucial, if not so publicly stressed corollary—that Japan's
rights and interests in the Northeast had to be preserved at all costs, and
regardless of China's civil wars. To do this was to preserve Chang Tso-lin
in office, and Shidehara, though he never said so, was committed to precisely that. When his subordinates spelled this out in so many words, however, he did not contradict them. His silence on the various suggestions of
how the situation should be met, from Yoshizawa in Peking favoring bribery, or from Funatsu in Mukden favoring armed intervention (see Chapter
4, pp. 139–42), suggests a fastidious desire on Shidehara's part not to be acquainted with the details of the execution of his policy—although he made
it clear eventually, on the eve of Feng Yü-hsiang's coup d'etat, that he
thought armed intervention to stop a Wu P'ei-fu march on Mukden was
perfectly compatible with "neutrality" (see above, p. 142). At this point
the latent contradiction in the China policy as enunciated under the Hara
cabinet became obvious. "Nonintervention," to Shidehara as much as to
Hara, was a diplomatic façade, concealing the reality of a determination to

---

*See above, Chapters 1, 2, and 4, pp. 38–39, 57–59, 134–39.

preserve at all costs the privileges that Japan had won in China by dint of successive wars, interventions, and threats. In the following year, 1925, the emptiness of the Shidehara pretense was demonstrated again as Chang was afforded massive Japanese aid to resist the challenge of the rebellious subordinate, Kuo Sung-ling. Thus, whatever conflicts and differences there were within Japan's China policy as a whole, the fundamental premise underlying policy toward the Northeast remained constant.

This point is of some importance, since scholars have, in general, taken the opposite view. Nobuya Bamba, for example, denies that there was Japanese intervention in the second Fengtien-Chihli war, and quotes with approval Shidehara's reputation as an "international law-abiding and peace-making man," a man who stood fast by "democratic and law-abiding principles of international relations."[4] Akira Iriye also insists, in relation to the 1925 rebellion, "Contrary to the generally accepted view there was no thought of openly assisting Chang Tso-lin against Kuo Sung-ling,"[5] a conclusion to which it is only possible to assent if the denial of open assistance is meant to suggest its granting covertly. Iriye is clearly right, however, on the larger issues at stake in comparing Shidehara and Tanaka diplomacy, when he concludes, "In effect, Tanaka carried on Shidehara's policy, but in circumstances that eventually made it a different policy,"[6] though his underlying assumption—that the 1920's are the period of "after imperialism" in the Far East—is one we find it impossible to agree with.

Well before the accession of the Tanaka ministry in April 1927, the pressures to exact from Chang a price for the 1924 and 1925 interventions on his behalf were mounting. Japanese demands were many, but most important was that he should withdraw from his involvements in North China and concentrate exclusively on restoring social order to the Northeast—to adopt what Yoshida Shigeru described as a policy of the "Greater Three Eastern Provinces" (see Chapter 6, p. 224). Japanese diplomats, officers, and other semiofficial representatives had repeatedly urged Chang to do this: it was the direction of the officially sanctioned plotting in 1916 (indeed in 1911 also), was reaffirmed at the 1921 Eastern Conference, remained the unstated assumption underlying Shidehara policy (not only unstated but unquestioned, since Yoshida and others continued to act upon it), and was given forceful restatement at Tanaka's Eastern Conference in 1927. Furthermore, the consensus of all wings of the Japanese government, civil and military, on these basic policy directions, is significant.

It is a striking historical irony that in the crucial years 1925–27 the most strident calls for active intervention in China, and for the severance of relations between the Northeast and the rest of the country, were issued not by Kwantung Army hotheads but by Yoshida Shigeru, a senior Foreign Ministry bureaucrat who was regarded as the epitome of cosmopolitan internationalism. Much later Yoshida was favored by the occupation forces as a "democrat," untainted by militarism and innocent of any responsibility for the China and Pacific wars, to serve as Japan's postwar premier, although it was precisely the course he recommended that, when carried into operation by the military, led directly to the establishment of Manchukuo, to the China war and all its consequences.

The bomb that blew up Chang Tso-lin's train in June 1928 thus had a long fuse, but one that shortened gradually and inexorably through the decade. Once Chang had established himself as the dominant figure in the Northeast, Japanese diplomats, officials, army officers, and businessmen strove assiduously to work through him to build up the Japanese position. Chang, for his part, was anxious to placate the Japanese and to be seen by them as the most unflagging proponent of closer Japanese ties in order to enjoy the many perquisites of Japanese favor, and above all in the hope of utilizing Japanese support and aid to attain his own ends in China. The intimate and frequently corrupt liaisons that developed between the two sides as a result were typical of the semicolonial relationship that developed between Japan and Northeast China. Until approximately 1925 the relationship was generally mutually satisfactory, but thereafter the pressures of awakening Chinese nationalism and Chang's stubborn ambition on the one hand, and impatient, implacable Japanese imperialism on the other, were increasingly irreconcilable. The only way collision might have been averted was through a fundamental reconsideration on Japan's side of its position in the Northeast, of the claims of Chinese nationalism, and of the fiction of a separate "Manchuria." No one in a position of power in Japan in the 1920's undertook such a reconsideration.

Reference Matter

Glossary

All Chinese place names have been romanized according to the principles set forth by G. William Skinner in his *Modern Chinese Society: An Analytical Bibliography* (3 vols.; Stanford, Calif., 1973), in Explanatory Notes. They are given in either of two forms: "in Post Office spelling, which never involves hyphenation, or in Wade-Giles transcription, which never combines syllables into an unhyphenated word." Post Office spelling is used only in cases where that form has been "securely established as scholarly idiom"; in all other cases Wade-Giles spelling is used. Thus, following Skinner, some former treaty ports and large cities are given here in Wade-Giles rather than Post Office form: Ch'in-huang-tao rather than Chinhwangtao, Niu-chuang rather than Newchwang, and Fu-shun rather than Fushun being notable examples.

Akatsuka Shōsuke 赤塚正助
Amau Eiji 天羽英二
an-min pao-ching 安民保境
An-shan 鞍山
An-ta 安達
An-tung 安東
Ang-ang-ch'i 昂昂溪
Ankuochün 安國軍
Araki Gorō 荒木五郎
Arita Hachirō 有田八郎
Azuma Otohiko 東乙彦

Babojab (Bavuujav) 巴布扎布
Bando Matsuzō 坂東末三
Banzai Rihachirō 坂西利八郎

Bōeichō senshishitsu 防衛庁戦史室

Chang Ching-hui 張景惠
Chang Chiu-ch'ing 張九卿
Chang Ch'ün 張羣
Chang Hai-p'eng 張海鵬
Chang Hsi-luan 張錫鑾
Chang Hsüeh-liang 張學良
Chang Hsün 張勲
Chang Huan-hsiang 張煥相
Chang K'uei-wu 張奎武
Chang Ming-chiu 張明九
Chang Shao-tseng 張紹曾
Chang Ssu 張思

Chang Tso-hsiang 張作相

Chang Tso-lin 張作霖

Chang Tso-t'ao 張作濤

Chang Tsung-ch'ang 張宗昌

Chang Yung 張瑢

Ch'ang-hsin-tien 長辛店

Changchun 長春

Chao Chieh 趙杰

Chao Ch'u-fei 趙鉚非

Chao En-chen 趙恩臻

Chao Erh-hsün 趙爾巽

Chao T'i 趙倜

Ch'en Fu-sheng 陳輔陞

Ch'en Kuang-yüan 陳光遠

Cheng-chia-t'un 鄭家屯

Cheng-chou 鄭州

Cheng-yen pao 正言報

Ch'eng Te-ch'üan 程德全

Chi-an 輯安

Chi Chin-ch'un 汲金純

Chi-tung 齊東

Ch'i En-ming 齊恩明

Ch'i Hsieh-yüan 齊燮元

chiang-chün 將軍

Chiang Kuei-t'i 姜桂題

Chiang Teng-hsüan 姜登選

Chien-chou 建州

Chien-tao 間島

Ch'ih-feng 赤峰

Chin-chou 錦州

Chin-chou 金州

Chin-yen chü 禁烟局

Chin Yün-p'eng 靳雲鵬

Ch'in Hua 秦華

Ch'in-huang-tao 秦皇島

ching-lüeh-shih 經畧使

Ching-tsin hsien-ping ssu-ling
京津憲兵司令

Chou P'ei-ping 周焙炳

Chou Tzu-ch'i 周自齊

Chou Yü-ping 周玉珃

Chu Ch'ing-lan 朱慶瀾

Chu-liu-ho 巨流河

Ch'u Yü-p'u 褚玉璞

Chuang-ho 莊河

chün-wu pang-pan 軍務幫辦

Chung-yü 鐘毓

Chūnichi jitsugyō 中日實業

Darkhan 達爾罕

Doihara Kenji 土肥原賢二

Erh-tao-kou 二道溝

Etō Toyoji 江藤豐二

Feng Kuo-chang 馮國璋

Feng Te-lin 馮德麟

Feng Yü-hsiang 馮玉祥

Feng-t'ien fang-sha-ch'ang
奉天紡紗廠

Fu-chou 復州

Fu-shun 撫順

Fukuhara Yoshiya 福原佳哉

Funatsu Tatsuichirō 船津辰一郎

Gaimushō 外務省

Giga Masaya 儀我誠也

Hai-ch'eng 海城

Hai-la-erh 海拉爾

Hai-lin 海偷

Hai-lung 海龍

Hai-yang-chen 海陽鎮

Han Lin-ch'ün 韓麟春

Hang-ching chü 航警局

Hara Kei 原敬

Harbin (Pin-chiang) 哈爾濱 (濱江)

Hayashi Kyujirō 林久治郎

Hayashi Yasakichi 林弥三吉

Hei-ho 黑，河

Hoiryong (Hui-ning, Kainei) 會寧

Honjō Shigeru 本庄繁

Hsi Hsia 熙洽

Hsiao-chan 小站

Hsiao Yao-nan 蕭耀南

Hsieh Chieh-shih 謝介石

Hsieh Yin-ch'ang 謝蔭昌

hsien 縣

hsien ta-yang 現大洋

Hsin-ch'iu 新邱

Hsin-li-t'un 新立屯

Hsin-min-t'un 新民屯

Hsing Shih-lien 邢士廉

hsiu-ts'ai 秀才

Hsü-chou 徐州

Hsü Shih-ch'ang 徐世昌

Hsü Shu-cheng 徐樹錚

Hsü Ting-lin 許鼎霖

hsün-an-shih 巡按使

hsün-fang-tui 巡防隊

hsün-fu 巡撫

Hu Ching-i 胡景翼

hu-chün-shih 護軍使

Hu-lan 呼蘭

Hu-lu-tao 葫蘆島

Hu-nan lu-chün hsüeh-t'ang 湖南陸軍學堂

Hu Yung-k'uei 胡永奎

Hua shen chih-ts'ai kung-ssu 華森製材公司

Huai-te hsien 懷德縣

Huang Fu 黃郛

Huang Mu 黃慕

Hui-ning (Hoiryong) 會寧

Hun-ch'un 琿春

hunghutzu 紅鬍子

Idokawa Tatsuzō 井戸川辰三

Ishii Kikujirō 石井菊次郎

Iwama Tokuya 岩間德也

Jen Yü-lin 任毓麟

K'ai-yüan 開元

Kamata Yasuke 鎌田弥助

K'an Chao-hsi 闞朝璽

Kao Shih-pin 高士儐

Kao Wei-yo 高維嶽

Kawashima Naniwa 川島浪速

Kenseikai 憲政会

Kikuchi Takeo 菊池武夫

Kirin 吉林

Kishi Yajirō 貴志彌治郎

Kōmoto Daisaku 河本大作

Korenaga Shigeo 是永重夫

Kou-pang-tzu 溝帮子

ku-wen 顧問

Kuan-ch'eng-tzu 寬城子

Kuang-hsin 廣信

Kuang-ning (Pei-chen) 廣寧
(北鎮)

K'uei Sheng (courtesy name
Hsing-chieh) 魁陞 (星階)

Kung-chu-ling 公主嶺

Kuo-chia-tien 郭家店

kuo-min ta-hui 國民大會

Kuo Sung-lin 郭松齡

Kuo Tsung-hsi 郭宗熙

Kuominchün 國民軍

Lan T'ien-wei 藍天蔚

Li Chen-sheng 李振聲

Li Ching-lin 李景林

Li K'uei-lin 李桂林

Li Shuang-k'ai 李爽塏

Li Tsung-jen 李宗仁

Li Yüan-hung 黎元洪

liang-ch'ien 糧餞

Liang Sheng-te 梁聲德

Liang Shih-i 梁士詒

Liao-yang 遼陽

lien-chuang-hui 聯莊會

lien-ho chi-chin-hui 連合急進會

Lien-shan 連山

Lin-chiang 臨江

Liu Hsiang-chiu 劉香九

Liu Shang-ch'ing 劉尚清

Lu Chan-k'uei 盧占魁

Lu Ch'eng-wu 陸承武

Lu-chün chiang-hsiao yen-
chiu-so 陸軍將校研究所

Lu-chün su-ch'eng hsüeh-
hsiao 陸軍速成學校

Lu-chün ta-hsüeh 陸軍大學

Lu Jung-t'ing 陸榮廷

Lu Yung-hsiang 盧永祥

Luan-chou 灤州

Ma Chün-ku 馬俊顧

Ma Chung-chün 馬忠駿

Ma Fu-hsiang 馬福祥

Ma Lung-t'an 馬龍潭

ma-tse 馬賊

Machino Takema 町野武馬

Man-chou (Japanese Manshū)
滿州

Man-chou-li 滿州里

Man-chou yüan-liu-k'ao 滿州源
流考

Manshū bōseki 滿州紡績

Mantetsu 滿鐵

Mantetsu chōsa geppō 滿鐵調
查月報

Mao-erh-shan 帽兒山

Matsui Iwane 松井石根

Matsui Nanao 松井七夫

Matsumiro Takayoshi 松室孝良

Matsuoka Yōsuke 松岡洋石

Meng-chiang hsien 蒙江縣

Meng En-yüan 孟恩遠

Mi-shan 窓山

Min-shih pao 民實報

Minami Jirō 南次郎

Mitsumura Yutaka 三村豊

Mo Te-hui 莫德惠

Morita Kanzō 森田寛藏

Mu Ch'ün 穆春

Muraoka Chōtarō 村岡長太郎

Nagao Hampei 長尾半平
Nan-k'ou 南口
Ni Ssu-ch'ung 倪嗣冲
Nieh Ju-ch'ing 聶汝清
Ning-ku-t'a 寧古塔
Nishihara Kamezō 西原亀三
Niu-chuang 牛荘
Nung-an 農安

Obata Yukichi 小幡酉吉
Ochiai Kentarō 落合謙太郎
Omotokyō 大本教

Pa-chiao-t'ai 八角台
Pa Ying-e 巴英額
Pai-Ch'ung-hsi 白崇禧
Pai-yin-t'ai-lai (T'ung-liao) 白音太来 (通遼)
P'an Fu 潘復
pao-ching an-min 保境安民
Pao Kuei-ch'ing 鮑貴卿
Pao Te-shan 鮑德山
Paoting 保定
Pei-chen (Kuang-ning) 北鎮 (廣寧)
P'ei Ch'i-hsün 裴其勲
P'ei Ch'ün-sheng 裴春生
Pen-ch'i-hu 裴溪湖
P'eng Chin-shan 彭金山
P'eng Hsien 彭賢
Pi Kuei-fang 畢桂芳
Pin-chiang (Harbin) 濱江 (哈爾濱)
Po-k'o-t'u 博克圖

Po-shan 博山
Pukow 浦口

Rikugunshō gunmukyoku 陸軍省軍務局

Saitō Minoru 斉藤稔
Saitō Tsune 斉藤恒
San-yü 三舍
Sang-yüan 桑原
Sasaki Tōichi 佐々木到一
Satō Yasunosuke 佐藤安之助
sha-fu chi-pin 殺富濟貧
Shan-hai-kuan 山海關
shang 晌
Shen-yang 瀋陽
sheng-chang 省長
Sheng-ching shih-pao 盛京時報
Shidehara Kijūro 幣原喜重郎
Shih Chi-ch'ang 史記常
Shih Te-shan 石得山
Shikan gakkō 士官学校
Shirakawa Yoshinori 白川義則
So-lun 索倫
Sonoda Kazuki 園田一亀
Ssu-p'ing-chieh 四平街
Su-chia-t'un 蘇家屯
Su Hsi-lin 蘇錫麟
Sui-fen 綏芬
Sui-hua 綏化
Sun Ch'uan-fang 孫傳芳
Sun Lieh-ch'en 孫烈臣
Sun Yat-sen 孫逸仙
Sun Yo 孫岳

Sung Che-yüan 宋哲元
Suzuki Yoshiyuki
鈴木美通

Ta-hu-shan 大虎山
Ta-lai 大賚
Ta-tao-hui 大刀會
Ta-t'ung 大同
ta-yang-p'iao 大洋票
ta-yüan-shuai 大元帥
Tachibana Shōichirō 立花小一郎
T'an Kuo-han 談國桓
Tanaka Giichi 田中義一
T'ang Shao-i 唐紹儀
T'ang Sheng-chih 唐紹智
T'ang Yü-lin 湯玉麟
T'ao-nan 洮南
Te-chou 德州
t'e-pieh ch'ü-yü 特別區域
Teranishi Hidetake 寺西秀武
tiao 吊
T'ieh-ling 鐵嶺
T'ien Chung-yü 田中玉
Ting Chao 丁超
tokumu kikan 特務機関
Ts'ai P'ing-pen 蔡平本
Ts'ai Yün-sheng 蔡運升
Ts'ai Yung-chen 蔡永鎮
Ts'ao Ju-lin 曹汝霖
Ts'ao K'un 曹錕
Tsitsihar 齊々哈爾
Tsou Fen 鄒芬
Tu Hsi-kuei 杜錫珪
Tu Li-shan 杜立山
T'u-men 圖們

Tuan Ch'i-jui 段琪瑞
Tuan Chih-kuei 段芝貴
tuchün 督軍
tuli 督理
Tun-hua 敦化
Tung-fang 東方
Tung-ning 東寧
Tung-pao 東報
Tung-pei 東北
Tung-san-sheng 東三省
Tung-san-sheng chin-yung
  cheng-li wei-yüan-hui 東三省
  金融整理委員會
Tung-san-sheng hsün-
  yueh-shih 東三省巡閱使
Tung-san-sheng kuan-yin-
  hao 東三省官銀號
Tung-san-sheng lu-chün
  chiang-wu-t'ang 東三省陸軍
  講武堂
Tung-san-sheng min-chih
  ts'u-chih-hui 東三省民治
  促進會
Tung-san-sheng min-pao 東三省
  民報
Tung-sheng 東省
Tung-ya t'u-mu 東亞土不
tupan 督辦
tut'ung 督統

Uchida Yasuya 內田康哉
Uchiyama 內山
Uehara Yūsaku 上原勇作
Ugaki Kazushige (Kazunari) 宇垣
  一成

Ura Sumie 浦澄江
Ushijima Yoshio 牛島吉郎

Wa-fang-tien 瓦房店
Wakatsuki Reijirō 若槻禮次郎
Wan Fu-lin 萬福麟
Wang Chan-yüan 王占元
Wang Chao-ming (Wang Ching-wei)
　汪兆銘 (汪精衛)
Wang Ch'eng-pin 王承斌
Wang Huai-ch'ing 王懷慶
Wang Yung-chiang 王永江
Wei Yi-san 魏益三
Wu-ch'ang 五常
Wu Ch'ao-shu 伍朝樞
Wu Ching-lien 吳景濂
Wu Chün-sheng 吳俊陞
Wu Lu-chen 吳祿貞
Wu P'ei-fu 吳佩孚

Yada Shichitarō 矢田七太郎
Yamamoto Jōtarō 山本条太郎
Yang-chou 陽州
Yang Ta-shih 楊大實

Yang Te-sheng 楊德生
Yang Yü-t'ing 楊宇霆
Yasuhiro Tomoichirō 安永伴一郎
Yeh Kung-ch'o 葉恭綽
Yen-chi 延吉
Yen Hsi-shan 閻錫山
Yen Hui-ch'ing (W.W. Yen)
　顏惠慶
Ying Hsün 英順
Ying-k'ou 營口
Yoshida Shigeru 吉田茂
Yoskioka Kensaku 吉岡顯作
Yoshizawa Kenkichi 芳澤謙吉
Yu-ning 裕寧
Yu Shen-ch'eng 于深澂
Yü Chen 于珍
Yü Ch'ung-han 于沖漢
Yü Ssu-hsing 于駟興
Yü-ta 裕大
Yü Yüan-p'u 于溱浦
Yüan Chin-k'ai 袁金鎧
Yüan Shih-k'ai 袁世凱
Yung-heng 永衡

Notes

INTRODUCTION

1. Egami, pt. 3, "Manshū," pp. 183ff; Lee, pp. 3–8.
2. Egami, pp. 218–29; Lee, pp. 7–8; Li Chi, "Manchuria in History," *CSPSR*, 16, no. 2 (1932): 227, 253–55.
3. Lee, p. 7.
4. Li Chi, *ibid.*, p. 228.
5. *Ibid.*, p. 227.
6. *MYB*, 1932–33, p. 34.
7. See, for example, Lee, pp. 8–9, 20–23, 182–84.
8. Sun, p. 3.
9. Cited in C. Walter Young, "Chinese Colonization and the Development of Manchuria," in Condliffe, p. 423.
10. Lee, p. 103; Sun, p. 11.
11. C. Walter Young, "Chinese Colonization," p. 423.
12. Lee, p. 60.
13. Oshibuchi, *passim*.
14. Lattimore, p. 67.
15. Manshikai, vol. 1, p. 30.
16. C. Walter Young, *Japanese Jurisdiction*, pp. 138–63.
17. Murphey, p. 48.
18. Chu, p. 380.
19. Amano, pp. 19–20; Sun, p. 3.
20. *MYB*, pp. 329–31.
21. Ho, p. 364; see also his table "Provincial Distribution of China's Industrialization," on p. 28.
22. Masamichi Royama, "Japan's Position in Manchuria," in Condliffe, p. 554.
23. Hsü Hsing-k'ai, pp. 391–92.
24. *Minami Manshū*, p. 651.
25. Ho, p. 346; *MYB*, p. 459.
26. Sheridan, *Chinese Warlord: The Career of Feng Yü-hsiang.* The major studies that have appeared since are as follows: Hsieh, "The Ideas and Ideals of a Warlord"; Gillin, *Warlord: Yen Hsi-shan in Shansi Province*; Ch'en, "Defining Chinese Warlords and Their Factions"; Chi, *The Chinese Warlord System*; Wou, *Militarism . . . in the Career of Wu P'ei-fu*; Pye, *Warlord Politics*; Hall, *The Provincial Warlord Faction in Yunnan*; Kapp, *Szechuan and the Chinese Republic*;

Lary, *Region and Nation*; Ch'i, *Warlord Politics in China*. (This last is a much revised and rewritten version of that cited above by the same author.)

27. Sheridan, p. 1.

28. There is no full-scale biography of Chang in English, although there are several in Chinese and Japanese, to which reference will be made in due course. A good brief account of Chang's life may be found in Boorman, vol. 1, pp. 115–22. However, it is a reflection of the absence of detailed monographic study of the Northeast that this standard Western-language reference work contains no entry whatever for several of the persons of major importance to this book—Wang Yung-chiang and Kuo Sung-ling, to name but two.

29. Nathan, p. 221.

30. *Ibid.*, p. 37.

31. Nathan, for example, classifies such ties into nine types (pp. 50–54); Hsi-sheng Ch'i, on the other hand, uses 12 categories, though of a similar nature (*Warlord Politics*, pp. 38–56).

32. Sheridan, p. 9.

33. *Pace* Suleski, who introduces his study with the claim: "Fortunately for Chang both powers [Japan and the USSR] were in a somewhat confused state regarding the role they wished to play in Manchuria, so that their policies toward Manchuria were in a quiescent period during the 1920s, and most of the time Chang was able to ignore their presence" (p. 18).

CHAPTER ONE

1. On Yüan Shih-k'ai see Jerome Ch'en, *Yüan Shih-k'ai*; for the others see Introduction, note 26.

2. For some general accounts of Chang's early years, see Sonoda, *Kaiketsu Chō Sakurin*; Asano, *Daigensui Chō Sakurin; Chang Tso-lin ch'üan-shih*; Tung Chien-chih, *Chang Tso-lin chih ch'i-mou ch'üan-shu*; Yü Ming, *Chang Tso-lin wai-chuan*; "Kaiketsu Chō Sakurin" (no author, no date, but may be assumed from the context and content to have been written in 1912 or 1913), in Matsumoto Bunko; and Hakuunsō Shujin, *Chō Sakurin*.

3. The principal authorities divide as follows on the date of Chang's birth:

1873: Boorman, vol. 1. p. 115; Ts'ao Te-hsuan, p. 24; and Gaimushō, *Gendai Chūka minkoku Manshūkoku jinmeikan* (1932), p. 235.

1875: Sonoda, *Kaiketsu Chō Sakurin*, supplement, "Chō Sakurin nenpyō" (A Chang Tso-lin chronology); Asano, p. 14; Hakuunsō Shujin, p. 1; Wang, *Tung-pei*, p. 7; *Chang ta-yüan-shuai ai-wan-lu*, Hsing-chuang, p. 1. This last source does not state categorically that Chang was born in 1875 but does establish that he was 54 years of age at the time of his death in June 1928. Assuming that this was calculated according to the traditional method of calculating age in China, which counted one's age at birth as already one, thus giving always an age one year older than Western calculations, it does, however, amount to the same thing. Finally, modern Japanese authorities seem to be agreed on 1875, among them Etō Shinkichi in "Gunbatsu konsen," p. 383; Kaizuka, vol. 6, p. 290; and Saeki, p. 236.

Between 1875 and 1879: Stauffer, in *Manchuria as a Political Entity*, cites as his authority an article by Dr. S. Washio, "The Bandit Governor," *Trans Pacific*, 17 (July 28, 1928): 5. After reviewing the various evidence, however, we take the view that there can be little doubt that 1875 is the correct date, particularly because of the "Mourning Record," which had at least semiofficial status, and the early Japanese biographies, in which the assistance of numerous senior officials and associates of Chang, including his son Hsüeh-liang, is acknowledged.

4. Lattimore, p.67.

5. *Ibid.*, pp. 187, 195, 223, 226; on early opium cultivation in the Northeast, see also Lee, p. 195.

6. *People's Revolutionary Movement*, p. 144.

7. On the question of bandits generally, see Billingsley.

8. T'ien Pu-i teng, p. 62.

9. Sonoda, *Kaiketsu Chō Sakurin*, pp. 38–39.

10. *Ibid.*, pp. 39–40.

11. *Ibid.*, p. 42; Asano, pp. 18–19; *People's Revolutionary Movement*, p. 146.

12. Tanaka Giichi denki kankōkai, vol. 1, pp. 324–25; Kokuryūkai, vol. 3, pp. 40–43.

13. Tōa dōbunkai, *Zoku taishi kaikoroku*, vol. 2, pp. 1287–88; on the generally pro-Japanese proclivities of the *hung-hu-tzu* at this time, see Watanabe, p. 37; "Chang Tso-lin wai-chuan," in Matsumoto Bunko, n.p.

14. Tanaka Giichi denki kankōkai, pp. 324–28.

15. "Chang Tso-lin wai-chuan," in Matsumoto Bunko; T'ien Pu-i teng, p. 63.

16. Li Shih-yüeh, p. 59; Lee, pp. 152–54, 170.

17. Sonoda, *ibid.*; Wang, "Chang Yü-t'ing," p. 31.

18. Li Shih-yüeh, p. 61; Ning Wu, "Tung-pei . . . chien-shu," p. 536.

19. *People's Revolutionary Movement*, p. 196.

20. Li Shih-yüeh, p. 60; *People's Revolutionary Movement*, pp. 191–93; Ning Wu, "Tung-pei . . . chien-shu," p. 536.

21. Li Shih-yüeh, p. 58.

22. *Ibid.*, pp. 56–57; *People's Revolutionary Movement*, pp. 169–72, 178.

23. *People's Revolutionary Movement*, pp. 178–79; Lee, p. 131.

24. Ning Wu, "Tung-pei . . . chien-shu," p. 543.

25. *Ibid.*, p. 541; for a biography of Chang Yung, see pp. 592–611 of this same volume: Ch'in Ch'eng-chih, "Hsin-hai ko-ming yü Chang Yung" (Chang Yung and the 1911 Revolution). See also *People's Revolutionary Movement*, pp. 189–90.

26. *People's Revolutionary Movement*, pp. 205–7; Powell, pp. 311–12.

27. Ning Wu, "Tung-pei . . . chien-shu," p. 546.

28. Powell, pp. 311–12.

29. *People's Revolutionary Movement*, pp. 211–12.

30. *Ibid.*, pp. 211–14; Powell, p. 312.

31. Ning Wu, "Tung-pei . . . yün-tung." (Ning Wu performed the unusual feat of publishing his memoirs of 1911 in Taipei in 1962 and Peking in 1963.) See also *People's Revolutionary Movement*, p. 213.

32. *People's Revolutionary Movement*, pp. 211–14; Wang, "Chang Yü-t'ing," pp. 31–34. This article is based on interviews conducted by its author with Chang Tso-hsiang in Mukden on Aug. 9, 1948, and with Wan Fu-lin in Taipei on Dec. 20, 1950. By this account Chang's liaison officer in Mukden, Chang Hui-lin, intercepted an order to Wu Chün-sheng to hurry to Mukden to assume responsibility for its defense from the unreliable New Army. As soon as he received this intelligence, Chang himself rushed to the capital, passing through Wu's territory en route

without mentioning the order, and on arrival in Mukden was appointed by Chao to command of the 15 battalions of provincial troops in the area, a force about sufficient to counterbalance any move by the New Army.

33. Ning Wu, "Tung-pei . . . yün-tung," pp. 373-74; Ning Wu, "Tung-pei . . . chien-shu," pp. 547-48; Li Shih-yüeh, p. 64; Wang, "Chang Yü-t'ing," p. 32.

34. *People's Revolutionary Movement*, p. 218.

35. *Ibid.*, p. 219; Ning Wu, "Tung-pei . . . chien-shu," p. 601; Li Shih-yüeh, p. 67.

36. *People's Revolutionary Movement*, p. 231; Ning Wu, "Tung-pei . . . yün-tung," pp. 375-76, and "Tung-pei . . . chien-shu," p. 548.

37. Li Shih-yüeh, pp. 67-68; *People's Revolutionary Movement*, pp. 232-33; Ch'in Ch'eng-chih, in Ning Wu, "Tung-pei . . . chien-shu," pp. 603-4; Sasaki Kōzaburō, p. 53. For a Western reaction to the terror, see Fulton, pp. 251-52.

38. *People's Revolutionary Movement*, pp. 238-40; Dazai, *Manshū gendaishi*, pp. 121-23.

39. Li Shih-yüeh, p. 69.

40. Nishimura, "Tōsanshō ni okeru Shingai kakumei," pp. 19-23.

41. *Ibid.*, p. 22.

42. *Ibid.*

43. Kurihara, "Dai ichiji dai niji Manmō dokuritsu undō to Koike Gaimushō Seimukyoku-chō no jishoku" (The first and second Manchuria and Mongolia independence movements and the resignation of Political Affairs Bureau Chief Koike of the Foreign Ministry), in Kurihara, p. 142. On Machino, see Table 5, p. 121.

44. Valliant, p. 4.

45. Sonoda, *Kaiketsu Chō Sakurin*, pp. 64-68.

46. Nishimura, "Tōsanshō ni okeru Shingai kakumei," p. 24.

47. Sonoda, *Kaiketsu Chō Sakurin*, p. 81.

48. Wang, "Chang Yü-t'ing, pp. 32, 33; Sonoda, *Tōsanshō no seiji to gaikō*, p. 67; "Chang Tso-lin wai-chuan," *Ch'un-ch'iu*, no. 225, Nov. 1966, pt. 1, p. 8; Tōa dōbunkai, *Taishi kaikoroku*, vol. 1, pp. 519-20.

49. Kurihara, pp. 145-47.

50. *Ibid.*, pp. 149-50.

51. *Ibid.*, p. 150.

52. Sonoda, *Kaiketsu Chō Sakurin*, pp. 77-78; Sasaki Kōzaburō, p. 104; Dazai, *Manshū gendaishi*, pp. 150-51.

53. Kurihara, pp. 151-52. For biographies of Yü, see Sonoda, *Hōten-ha no shinjin to kyūjin*, pp. 54-55; Gaimushō, *Gendai Chūka minkoku Manshūkoku jin-meikan* (1932), pp. 431-32.

54. Kurihara, pp. 151-52; Sonoda, *Tōsanshō no seiji to gaikō*, pp. 69-71.

55. *NGN*, vol. 1, bunsho, pp. 437-38; Morley, p. 14.

56. Morley, pp. 69-71; Sonoda, *Tōsanshō no seiji to gaikō*, pp. 69-71; Koo, vol. 2, pp. 576-80.

57. "Chang Tso-lin wai-chuan," pt. 2, *Ch'un-ch'iu*, no. 226, Dec. 1966, p. 8; Sonoda, *Kaiketsu Chō Sakurin*, pp. 106-18; Dazai, *Manshū gendaishi*, pp. 178-79.

58. Sonoda, *Shina shinjin kokki*, p. 595.

59. *Ibid.*; Ning Wu, "Tung-pei . . . chien-shu," p. 548; *People's Revolutionary Movement*, p. 63.

60. Sonoda, *Kaiketsu Chō Sakurin*, p. 115.

61. *Ibid.*, pp. 120–22, 137–41; Dazai, *Manshū gendaishi*, pp. 188–95.

62. The 29th Division was authorized by Peking in May 1917. Sonoda, *Kaiketsu Chō Sakurin*, p. 122.

63. Gaimushō, *Gendai Chūka minkoku Manshūkoku jinmeikan* (1932), p. 464.

64. Sada, pp. 18–19; Entō jijō kenkyūkai, no. 47, "Hoten-sho zaisei no shi-teki kōsatsu" (A historical investigation of the finances of Fengtien province), pt. 3, Aug. 28, 1924. (These materials are introduced and discussed by Imai, in "Sen kyū-hyaku nijū yon nen no Tōsanshō," pp. 21–26.) For another recent study, much of which is devoted to the career of Wang Yung-chiang, see Suleski, *Manchuria under Chang Tso-lin*.

65. Sonoda, *Shina shinjin kokki*, pp. 73–75.

66. "Chang Tso-lin wai-chuan," pt. 3, *Ch'un-ch'iu*, no. 227, Dec. 1966, p. 11.

67. Sonoda, *Tōsanshō no seiji to gaikō*, p. 77; Dazai, *Manshū gendaishi*, pp. 196–99.

68. Sonoda, *Kaiketsu Chō Sakurin*, pp. 144–48; Sonoda, *Shina shinjin kokki*, p. 593.

69. Dazai, *Manshū gendaishi*, p. 237.

70. "Chang Tso-lin wai-chuan," pt. 3, *Ch'un-ch'iu*, no. 227, Dec. 1966, p. 12; Sonoda, *Kaiketsu Chō Sakurin*, pp. 154–56; *Chang Tso-lin ch'üan-shih*, pp. 30–31.

71. Sonoda, *Tōsanshō no seiji to gaikō*, pp. 81–84; Morley, p. 110.

72. Sonoda, *ibid.*, p. 89.

73. Meng's announcement to the closing session of the Kirin Provincial Assembly, June 10, 1919, as cited in Hayashi, p. 124.

74. *Ibid.*, p. 125.

75. *NGN*, vol. 1, bunsho, pp. 437–38.

76. Morton, "The Tanaka Cabinet's China Policy," p. 50.

77. See the table on pp. 190–202 of Chang Yen-shen.

78. *Ibid.*, p. 91.

79. *Ibid.*, pp. 130–31.

80. Hayashi, pp. 125–26.

81. *Ibid.*, p. 128.

82. *Ibid.*, p. 129.

83. "Chang Tso-lin wai-chuan," pt. 3, *Ch'un-ch'iu*, no. 227, Dec. 1966, p. 13.

84. Ishida, pp. 543–45.

85. Chang, pp. 133–34.

86. Sokolsky, p. 36; Nakahama, p. 4; Dazai, *Manshū gendaishi*, pp. 257–60.

87. Sonoda, *Kaiketsu Chō Sakurin*, pp. 287–88.

88. Dispatch from Morita, Kirin Consul General, June 2, 1921, JFMA, F 192 7, p. 1544; also Morita dispatch of Aug. 17, JFMA 1614 2-12, pp. 3276–78. (Note that Japanese Foreign Ministry archives are cited here according to the code numbers by which they are classified in the Foreign Ministry archives in Tokyo. These do not always correspond with the numbers given in Uyehara, according to which the microfilm copies of this material are available outside Japan. Furthermore, where Japanese diplomatic dispatches are addressed, as commonly, to the Minister of Foreign Affairs, that fact is omitted from the citation.)

89. *NGN*, vol. 1, bunsho, p. 516.

90. Sonoda, *Kaiketsu Chō Sakurin*, pp. 293–96.

91. *Ibid.*, pp. 297–98; *NGN*, vol. 1, bunsho, p. 517.
92. *CYB*, 1921–22, p. 608; Dazai, *Manshū gendaishi*, pp. 265–73.
93. Sonoda, *Kaiketsu Chō Sakurin*, pp. 306–7.
94. Dazai, *Manshū gendaishi*, pp. 150–51.
95. Sonoda, *Kaiketsu Chō Sakurin*, pp. 201–3.
96. *Ibid.*, pp. 293, 296.
97. *Ibid.*, p. 299.

CHAPTER TWO

1. Hatano, *Chūgoku kindai gunbatsu no kenkyū*, p. 300; Usui, *Nihon to Chūgoku*, p. 108.
2. Li Chien-nung, p. 364.
3. Asano, pp. 55–56; Sonoda, *Kaiketsu Chō Sakurin*, p. 168; Dazai, *Manshū gendaishi*, pp. 216–17; Ch'i, *Warlord Politics*, p. 22.
4. Usui, *Nihon to Chūgoku*, p. 122.
5. Roberts, p. 187. Roberts's account, however, does not name Takada Shōkai, the third of the companies concerned, merely suggesting, wrongly, that it was a Mitsubishi affiliate. I am indebted to Professor Imai Seichi for pointing this out to me.
6. *NGN*, vol. 1, nenpyō, p. 219.
7. Usui, *Nihon to Chūgoku*, p. 122; Sonoda, *Kaiketsu Chō Sakurin*, pp. 168–99; Sonoda, *Tōsanshō no seiji to gaikō*, pp. 84–87.
8. Sonoda, *Kaiketsu Chō Sakurin*, p. 173; T'ao Chü-yin, *Tuchün-t'uan chuan*, p. 197ff.
9. Ch'i, p. 23.
10. *Ibid.*, p. 25.
11. Sonoda, *Kaiketsu Chō Sakurin*, pp. 168–99 *passim*; Dazai, *Manshū gendaishi*, pp. 220–26.
12. Sonoda, *ibid.*, p. 197; Dazai, *ibid.*, p. 227.
13. For a detailed study of clique and faction relationships at this time, see Nathan, pp. 128–75.
14. Nathan, p. 164; Clubb, pp. 94–96. Note that Chihli and Anhwei are here to be understood as referring to the cliques organized around leaders whose original or main interest lay in those provinces. Chihli strength was actually concentrated at this time on the Yangtze. On Hsü in Mongolia, see Tang, pp. 362–64; Carr, *The Bolshevik Revolution*, p. 496.
15. Sonoda, *Kaiketsu Chō Sakurin*, pp. 227–32. The eight-province alliance— (southern) Chihli, Honan, Kiangsu, Kiangsi, Hupeh, Fengtien, Kirin, and Heilungkiang—was somewhat more clearly defined than the five-province alliance around Tuan, which consisted primarily of Anhwei, Chekiang, Fukien, Shantung, and Shensi, but which may also be considered to have included the three Inner Mongolian special administrative areas of Jehol, Chahar, and Suiyuan, which would make for a rough equality on both sides. For a map of territorial distribution of the eve of the Anhwei-Chihli war, see Watanabe, p. 61. See also Ch'i, p. 210.
16. Hara, vol. 8, p. 249 (June 19, 1919); Usui, *Nihon to Chūgoku*, p. 169. (This was, of course, at the time the anti-Japanese movement was at its height.)
17. Uchida Yasuya (Foreign Minister) to Obata Yūkichi (Minister in Peking), June 16 and July 9, and public government statement of July 16, 1919, JFMA 1614

2-12, pp. 166, 766–68, 1250–55, and English-translated text at p. 1408; Fujii, pp. 58–62.

18. Major General Sato (Yasunosuke) to Army Vice-Minister, July 13, 1920, JFMA 1614 2-12, pp. 1450–51.

19. Report dated Aug. 21, 1920, *ibid.*, p. 3408; Fujii, p. 63.

20. Ohashi, Acting Consul General, Mukden, July 11, 1920, *ibid.*, pp. 965–69; Fujii, p. 62.

21. Fujii, p. 62.

22. For military details see JFMA file, *passim*, battle maps at pp. 3870–75. A résumé of the political developments is given in a Ministry of Foreign Affairs report of Oct. 14, 1920, JFMA 1614 2-12, pp. 3520–67.

23. Of the money advanced to the Anhwei group by Japan (the so-called "Nishihara loans"), approximately 150 million yen in all, only about 5 million was ever repaid; Morton, p. 49.

24. Sonoda, *Kaiketsu Chō Sakurin*, p. 265.

25. *Ibid.*, p. 271.

26. Inaba, "Shingai kakumei yori Manshū jihen zengo made no Nitchū kankei," p. 156; Quarterly Intelligence Report from (British) Consul General Wilkinson for the quarter ended Dec. 31, 1920, FO 371 6634 F309/309/10.

27. Sonoda, *Kaiketsu Chō Sakurin*, pp. 278–80.

28. *Ibid.*, pp. 280–82.

29. *Ibid.*, pp. 333–46; Li Chien-nung, p. 410.

30. Sonoda, *Kaiketsu Chō Sakurin*, pp. 339–40.

31. *Ibid.*, pp. 340–44.

32. MacKinnon, "Liang Shih-i and the Communications Clique."

33. Li Chien-nung, p. 384; Morley, p. 120; Nathan, pp. 86–87, 122–23, 245–53.

34. Sonoda, *Kaiketsu Chō Sakurin*, pp. 353–54.

35. *Ibid.*, pp. 368–72.

36. *Ibid.*, pp. 353–54. Other sources give a smaller figure for the grant to Chang: 500,000 yüan in Tang, p. 369, for example.

37. Tang, p. 368.

38. Carr, *The Bolshevik Revolution*, p. 507; Tang, p. 369.

39. Sonoda, *Kaiketsu Chō Sakurin*, pp. 356–63; Asano, pp. 48–49. For a discussion, not altogether convincing, of the theory that the delay on Chang's part was due to collusion with Ungern-Sternberg, see Weigh, pp. 200–202.

40. Sonoda, *Kaiketsu Chō Sakurin*, pp. 363–64; Tang, p. 370; Carr, *ibid.*, pp. 507–8.

41. Sonoda, *Kaiketsu Chō Sakurin*, pp. 365–66; Ts'en, vol. 2, p. 210.

42. To Major General Kishi (Yajirō) of the Kwantung Army on Sept. 15; Kwantung Army Headquarters, Special Report, China, no. 32, JFMA 1614 2-12, p. 3476. Also Fujii, p. 66.

43. Remark to Machino Takema, reported in Commander in Chief, Tientsin, to Uehara Yūsaku, Chief of the General Staff, Aug. 4, 1920, cited in Hayashi, p. 136.

44. Machino to Akatsuka, Aug. 7, 1922, cited in Fujii, p. 66.

45. Press conference on July 16 at Tientsin to all the foreign press; Aug. 13 at Peking to the Japanese press; Aug. 31 at Peking to the American press; Sonoda, *Kaiketsu Chō Sakurin*, pp. 273–78.

46. Interviews with Kishi Yajirō, Sept. 15, and with Tachibana Shōichirō (Kwantung Army Commander in Chief) on Sept. 23. Kwantung Army Staff Office Report, Sept. 24, 1921, in Hayashi, p. 140.

47. Hayashi, pp. 137–39.

48. John W. Young, "The Hara Cabinet," p. 133.

49. Dec. 16, 1920. "Tōsanshō kun-etsu-shi Chō Sakurin shōgun ni kansurū hiken" (My opinion about Chang Tso-lin, Inspector General of the Three Eastern Provinces), in Bōeichō senshishitsu, *Mitsu dai nikki*, 1921, vol. 6. See also John W. Young, "The Hara Cabinet," pp. 134–36.

50. Shidehara heiwa zaidan, p. 116. See also the revealing entry in Hara's diary for Sept. 29, 1917, quoted in John W. Young, "The Hara Cabinet," p. 141.

51. Hara Keiichirō, Nov. 19 and 24, 1920, vol. 9, pp. 135–36, 138–39.

52. *Ibid.*, p. 136.

53. For a full record of the conference, see JFMA PVM 12, pp. 14650–90; for cabinet decisions of May 13 and 17, see also *NGN*, vol. 1, bunsho, pp. 523–25; also Hara Keiichirō, vol. 9, pp. 308–10. The conference is also discussed in the article already cited by John W. Young, "The Hara Cabinet," at pp. 137–40. This article, to which my attention was drawn while this manuscript was in process of revision, reaches a conclusion (at p. 142) strikingly similar to my own.

54. Quarterly Intelligence Report, British Consul General, Mukden, Sept. quarter, 1921; FO 371 6635.

55. Japanese Consul Hojo at Ch'ih-feng, Oct. 24, 1921; JFMA 1614 25, p. 7091.

56. Consul Hojo, Feb. 22, 1922, *ibid.*, p. 7202.

57. *Chang Tso-lin ch'üan-shih*, p. 36.

58. Cable dated Sept. 18, 1921, a copy of which was sent by the Japanese Consul General in Mukden to Foreign Minister Uchida, Sept. 24, 1921; JFMA 161 425, p. 7076.

59. The actual conference lasted only from October 10 to 18. However, most of the delegates were reported to have arrived beginning Sept. 22. Report by Chief of Police, Kwantung Province, Nov. 5, 1922, *ibid.*, p. 7095.

60. Memorandum submitted by General Chang Huan-hsiang from Harbin to General Chang Tso-lin on "The General Situation in Manchuria," a copy of which is printed in *The Peking and Tientsin Times*, Feb. 3 and 4, 1921. I have not been able to locate an original Chinese text of this memo, but since "Three Eastern Provinces" was conventionally translated into English as "Manchuria," the use of that term here is quite consistent with the point just made above.

61. Report by Chief of Police, Kwantung Province, Nov. 5, JFMA 1614 25, p. 7099.

62. Quarterly Intelligence Report, British Consul General, Mukden, Sept. quarter, 1920, FO 228 3290. Baker eventually resigned in June 1923; *GSS*, 31: 233.

63. Chang Yen-shen, p. 139.

64. *Ibid.*, p. 140.

65. Sonoda, *Kaiketsu Chō Sakurin*, p. 377. Compare the opinion of the British Consul General that "Chang, far from being a Japanese puppet, is actually most friendly to the Americans, seeing them as most likely allies in an eventual struggle between China and Japan." Quarterly Intelligence Report, Sept. quarter, 1920, FO 228 3290.

66. Entō jijō kenkyūkai, *Chōsa shiryō*, no. 47, Aug. 28, 1924.

67. Sonoda, *Kaiketsu Chō Sakurin*, p. 397; Ts'en, vol. 2, p. 177ff. The terms of this loan were not published, but were believed to have been discount at 95 percent and repayment within six months at 12 percent interest (according to the *Chōsa shiryō* report cited in the previous note).

68. Chang Tzu-sheng, p. 5. On the escape of Tuan and Hsü, see Ikei, "Dai ichiji Hōchoku sensō to Nihon," pp. 163–91, at pp. 178–80.

69. Sonoda, *Kaiketsu Chō Sakurin*, p. 336.

70. Sun Yat-sen to Chicherin, Aug. 28, 1921; Eudin and North, p. 220.

71. *The Times* (London), Dec. 27, 1921.

72. Uchida to Obata (Minister in Peking), Jan. 6, 1922, JFMA 1614 11, pp. 135–41.

73. Quarterly Intelligence Report, British Consul General, Mukden, March quarter, 1922, FO 371 6635; Chang Tzu-sheng, pp. 7–8.

74. "Documents on the Comintern and the Chinese Revolution," introduced by Harold Isaacs, *China Quarterly*, 45, Jan.–March, 1971, p. 103.

75. *The Times* (London), March 11, 1922.

76. On Jan. 8 and 15; Obata to Uchida, Jan. 15, and Kwantung Army Chief of Staff to Deputy Chief of (General) Staff, Jan. 15, JFMA 1614 11, pp. 241–58, 372–73.

77. Kwantung Army Chief of Staff to Deputy Chief of (General) Staff, Jan. 14, 1922, *ibid.*, pp. 307–8. Items requested were 10,000 rifles, with 10 million bullets; 100,000 artillery shells; 200 machine guns, or at least 100, with 5 million bullets; Akatsuka, Jan. 14, 1922, JFMA 1614 11, pp. 261–69.

78. *Ibid.*, pp. 307–8.

79. In Jan. 1922, Akatsuka contributed a preface to Sonoda Kazuki's biography of Chang (*Kaiketsu Chō Sakurin*), in which he described him as "looking over the whole of China with the power of the rising sun," adding that he could not but hope that "together with other dedicated men, Chang might succeed in the difficult task of uniting North and South and leading the people of the four hundred and more provinces [*sic*] to the tranquillity of T'ai-shan."

80. Akatsuka, Jan. 14, 1922, JFMA 1614 11, pp. 261–69.

81. Obata to Uchida, Jan. 15, 1922, JFMA 1614 11, pp. 241–58.

82. Major General Banzai (Rihachirō) to Chief of General Staff, Jan. 10, 1922, *ibid.*, pp. 221–25.

83. Akatsuka to Uchida, Jan. 14, 1922, JFMA 1614 11, pp. 261–69.

84. Kishi to Deputy Chief of Staff, Jan. 19, 1922, *ibid.*, pp. 470–71.

85. Kwantung Army Chief of Staff to Deputy Chief of Staff, Jan. 21, 1922, *ibid.*, pp. 530–33.

86. Military Attaché (Peking) to Army Vice-Minister, Jan. 17, 1922, *ibid.*, pp. 328–29.

87. Uchida to Akatsuka, Jan. 19, 1922, *ibid.*, pp. 408–22.

88. Uchida to Akatsuka, Jan. 23, 1922, *ibid.*, pp. 523–27.

89. Ikei, "Dai ichiji Hō-choku sensō to Nihon," pp. 175–76.

90. Akatsuka to Uchida, Jan. 25, 1922, JFMA 1614 11, pp. 625–28.

91. See discussion in Ikei, "Dai ichiji Hō-choku sensō to Nihon," pp. 177–78.

92. At a dinner party given by Chang for a group of 29 Japanese in Mukden on March 25, Akatsuka responded for the guests as follows: "Though it is the most earnest desire of all Japanese, who bear a special relationship with the Three East-

ern Provinces, to want to help you as their friend, Your Excellency, because of the present situation in international relations and because of the confusion in China, we cannot do this actively, and would just like you to know that passively we are completely favorably disposed to you." Akatsuka to Uchida, March 28, 1922, JFMA 1614 11, pp. 1662-72.

93. Draft dated April 21, 1922, JFMA 1614 11, pp. 2083-93.

94. What is included in *NGN*, vol. 2, bunsho, pp. 22-23, as a cabinet decision on this matter is an amended version, dated April 22, of a draft first drawn up the previous day. The former appears in the JFMA file at pp. 2137-41; the latter is at pp. 2083-93. The April 22 draft was further amended, as can be seen from the same file at pp. 2142-46, whereupon it was decided not to refer it to the cabinet at all. See also Ikei, "Dai ichiji Hō-choku sensō to Nihon," p. 186.

95. Statement by Chief of the Asia Bureau of the Ministry of Foreign Affairs, April 22, 1922, JFMA 1614 11, pp. 2147-52.

96. This is according to the account by Machino. See also "Aizu shikon fūun-roku, pp. 148-49; and Tōa dōbunkai, *Zoku taishi kaikoroku*, vol. 2, p. 855.

97. JFMA 1614 11, pp. 2153-57.

98. As forwarded in a letter from Matsuoka Yōsuke to Baron Ijūin dated April 13, 1922, contained in JFMA 1614 11, pp. 2065-68.

99. For the text of Wu's telegram and Chang's reply in defense of Liang, see Chang Tzu-sheng, pp. 5-7; also Li Chien-nung, pp. 411-12. The loan amount under consideration was 96 million yüan, sufficient to arouse fears among his opponents that Chang might, from such economic strength, achieve permanent dominance over them. T'ao Chü-yin, *Pei-yang chün-fa t'ung-chih shih-ch'i shih-hua*, vol. 6, p. 99; *The Times* (London), March 11, 1922. Another, perhaps equally important, reason for Wu's hostility is in the fact that the Liang cabinet refused to pay expenses previously promised to Wu (Ch'i, *Warlord Politics*, p. 211).

100. Chang Tzu-sheng, p. 8; *Peking and Tientsin Times*, March 20, 1922.

101. *CYB*, 1923, pp. 573-74.

102. Chang's fourth son, child of his fifth wife, Wang, was betrothed to Ts'ao's sixth daughter; Sonoda, *Kaiketsu Chō Sakurin*, p. 25.

103. T'ao Chü-yin, *Pei-yang*, vol. 6, pp. 98-99. Ts'ao K'un's brother, Ts'ao Jui, Civil Governor of Chihli province, also journeyed to Mukden to convey goodwill between the two (*ibid*., p. 100).

104. Ikei, "Dai ichiji Hō-choku sensō to Nihon," p. 184.

105. Li Chien-nung, pp. 414-19.

106. Chang Tzu-sheng, p. 17; also *Peking and Tientsin Times*, March 30, 1922.

107. Chang Tzu-sheng, p. 17.

108. *Ibid*., p. 18; *CYB*, 1923, p. 574; Sheridan, pp. 110-12.

109. Dazai, *Chūka minkoku dai jūichi nen shi*, pp. 83-84; Chang Tzu-sheng, p. 18; T'ao Chü-yin, *Pei-yang*, vol. 6, pp. 103-5.

110. T'ao Chü-yin, *Pei-yang*, vol. 6, p. 105. Both Lu and Tuan Ch'i-jui may also have been put off, as a Ministry of Foreign Affairs paper suggests, by repugnance at engaging in any dealing involving Chang Hsün; JFMA, 1614 11, at p. 1881.

111. The "telegraphic warfare" that preceded the actual fighting is reproduced at length in Ts'en Hsüeh-lü, vol. 2, pp. 181-221.

112. *CYB*, 1923, gives Chang 84,000 men and Wu 64,000 (p. 574). The

Japanese *Yomiuri shinbun* (April 18) gives Chang 80,000 and Wu between 70,000 and 80,000. The highest estimate given is in Chang Tzu-sheng, p. 27: Chang 120,000 and Wu 100,000. Some observers, however, were highly impressed by Chang's armies, especially their equipment. For a report of a visit to the Fengtien army lines by a British correspondent on April 27, see *The Times* (London), June 24, 1922.

113. Chang Tzu-sheng, p. 140; Tōa dōbunkai, *Taishi kaikoroku*, vol. 1, p. 545; also Chi Chen-chü, chuan 3, pp., 20–21.

114. T'ao Chü-yin, *Pei-yang*, p. 108; Sonoda, *Tōsanshō no seiji to gaikō*, p. 109, gives both reasons. See also further discussion in following text.

115. These divisions actually remained neutral. Presumably efforts were made by both sides to involve them, however. On Chang's behalf Communications clique representatives had tried unsuccessfully to bribe them into open alliance with him. See Kwantung Army Staff Office report, "Investigation into the Reasons for the Defeat of the Fengtien Army," forwarded to Tokyo by the Kwantung Province Police Bureau, May 31, 1922, JFMA 1614 11, pp. 4917–30.

116. "*Aizu shikon fūunroku*," pp. 147–48.

117. Sonoda, *Kaiketsu Chō Sakurin*, p. 48.

118. *Ibid.*, pp. 38–39.

119. "Investigations into the Reasons for the Defeat of the Fengtien Army," JFMA, 1614 11, pp. 4917–30.

120. T'ao Chü-yin, *Pei-yang*, p. 108.

121. Sonoda, *Kaiketsu Chō Sakurin*, p. 39.

122. "Investigations into the Reasons . . .," JFMA, 1614 11, pp. 4917–30. Also Chang Tzu-sheng (p. 42) estimated that 20,000 men under Chang Tso-hsiang simply broke ranks and fled.

123. Yang Yü-t'ing, for example, Chang's Japanese-trained Chief of Staff, opposed the war from its inception and also opposed the appointment of Tsou Hua; *ibid.* See also "*Aizu shikon fūunroku*," pp. 148–49.

124. "*Aizu shikon fūunroku*, p. 149. Tōa dōbunkai, *Zoku taishi kaikoroku*, vol. 2, p. 876.

125. Chang Tzu-sheng, p. 52.

126. T'ao Chü-yin, *Pei-yang*, p. 110, 112.

127. Chang Tzu-sheng (p. 53) gives 3,000 casualties on each side; Machino thought a total of 10,000 (*Aizu shikon fūunroku*," p. 150).

128. For details of the cease-fire terms, see Chang Tzu-sheng, pp. 53–54.

129. Lattimore's concept of the function of the "reservoir" region of "Manchuria" as key to the sovereignty of North China is relevant here. See Lattimore, p. 41, for example.

CHAPTER THREE

1. Sonoda, *Tōsanshō no seiji to gaikō*, p. 112.

2. Akatsuka, Consul General at Mukden, July 26, 1922, JFMA 1614 6, p. 7583. For biographies of Wu Chün-sheng, see Sonoda, *Shina shinjin kokki*, p. 151; and Gaimushō, *Gendai Chūka minkoku Manshūkoku jinmeikan*, 1932, p. 111.

3. Kwantung Province Police Department, report of May 31, 1922; JFMA 1614 6, p. 7258. For details of the railway plans, see *GSS*, vol. 31 (Mantetsu vol. 1), pp.

447–57. The principal project was for a line from Harbin north to the Amur River at Heiho.

4. *Ibid.* (Kwantung Province). Also report by the same source dated June 14, 1922; JFMA 1614 6, p. 7255.

5. Kwantung Province Police Report, May 31, 1922; JFMA 1614 6, p. 7258.

6. *Ibid.*

7. Kwantung Province Police Report, May 21, 1922; *ibid.*, p. 7255.

8. Akatsuka, July 26; Nakayama, Kwantung Province Police Chief, Oct. 30, 1922; *ibid.*, p. 7794.

9. Nakayama, report of Oct. 26; *ibid.*, p. 7782.

10. Strong local opposition to Wu in the Provincial Assembly might have afforded Chang a pretext for dismissing him. See Nakayama, report of Nov. 13; *ibid.*, p. 7830.

11. Sonoda, *Tōsanshō no seiji to gaikō*, p. 111; T'ao Chü-yin, *Pei-yang*, vol. 6, pp. 111–12; Kwantung Province Police Report, June 5, 1922, JFMA 1614 6, p. 7289; *North-China Herald*, June 3 and 17, 1922.

12. Reports, as in the *North-China Herald*, July 1, of his death in late June seem to have been premature; he appears to have escaped the initial assault of Chang Tsung-ch'ang's troops but been captured and shot in August. Kishimoto, Kwantung Province Police Chief, report of Aug. 24, 1922, JFMA 1614 6, p. 7642.

13. Sonoda, *Tōsanshō no seiji to gaikō*, pp. 111–12.

14. *Ibid.*, pp. 113–14. Chang Tso-lin was not known for his wit, and the irony of his rhetoric on this occasion must be presumed unconscious.

15. See, for example, Chesneaux, "Le Mouvement fédéraliste en Chine."

16. Kwantung Province Police Report, June 8, 1922, JFMA 1614 6, p. 7294. The seals of office were actually handed over to Chang on May 31, though the decision was not formally adopted by the Assembly until June 4. Takahashi, p. 243.

17. Dazai, *Manshū gendaishi*, p. 243.

18. Nishimura, "Tōsanshō ni okeru Shingai kakumei," p. 15.

19. Fincher, pp. 209–11.

20. Takahashi, pp. 266–67.

21. Chai and Tsang, chüan 142.

22. Hsieh, p. 223.

23. Dazai, *Manshū gendaishi*, pp. 395–96.

24. Kwantung Province Police Report, June 19 and July 10, 1922, JFMA 1614 6, pp. 7363, 7432.

25. Akatsuka to the Minister of Foreign Affairs, Sept. 7, 1922, JFMA 1614 6, p. 7809. For an English text of the "Peace Preservation Principles," see the *North China Star*, Sept. 3, 1922.

26. For biographies of Wang Yung-chiang, see Sonoda, *Shina shinjin kokki*, p. 595; Tanabe, pp. 79–80; and Tajima, pp. 102–8 (based on information obtained from Wang's friend and adviser Iwama Tokuya). For another, detailed account of Wang's career, see Suleski.

27. Kwantung Province Police Department, report of June 8, 1922, JFMA 1614 6, p. 7294; Mukden Political and Intelligence Reports, (British) Consul General Wilkinson, June quarter, 1922, FO 371 6635.

28. Kwantung Province Police Report, June 26 and July 5, 1922, JFMA 1614 6, pp. 7830, 7395; "Summary of Events for 1922," *MCG*, Jan. 1, 1923.

29. *MCG*, July 1, 1922, p. 401: 4 million yüan in copper coin, 5 million in Communications Bank *ta-yang* notes, and 2 million in silver coin.

30. Kwantung Province Police Report, July 5. The credit balance in the treasury was reported to be down from $17 million yüan to 4 million anyway; Consul General Wilkinson Report, June 1922, FO 371, 6635.

31. Kwantung Province Police Report, July 14, 1922, JFMA 1614 6, p. 7467.

32. *Ibid.*, Aug. 9, 1922, p. 7620.

33. *Ibid.*, Aug. 18, 1922, p. 7627.

34. *Ibid.*

35. During the war of 1922 many Kiriners were reported to be hoping for the defeat of Chang Tso-lin; Kwantung Province Police Report, May 22, 1922, JFMA 1614 11, p. 4319.

36. Kwantung Province Police Department, report by Kwantung Army Chief of Staff, July 11, 1922, JFMA 1614 6, p. 7441.

37. Kwantung Province Police Department, report by Changchun Police Chief, July 5, 1922, JFMA 1614 6, p. 7401.

38. *Ibid.*, and Consul General Morita, Kirin, July 3, 1922, JFMA 1614 6, p. 7382. K'uei is actually referred to in these sources as K'uei Hsing-chieh, i.e. by his courtesy name rather than by his correct given name, although both seem to have been used interchangeably. See Table 2.

39. Reports of July 11 and 5, as in notes 36 and 37 above.

40. Kwantung Province Police Department, reports of Aug. 4 and Dec. 13, 1922, and *Tōhō Tsūshin* (Fengtien), Dec. 21, 1922, JFMA 1614 6, pp. 7610, 7897, 7902.

41. *North-China Herald*, June 24, 1922.

42. Letter from the Association of Kirin Students returned from Japan, dated May 24, in *Chi-ch'ang jih-pao* (Kirin-Changchun daily), June 3. Enclosures in dispatch from Consul General Morita, Kirin, June 6, 1922; JFMA 1614 6, p. 7280.

43. Sonoda, "Kokuryūkōshō seikyoku no kaibō," report prepared for *Tōhō Tsūshin* and contained in dispatch from Mukden Consul General Funatsu dated July 15, 1924. JFMA 1614 6, pp. 9218–43.

44. Kwantung Province Police Report, May 26, 1922; JFMA 1614 11, p. 4718.

45. Kwantung Province Police Reports, July 3 and Aug. 2, 1922, JFMA 1614 6, pp. 7410, 7603. Chang Tsung-ch'ang's 4th Mixed Brigade was also ordered to assist in case the Assembly needed "persuasion" to make it submit.

46. Changchun Police Department Chief Minami to Changchun Consul, Feb. 9, 1923; JFMA 1614 6, pp. 8078–83.

47. See, for example, Quarterly Intelligence Report, British Consul, Mukden, Sept. quarter, 1922; FO 371 6635.

48. Report by Kwantung Province Police Chief, Oct. 26, 1922; JFMA 1614 6, p. 7784.

49. Chai and Tsang, chüan 144, p. 148.

50. Entō jijō kenkyūkai, no. 18, March 28, 1924: "Tōsanshō minji sokushinkai no kaibō" (An analysis of the Association for the Promotion of Civil Government in the Three Eastern Provinces). (See below, n. 85).

51. *MCG*, March 1, 1925, p. 10.

52. According to a brief biography in Tanabe, p. 155.

53. Otsuka, pp. 34–35.

54. From Sept. 1921. Nangō, p. 117.

55. *Ibid.*, p. 102. For a chart of annual exchange rates for all important Manchurian currencies, averaged out per year from 1912 to 1930, see Tōa Keizai Chōsakyoku, *Manmō seiji keizai teiyō*, pp. 471–72.

56. Nangō, p. 102.

57. *Ibid.*, p. 118.

58. *Ibid.*, pp. 116–18; "Feng-Chih war and the world of commerce," *MCG*, July 1922, pp. 1–15, 393ff; and "Fluctuating relations between the Fengtien p'iao and the Japanese silver- and gold-backed bank notes," *MCG*, Dec. 1924, p. 23.

59. Average annual exchange rates from 1920 to 1930 for 100 yüan of Fengtien p'iao as against the Japanese 100 yen (gold) note follow (taken from Tōa Keizai Chōsakyoku, *Manmō seiji keizai teiyō*, pp. 471–72).

1920	100	1923	139	1926	359	1929	5,683
1921	139	1924	138	1927	957	1930	10,036
1922	135	1925	168	1928	2,510		

Currencies of Kirin and Heilungkiang provinces suffered even worse decline, as figures given by this source indicate.

60. *Peking and Tientsin Times*, July 11, 1922; *The Times* (London), July 12, 1922.

61. Net surplus of revenue over expenditure dropped as follows: 1920, 14,617,740 yüan; 1921, 12,470,092 yüan; 1922, 7,756,950 yüan; 1923, 6,951,447 yüan; and 1924, 5,596,633 yüan (*MYB*, 1932–33, pp. 269–70). Some sources have speculated that seizure of the line meant as much as $15 million (yüan) a year to Chang, but it seems impossible to justify such a figure (Stauffer, p. 158).

62. Ying-k'ou Consul Suzuki, dispatches of May 20 and 22; Antung Consul Fukuda, of May 21; and Mukden Consul General Akatsuka, of May 22, 1922; JFMA 1614 11, pp. 3783, 3861, 3838, 3934; also *CYB*, 1924–25, pp. 796–97; *MYB*, 1931, p. 89. The Haikwan tael was worth just over 1½ yüan in 1920 (Nathan, p. xiii), progressively more thereafter.

63. "The situation in the Three Eastern Provinces in mid-January, 1923," *MCG*, Feb. 1923, p. 112.

64. Sada, pp. 21–22.

65. In Jan. 1924, JFMA 1614 6, p. 8651.

66. Drage, p. 172.

67. *North-China Herald*, Feb. 9, 1924.

68. Dispatch from Changchun Police Department Chief, Aug. 19, 1923, JFMA 1614 6, p. 8383 (reporting a meeting of school principals from 39 hsien in Kirin province, together with citizens interested, etc., in Changchun on August 17 to demand increased educational and reduced military expenditure; the figure cited here refers to budgetary allocation).

69. Report quoted from the *Min-pao* in *MCG*, Feb. 1, 1923, p. 116.

70. *MYB*, 1932–33, p. 247. This estimate refers to pre–World War I, but it is used here, since the only railway construction undertaken in the Northeast between then and 1932 was the 426 kilometers of the line between Ssu-p'ing-chieh and T'ao-nan, and that was built with Japanese loan funds.

71. *CYB*, 1924–25, p. 321; *The Times* (London), Aug. 2, 1923; *Nichi-nichi shinbun*, Dec. 11, 1922.

72. The British were considerably irked by this "illegal" second mortgage on property for which they had not yet been fully paid, an insult added to the injury of Chang's seizure of half the line. See the *Times* (London), Aug. 2, 1923.

73. This committee is first mentioned in a report by the Harbin Branch Office Chief of the South Manchuria Railway, May 14, 1924; *GSS*, 32: 403. For a detailed discussion of railway development issues, see Chapter 6.

74. "China Policy General Plan," Agreement of the Foreign, Army, Navy, and Treasury Ministries of the Kiyoura Cabinet, May 1924; *NGN*, vol. 2, bunsho, p. 61.

75. "Recent circumstances of the spinning industry in Manchuria," *MCG*, March 15, 1923, p. 108.

76. *Ibid.*

77. Report from the Mukden Office of the South Manchuria Railway Company, June 13, 1923; *GSS*, 31: 512.

78. Yanaihara, p. 248. Note that the brief account in Sun, p. 73, incorrectly gives 1921 as the date of establishment of the Chinese mill.

79. Yamauchi Shirō, Harbin Consul General, Feb. 8, 1924; JFMA 1614 6, p. 8781.

80. Amano, pp. 50–51. For detailed tables of all electrical enterprises in Manchuria, capitalization, date of establishment, output, ownership, etc., see Manshikai, vol. 2, pp. 516–21.

81. For another example, see report of the conference of July 22–28, 1924, which was attended by civilians from the rank of *Tao-yin* up and military men of the rank of brigade commander. Funatsu, Mukden Consul General, Aug. 16, 1924, JFMA 1614 6, p. 9280.

82. Mantetsu, Changchun Local Office Report, Aug. 16, 1923, *GSS*, 31: 515; Itō, *China's Challenge in Manchuria*, p. 90; Asada, p. 187, n. 14.

83. *MCG*, March 15, 1923, pp. 105–6.

84. *Ibid.*, April 15, 1923, p. 67.

85. Tōa dōbunkai, *Taishi kaikoroku*, vol. 1, p. 549; Imai, "Sen kyū-hyaku nijū yon nen no Tōsanshō," p. 22. I am indebted to Professor Imai for a copy of this article, and for copies of the materials introduced in it. These are a series of reports prepared by an organization called the Entō jijō kenkyūkai (Society for the study of Far Eastern Affairs) and entitled simply *Kenkyū shiryō* (Research materials). The reports, dated from no. 10, of Feb. 21, 1924, to no. 81, of Feb. 26, 1925, were bound under the title *Tōsanshō jōhō* (Reports on the Three Eastern Provinces). They came by chance into the possession of Professor Imai, and although it is not clear under what circumstances or for whom they were compiled, they are clearly a valuable and detailed source of information on political and economic developments of the period, and they are written from a position of opposition to Japanese intervention in Chinese affairs.

86. *Tung-san-sheng min-pao*, Aug. 26, 1924, from the Japanese translation contained in JFMA 1614 6, p. 9333.

87. Niijima Atsuyoshi, "Manshū kyōiku shi oboegaki" (A note on the history of education in Manchuria), pt. 1, in Mantetsu shi kenkyū gurūpu, no. 8, 1962, p. 15.

88. *Ibid.*; Manshikai, vol. 3, p. 94.

89. Mantetsu, Mukden Office Reports, July 28 and 31, 1923, *GSS*, 31: 595.

90. Niijima, in Mantetsu shi kenkyū gurūpu, no. 8, pp. 15–17.

91. *Ibid.*, p. 17. (Students had to complete two years of preparatory work before

being admitted to the four-year course proper—thus six years from time of establishment of the university until its first graduating class.)

92. Manshikai, vol. 3, pp. 79–83. The principal Japanese-run institutions of higher learning to which Chinese were admitted were the Manchurian Medical University in Mukden and the Engineering College in Port Arthur (*ibid.*, p. 87). For a brief and uncritical account in English of the Japanese educational system, see *MYB*, 1932–33, pp. 466–68.

93. Dazai, *Manshū gendaishi*, p. 411; Imai, "Sen kyū-hyaku niju yon nen no Tōsanshō," p. 22.

94. Kwantung Province Police Report, April 17, 1924; JFMA 1614 6, p. 8954.

95. Mantetsu, Kung-chu-ling Office Chief, March 31, 1924, *ibid.*, p. 8941.

96. Changchun Consul Report, April 11, 1924, *ibid.*, p. 8937.

97. Wieger, p. 130.

98. Imai, "Tōsanshō," pp. 23–24; Kikuchi and Nakajima, p. 283. Circulation figures of the *Sheng-ching shih-pao* in June 1926 were 30,000, so far in advance of any other paper—next in size being the *Tung-san-sheng min-pao* at 8,000, for example—that we can assume it enjoyed at least a substantial command by 1924 (Otsuka, pp. 33–35).

99. Wieger, p. 129.

100. The Japanese Consul General in Mukden was visited by Hsieh on May 2, in connection with this issue. Dazai, *Manshū gendaishi*, p. 411; Imai, "Tōsanshō," p. 23. On the decision by the Mantetsu directorate, see *GSS*, 32; 10, 117.

101. Kikuchi and Nakajima, p. 283. Among the demands voiced in the *Min-pao*'s September editorials were those for the refusal of Japanese Chōsen Ginkō banknotes, for the refusal of any joint enterprises with Japanese, and for an end to subscriptions to Japanese-run Chinese newspapers.

102. Wen, vol. 1, pp. 52–53.

103. *Ibid.*, and Chapter 2 above. Chang Tso-hsiang, together with Sun Lieh-ch'en, tuchün of Kirin and another key subordinate of Chang Tso-lin's who had come to be regarded as unreliable before the war (Kwantung Province Police Report, Nov. 15, 1921; JFMA 1614 6, p. 7095ff), submitted his resignation to Chang in July. Both resignations were declined (Kwantung Province Police Report, July 14, 1922; JFMA 1614 6, p. 7470).

104. Kwantung Province Police Report, July 20, 1922; JFMA 1614 6, p. 7500. Pao Te-shan particularly was an early affiliate of Chang Tso-lin, having been a battalion commander in his 27th Division since 1915 (Sonoda, *Kaiketsu Chō Sakurin*, appendix 2, p. 14). Looting carried out by his troops as they retreated through Jehol was cited as one reason for his arrest and execution (*North-China Herald*, July 15, 1922). On the execution of Chang K'uei-wu, see Dazai, *Manshū gendaishi*, p. 397. A third general reported executed in Mukden after the war was Chia Chen-kuo, commander of a brigade serving with the Chang Tsung-ch'ang detachment that had been supposed to open a Shantung front in the war. Pretext for his execution was alleged misuse of 200,000 yüan of war funds provided by Chang Tso-lin to pay various bandit groups and to work in collusion with Chihli. However, the promptness and readiness with which Chia returned to Mukden after the war, and the promptness with which Chang Tsung-ch'ang then had him shot, suggest that perhaps after all the guilty one may have been Chang Tsung-ch'ang. Kishimoto, report of June 5, 1922; JFMA 1614 6, p. 7285.

105. Report by Police Captain Kurehashi Kōjirō to Consular Representative

Tanaka Bunichirō at Manchouli, August 18, 1922; *ibid.*, p. 7643. Later 86 ringleaders of this mutiny were reported shot, and the rest were expelled from the army, branded on the chest with acid to avoid any possibility of their reenlisting; *North-China Herald*, Oct. 7, 1922.

106. *Inter alia*, on these events, see Reports of the Chōsen Army Chief of Staff, Sept. 8; *Tōhō Tsūshin* of Sept. 7; Assistant Consul T'ou-tao-kou, Sept. 6; and Tsitsihar Consul Yamazaki, Sept. 21; at JFMA 1614 6, pp. 7687, 7688, 7707, 7717.

107. Kwantung Province Police Chief, report of July 24, 1922, JFMA 1614 6, p. 7529.

108. Account of these reforms is taken from Wen, vol. 1, pp. 53–54; Dazai, *Manshū gendaishi*, pp. 396–99.

109. The Three Eastern Provinces "lu-chün chiang wu-t'ang" was originally set up in Mukden by Chao Erh-hsün in 1906. Training periods ranged from 6 to 18 months. After a lapse from 1915 to 1919, when the school did not function at all, it was set up again under Chang Tso-lin in March 1919. Students were supposed to be selected equally from each division, brigade, etc., and to study there for an 18-month term. From 1920 to 1925, the groups numbered 222, 352, 391, 335, 324, and 406. Chai and Tsang, chüan 171, p. 12.

110. Dazai, *Manshū gendaishi*, pp. 396–97.

111. Wou, pp. 103–4.

112. Sheridan, *passim*.

113. Quarterly Intelligence Report, Consul General Wilkinson, Mukden, Sept. quarter, 1922; FO 371 6635.

114. *North-China Herald*, Aug. 26, 1922.

115. For a general biography, see Sonoda, *Shina shinjin kokki*, p. 152; also Chou, "The Profile of a Warlord."

116. *Manchuria Daily News*, Aug. 25, 1922.

117. Mantetsu, Harbin Office Chief, report of Dec. 20, 1924, "Manshū bazoku ni tsuite" (On Manchurian bandits), *GSS*, 32: 796–97; on the Yü-ning company, see also Chang Yen-shen, p. 137.

118. *CYB*, 1924–25, p. 564.

119. Cited in Merrill, p. 91. "Though opium was still legally prohibited, land sowed with poppies was actually taxed by means of 'fines.' Temporary permits were issued to addicts 'until they were able to cure themselves,' while 'suppression bureaux' levied heavy taxes on opium sales, which in many cases were made quite openly" (p. 92). Many Fengtien militarists were thus involved, and the profits of the trade must have been considerable. The role of opium colonization, as "of all forms of unassisted migration in Manchuria, the most creative, fruitful and beneficial, with the single exception of the remarkable Shantung type of migration," has been stressed by Lattimore (p. 187).

120. Kwantung Province Police Chief, report of Nov. 27, 1922. JFMA 1614 6, p. 7850.

121. Chai and Tsang, chüan 171, p. 7.

122. Drage, pp. 168–73. (Though a biographical rather than autobiographical account, this book draws heavily on Sutton's papers, and I have assumed that the words of the description quoted here are Sutton's own.)

123. Chai and Tsang, chüan 171, p. 9.

124. A report in the JFMA file on the Fengtien-Chihli war, dated April 23, 1923,

and signed only by "Sa," is as follows: "There are three arsenals in Mukden. Two are old institutions able to produce about 250,000 cartridges per day, which will be brought up to 1,000,000 per day. Machinery in the third arsenal doesn't come up to expectations and is worn out. Englishman Mr Setton [sic] is working on inventing new and advanced guns for Chang Tso-lin. A Russian is trying to construct gas bombs" (JFMA 1614 11, p. 5578). The production goal was apparently an annual 200 artillery pieces, 200,000 shells, 600,000 rifle bullets, over 100 tons of smokeless gunpowder, and an unspecified number of Sutton's trench mortars (Wen, vol. 1, p. 54).

125. Sasaki Kōzaburō, pp. 158–60.

126. Yanaihara, p. 86.

127. Manshikai, *Manshū kaihatsu yonjū nen shi*, vol. 2, p. 492. By 1928 its output was almost equal to the combined output of all other Chinese arsenals together (Ch'i, p. 119).

128. Generally on the embargo, see Ch'i, pp. 121–22. For a "Chart of arms sales by the powers to China from Jan. 1922 to Oct. 1923," by Ushijima Yoshio of the South Manchuria Railway Research Department, see *GSS*, 31: 245–48.

129. Drage, pp. 174–77.

130. Reports from the Japanese Consul, Ying-k'ou, of May 1, 2, 8, 17, and July 31, 1923, especially the last of these; *GSS*, 31: 220, 221, 225, 228, 235.

131. Drage, p. 183. Sutton was aided in this operation by two Britishers—Talbot-Lehmann, an aeronautical adviser, and a New Zealander of Scots descent named Mackenzie. *The Times* (London), Dec. 22, 1923, also reports the arrival of these planes.

132. Wen, vol. 1, p. 54.

133. *MCG*, March 1, 1925.

134. Report by Gō Satoshi, Mantetsu Mukden Office, Sept. 10, 1924; *GSS*, 32: 275–77.

135. Chai and Tsang, chüan 171, p. 15.

136. SMR Changchun Local Office Report, July 14, 1923, "Formation of a Three Eastern Provinces Navy," *GSS*, 31: 234; Consul Nishi in Changchun, report of Jan. 31, 1924; JFMA 1614 6, p. 8740.

137. Funatsu, Consul General, Mukden, Jan. 29, 1924; JFMA 1614 6, p. 8651.

138. Funatsu, May 23, 1924; JFMA 1614 6, p. 9093.

139. Funatsu, Jan. 29, *ibid.*, p. 8651.

140. At the time Chang Ching-hui, because of the apparent dominance of new men in the clique, was reluctant to return. Mantetsu Mukden Office, report of Aug. 24, 1923; *GSS*, 31: 236.

141. The new military men—Yang Yü-t'ing, Chiang Teng-hsüan, Chang Hsüeh-liang, and Han Lin-ch'ün—were joined in the desire for battle by Chang Tsung-ch'ang, whose ambition lay in the direction of his home province, Shantung; *MCG*, Feb. 1, 1923. Report of the Military Conference of July 1923, *GSS*, 31: 234. Funatsu, Dec. 8, 1923, JFMA 1614 6, p. 6020.

CHAPTER FOUR

1. Good general coverage on the Chinese Eastern Railway problem may be found in the following: Tao Shing-chang, *International Controversies over the Chinese Eastern Railway*; C. Walter Young, *The International Relations of Manchuria*; *China Year Book,* 1926; Sokolsky, *The Story of the Chinese Eastern Railway*;

Chinese Eastern Railway Printing Office, *North Manchuria and the Chinese Eastern Railway*; Carr, *The Bolshevik Revolution*, vol. 3, p. 484ff; Tang, *Russian and Soviet Policy in Manchuria and Outer Mongolia*, p. 114ff; Whiting, *Soviet Policies in China*. On Chinese moves to establish control over the line in 1917 and 1918, see also above, pp. 35, 40.

2. Carr, *The Bolshevik Revolution*, p. 496; Tang, pp. 121–25. Text of the Sino-Japanese military agreement is in Morley, *The Japanese Thrust into Siberia, 1918*, pp. 363–65.

3. Tang, pp. 114–31 *passim*; Tao Shing-chang, pp. 101–4; Sokolsky, pp. 36–37.

4. Carr, *The Bolshevik Revolution*, p. 496; Tang, pp. 135–36.

5. The controversy over the "Karakhan Declaration" of May 1919 is thoroughly analyzed in Whiting, chap. 2 *passim*. On the treaty, see Whiting, chap. 11 and pp. 276–82; also C. Walter Young, *The International Relations of Manchuria*, pp. 283–87.

6. C. Walter Young, *ibid.*, pp. 288–91.

7. For various correspondence concerning Chang's reasons for entering negotiations with the Soviet Union, see "Hō-Ro kyōtei mondai" (The problem of the Mukden-Russian agreement), *GSS*, 32: 308–26. It is also possible that Chang was somewhat favorably disposed toward Karakhan by the fact that when Karakhan first arrived in China, in August 1923, he presented Chang with "a golden sword studded with diamonds." Weale, *Why China Sees Red*, p. 77; Carr, *Socialism in One Country*, vol. 3, p. 694.

8. C. Walter Young, *ibid.*, pp. 295–300

9. *GSS*, 32: 309, 364–65.

10. *North-China Daily News*, May 2, 1925; cited in Sokolsky, p. 48.

11. *Ibid.* Whether this imbalance continued or was eliminated later seems a matter of dispute. According to Tang (p. 191): "On January 1, 1929, of the 12,000 officers on the regular payroll of the Chinese Eastern Railroad the Chinese numbered less than 3,000. The rest were Soviet citizens." Louis Fischer, on the other hand (*The Soviets in World Affairs*, vol. 2, p. 798) claims that in July 1929 there were 17,841 Chinese, and 13,300 Russian employees.

12. *GSS*, 32: 327–36; *CYB*, 1926, p. 823; Tao Shing-chang, p. 134.

13. Kwantung Province Police Department Report, Oct. 13, 1922, JFMA 1614 6, p. 7761; *Tōhō Tsūshin*, Dec. 18, 1922, *ibid.*, p. 7896.

14. Mukden SMR Office Report, July 14, 1923, *GSS*, 31: 203. A short biography of Yang may be found in Tanabe, pp. 179–80.

15. Pye, p. 83. Lu Hsiao-chou's mission was to obtain "financial support as well as munitions from the Mukden arsenal."

16. Pye, p. 82.

17. *CYB*, 1924–25, at p. 1182 says March 1923; Ikei, "Dai niji Hōchoku sensō to Nihon" (pp. 193–224), at p. 196 gives April 1924.

18. Pye, pp. 181–87, takes a similar view.

19. Letter of Nov. 25, 1923. Facsimile in Wang, *Tung-pei chün-shih shih lüeh*, pp. 1–3.

20. This episode is treated in *GSS*, 31: 249–54; also reports by Fukazawa, Acting Consul General in Kirin, dated July 9; Changchun Consul Nishi, dated Sept. 28; and Changchun Police Chief, dated Oct. 12, 1923, all in JFMA 1614 6, at pp. 8820, 8405, 8441.

21. The figure of 15,000 is given by Consul Nishi; the Changchun Police Report, however, gives only about 2,500 men, an enormous discrepancy.

22. Report by Kirin SMR Office, July 14, 1923. *GSS*, 31: 253. It may be significant that Hsü had earlier been dismissed from his post as Civil Governor in Kirin in 1920 under Japanese pressure because of his alleged anti-Japaneseness and efforts to encourage the introduction of American capital in the development of the province. See above, Chapter 1, p. 41.

23. Report by Mukden SMR Office Chief Kamata, dated Jan. 16, 1924; JFMA 1614 6, p. 8623.

24. *Ibid.*

25. *Ibid.*, also Funatsu, Mukden Consul General, April 30, 1924, *ibid.*, p. 9025.

26. Funatsu, *ibid.*

27. Kwantung Province Police Report, May 31, 1924; JFMA 1614 6, p. 9116.

28. Other reports differ somewhat on the numbers involved; 7,000 is the estimate of the Cheng-chia-t'un Police Chief, May 2, 1924; *ibid.*, p. 9066.

29. Funatsu, April 30, 1924, *ibid.*, p. 9025.

30. *Ibid.* Although there is no evidence either way on this point, it is possible that other Japanese interests were also involved, using the Lu expedition to push Japanese interests in Mongolia. Later, when difficulties arose between Lu's forces and regular troops in the area, Lu dispatched a delegation of Japanese to Chang Tso-lin to try to straighten them out. Takahashi Sutejirō, "Manshū bazoku ni tsuite" (On the Manchurian mounted bandits), *GSS*, 32: 795–805, at pp. 803–5, "The death of Lu Chan-k'uei." For a brief account of Omotokyō and Deguchi, see Offner and Van Straelin, p. 63ff. On the Lu Chan-ku'ei affair in general, and for details of Deguchi's aspirations in the context of Japanese imperialist ambition toward Mongolia, see Kokuryūkai, vol. 3, pp. 28–39.

31. Takahashi Sutejirō, *GSS*, 32: 803–5; also Kuchiki, vol. 1, pp. 285–96.

32. Taga, 1931, pp. 22–23; Powell, p. 161.

33. Powell, p. 161.

34. Imai, "Taishō-ki," p. 107.

35. JFMA S 1612 2, p. 207.

36. On the latter, see Vespa, pp. 1–12.

37. "On the seconding of soldiers on the active service list as advisers (*ku-wen*) to the central government or to local officials in China," Decision of July 27, 1922; *NGN*, vol. 2, bunsho, pp. 25–26.

38. *Ibid.*

39. Instructions from the Army Minister to Kikuchi on taking up his appointment; Sept. 20, 1924. Cited by Ikei, "Dai niji Hōchoku sensō to Nihon," pp. 221–22. For a set of almost identical instructions, issued to Doihara Kenji in March 1928, at a time when he was due to assume the position of adviser under Chang Tso-lin, see Doihara Kenji kankōkai, p. 529.

40. Tōa dōbunkai, *Zoku taishi kaikoroku*, vol. 2, pp. 1118–20.

41. I am grateful to Mr. Etō, then aged 88, for his discussions with me in Tokyo on July 21 and 23, 1970, on his experiences, first in Tientsin and then in Mukden, as Mitsui representative, and from 1923 in Peking as representative of Chūnichi Jitsugyō (Sino-Japanese Industrial Company), technically a joint concern, of which Sun Yat-sen was first president, but actually a funnel through which Japanese *zaibatsu* funds were transmitted to successive Chinese governments.

42. On this see Imai, "Taishō-ki," p. 112.

43. C. Walter Young, *The International Relations of Manchuria*, p. 197ff.

44. Discussion between Chang Tso-lin and President Kawamura, Jan. 7, 1923, reported in Kwantung Army Chief of Staff to Deputy Chief of (General) Staff, Jan. 9, 1923; JFMA 1614 6, p. 7962.

45. Pekin Tokuhō (Peking Special Report), April 23, 1923, "Policy Decided by the Mukden Conference," *GSS*, 31: 406.

46. As reported in Report by Kirin SMR Office, May 25, 1923, *GSS*, 31: 456; on this line see Chapter 6 for a more detailed discussion.

47. Ijūin, Kwantung province Governor, to Minister of Foreign Affairs, Aug. 4, 1923; JFMA 1614 6, p. 8261.

48. At least from October, Chang was pressing Honjō on this point (Report by Mukden SMR Office, Oct. 16, 1923; *GSS*, 31: 242); Ikei, "Dai niji," p. 200.

49. As reported by Mukden Consul General Funatsu to Minister of Foreign Affairs, Jan. 11, 1924; Ikei, "Dai niji," p. 200.

50. *Ibid.*

51. *Ibid.*, p. 199. The only concrete suggestion specified in this paper, however, was that some "Japanese statesman or influential financier" might be sent to attempt to negotiate a settlement of the disputes in China.

52. *Ibid.*, p. 203. In January 1924, as Yang Yü-t'ing was expected in Tokyo on a visit, the position in the Ministry of Foreign Affairs was spelled out once again—that no arms could be supplied to Chang's forces. JFMA Report, Jan. 1924; JFMA 1614 6, p. 8603.

53. Ikei, "Dai niji," p. 203.

54. Shidehara to Funatsu, Sept. 8, 1924 (draft reply), *ibid.*, p. 205.

55. Sheridan, pp. 130–31. On the crisis of that spring and early summer, see "Hōchoku wagi kōshō oyobi sore ni tomonau seijō narabini gunjō" (Peace negotiations between Fengtien and Chihli and the political and military situation at the time), *GSS*, 31: 220–48. The latter file covers the period from April to November 1923.

56. The delegates were Sun Lieh-ch'en and Yü Ch'ung-han for Fengtien, and Wang Ch'eng-pin as the principal delegate for Chihli. Terms of the agreement were as follows (*GSS*, 31: 231): (1) Fengtien not to offer opposition on the greatest problems; (2) Fengtien to negotiate directly with the Ministry of Communications about the railway cars it is retaining; (3) Fengtien to discuss the salt tax with the Ministry of Finance; (4) one brigade of reinforcements recently sent from Jehol for suppression of bandits in the K'ai-lu area to be withdrawn, the same bandits to be suppressed by joint operation; and (5) searches of trains and passengers to be suspended by both sides. This agreement was followed in August by a similar one between the respective allies and protégés of Chihli and Fengtien—Chi Hsieh-yüan of Kiangsu and Lu Yung-hsiang of Chekiang (Pye, p. 186, n.30).

57. Sheridan, p. 131.

58. Pye, pp. 28–29; Sheridan, p. 131. Shanghai was known as one of the largest opium traffic centers in the world, and as the *China Year Book* pointed out (1926, p. 634): "Millions of money can be made out of opium, and this is the easiest way to raise funds for civil wars and the maintenance of armies." One source estimates the annual opium revenues in Shanghai to have amounted to $20 million (Jermyn Lynn, p. 136).

59. On the course of this war, see Wen, vol. 2, pp. 160–80. On Lu's appeal for aid, see Pye, pp. 85–86.

60. Li Chien-nung, pp. 462–64.

61. A Mukden leadership conference, July 22–28, attended by civil officials over the rank of tao-yin and military officials over that of brigade commander, was reported to have accorded the policy toward Chihli only thirteenth in priority among matters decided, and to have held that preparations for the showdown between the Chihli and Fengtien forces were not yet complete and that a clash was to be avoided for the time being (Funatsu, Mukden Consul General, Report of August 6, 1924; JFMA 1614 6, pp. 9280–85). A military conference at the end of August did little more than urge President Ts'ao K'un to order a cessation of hostilities (Dazai, *Manshū gendaishi*, p. 412). *The Times* (London) of Sept. 4 reported there was "strong reason to believe" that this four-month salary advance was paid by Chang.

62. The issue of orders for the punishment of Lu by Ts'ao K'un on Sept. 9 seems to have been decisive for Chang. Dazai, *Manshū gendaishi*, p. 413.

63. Pye, p. 28.

64. *Ibid*., p. 48.

65. Wen, pp. 177–78; Sheridan, p. 132.

66. On the general course of the war, see Asano, p. 87ff; Dazai, *Manshū gendaishi*, p. 412ff; Sonoda, *Tōsanshō no seiji to gaikō*, p. 128ff.

67. Sheridan, *passim*.

68. Pye, p. 29.

69. Ikei, "Dai niji," p. 217.

70. *Ibid*.

71. Sheridan, pp. 126–32.

72. Pye, p. 29.

73. Sheridan, p. 333, n.90, for a discussion of these rumors and their source.

74. Ikei, "Dai niji," p. 218. Teranishi was almost certainly involved in the plotting from an early stage. A dispatch from Yoshizawa in Peking, dated Oct. 12, eleven days before the coup, reports information from Teranishi to the effect that Feng had already agreed on cooperation with Tuan, and that he would effect a coup within the next few days to take Peking in Wu's absence. Yoshizawa to Shidehara, Oct. 12, 1924, JFMA PVM 12, vol. 3, p. 19750.

75. "Aizu shikon fūunroku," p. 156.

76. Sheridan, p. 142.

77. Ikei, "Dai niji," p. 219.

78. "Chung-kuo kung-ch'an-tang ti san-tz'u tui-yu shih-ch'i hsüan-yen," *Ying-hsiang*, no. 82, Sept. 10, 1924, pp. 657–60. On French involvement in the building up of Chang's air force, see p. 108, and on French diplomatic support, see p. 216.

79. General strategic considerations are thoroughly dealt with in Sheridan, pp. 141–42.

80. Given the agreement of so many sources on the fact of the bribe, we are not here greatly concerned with its precise amount. Sheridan (p. 142, p. 334, n.91) concludes that it was one and a half million yen, with perhaps a promise of more to be paid later. Ikei, "Dai niji," (p. 218) and "Aizu shikon fūunroku" (p. 160) give one million yen. In an October 1927 report by Etō Toyoji of a conversation between Chang and the head of Mantetsu's Mukden office, Kamata Yasuke, attended personally by Etō, the sum of 2.4 million yen was discussed. Chang on this occasion was pressing Mantetsu to return him the deeds he had then proffered in security for

the loan—in other words, to convert the loan to a gift. Yoshizawa to Tanaka, Oct. 20, 1927, JFMA F 1.9.2. 43, p. 1164. On this point see also pp. 242–43.

81. Ikei, "Dai niji," p. 218.

82. *Ibid.*

83. *Ibid.*; Sheridan, p. 144. Apart from Matsumuro, the others involved in effecting the delivery of the cash to Feng were said by Matsumuro to have been Tuan Ch'i-shu and Wang Nai-mu (Ikei, "Dai niji," p. 218).

84. *Ibid.*

85. Ugaki, p. 42.

86. Gensui Uehara Yūsaku denki hensan iinkai, *Gensui Uehara Yūsaku-den* (Biography of Field Marshal Uehara Yūsaku), cited in Ikei, "Dai niji," p. 228.

87. Sheridan, p. 144.

88. Uehara biography, cited in Ikei, "Dai niji," p. 220.

89. Sheridan, pp. 143–44.

90. Drage, pp. 187–88.

91. Tōa dōbunkai, *Zoku taishi kaikoroku*, vol. 2, p. 900. On Korenaga's activity on the T'ung-liao front, see SMR Cheng-chia-t'un office, report of Sept. 22, 1924; *GSS*, 32: 287. I have no other information on the identity of Major Hamamoto.

92. Funatsu-Wü Chun-sheng conversation of Dec. 9, reported in Funatsu's dispatch of Dec. 10, 1924; JFMA 1614 6, p. 9562.

93. *NGN*, vol. 2, pp. 62–63.

94. See his maiden speech as Minister of Foreign Affairs to the 49th session of the Diet, which met from July 1, 1924; Shidehara heiwa zaidan, pp. 262–66.

95. On his insistence on these, see Iriye, p. 111.

96. See, for example, Bamba, pp. 238–41, for the most recent statement of this view.

97. Funatsu to Debuchi, Sept. 5, 1924, cited in Ikei, "Dai niji," p. 204.

98. Shidehara to Dunatsu, Sept. 8, 1924; *ibid.*, p. 205.

99. Matsuoka to Chief Cabinet Secretary Egi, General Tanaka Giichi, Kwantung Province Governor and Kwantung Army Chief of Staff, Oct. 1, 1924; *GSS*, 32: 292.

100. Ikei, "Dai niji," pp. 206–8.

101. *Ibid.*, pp. 205–6.

102. Shidehara to Funatsu, Sept. 8, 1924; *ibid.*, p. 205.

103. *Ibid.*, pp. 206, 209–10.

104. *Ibid.*, p. 212.

105. *Ibid.*, pp. 210–12. For text of the warning and Chang's reply, see Sonoda, *Tōsanshō no seiji to gaikō*, pp. 210–11.

106. Asano, p. 91. On the heavy losses at the Shan-hai-kuan battle, see Wen, vol. 2, p. 192.

107. *Ibid.* As the Fengtien armies closed in on him, Wu was given a friendly warning through Machino to leave Tientsin before 10 o'clock the following morning, when the Tangku escape route would be cut off ("Aizu shikon fuūnroku," p. 156).

108. Sheridan, pp. 136, 146–48, 159–63.

109. Pye, p. 31. Chang made a further, unsuccessful approach to Japan for extra weapons before setting out himself, on November 8, for Peking. His request on this occasion was directed to the Kwantung Army and to South Manchuria Railway

Company Director Matsuoka Yōsuke through the local Mukden office chief of the railway company, Kamata. The reply, through Matsuoka, was a simple negative. *GSS*, 32: 303.

110. *Ibid.*; Li Chien-nung, pp. 474–77.

111. The death of Sun Yat-sen during the negotiations in Peking, on March 12, 1925, should also be noted here. General summaries of these events may be found in Pye, Li Chien-nung, Asano, Lai Hsin-hsia, etc. On the words *tuli, tutung, tupan*, all equivalent in meaning to *tuchün*, see p. 28n.

112. Tuan Ch'i-jui was immediately provided with a half-million Japanese yen in funds by the (Japanese) Okura company (Usui, *Nihon to Chūgoku*, p. 195).

CHAPTER FIVE

1. Wen, vol. 1, p. 87.

2. Funatsu to Shidehara, Nov. 29, 1924; JFMA 1618 53, p. 904. Acting Consul General Uchiyama, Mukden, Jan. 31, 1925; JFMA 1614 6, p. 9679.

3. According to Chang Tso-lin, in conversation with Funatsu on May 25, 1925. Funatsu, May 26, 1925; JFMA PVM 13, p. 824.

4. Kwantung Province Police Chief, March 26, 1926; JFMA 1614 6, pp. 10407–11. Consul General Yoshida Shigeru, Mukden, Jan. 10, 1926; JFMA 1614 6, p. 10166. Miscellaneous secret military expenditure authorized by Chang was said to amount to another 10 million yüan annually; Nangō, p. 168.

5. For brief reports of this conference, see Funatsu, April 25, 1925, JFMA 1614 6, p. 9822; and Mantetsu, Mukden Branch Office Chief, report of April 25, 1925, *GSS*, 33: 127.

6. *Ibid.*

7. Funatsu, April 16, 1925, JFMA 1614 6, p. 9792, reporting his conversation with Chang over a private dinner together the previous evening.

8. One example of this is the long-delayed project for the construction of a railway from Harbin to the Amur River, which it was hoped might be done with Chinese funds. At a conference in Mukden in August 1925, the Heilungkiang Tupan, Wu Chün-sheng, was reduced to arguing that the problem could be met by simply issuing paper money to the amount desired. Funatsu, Aug. 17, 1925, JFMA 1614 6, p. 9974.

9. One quarter of this ten million yüan was to cover the cost of expansion of the arsenal and air force (Mantetsu, Harbin Office Chief, conveying intelligence received from Lieutenant Colonel Takahashi, May 22, 1925, *GSS*, 33: 130). Another report of this note issue (*MCG*, June 1925, p. 71) simply mentions that it was to cover arsenal and air force costs. A further 10 million was reportedly issued in October to meet arsenal costs and construction expenditure on new railway lines (*MCG*, Oct. 1925, p. 31).

10. The division was reinstituted in March 1925. Of the 18 divisions created in this reorganization, eleven were directly attached to Fengtien province; and the appointees to positions of divisional, brigade, and regimental commanders were very largely men of the old Fengtien 27th and 28th divisions. For a full table of army positions at this time, see Sonoda, *Tōsanshō no seiji to gaikō*, pp. 338–43.

11. Itō, "Minkoku jūyon nendo han-Hō senran shi," p. 60.

12. Pye, p. 51 (Kiangsu): Wen, p. 207; Itō, "Minkoku jūyon nendo han-hō senran shi," p. 60 (Jehol).

13. For the standard details of Kuo's biography, see Sonoda, *Shina shinjin kokki*,

p. 616; Gaimushō, *Gendai Chūka minkoku Manshūkoku jinmeikan*, p. 62. Some additional detail is included in Gotō, p. 34. For the suggestion that Kuo may have become a Kuomintang member while in the South, see Lynn, p. 186.

14. See, for example, Kapp, p. 34ff.

15. Falconeri, pp. 89–100; Usui, "Shidehara gaikō oboegaki," p. 64.

16. "Aizu shikon fūunroku," pp. 177–78.

17. *Osaka Mainichi Shinbun*, May 30, 1925; *Tokyo Asahi Shinbun*, May 31, 1925, cited in Falconeri, p. 96; Usui, *Nihon to Chūgoku*, p. 206.

18. Falconeri, p. 96.

19. Usui, *Nihon to Chūgoku*, pp. 206–7.

20. *Ibid.*, p. 208.

21. "Aizu shikon fūunroku," p. 178.

22. Usui, *Nihon to Chūgoku*, pp. 208–9.

23. Chesneaux, *The Chinese Labor Movement*, p. 276.

24. Chang Wei-ying, p. 90. Chang Tso-lin's advisers were so embarrassed by the hostility generated in Shantung by Chang Tsung-ch'ang's regime that they planned to bring Yü Ch'ung-han down from Harbin to replace him. Strong Japanese pressure was brought to bear both through Mantetsu representatives and through Chang Tso-lin's advisers to defeat this move, ostensibly on grounds of Yü's importance to negotiations with the Russians in the North. See the October 1925 correspondence between Matsuoka Yōsuke (Mantetsu director), Kamata Yasuke (Mukden office chief for Mantetsu), and Honjo Shigeru (adviser), *GSS*, 33: 121–22.

25. Ho, pp. 360–62.

26. Quoted in Myers, p. 264.

27. Tientsin *Ta Kung Pao*, May 23, 1934, cited in Nishimura, "Dai kakumei-ki ni okeru Tōsanshō, p. 42.

28. Myers, p. 264. The question of taxes is a difficult one to square in the sources. Fang assembles figures (pp. 955–56) to show that, in eight provinces for which statistics are quoted, the surtax in the years 1931–33 varied between a minimum 95 percent and a maximum of 156 percent of the basic tax rate. Shantung was not included, but the discrepancy is nevertheless striking.

29. Lynn, pp. 183–84; Nishimura, "Dai kakumei-ki ni okeru Tōsanshō," p. 42; Lai, "Pei-yang chün-fa . . . fang shih," p. 9.

30. Ho, pp. 361–62.

31. *Ibid.* On the Shantung immigration to the Northeast, see also Nishimura, Dai kakumei-ki ni okeru Tōsanshō," pp. 40–42.

32. Myers, p. 277.

33. Gunther, p. 280; otherwise on Chang Tsung-ch'ang, see above, Chapter 3, pp. 105–6.

34. Chesneaux, *The Chinese Labor Movement*, p. 276; *GSS*, 33: 499–500, also 474, 485.

35. Consul General Uchiyama, Sept. 6, 1925, JFMA, 1614 6, p. 10037. On the eve of the Kuo rebellion, Chang Tso-lin himself expressed doubts whether Chang Tsung-ch'ang would still obey orders from him (Yoshida to Shidehara, Nov. 14, 1925, JFMA, PVM 12, p. 21973). Lynn (pp. 178–79) reports Li Ching-lin's involvement in a plot against Chang Tso-lin's life in December 1924. And for Yü Ch'ung-han's assessment of Li, see Uchiyama to Shidehara, Jan. 20, 1925, JFMA 1614 6, p. 9666.

36. Gotō, p. 10; *GSS*, 33: xviii.

37. Li Chien-nung, p. 486. On the assurance given Japanese Consul Yada, see Falconeri, p. 133.

38. Falconeri, p. 133; also Chesneaux, *The Chinese Labor Movement*, p. 269.

39. Representations from a director of Jardine Matheson to the Foreign Office, pressing the view of the company's Shanghai office, which were said to be shared also by other major China coast companies; June 24, 1925, and minutes of June 25 and June 29 by the head of the Foreign Office Far Eastern Department, and comment by the Foreign Minister, FO 371/10919 (F2575/2/10).

40. Minutes of the cabinet meeting of May 19, 1927, CAB 23/55, and Foreign Office Memorandum of May 16, CAB 24/187 (CP 156). I am indebted for this and the previous reference to David Wilson, from whose doctoral dissertation they are drawn.

41. Sheridan, pp. 177–78 (footnote).

42. Schurmann, U.S. Minister in China, to the Secretary of State, March 21, 1925; *Foreign Relations of the United States*, 1925, vol. 1, p. 600. Chang had convened the British and U.S. consuls and "made it plain first that he was determined to oust Feng, Hu and Sun; second, that he and Wu P'ei-fu were on excellent terms; and, third, that hostilities would start in the very near future."

43. Li Chien-nung, p. 485; Sheridan, p. 178. Wen, vol. 2, p. 205.

44. On the tariff conference, see Iriye, pp. 71–80. The figure of 20 million yüan is suggested in Gotō, p. 14. This estimate is presumably based on the increases proposed by Japan at the conference—2.5 percent surtax on ordinary goods and 5 percent on luxury imports. See also Asano, p. 112; *MCG*, Nov. 1925, p. 1.

45. According to a memorandum presented by the Chinese delegation to the tariff conference, the revenue from likin to all provinces in China amounted to a total of 70 million yüan; *CYB*, 1926, p. 1134.

46. Iriye, p. 72.

47. See Sheridan, pp. 179–80; Asano, pp. 112–18; Gotō, pp. 14–31; and Li Chien-nung, pp. 486–90, for basically corroborative accounts of the following events. For a detailed, unpublished account, see Yoshida Shigeru, "Hōten-ha o chūshin to suru Minkoku jūyon-nen dōran kiyō" (A memoir of the disturbances of 1925 based on the Mukden clique), Feb. 6, 1926 (secret); JFMA, 161 86, vol. 1, pp. 1192–1232.

48. Sheridan, p. 180.

49. *CBY*, 1926, p. 1023.

50. Wou, p. 293.

51. Gotō, p. 25.

52. Mantetsu Harbin Office Chief, report of Nov. 21, 1925, *GSS*, 33: 147.

53. *CYB*, 1926, p. 1025.

54. Gotō, pp. 27–30; *CYB*, 1926, p. 1025; Yoshida, in JFMA, 161 86, vol. 1, p. 1208.

55. Wen, vol. 2, pp. 209–10.

56. Fuse, pp. 122–24.

57. *Ibid.* Also Commander in Chief, China Station Army (Tientsin) to Vice-Chief of General Staff, Nov. 26, 1925; JFMA 161 86, vol. 1, p. 154.

58. *Ibid.*, pp. 150–51.

59. Gotō, pp. 47–48.

60. *Ibid.*; Yoshida, in JFMA, 161 86, vol. 1, pp. 1216–19; Wen, vol. 2, p. 213.

61. Sheridan, p. 183 ("It was evident that the defeat of Chang Tso-lin would be followed by an expansion of Feng's influence in northern China, and the most obvious area for that expansion was the province of Chihli"). See also *CYB*, 1926, p. 1026.

62. Gotō, p. 48.

63. Wen, vol. 2, pp. 209–10.

64. Sheridan, p. 182.

65. *CYB*, 1926, p. 1026.

66. Initially Li at least vacillated about which side he would support. His cable of November 25 was issued after conferring with Kuo in Tientsin that day, but even then he appears to have had reservations about allying himself with the Kuominchün, which he saw as a Red force (Commander in Chief, China Station Army, Tientsin, to Vice-Chief of General Staff, Nov. 25, 1925, JFMA, 161 86, vol 1, p. 148). He appears to have made great efforts to secure Chang Tsung-ch'ang's agreement to a common stand of neutrality. When this failed, he cabled Wang Yung-chiang in Mukden, explaining that he had been suffering from "nervous trouble," had been unable to cope with his work, and had had no alternative but to act as he did (Consul General Arita, Tientsin, Nov. 28, *ibid.*, p. 179; Nomura to Matsuoka Yōsuke, Nov. 30, *ibid.*, p. 246). On Dec. 2 he made public his continued loyalty to Chang (Sheridan, p. 182).

67. Li sent at least one cable to Yoshida Shigeru, urging him to see to the protection of his mother in Mukden (Nomura to Matsuoka, Dec. 3, 1925; JFMA 161 86, vol. 1, p. 306).

68. Nomura to Matsuoka, Dec. 1, 1925, *ibid.*, p. 249.

69. Wen, vol. 2, p. 213. These three commanded, respectively, the 15th, 9th, and 13th divisions.

70. Kwantung Army Staff Office, "Chō-Kaku sen ni okeru Shina guntai ni kansuru sho kansatsu oyobi ni hon senran ni kansuru sho mondai" (Various observations concerning the Chinese armies in the Chang-Kuo war and problems concerning this war), 1926, pp. 2–3, as cited in Eguchi, p. 76.

71. "Han Hōten funjō jiken senkyo" (The military situation in the anti-Mukden clique disturbances), Ministry of Foreign Affairs report prepared in Feb. 1926 and marked "For Diet use," JFMA 161 86, vol. 2, p. 1100.

72. Wang Yung-chiang conversation with Yoshida Shigeru, as reported in Yoshida, Dec. 5, 1925; JFMA 161 86, vol. 1, p. 378.

73. Nomura to Matsuoka, Dec. 8, 1925; *ibid.*, vol. 1, p. 462.

74. Nomura to Matsuoka, *ibid.*, p. 464.

75. Consul General, Harbin, report of Jan. 15, 1926; JFMA 1614 6, p. 10236.

76. *Ibid.*; also Consul General, Changchun, report of Dec. 17, 1925; JFMA 161 86, vol. 2, pp. 290–91.

77. Consul General, Mukden (Yoshida Shigeru), Jan. 7–8, and Consul General, Harbin (Amao Eiji), Feb. 12, 1926; JFMA 161 4, pp. 10159, 10324.

78. Yoshida, Jan. 16, 1926; *ibid.*, p. 10183.

79. Kwantung Army Staff Office, "Chō-Kaku sen . . . ," cited in Eguchi, p. 76.

80. Funahashi, pp. 9–11.

81. Kamata, Mantetsu Mukden Office Chief, report of Jan. 20, 1926. K'an announced his resignation on Jan. 12; JFMA 1614 6, p. 10193.

82. Yoshida, Feb. 23, 1926; JFMA 1614 6, p. 10352. It is to be noted that the statement in Li Chien-nung (p. 490), that upon the outbreak of the rebellion "the

military head of Jehol rushed with his troops to the rescue of Fengtien," is not correct.

83. Kwantung Army Chief of Staff to Army Vice-Minister, Dec. 9, 1925; JFMA PVM 12, "Kō-setsu narabini Hōchoku funjō kankei ikken" (The Kiangsu-Chekiang and Fengtien-Chihli disturbances), p. 22639. (This five-volume series is also included in the JFMA archives under the series number 16185.) Wu's position was somewhat complicated by the reports that he said had come in from Man-chou-li of Soviet army concentrations along the Soviet-Chinese border, presumably acting as a diversion to tie up as many of Chang Tso-lin's troops as possible and thus to aid the Feng-Kuo alliance against him. Deliverate Soviet pressure *may* have been applied through Chinese Eastern Railway manager Ivanov, since a visit by him to Wu on December 24 immediately preceded the cancellation of Wu's plans to go to Chang's aid. See also Weale, *The Vanished Empire*, p. 308, for a detailed account.

84. Nomura to Matsuoka, Dec. 2, 1925 (reporting conversation with Wang Yung-chiang), JFMA 161 86, vol. 1, p. 251; also Kwantung Army Chief of Staff to Army Vice-Minister, Dec. 12, 1925, *ibid*. vol. 2, p. 655.

85. Kwantung Army Staff Office, "Chō-kaku sen . . . ," *passim*, in Eguchi, p. 77.

86. Ugaki, p. 44, entry for the beginning of 1925.

87. *Ibid.*

88. Sakurai, pp. 485–86

89. On the origins of the Kwantung Army, see Shimada, pp. 39–40. On the question of "railway guards," see C. Walter Young, *Japanese Jurisdiction in the South Manchuria Railway Areas*, chap. 10, p. 261ff. The Japanese claimed the right to station 15 guards per kilometer of railway under their control, the figure specified in the Treaty of Portsmouth, by which control of the South Manchuria Railway was transferred from Russia to Japan. The dubious legality of this claim is dealt with by Young. Since the principal lines over which Japan assumed control under this treaty were the Dairen–Changchun (704 kilometers) and the Antung–Mukden (260 kilometers), this would mean entitlement to a force of 14,460 guards. See also Koo, vol. 1, pp. 195–217, doc. 7, "Memorandum of the 'guards' of the South Manchuria Railway."

90. Ministry of Foreign Affairs, "Manshū chūsatsugun zenbu Kantōshū sokaichi o fukumu" (The full strength of the army stationed in Manchuria, including the leased territories in Kwantung province), a one-page résumé of troop strengths and movements during the Kuo affair, prepared on Dec. 28, 1925; JFMA 161 861, p. 921.

91. *Ibid.*; also Eguchi, p. 77.

92. Eguchi, p. 78.

93. The 2d Battalion of the 39th Brigade of the Liao-yang Division, plus one company of engineers and 110 auxiliary police from Kwantung province; Sasaki, p. 172.

94. *Ibid.*

95. Ura's version of these talks is contained in Kwantung Army Staff Office, *Kaku Shō-rei to Ura sambō no kaidan no yōshi* (Summary of the talks between Kuo Sung-ling and Staff Officer Ura). Talks were held first on November 27 at Chang-li, and then on December 10 and 11 at Chin-chou. The complete documents are repro-

duced in Inaba, "Chō-Kaku sensō shiryō," from Bōeicho senshishitsu, *Mitsu dai nikki*, 1926, vol. 6.

96. Kwantung Army Staff Office, "Taishō juyon nen Shina jikyoku shōhō" (Detailed reports on the situation in China in 1925), cited in Eguchi, p. 79.

97. *Osaka Asahi Shinbun*, Dec. 2, 1925.

98. Yoshida to Shidehara, Dec. 5, (2:20 p.m.), 1925; JFMA 161 861, pp. 176–78.

99. Shidehara to Yoshida, Dec. 7, 1925, quoted in Falconeri, p. 225.

100. *Ibid.*

101. JFMA 161 861, p. 46.

102. Usui, "Shidehara gaikō oboegaki," p. 63.

103. JFMA 161 861, vol. 1, p. 267.

104. Matsuoka to Shidehara, JFMA 161 861, pp. 146–56. This document is undated, but from its content and sequence in the Foreign Ministry file it may be assumed to be from approximately the beginning of December 1925.

105. *China Weekly Review*, Jan. 2, 1926, vol. 35, no. 5, p. 121, reports a Shanghai story to the effect that the company had stood to lose 60 million p'iao if Chang's paper currency had collapsed.

106. Nangō, p. 156; *MCG*, Jan. 1926, p. 29.

107. Report by the governor of the Bank of Korea (Chōsen Ginkō Sōsai), Jan. 8, 1926, to the head of the Foreign Ministry's commercial section (Tsūshō-kyokuchō); JFMA 161 86, vol. 2, p. 1159.

108. Letter from Kuo to Minister Yoshizawa in Peking, Dec. 2, 1925, quoted in Nangō, p. 154. To quell the fears aroused by this announcement, Kuo sent his spokesman on foreign affairs, Yin Ju-keng, to Dairen to explain that the issue of a new currency would be necessary because of the overissue of unbacked notes by the Chang regime, but that the new notes would be issued in exchange for the Fengtien p'iao at "current rates of value," and that foreign loans would be negotiated to finance the issue of the new, convertible currency; *ibid.*, p. 155.

109. Hsiao Chu, "Manchuria: A statistical survey of its resources, industries, trade, railways and immigration," in Condliffe, p. 408.

110. See table of conversion rates on p. 282, note 59 to Chapter 3. Mantetsu profits amounted to approximately 26.7 million yüan in 1923, 29 million in 1924, and 34 million in 1925. Hsiao Chu, in Condliffe, p. 408; Sada, pp. 21–22, 454; Nangō, p. 234.

111. The Kwantung government office on December 3 instructed its Tokyo office to take steps to request a dispatch of troops to deal with the rapidly deteriorating situation; JFMA 161 86, vol. 1, p. 301. Machino, Chang's adviser, also related that Governor Kodama Hideo was partly responsible for encouraging Yang Yü-t'ing, who had fled to Port Arthur as soon as he heard of Kuo's rising, and Chang Hsüeh-liang, who also came to see Kodama in Port Arthur after being refused an interview with Kuo to discuss his demands, to return to Mukden and prepare to fight with Kuo ("Aizu shikon fūunroku").

112. Falconeri, p. 205; Eguchi, pp. 76, 82; Yoshida to Shidehara, Dec. 6, 1925; JFMA 161 861, p. 337.

113. Ugaki, pp. 46–47.

114. Usui, "Shidehara," p. 63.

115. Army Vice-Minister to Kwantung Army Chief of Staff and Commander in

Chief of China Station Army, Nov. 30, 1925, and Army Vice-Minister to Kwantung Army Chief of Staff, Dec. 3, 1925; quoted in Eguchi, pp. 80, 81.

116. General Staff Headquarters, "Shina no gen jikyoku ni kaerimi waga seisakujō no chakui" (Our policy considerations in view of the present situation in China). Dec. 1924; quoted in Eguchi, p. 79.

117. JFMA, 161 861, pp. 132–41; Usui, "Shidehara," p. 63. The line so decided by the cabinet was communicated the following day to Yoshizawa in Peking and Yoshida in Mukden. JFMA 161 861, p. 161.

118. JFMA, 161 861; Eguchi, pp. 82–83.

119. Eguchi, p. 83.

120. JFMA, 161 861, p. 200.

121. Eguchi, p. 84.

122. Inaba, "Chō-Kaku sensō shiryō," for Ura's record of these talks.

123. Ibid. According to Falconeri (p. 229), Kuo was also told that the Kwantung Army would countenance no fighting in or near Mukden, "which is too near to the area under Japanese guard."

124. Shirakawa noted that whereas Chang willingly acceded to the warning, Kuo tossed the paper away, showing disdain for the Japanese position; Falconeri, p. 229.

125. Usui, "Shidehara," p. 63; Shimada, p. 45; Kikuchi and Nakajima, pp. 662–63.

126. Eguchi, p. 84

127. Kikuchi and Nakajima, p. 662. Usui, "Shidehara," p. 63; MCG, Jan. 1926, pp. 7–10.

128. Weale, The Vanished Empire, p. 270.

129. Usui, "Shidehara," p. 63.

130. Ibid.

131. Usui, "Shidehara," p. 64; Shimada, p. 45. The Ministry of Foreign Affairs file for this period also includes a chart of the Japanese defense system, clearly marked so as to indicate that, whereas military operations were to be forbidden within the 12-kilometer band on either side of the railway, even the entry of armies under arms was to be forbidden in the case of the 14 main towns along the railway, including Ying-k'ou, and the belt of 12-kilometer radius around them. This too was at variance with Shidehara's interpretation of Ugaki's instructions. JFMA 161 861, p. 368.

132. Inaba, "Chō-Kaku sensō shiryō," p. 88. For the text of Kuo's reply to Shirakawa, dated Dec. 18, see JFMA 161 861, p. 723.

133. Tokyo Nichi Nichi Shinbun for Dec. 12, 1925, cited in Falconeri, p. 228. For a report of Matsui's discussions at the Ministry of Foreign Affairs on December 12, see JFMA 161 86, vol. 1, p. 626.

134. Kwantung Army Chief of Staff to Army Vice-Minister, Dec. 12, 1925, JFMA 161 86, vol. 1, p. 655. The last requests for troop reinforcements were submitted by both the Kwantung government and the Kwantung Army on the morning of December 15, the day the decision to allow the request was taken (Eguchi, p. 85).

135. On this, see Falconeri, esp. p. 231ff.

136. Quoted in Falconeri, p. 223.

137. Shidehara to Yoshida, Dec. 15, 1925 (9:30 p.m.), JFMA 161 861, pp. 434–37.

138. Sasaki Tōichi, pp. 123–24.

139. Nomura to Matsuoka, Dec. 8, 1925 (10:30 p.m., reporting plans as revealed to him by Wang Yung-chiang), JFMA 161 86, p. 467. On the recovery of confidence by Chang, see also Kamata to Matsuoka, Dec. 9, 1925, *ibid.*, p. 465; and Funatsu to Vice-Minister of Foreign Affairs, Dec. 15, 1925, quoted in Ikei, "Funatsu Tatsuichirō," p. 82.

140. "Zai Hōten Haraguchi zen-Man zairyūmin rengō kaigi gichō hōkoku" (report from Haraguchi, president of the Association of All-Manchurian Residents, in Mukden), Dec. 16, 1925, JFMA 161 681, pp. 555–58. Araki entered Chang's service as an adviser (ku-wen) under the Chinese name of General Huang Mu. Yoshida describes this unit as having been privately recruited on December 16 and not being the responsibility of the Japanese authorities. Yoshida to Changchun Consul General Amao, Jan. 16, 1926, JFMA 161 86, vol. 2, pp. 1086–94, at pp. 1092–93. However, military historian Inaba Masao states that arrangements for the supply of this unit were made by the Kwantung Army commander, General Shirakawa (*Hiroku: Doihara Kenji*, p. 168).

141. Both Wu Chün-sheng and Chang Tso-hsiang were reported by the Kwantung Army to have been strongly influenced in this way. Kwantung Army Staff Office, "Chō-kaku sen ni okeru . . . sho mondai," 1926, pp. 148–49, quoted in Eguchi, p. 86. On Chang Tso-hsiang, see also Changchun Consul Kurihara to Foreign Minister, Dec. 11, 1925, JFMA 161 86, vol. 1, p. 579, and Kirin Consul Kawakoshi, Dec. 12, 1925, *ibid.*, p. 606.

142. A detailed report on the battle, taken from the pages of the Dairen Japanese daily, *Ryōtō Shimpō* (Liaotung news), is included in Kikuchi and Nakajima, pp. 765–70. A Ministry of Foreign Affairs Report, prepared for use in the Diet, dated Feb. 1926, is included in JFMA 161 86, vol. 2, pp. 1100–1102.

143. Tōa dōbunkai, *Zoku taishi kaikoroku*, vol. 2, p. 952; "Aizu shikon fūunroku," p. 169. Machino himself also appears to have played an active role, and claims not to have slept a wink for 11 days during the crisis. He also claims to have argued very strongly, after Kuo's capture, in favor of his immediate execution, an argument that, despite the initial opposition of both Chang Tso-lin and Yang Yü-t'ing, was accepted (*ibid.*, pp. 166, 170).

144. Wei Yi-san, Kuo's Chief of Staff, was the solitary commander to continue the fight; Gotō, p. 58.

145. *MCG*, Jan. 1926, p. 32; also Ministry of Foreign Affairs Report of Feb. 1926, JFMA 161 86, vol. 2, p. 1102.

146. See his remarks to the 51st Diet in defense of his policy during the Chang-Kuo war, quoted in Eguchi, pp. 87–88. See also Iriye, pp. 111, 114.

147. JFMA 161 861, p. 474.

148. Shidehara to Yoshida, Dec. 17, 1925, JFMA 161 861, pp. 508–9.

CHAPTER SIX

1. After a conference with his chief advisers on December 26; Funahashi, p. 9.

2. *Ibid.*, p. 12.

3. Sada, p. 23.

4. *Ibid.*, p. 24–25.

5. *Ibid.*, pp. 25–27.

6. For Wang's letters, dated March 2 and 5, 1926, see *MCG*, March 1926, p. 2; Nangō, pp. 169–72; JFMA, 1614 6, p. 10407ff; Sada, pp. 127–30.

7. Tajima, pp. 105–6.

8. Wang was more congenial to the Japanese, as was Chang's other right-hand man, Yü Ch'ung-han, than was Chang. See League of Nations Association of Japan, *Observations of the Japanese Government on the Report of the Commission of Enquiry Appointed by the Resolution of December 10, 1931, of the Council of the League of Nations* (English text), Nov. 21, 1932, p. 36.

9. For biographies of Mo Te-hui, see Nangō, pp. 191–92; Gaimushō, *Gendai Chūka minkoku Manshūkoku jinmeikan*, p. 315.

10. On Liu Shang-ch'ing, see Gaimushō, *ibid.*, p. 399.

11. Nangō, p. 175.

12. *Ibid.*, p. 193–94, 208–10.

13. *MCG*, Jan. 1928, pp. 63–66; March 1928, pp. 47–52.

14. Nangō, pp. 196–203

15. Takahisa, pp. 8, 24–25.

16. Quoted in Nishimura, "1920 nendai," p. 138.

17. Amano, pp. 63–64. Amano, however, subsequently revised his estimate down to 1,167 million. See Manshūshi kenkyūkai, pp. 120–21.

18. Nishimura, "1920 nendai," p. 138.

19. For tables of the rapidly expanding note issue and the rapidly declining exchange value of the Kirin provincial notes between 1911 and 1931, see Ishida, pp. 543, 544.

20. Nangō, pp. 234–35.

21. *MCG*, April 1927, pp. 75–79.

22. Takahisa, pp. 36–77, 43–45; Sada, pp. 30–33.

23. "Tung-san-sheng chin-yung cheng-li wei-yüan-hui pao-kao shu" (Report of the Currency Reorganization Committee of the Three Eastern Provinces), May 1931, Japanese text in *MCG*, Nov. 1932, pp. 113–74, at pp. 154–55.

24. Takahisa, pp. 34–36; Sada, p. 454; *MCG*, Nov. 1926, pp. 97–100.

25. *MCG*, Jan. 1928, pp. 63–66; *MCG*, May 1928, pp. 31–33.

26. Yen Ch'uan-fu, pt. 4, Sept. 1932, pp. 184–264, at pp. 193–99, 256–58.

27. Takahisa, pp. 20–21

28. *Ibid.*, pp. 4, 35; Sada, p. 454; also Acting Consul General Hachitani Teruo, Mukden, Feb. 16, 1928, JFMA S1612 2, p. 114ff, at PP 120–24.

29. *MCG*, 1928, pp. 63–66.

30. Chang's close friendship with Etō Toyoji, formerly Mitsui Bussan representative for various Sino-Japanese trading interests, stemmed, according to Etō, partly from Chang's appreciation of Etō's investment tips. In Chang's early years in Mukden, Etō secured the contract for supply of weapons and equipment to Chang's 27th Division, and in return put to best advantage the information he could secure from his company to advise Chang on when to buy and sell soy beans, so that on his first venture Chang was able to make a 100 percent profit.

31. For a table of business concerns directly affiliated to each of the three central banks of the Northeastern provinces, see Amano, pp. 60–61. The Chang family (Tso-lin and Hsüeh-liang), as well as their extensive investments in the central provincial banks—the Official Bank of the Three Eastern Provinces, the Yungheng Bank (Kirin), and the Heilungkiang Bank—actually owned their own private bank, the Pien-yeh (Frontier Bank), which also enjoyed the right to issue its own notes.

32. In the 1926–27 season, in certain areas in the West, as much as 90 percent of

the crop was disposed of in these future deals. Nishimura, "1920 nendai," p. 147. For a description of how the system worked in detail, see Feng, pp. 1041–42.

33. On this point see Bix, pp. 431–34. Bix perhaps overemphasizes the degree to which Japanese control reached down, through control of credit, etc., to the initial stages of the bean business. This may be the result of telescoping the developments of such a long period. It is clear though, at least from the mid-1920's, that Japanese business concerns greatly resented the extremely active, monopolistic practices of the Chinese warlord banking concerns, which they claimed were grabbing at least half the entire bean crop. See Consulate General of Japan, p. 44; also Itō, p. 50.

34. Nangō, pp. 217–18.

35. Ibid.

36. Takahisa, pp. 38–39. For a report on the early activities in purchase of futures in this season, see MCG, July 1926, pp. 72–73.

37. Ishida, p. 577.

38. Ibid., pp. 547, 548, for a table of the enterprises affiliated with this bank in 1918 and 1933. For an estimate of bean purchases by the Kirin banking group in the 1930 season, see MCG, Dec. 1931, p. 197. See also Amano, p. 60.

39. Consulate General of Japan, p. 42. (Though the general position adopted by this work is quite unacceptable, on points of pure factual detail it serves to corroborate other sources.)

40. For a short history of this bank, and a table of enterprises that it either set up or came to control between 1919 and 1931, see Ishida, pp. 556–59.

41. Ishida notes (p. 552) that the credits granted by the Yung-heng bank were overwhelmingly granted either to the government or to Chang Tso-hsiang himself, and that, even of the remainder, over 90 percent were loans granted to affiliate businesses.

42. MCG, Dec. 1926, pp. 59–61.

43. Consulate General of Japan, p. 42.

44. Ishida, p. 548; Manshūshi kenkyūkai, pp. 131, 139.

45. Bix, p. 432.

46. For a brief biography of P'eng, see Gaimushō, Gendai Chūka minkoku Manshūkoku jinmeikan, p. 482. For P'eng's wealth, see the table in Takahisa, appendix 1, pp. 8–9; for further details on P'eng's relationship with Chang and his household, see the dispatch referred to above, in note 28: Acting Consul General Hachitani Teruo, Mukden, Feb. 16, 1928, JFMA S1612 2, pp. 117–18. Hachitani reports that P'eng borrowed funds from the bank to set himself up in the grain business, and that by early 1928 he had no fewer than 26 grain shops. Suleski (p. 159) mistakenly describes P'eng as a protégé of Wang Yung-chiang.

47. Takahisa, p. 3. A higher estimate of his wealth—70 to 80 million yüan—was given by a former Japanese consul general in Mukden (see Hakuunsō Shujin, preface, p. 8). Hatano Yoshihiro has calculated the relative wealth of some of the prominent warlords as follows: Ts'ao K'un, 4 million yüan; his younger brother and for some years civil and military governor of Chihli, Ts'ao Jui, 20 million; Ni Ssu-ch'ung (Anhwei warlord), 80 million; Wang Chan-yüan, 50 to 60 million; Chao Chieh, 30 million; Chiang Kai-shek, 100 million (Hatano, "Gunbatsu konsen no soko ni aru mono," p. 26).

48. "Tōsanshō kanken yūryokusha no shisankō oyobi tōshi jigyō shirabe" (An investigation of the level of wealth and enterprises invested in by influential officials of the Three Eastern Provinces), Takahisa, pp. 1–12.

49. On the Packard, see Adelaide Nichols, "Chinese Walls within Walls," *New York Times*, May 6, 1923.

50. During the crisis of late 1925, deposits in Japanese banks in the South Manchuria Railway zone went up from 15.75 million yen at the end of October to 26.13 million at the end of November and to 35.65 million at the end of December. Chang Tso-lin himself was reported to have transferred 4 million in cash to these banks, as well as depositing 2 million yen in the Chōsen Ginkō and 5 million in the Yokohama Specie Bank (Nangō, pp. 157–58, 190).

51. Nishimura, "Dai kakumei-ki ni okeru Tōsanshō," *Ajia Kenkyū*, Oct. 1972, p. 52. (This article hereafter cited as Nishimura, "Dai kakumei-ki.")

52. Nishimura, "1920 nendai," p. 141.

53. Takahisa, p. 27; *MCG*, March 1928, p. 51.

54. See table in Nishimura, "Dai kakumei-ki," p. 52; also *MCG*, Nov. 1932, pp. 37–38.

55. *North-China Herald*, Oct. 29, Dec. 10, 1927.

56. Takahisa, p. 27.

57. *MCG*, Nov. 1932, p. 32. It is rather difficult to square these figures, given by Ishida Shichirō in this *MCG* article entitled "Manshu keizai kankei no ichi kōsatsu" (An inquiry into the economic relations between Manchuria and China), with those given for 1935, in a survey of 569 farming households in Fengtien province and quoted by Asada Kyōji in *Nihon teikokushugi to kyū shokuminchi jinushisei*, p. 174. Asada's figures show only 32.5 percent landless peasants. Even the assumption that the process of peasant pauperization may have proceeded more rapidly in the two hsien studied in the Ishida article can scarcely explain such a wide discrepancy. Asada's figures are quoted in English in Bix, p. 433.

58. *MCG*, Sept. 1932, p. 257; Nishimura, "1920 nendai," p. 136.

59. Feng, pp. 1006, 1030–31.

60. On pawnshop rates, *ibid.*, pp. 1044–45; on advance sales (*ch'ing-t'ien*), see above, p. 198.

61. *MCG*, Feb. 1928, p. 50.

62. Nishimura, "1920 nendai,", p. 147. Also Takahisa, pp. 14–16, deals with the suppression campaign.

63. Asada, p. 211.

64. *MCG*, Feb. 1928, p. 51. The latter incident occurred on January 31. For details of strikes in "South Manchuria" in the month of February 1928, see *MCG*, March 1928, pp. 98–99. As the Fengtien-p'iao hit 2,000 yüan on the exchanges in January, some 5,000 businesses were reported to have closed or suspended business at least temporarily; Kojima, p. 561.

65. Wou, p. 298. On the negotiations leading to the alliance, see Funahashi, pp. 31–32, and Asano, pp. 130–31.

66. Lynn, p. 192; also Sheridan, pp. 187–88, and Wou, p. 300.

67. Lynn, p. 193.

68. Funahashi, pp. 16–17.

69. Lynn, p. 195; Funahashi, pp. 37–39.

70. Funahashi, p. 39.

71. Gillin, p. 103.

72. Funahashi, pp. 41–42; Carr, *Socialism in One Country*, p. 793.

73. Funahashi, pp. 41–51.

74. Asano, pp. 131–32; *MCG*, May 1926, pp. 13–16; Funahashi, pp. 52–53, 57–64.

75. Funahashi, pp. 65–67; *MCG*, July 1926, pp. 1–7; Asano, p. 132.

76. Sheridan, pp. 190–93; Lynn (p. 199) gives the grossly inflated figure of one million as the allied army strength. The Fengtien Army strength at this point is estimated in Funahashi, p. 69.

77. Asano, p. 135; Wou, p. 310; Lynn, p. 201.

78. Sheridan, p. 193.

79. Funahashi, p. 202; Wou, pp. 306–7, 309. For an account by Chang's adviser, Machino, of Sun's arrival in Tientsin and interview with Chang, see "Aizu shikon fūunroku," pp. 173–74.

80. Wu P'ei-fu actually requested arms and cash from Chang, but Chang was prepared only to send an army, which Wu refused. Sun Ch'uan-fang was also asked by Wu to take action jointly against the Northern Expedition armies, but gave only vague replies and took no action (Wou, pp. 311–12, 309). Chang Tsung-ch'ang then declined to go to Sun's aid when need arose. (*MCG*, Dec. 1926, p. 5). On Yen Hsi-shan's attitude toward the Ankuochün, see Gillin, p. 105.

81. Asano, pp. 159–61.

82. *MCG*, Dec. 1926, pp. 5–12; Funahashi, pp. 73–84; Asano, pp. 139–44. Chang's declaration of policy was stated to the diplomatic body on December 28 (Funahashi, pp. 80–81); for a list of the Koo cabinet, see *ibid.*, p. 82. On the debate in the Wu camp on whether to accept subordinate status within the Ankuochün plus a military expedition of Fengtien troops, see Wou, pp. 312–14.

83. Yü Ch'ang-fu, Director of the Board, T'ao-nan–Ang-ang-ch'i railway, and shortly afterward appointed Secretary to the Communications Board in P'an Fu's government, speaking to Kamata Yasuke, Mantetsu's Mukden Office Chief, Sept. 29, 1927; Kamata to Mantetsu Directorate, Sept. 30, 1927; JFMA F 1926, p. 324. Etō Toyoji, who was closely involved with Chang's administration at this time, confirms this impression. According to him, Chang and leading members of his administration played mah-jongg nightly until around midnight. Discussions of July 21 and 23, 1970, with the author. See also Houn, pp. 158–59.

84. Lynn, p. 213.

85. Funahashi, pp. 83–85; Sheridan, pp. 220–24; Lynn (p. 204–8) emphasizes the treachery of Chang's newfound allies within the Wu camp as a major factor in the Ankuochün defeat. Wu P'ei-fu retired permanently from politics with the fall of Honan to the south, on June 14, 1927 (Wou, p. 314).

86. For a detailed treatment of the Shantung expedition, see Baba.

87. Funahashi, pp. 90–92. For a good statement of Yang's views at this time, see also Asano, pp. 207–9.

88. Among the vague generalities of the program published by the political commission of the Ankuochün in early March, two items stand out: abolition of the unequal treaties, and what was euphemistically described as "co-operation between capital and labour"; *The Times* (London), March 4, 1927.

89. Funahashi, pp. 93–95, Gillin, pp. 106–7.

90. For a list of cabinet members, see Funahashi, p. 103; for Chang's speech on accesssion to the office of generalissimo, see Asano, pp. 211–12. Also *CSPSR*, 11, no. 3 (July 1927): 133–36. Details of background and affiliation of the members of the new cabinet are taken from Gaimushō, *Gendai Chūka minkoku manshūkoku*

jinmeikun. A convenient table showing all military as well as civil officeholders in the new administration is given in Wang, *Tung-pei chün-shih shih-lüeh*, pp. 67–68.

91. I do not wish to suggest that these agreements were perfect—far from it. Many differences remained within the new united front. Without consideration of the finer details, however, the contrast between the two sides was still marked. See Sheridan, pp. 229, 233–34.

92. *Ibid.*; Funahashi, pp. 144–47.

93. Sheridan, p. 234; Funahashi, pp. 159–61.

94. Gillin, pp. 107–8. Considerable detail on this war may be found in Funahashi, pp. 170–91. On the negotiating positions of both sides in early 1928, see Mantetsu shomubu chōsaka, pp. 12–15.

95. Asano, pp. 194–98: Mantetsu shomubu chōsaka, pp. 19–20.

96. Asano, pp. 216–21; Mantetsu shomubu chōsaka, pp. 20–23; Sheridan, pp. 237–38.

97. Wang, *Tung-pei chün-shih shih-lüeh*, pp. 70–71.

98. For a description of the scene as Chang left Peking, see Bamba, p. 339; Asano, pp. 223–25. The explosion itself is discussed in the section following, on Japanese policy.

99. FO 371 12471, F 1224/1224/10.

100. Lampson (to Foreign Minister), Dec. 23, 1926, FO 371 11664, F 5715/10/10; Jan. 25, 1927, FO 371 12399, F 723/2/10; Jan. 5, 1927, FO 371 12398, F 90/2/10; and Jan. 27, 1927, FO 371 12400, F 847/2/10.

101. Lampson, March 9, 1927, FO 371 12420, F 2301/28/10. For Polish reaction, see F 2905/28/10 of the same volume.

102. French Ambassador, London, to Foreign Office, Aug. 13, 1925, FO 371 10916, F 3926/1/10.

103. Minutes of Jan. 29, FO 371 12400, F 847/2/10.

104. Minutes of Jan. 31, FO 371 12400, F 873/2/10.

105. See, for example, Lampson to Wellesley, Sept. 2, 1927, FO 371 12505, F 9218/4382/10; and, after Chang's death, Lampson to Austen Chamberlain, July 3, 1928, FO 371 13171, F 4598/7/10.

106. See especially Lampson, May 5, 1927, and Oct. 27, 1927, FO 371 12506, F4394/4394/10, and FO 371 12514, F9077/9077/10. Minutes and replies attached.

107. See, for example, U.S. Minister Schurman to the Secretary of State, March 21, 1925, FRUS 1925, col. I, p. 600ff.

108. See, in general, JFMA 173 97, "Chōsai tetsudō kankei ikken" (Concerning the T'ao-nan to Tsitsihar railway), and JFMA F 1926, "Chōkō tetsudō kankei ikken" (Concerning the T'ao-nan to Ang-ang-chi railway). See also C. Walter Young, *The International Relations of Manchuria*, pp. 209–12; *Survey of International Affairs* (Royal Institute of International Affairs, C. A. Macartney et al., eds., 1928), 1925, vol. 2, pp. 353–55; Kingman, pp. 19–21; *MYB*, 1932–33, pp. 261–62.

109. The only other connection to the Chinese Eastern Railway was the spur from Changchun to Harbin, which was actually a section of the CER, on the nonstandard Russian five-foot gauge.

110. *The Times* (London), March 12, 1926, cited in *Survey of International Affairs*, ibid., p. 354. See also the *Christian Science Monitor*, June 3, 1925, clipping in JFMA 173 97, p. 845.

111. JFMA series, *passim*; Kingman, p. 20.

112. Tao Shing-chang, p. 129; Kingman, p. 63.

113. C. Walter Young, *The International Relations of Manchuria*, p. 229.

114. *Ibid.*, p. 130.

115. *Pace*, Carr, *Socialism in One Country, p.* 782, and Tao Shing-chang, p. 131, where it is stated that Ivanov's action took place during the Kuo Sung-ling affair. The Kuo affair was settled on December 23. See Chapter 5 above.

116. C. Walter Young, *ibid.*, pp. 229–31; Kingman, p. 63; Sokolsky, pp. 50–52.

117. Tao Shing-chang, p. 135; Young, *ibid.*, p. 234; Stauffer, pp. 172–74; *MYB*, 1932–33, p. 35; Kingman, pp. 64–67.

118. Carr, *ibid.*, p. 780, n.2, where it is noted that "of eighteen articles or items about China in *Internationale Presse-Korrespondenz* for the first three months of 1926, nine were devoted to relations with Chang Tso-lin and only two to relations with Canton."

119. *Ibid.*, p. 795; also pp. 916–17. Deutscher, p. 322.

120. Carr, *ibid.*, pp. 916–17; Tao Shing-chang, p. 135. *Survey of International Affairs*, *ibid.*, p. 356, is more dubious about the achievements of the Serebryakov mission than the Pravda account cited by Carr (*ibid.*, p. 217).

121. Sokolsky, p. 53; disposition of profits was one of the matters left open in the 1924 agreements, *ibid.*, p. 47. See also Kingman, p. 69.

122. Sonoda, *Kaiketsu Chō Sakurin*, p. 381.

123. Army Vice-Minister to General Matsui (adviser to Chang), Aug. 21 and 30, 1926, Bōeicho senshishitsu. 1926.

124. *MCG*, Nov. 1926, pp. 57–59.

125. Iriye, pp. 113–14, citing various Foreign Ministry studies of late 1926.

126. *MCG*, Oct. 1927, pp. 55–56. Reports that an agreement had been reached appeared in the Chinese press at the time. See *Yi-shih-pao*, Dec. 9, 1925, cited in *MCG*, Dec. 1925. Evidently Chang Hsüeh-liang also made a special trip to see General Shirakawa, Kwantung Army commander, at the critical time in December 1925, and it is worth noting that Chang Tso-lin made a special, and most unusual, visit to Shirakawa in the summer of 1926 to express thanks for the aid given him. Sakurai, pp. 495, 506.

127. See unsigned Navy Ministry report dated July 18, 1926, on the significance of the line, JFMA F 1927, p. 2105. In the Japanese Foreign Ministry archives there are no fewer than ten thick volumes of correspondence and papers relevant to this line, attesting both to its importance and to the difficulties the Japanese experienced in making progress on it. The F 1927 series listed above is entitled "Kikkai tetsudō kankei ikken" (Concerning the Kirin to Hoiryong railway) and consists of seven volumes, and another three volumes are entitled "Kitton tetsudō kankei ikken" (Concerning the Kirin to Tun-hua railway) and are listed under the number F 1924 3.

128. Morita, Consul General, Kirin, report of Oct. 19, 1920, JFMA F 1927, p. 849. Numerous references to Hsieh's activities are contained in the file subsequent to this report. A brief biography of Hsieh may be found in Gaimushō, *Gendai Chūka minkoku Manshū jinmeikan*, p. 447. After the Mukden Incident of 1931, Hsieh immediately resumed office as Commissioner for Foreign Affairs in Kirin, and the following year became Manchukuo's Foreign Minister and Secretary-General of the Kyōwakai, or Concordia Association.

129. Nakayama, Chief of the Kwantung Government Police Department, report of Feb. 20, 1924, JFMA F 1924 3, p. 16–17. These secret dealings by a local Japanese businessman, Minehata Yoshimitsu, greatly annoyed the official consul general in Kirin, Fukazawa Noboru, who complained that Minehata, whom he described as an "untrustworthy charlatan," had more influence than he did in Kirin (Fukazawa, report of Feb. 12, 1925, to Foreign Minister, and private letter to Kimura, head of the Asia Bureau of the Foreign Ministry, March 30, 1925; *ibid.*, pp. 25–54, 61–74).

130. Yoshizawa, Minister at Peking, report of Dec. 27, 1925, *ibid.*, pp. 208–10.

131. The figure of 500,000 yen is mentioned in reports in *Asahi Shinbun*, Jan. 19, 1928, and *Chi-Ch'ang jih-pao* (Kirin and Changchun daily), Oct. 29, 1928 (both clippings in *ibid.*, vol. 3, unpaginated). Some payment seems likely in view of the importance of the deal, the length of Chinese opposition, and the procedures commonly employed by Mantetsu (see text, pp. 226–27). Japanese Foreign Ministry officials were totally ignorant of the negotiations leading up to signature, as Minister Yoshizawa complained to Tokyo (Yoshizawa, Jan. 12, 1926, JFMA F 1924 3, p. 305.

132. On the circumstances surrounding this, see Yoshizawa, Dec. 28, 1925; Harbin Consul General Amau Eiji, Jan. 4, 1926; *Asahi Shinbun*, Dec. 28, 1925, and Jan. 8, 1926 (*ibid.*, pp. 275, 295, 211, 282).

133. *Chi-Ch'ang jih-pao*, Jan. 28, 1926, *ibid.*, vol. 3, unpaginated.

134. Suzuki Yōtarō, Chien-tao Consul General, April 5, 1927, JFMA 1927, pp. 2461–64.

135. Amau Eiji, "Hokuman mondai to taisaku" (The North Manchurian problem and measures to deal with it), May 31, 1927, JFMA, PVM 41 (Tōhō kaigi kankei ikken; Concerning the Eastern Conference), pp. 54–109.

136. Etō Shinkichi, "Kei-Hō sen shadan mondai no gaikō katei," pp. 194–95. Etō also cites a veiled caution administered to Yoshida by Kimura Eichi, Chief of the Asian Bureau of the Foreign Ministry, in a private letter dated March 24, 1927 (*ibid.*, p. 196).

137. In conversation with Honjō Shigeru, Honjō to Minami Jirō, Vice-Chief of Staff, Aug. 9, 1927, cited in *ibid.*, p. 196.

138. Koo, vol., 2, pp. 529–30; Kingman, p. 14.

139. "Tōsanshō kankei Nisshi-kan ken-an mokuroku narabini tekiyō" (Enumeration and outline of the matters at issue between Japan and China in the Three Eastern Provinces), private letter from Debuchi Katsuji, Vice-Minister for Foreign Affairs, to Chinese Minister in Tokyo, Aug. 12, 1927, JFMA, PVM 23, p. 278 (cited hereafter as "Mokuroku narabini tekiyō").

140. Itō, *China's Challenge in Manchuria*, p. 31.

141. MacMurray, vol. 1, p. 554. For a convenient discussion of the question of this disputed protocol, see Kingman, p. 6ff.

142. Kingman, pp. 11–12; Koo, pp. 446–48, 528; on the plans in 1923, see above, Chapter 3.

143. "Mokuroku narabini tekiyō," JFMA, PVM 23, p. 279; Koo, pp. 446–48; Itō, *China's Challenge in Manchuria*, p. 32.

144. Itō, *ibid.*

145. Borg, p. 135.

146. "Mokuroku narabini tekiyō," JFMA, PVM, pp. 283–85.

147. *Ibid.*, pp. 285–86.

148. Morishima, pp. 14–15.

149. "Mokuroku narabini tekiyō," JFMA, PVM 23, p. 280–83, 287–96.

150. Yoshida to Kimura Eiichi, April 21, 1927, JFMA, PVM 23, p. 23ff; Etō, *ibid.*, pp. 200–201.

151. Iriye (*After Imperialism*), who gives a résumé of this letter at p. 162, attaches no particular significance to it. This may be partly because he construes the first clause as referring only to areas along Japanese-owned or -financed railways, in which there might be some justification, however tenuous, for Japanese intervention on grounds of protecting its property or security of its investment. Yoshida, however, simply says, "*tetsudō fuzokuchi naigai o towazu*," literally "not asking whether within the railway zone or not," which is very clear and very sweeping.

152. JFMA, PVM 41, pp. 5–8.

153. Iriye, pp. 165–67.

154. The Eastern Conference has been written about relatively extensively. A brief treatment is necessary here, however, since it introduces and conditions the final act in Chang Tso-lin's career. Two reliable accounts in English of the conference are Iriye, pp. 169–72, and Bamba, pp. 293–303. Both works contain exhaustive bibliographies.

155. JFMA PVM 41, pp. 351–54.

156. *Ibid.*, pp. 422–30; Etō, *ibid.*, pp. 208–9.

157. Bamba, pp. 299–300.

158. Inau, pp. 73–87; Stephan, pp. 733–45.

159. Etō, *ibid.*, pp. 210–12; Iriye, p. 173.

160. Etō, *ibid.*, pp. 212–21; Iriye, pp. 173–75; Nihon kokusai seiji gakkai, *Taiheiyō sensō e no michi*, vol. 1, p. 292 (cited hereafter as *Taiheiyō sensō*).

161. Etō, *ibid.*, pp. 221–22.

162. *Ibid.*

163. *MCG*, Sept. 1927, pp. 47–54. (The first such association was formed on August 2.)

164. *Ibid.*, p. 50.

165. *Ibid.* The figure of 20,000 is given in the *Japan Weekly Chronicle*, Sept. 15, 1927, pp. 270–71; 6,900 is the *MCG* figure.

166. Kingman, p. 25.

167. *MCG*, Sept. 1927, pp. 53–54.

168. *MCG*, Oct. 1927, p. 49.

169. *Ibid.*, p. 50 (4,500); the *Japan Weekly Chronicle*, Sept 22, 1927, p. 308, gives 12,000.

170. *MCG*, Oct. 1927, p. 52.

171. *Ibid.*, pp. 52–53.

172. *Ibid.*, pp. 53–55. (On some of the reasons for poor relations between Chang and Mo Te-hui, see the first section of Chapter 6.)

173. Iriye, pp. 178–79; Army Vice-Minister to Kwantung Army Chief of Staff, Sept. 10, 1927, Bōeicho senshishitsu, 1927. Military dispatches at this time are full of concern that Chang might somehow be behind the rising tide of anti-Japanese movement.

174. "Some Developments in the SMR Loan Question," *China Weekly Review*, Dec. 17, 1927, p. 65.

175. Kingman, p. 31 (quoting *New York Times* report).

176. *Ibid.*; also *Foreign Relations of the United States,* 1927, vol. 2, pp. 482–92, on the background of the loan generally and the opposition to it.

177. *The Times* (London), Nov. 30, 1927.

178. *China Weekly Review*, Dec. 10, 1927, p. 70

179. *The Week in China*, Oct. 19, 1927, p. 4. For a detailed account of the local opposition movement to proposed Japanese railway extensions in the Northeast in October and November 1927, see "Wagahō no Manmō tetsudō koshō ni taisuru Shinagawa saikin no hantai undō" (The recent Chinese opposition movement against our Manchurian and Mongolian railway negotiations), unsigned Foreign Ministry report, JFMA, F 1924 3, p. 1176ff.

180. *Taiheiyō sensō*, vol. I, pp. 296–97.

181. JFMA, PVM 23, pp. 459–64.

182. Iriye, pp. 164, 176–77; Bamba, pp. 315–16.

183. Conversation with the author, July 23, 1970.

184. Iriye, pp. 176–81; Bamba, pp. 317–18; *Taiheiyō sensō*, vol. I, p. 294–95.

185. Iriye, p. 180.

186. Yoshizawa to Tanaka, Oct. 20, 1927 (nos. 1112 and 1113), JFMA, F 1924 3, p. 1164ff.

187. *Ibid.* Also Yoshizawa to Tanaka, Oct. 15, 1927, *ibid.*, pp. 1158–61. On opposition among members of the government, see also Bamba, p. 317.

188. *Taiheiyō sensō*, vol. I, p. 294.

189. Yoshizawa to Tanaka, Oct. 20, 1927, JFMA, F 1924 3, p. 1164.

190. *Taiheiyō sensō*, vol. I, p. 294.

191. Bamba, p. 317.

192. *Taiheiyō sensō*, vol. I, p. 295; Iriye, pp. 181–82.

193. Iriye, *ibid.*

194. News of the Chang-Yamamoto agreement was leaked, perhaps deliberately, by Chang, leading to a fresh outburst of the anti-Japanese and railway rights protection movement, principally against the projected extension of the Kirin-Tun-hua line to the Korean border. Meetings, demonstrations, petitions, and conferences occurred throughout Kirin province from October 11 through November. See the unsigned Foreign Ministry Report cited in note 179 above.

195. *Taiheiyō sensō*, vol. I, p. 298.

196. *Ibid.*, pp. 297–98; Suzuki, p. 25.

197. Yoshizawa to Tanaka, March 28, 1928, JFMA, PVM 23, pp. 687–89.

198. *Taiheiyō sensō*, vol. I, p. 299. JFMA PVM 23, pp. 690–703; for a comprehensive statement of Yoshida's views as of April 27, see his "TaiMan seisaku shiken" (A personal view of Manchurian policy), *ibid.*, pp. 713–29.

199. On the Tsinan Incident and dispatch of troops to Shantung, see Morton, "Sainan jiken," pp. 103–4; also Iriye, pp. 195–98; *Taiheiyō sensō*, vol. I, pp. 299–303.

200. Bamba, pp. 331–32.

201. Usui, "Chō Sakurin bakushi no shinsō," p. 29; Iriye, p. 211; Usui, "Shōwa shoki no Chū-Nichi kankei," p. 1670.

202. *NGN*, vol. 2, p. 116.

203. Tanaka to Yoshizawa and Yada, May 16 and 17, 1928, JFMA S 1615 31; *Taiheiyō sensō*, vol. I, pp. 304–5; Iriye, p. 210; Usui, "Shōwa shoki no Chū-Nichi kankei," p. 1669.

204. JFMA S 1616 31; Usui, *ibid.*, pp. 1669–70.

205. For some of the most recent cases of such advice, see Bamba, p. 336.

206. Usui, "Chō Sakurin bakushi no shinsō," p. 29; *Taiheiyō sensō*, vol. 1, p. 305.

207. Bamba, p. 339; supra, p. 214.

208. *Taiheiyō sensō*, vol. 1, p. 306 (citing Staff Headquarters reports).

209. *Ibid.*, pp. 306–8.

210. *Ibid.*, pp. 308–9.

211. For the main accounts of the assassination, see Kōmoto; Dull; Usui, "Chō Sakurin bakushi no shinsō"; Baba, "Tanaka gaikō to Chō Sakurin bakusatsu jiken"; Mori Yoshiaki.

CONCLUSION

1. On Chang's family, see Sonoda, *Kaiketsu Chō Sakurin*, p. 19; *Chang ta-yüan-shuai ai-wan lu*, book 1, "Hsing-chuang" (Deeds), p. 17. References to Chang's gambling propensity are numerous. The fondness for poker is mentioned in a posthumous appraisal of Chang by British Minister to China Sir Miles Lampson to Austen Chamberlain, July 3, 1928; FO 371 13171 F4598/7/10.

2. Sonoda, *Kaiketsu Chō Sakurin*, p. 31.

3. See also comment on this point in Nomura, pp. 76–77.

4. Bamba, pp. 238, 239, 241; for similar statements, see also pp. 113, 208.

5. Iriye, p. 79.

6. *Ibid.*, p. 125; for a similar statement, see p. 191.

Bibliography

CYB   *China Year Book*. London and New York, 1912–
CSPSR   *Chinese Social and Political Science Review*.
FO   *Foreign Office, Great Britain, Archives*.
GSS   *Gendaishi shiryō* (Materials on contemporary history), vols. 31–33 (Mantetsu vols. 1–3). Itō Takeo, Ogiwara Kiwamu, and Fujii Masuo, eds. Tokyo, 1966.
JAS   *Journal of Asian Studies*.
JFMA   Japanese Foreign Ministry Archives.
MCG   *Mantetsu chōsa geppō* (Monthly Research Bulletin of the South Manchuria Railway Company). Dairen, 1919– . The bulletin was actually known for most of the 1920's as *Chōsa jihō*, but for convenience all references to it have been standardized under this abbreviation.
MYB   *Manchuria Year Book*, 1932–33. Tōa Keizai Chōsakyoku (East Asiatic Economic Investigation Bureau). Tokyo, 1932.
NGN   *Nihon gaikō nenpyō narabini shuyō monjo* (Chronology and important select documents in Japanese diplomacy). 2 vols. Tokyo, 1965–66.
SMR   South Manchuria Railway.

Adachi, Kinnosuke. Manchuria: A Survey. New York, 1925.
"Aizu shikon fūunroku" (Tales about the samurai spirit of Aizu), a privately prepared and circulated biography of Machino Takema. Tokyo, 1961.
Amano Motonosuke. "Manshū keizai no hattatsu" (The development of the Manchurian economy), *MCG*, July 1932.
Andō Hikotarō. Mantetsu: Nihon teikokushugi to Chūgoku (Mantetsu: Japanese imperialism and China). Tokyo, 1965.
Araki Gorō. "Uridasareta Manshūkoku" (Manchukuo for sale), *Bungei shunjū*, April 1964, pp. 262–70.
Asada Kyōji. Nihon teikokushugi to kyū shokuminchi jinushisei (Japanese imperialism and the old colonial landlord system). Tokyo, 1968.
Asano Torasaburō. Daigensui Chō Sakurin (Generalissimo Chang Tso-lin). Dairen, 1928.

Baba Akira. "Dai ichiji Santō shuppei to Tanaka gaikō" (Tanaka diplomacy and
  the first dispatch of troops to Shantung), *Ajia kenkyū* (Asian Studies), Oct. 1963,
  pp. 50–77.

———. "Tanaka gaikō to Chō Sakurin bakusatsu jiken" (Tanaka diplomacy and
  the assassination of Chang Tso-lin), *Rekishi kyōiku* (Historical education), Feb.
  1960, pp. 41–48.

Bamba, Nobuya. Japanese Diplomacy in a Dilemma: New Light on Japan's China
  Policy, 1924–1929. Kyoto, 1972.

Billingsley, Philip Richard. "Banditry in China, 1911–1928, with Particular Reference to Henan Province." Doctoral dissertation, Leeds University, 1974.

Bix, Herbert P. "Japanese Imperialism and the Manchurian Economy, 1900–
  1931," *China Quarterly*, 51 (July–Sept. 1972): 425–43.

Bōeichō senshishitsu (Defense Agency, Military History Section). Mitsu dai nikki
  (Secret daily records of important affairs). 1921, 1926, 1927, various volumes,
  unpaginated.

Boorman, Howard L. Biographical Dictionary of Republican China. 4 vols.; New
  York and London, 1967–71.

Borg, Dorothy. American Policy and the Chinese Revolution, 1925–1928. New
  York, 1947.

Carr, E. H. The Bolshevik Revolution, 1917–1923, vol. 3. Baltimore, 1966. Originally published in 1953.

———. Socialism in One Country, 1924–1926, vol. 3. Baltimore, 1972. Originally published in 1958.

Chai Wen-hsüan and Tsang Shih-i, eds. Feng-t'ien t'ung-chih (A comprehensive
  gazetteer of Fengtien province). 260 chüan, Mukden (?), 1934.

Chang ta-yüan-shuai ai-wan-lu (Morning Register for Generalissimo Chang).
  Mukden (?), 1928(?).

Chang Tso-lin ch'üan-shih (A complete history of Chang Tso-lin). No author.
  Shanghai, 1922.

"Chang Tso-lin wai-chuan" (An unofficial biography of Chang Tso-lin), by
  Tung-pei chiu-lü (Old companion from the Northeast), *Ch'un-ch'iu* (Hong
  Kong), Nov.–Dec. 1966, nos. 225–27.

Chang Tso-lin wai-chuan (An unofficial biography of Chang Tso-lin), *see below*,
  Yü Ming.

Chang Tzu-sheng. Feng-chih chan-cheng chi-shih (An account of the Fengtien-
  Chihli war). Shanghai, 1924. Reissued in Ch'en Yün-lung, ed., Chin-tai
  Chung-kuo shih-liao ts'ung-k'an (Collection of reprinted materials on modern
  Chinese history), no. 10. Taipei, 1967.

Chang Wei-ying. "Wu-sa yün-tung chung ch'üan-kuo jen-min fan-ti tou-cheng ti
  kai-k'uang" (A sketch of the anti-imperialist struggle of the people during the
  May 30th Movement), in Lai Hsin-hsia, ed., Ti-i-tz'u kuo-nei ko-ming chan-
  cheng shih-lun-ch'i (Collection of articles on the history of the first revolutionary
  civil war). Peking, 1957.

Chang Yen-shen. Jih-pen li-yung so-wei "ho-pan shih-yeh" ch'in hua te li-shih (A
  history of the use of the so-called "joint ventures" by Japan in its aggression
  against China). Peking, 1956.

Ch'en, Jerome. "Defining Chinese Warlords and Their Factions," *Bulletin of the
  School of Oriental and African Studies*, 31, pt. 3 (1968): 563–600.

————. "Historical Background," in Jack Gray, ed., Modern China's Search for a Political Form. London, 1969.

————. Yüan Shih-k'ai. 2d ed. Stanford, Calif., 1972.

Chesneaux, Jean. The Chinese Labor Movement, 1919–1927. Translated from the French by H. M. Wright. Stanford, 1968.

————. "Le Mouvement fédéraliste en Chine, 1920–1923," Revue historique, 236 (1966): 347–84. English version in Jack Gray, ed., Modern China's Search for a Political Form. London, 1969.

Chi Chen-chü. Feng-chih ta-chan chi (A history of the Fengtien-Chihli war). Shanghai, 1922.

Chi, Hsi-hseng. The Chinese Warlord System, 1916–1928. Washington, D.C., 1969.

Ch'i, Hsi-sheng. Warlord Politics in China, 1916–1928. Stanford, 1976.

China Monthly Review. Shanghai, 1917– ; from June 1923 became China Weekly Review.

Chinese Eastern Railway Printing Office. North Manchuria and the Chinese Eastern Railway. Harbin, 1924.

Chou Tsun-shih. "The Profile of a Warlord," Ch'üan-chi wen-hsüeh, 7, no. 3 (Sept. 1965): 42–47. Translated in Dun J. Li, The Road to Communism: China since 1912. New York, 1969, pp. 10–18.

Chow Tse-tsung. The May Fourth Movement: Intellectual Revolution in Modern China. Cambridge, Mass., 1960.

Chu, Hsiao. "Manchuria: A Statistical Survey of Its Resources, Industries, Trade, Railways and Immigration," in J. Condliffe, ed., Problems of the Pacific. Kyoto, 1929.

Chung-kuo k'o-hsüeh-yüan Chi-lin sheng fen-yüan li-shih yen-chiu-so Chi-lin shih-fan ta-hsüeh li-shih shih (Chinese Academy of Science, Kirin Provincial Branch, Institute of Historical Research, Kirin Normal University Historical Section). Chin-tai tung-pei jen-min ko-ming yün-tung shih (A History of the people's revolutionary movement in the Northeast in modern times). Changchun, 1960.

Clubb, O. Edmund. Twentieth Century China. New York and London, 1964.

Condliffe, J., ed. Problems of the Pacific. Proceedings of the Third Conference of the Institute of Pacific Relations. Kyoto, 1929.

Consulate General of Japan, Harbin. Sino-Japanese Relations: Improbity and Corruption Practised by Former Military Cliques in North Manchuria. Harbin, 1932.

Dazai Matsusaburō. Chūka minkoku dai jūichi nen shi (History of the 11th year of the Chinese Republic). Dairen, 1923.

————. Manshū gendaishi (A contemporary history of Manchuria). Mantetsu chōsa shiryō, no. 47. Dairen, 1925.

Deutscher, Isaac. The Prophet Unarmed: Trotsky, 1921–1929. London, 1959.

Doihara Kenji kankōkai. Hiroku: Doihara Kenji (Secret Records: Doihara Kenji). Tokyo, 1972.

Drage, Charles. General of Fortune: The Story of One-Armed Sutton. London, 1963.

Dull, Paul S. "The Assassination of Chang Tso-lin," Far Eastern Quarterly, 11, no. 4 (Aug. 1952): 453–63.

Egami Namio. Kita Ajia shi (History of Northeastern Asia). Tokyo, 1956.

Eguchi Keiichi. "Kaku Sho-rei jiken to Nihon teikoku-shugi" (Japanese imperialism and the Kuo Sung-ling Incident), *Jinbun gakuhō* (Kyoto University, Fa-
culty of Letters), no. 17, Nov. 1962.
Entō jijō kenkyūkai (Society for the study of Far Eastern affairs). *Kenkyū shiryō*
(Research materials), no. 10, Feb. 21, 1924, to no. 81, Feb. 26, 1925. Bound
under the title Tōsanshō jōhō (Reports on the Three Eastern Provinces).
Etō Shinkichi, "Gunbatsu konsen" (Warlord wars), in Eguchi Bokurō, ed., Sekai
no rekishi (World history). Tokyo, 1969, vol. 14, pp. 371–404.
————. "Kei-Hō sen shadan mondai no gaikō katei: Tanaka gaikō to sono haikei"
(The diplomatic processes concerning the problem of interception of the
Peking–Mukden railway line: Tanaka diplomacy and its background), in Etō
Shinkichi, ed., Higashi Ajia seiji-shi kenkyū (Studies in East Asian political
history). Tokyo, 1968, pp. 177–252. An English translation of this article is
available in Tōhō gakkai, *Acta Asiatica* (Bulletin of the Institute of Oriental
Culture), no. 14, 1968, pp. 21–71. References to this work cited here are all to
the Japanese text.
Etō Toyoji. Interviews in Tokyo with the author, July 21 and 23, 1970.
Eudin, Xenia Joukoff, and Robert C. North. Soviet Russia and the East, 1920–
1927: A Documentary Survey. Stanford, 1957.
Falconeri, Gennaro. "Reactions to Revolution: Japanese Attitudes and Foreign Pol-
icy toward China, 1924–1927." Doctoral dissertation, University of Michigan,
1967.
Fang Hsien-t'ing. Chung'kuo ching-chi yen-chiu (Studies on the Chinese
economy). 2 vols. Changsha, 1930.
Feng Ho-fa. Chung-kuo nung-ts'un ching-chi tzu-liao (Materials on the Chinese
village economy). Shanghai, 1943.
Fincher, John. "Political Provincialism and the National Revolution," in Mary C.
Wright, ed., China in Revolution: The First Phase, 1900–1913. New Haven,
1968, pp. 185–228.
Fischer, Louis. The Soviets in World Affairs. 2 vols. London, 1930.
Foreign Relations of the United States. Washington, D.C.
Fujii Shōzō. "Sen kyū-hyaku nijū-nen Anchoku sensō o meguru Nitchū kankei no
ichi kōsatsu: henbōgun mondai o chūshin ni" (An investigation into Sino-
Japanese relations in the Anhwei-Chihli war of 1920: Concerning especially the
Frontier Defense Army). In Nihon kokusai seiji gakkai, Nihon gaikōshi kenkyū:
Nitchū kankei no tenkai.
Fulton, Austin. Through Earthquake, Wind and Fire: Church and Mission in Man-
churia, 1867–1950. Edinburgh, 1967.
Funahashi Hanzaburō. Nyūkan go ni okeru Hōten-ha (The Mukden clique after its
entry into the passes). Mantetsu shomubu chōsaka (Mantetsu, Research Section,
General Affairs Department), Dairen. Pamphlet no. 40, Jan. 15, 1928.
Fuse Katsuji. Shina kokumin kakumei to Hyō Gyoku-shō (Feng Yü-hsiang and the
Chinese National Revolution). Tokyo, 1929.
Gaimushō (Ministry of Foreign Affairs). Gendai Chūka minkoku Manshūkoku jin-
meikan (Biographical dictionary of the contemporary Republic of China and
Manchukuo). Tokyo, 1932.
————. Nihon gaikō bunsho (Japanese diplomatic documents). Tokyo, 1868–
1921 (as of 1975 no documents beyond 1921 had been published).
————. Shina (fu Hon Kon) ni okeru shinbun oyobi tsūshin ni kansuru chōsa (A

survey of newspapers and communications in China, including Hong Kong). Tokyo, May 6, 1924.

Gillin, Donald G. Warlord: Yen Hsi-shan in Shansi Province, 1911–1949. Princeton, N.J., 1967.

Gotō Hideo. Minkoku jūyon nendo ni okeru Hōten-ha nyūkan shoshi (A brief history of the Mukden clique's entry into the passes in 1925). Mantetsu shomubu chōsaka (Mantetsu, Research Section, General Affairs Department), Dairen. Pamphlet no. 20, Jan. 1926.

Gray, Jack, ed. Modern China's Search for a Political Form. London, 1969.

Gunther, John. Inside Asia. New York and London, 1939.

Hakuunsō Shujin (pseud.). Chō Sakurin. Tokyo, 1928.

Hall, J. C. S. "The Provincial Warlord Faction in Yunnan, 1927–1937." Doctoral dissertation, University of Leeds, 1972.

Hara Keiichirō, ed. Hara Kei nikki (Hara Kei's diary). 9 vols. Tokyo, 1950–51.

Hashikawa Bunzō. "Tanaka Giichi to Shidehara Kijūrō," Asahi jānaru, Jan. 21, 1972.

Hatano Yoshihiro. Chūgoku kindai gunbatsu no kenkyū (Studies on the modern warlords of China). Tokyo, 1973.

———. "Gunbatsu konsen no soko ni aru mono" (On the nature of warlords), Rekishi kyōiku, no. 1, 1963, pp. 20–27.

Hayashi Masakazu. "Chō Sakurin gunbatsu no keisei katei to Nihon no taiō" (The process of formation of Chang Tso-lin's warlord clique and Japan's response). In Nihon kokusai seiji gakkai, Nihon gaikōshi kenkyū: gaikō to yoron.

Hirano Reiji. Manshū no inbōsha: Kōmoto Daisaku no unmei teki na ashiato (Conspirator in Manchuria: fateful footsteps of Kōmoto Daisaku). Tokyo, 1959.

Ho, Franklin L. "Population Movement to the Northeastern Frontier of China," Chinese Social and Political Science Review, 15 (1931–32).

Houn, Franklin W. Central Government of China, 1912–1928. Madison, Wis., 1959.

Hsieh, Winston. The Ideas and Ideals of a Warlord: Ch'en Chiung-ming (1878–1933). East Asian Research Center, Harvard University, Papers on China, no. 16, 1962, pp. 198–252.

Hsü Chin-ch'eng. Min-kuo yeh-shih (An unofficial history of the Republic). Hong Kong, 1955.

Hsü Hsing-k'ai. Jih-pen ti-kuo-chu-i yü Tung-san-sheng (Japanese imperialism and the Three Eastern Provinces). Shanghai, 1930. Translated into Japanese as Manmō to Nihon teikokushugi, by Matsuura Keizō. Tokyo, 1932.

Ikei Masaru. "Dai ichiji Hōchoku sensō to Nihon" (The first Fengtien-Chihli war and Japan), and "Dai niji Hōchoku sensō to Nihon (The second Fengtien-Chihli war and Japan), in Kurihara Ken, ed., Tai Manmō seisaku-shi no ichimen (An account of the history of policy toward Manchuria and Mongolia). Tokyo, 1966.

———. "Funatsu Tatsuichirō zen-Hōten sōryōji yori Debuchi gaimu jikan ate Manshū Chūgoku shutchō genchi hōkoku shokan" (On-the-spot reports to Vice-Minister of Foreign Affairs Debuchi from Funatsu Tatsuichirō, former Consul-General, Mukden, during his official visit to China and Manchuria), Hōgaku kenkyū, 36, no. 7 (July 1963), pp. 81–98.

Imai Seiichi. "Sen kyū-hyaku nijū yon nen no Tōsanshō" (The Three Eastern Provinces in 1924), Chūgoku, no. 23 (Tokyo, 1975), pp. 21–26.

———. "Taishō-ki ni okeru gunbu no seiji-teki chii" (The political position of the military during the Taisho Period), pt. 2, *Shiso*, no. 402, Dec. 1957, pp. 106–22.

Inaba Masao. "Chō-Kaku sensō shiryō" (Materials on the Chang-Kuo war), *Gunji shigaku*, 4, pt. 1, no. 14 (Aug. 1, 1968): 76–88.

———. "Shingai kakumei yori Manshū jihen made no Nitchū kankei" (Sino-Japanese relations from the 1911 Revolution up to the Manchurian Incident), in Doihara Kenji kankōkai.

Inau Tentarō. "Tanaka jōsōbun o meguru ni-san no mondai" (Two or three problems concerning the Tanaka Memorandum). In Nihon kokusai seiji gakkai, Nihon gaikōshi no sho mondai, pp. 73–87.

Iriye, Akira. After Imperialism: The Search for a New Order in the Far East, 1921–1931. Cambridge, Mass., 1965.

Isaacs, Harold. "Documents on the Comintern and the Chinese Revolution," *China Quarterly*, 45, Jan.–March 1971.

Ishida Kōhei. Manshū ni okeru shokuminchi keizai no shiteki hatten (The historical development of a colonial economy in Manchuria). Kyoto, 1964.

Itō Takeo [Takeo Itoh]. China's Challenge in Manchuria: Anti-Japanese Activities in Manchuria prior to the Manchurian Incident. Dairen, 1932.

———. Mantetsu ni ikite (Living in the South Manchurian Railway Company). Tokyo, 1964.

———. "Minkoku jūyon nendo han-Hō senran shi" (Record of the anti-Mukden disturbances of 1925), *Pekin Mantetsu geppō*, Tokkan, no. 3, 1926.

"Kaiketsu Chō Sakurin" (The prodigious Chang Tso-lin) (no author, no date), in Matsumoto bunko (may be assumed from context and content to have been written in 1912 or 1913).

Kaizuka Shigeki. Ajia rekishi jiten (Dictionary of Asian history). 10 vols. Tokyo, 1968.

Kapp, Robert A. Szechuan and the Chinese Republic: Provincial Militarism and Central Power, 1911–1938. New Haven and London, 1973.

Kikuchi Akishirō and Nakajima Ichirō. Hōten nijū-nen shi (A twenty-year history of Mukden). Mukden, 1926.

Kingman, Harry L. Effects of Chinese Nationalism upon Manchurian Railway Developments, 1925–1931. Berkeley, Calif., 1932.

Kojima Shōtarō. Shina saikin daiji nenpyō (Chronology of recent important events in China). Tokyo, 1942.

Kokuryūkai (Amur River Society). Tōa senkaku shishi kiden (Biographies of East Asian pioneers). Tokyo, 1936. Reprinted in 3 vols., 1966.

Kōmoto Daisaku. "Watakushi ga Chō Sakurin o koroshita" (I killed Chang Tso-lin), *Bungei shunjū*, 32, no. 12 (Dec. 1954): 194–201.

Koo, V. K. Wellington (Ku Wei-chün). Memoranda Presented to the Lytton Commission. 3 vols. Chinese Cultural Society, New York, 1932–33.

Kramer, Irving. Japan in Manchuria. Foreign Policy Association of Japan, Tokyo, 1954.

Kuchiki Kanzō. Bazoku senki: Kohinata Hakurō to Manshū (Chronicle of mounted-bandit wars: Kohinata Hakurō and Manchuria). 2 vols. Tokyo, 1966.

Kuo Ting-yee, comp., and James W. Morley, ed. Sino-Japanese Relations, 1862–1927: A Checklist of the Chinese Foreign Ministry Archives. East Asian Institute, Columbia University, New York, 1965.

Kurihara Ken. Tai Manmō seisaku shi no ichimen (An account of the history of policy toward Manchuria and Mongolia). Tokyo, 1966.

Lai Hsin-hsia. Pei-yang chün-fa shih-lüeh (Outline history of the Peiyang warlords). Hu-pei jen-min ch'u-pan-she, 1957. Translated into Japanese as Chūgoku gunbatsu no kōbō. Tokyo, 1969.

————. "Pei-yang chün-fa tui-nei sou-kua te chi chung fang-shih (Various methods used by the Northern warlords to carry out their internal exploitation), Shih-hsüeh yüeh-k'an (Historical studies monthly) (Kaifeng), vol. 8, no 11, (March 1957), pp. 8–11.

Lary, Diana. Region and Nation: The Kwangsi Clique in Chinese Politics, 1925–1937. New York, 1974.

Lattimore, Owen. Manchuria: Cradle of Conflict. New York, 1932.

Lee, Robert H. G. The Manchurian Frontier in Ch'ing History. Cambridge, Mass., 1970.

Li Chien-nung. The Political History of China, 1840–1928. Translated by Teng Ssu-yu and Jeremy Ingalls. New York, 1956.

Li Shih-yüeh. "Hsin-hai ko-ming shih-ch'i tung-san-sheng ko-ming yü fan ko-ming te tou-cheng" (The struggle between revolution and counterrevolution in the Three Eastern Provinces at the time of the 1911 Revolution). Li-shih yen-chiu (Historical studies), Peking, 1959, no. 6, pp. 56–70.

Lynn, Jermyn Chi-hung. Political Parties in China. Peking, 1930.

McAleavy, Henry. "China under the Warlords," History Today, vol. 12, April 1962, pp. 227–33; May 1962, pp. 303–11.

Machino Takema. "Chō Sakurin bakushi no zengo" (Before and after the assassination of Chang Tso-lin), Chūō kōron, Tokyo, Sept. 1949, pp. 72–80.

MacKinnon, Stephen R. "Liang Shih-i and the Communications Clique," Journal of Asian Studies, 29, no. 3 (May 1970): 581–602.

MacMurray, John V. A. Treaties and Agreements with and Concerning China, 1894–1919. 2 vols. Washington, D.C., 1921.

Manshikai (Manchurian History Society). Manshū kaihatsu yonjū nen shi (A history of forty years of Manchurian development). 3 vols. Tokyo, 1964.

Manshūshi kenkyūkai (Society for Research into Manchurian History). Nihon teikokushugi ka no Manshū: Manshūkoku seiritsu zengo no keizai kenkyū (Manchuria under Japanese imperialism: economic studies on the period before and after the founding of Manchukuo). Tokyo, 1972.

Mantetsu shi kenkyū gurūpu (Research Group on the History of Mantetsu). Kenkyū nōto: Nitchū mondai (Research notes; problems in Sino-Japanese relations). Waseda University, Tokyo, 1959–65, nos. 1–10.

Mantetsu shomubu chōsaka (Mantetsu, Research Section, General Affairs Department). Shōwa san-nen Manshū seiji keizai jijō (Manchurian political and economic affairs in 1928). Dairen, May 30, 1929.

Matsumoto Bunko (Matsumoto Library). Chūgoku kankei shinbun kirinuki shū (Collection of newspaper clippings relating to China), 1908–23. Tokyo, 1967.

Merrill, Frederick T. Japan and the Opium Menace. New York, 1942.

Minami Manshū tetsudō kabushiki kaisha sanjū nen ryakushi (The South Manchuria Railway Company: an abridged history of thirty years). Dairen, 1937.

Ministry of Foreign Affairs, see Gaimushō.

Mitarai Tatsuo. Minami Jirō. Tokyo, 1957.

Mizutani Kunikazu. Zoku Tōsanshō kanken no shisei naijō (The facts about the administration of the officials of the Three Eastern Provinces, continued). Dairen, 1929.

Mori Yoshiaki. "Chō Sakurin bakushi to Machino Takema" (Machino Takema and the assassination of Chang Tso-lin), Nihon shūhō, March 25, 1957.

Morishima Morito. Inbō ansatsu guntō: gaikōkan no kaisō (Plots, assassinations, swords: memoirs of a diplomat). Tokyo, 1950.

Morley, James. The Japanese Thrust into Siberia, 1918. New York, 1957.

Morton, Willian Fitch. "Sainan jiken" (Tsinan Incident) in Nihon kokusai seiji gakkai, Nihon gaikōshi kenkyū: Nitchū kankei no tenkai, pp. 103–18.

————. "The Tanaka Cabinet's China Policy, 1927–1929." Doctoral dissertation, Columbia University, 1969.

Murphey, William Rhoads. The Treaty Ports and China's Modernization: What Went Wrong?, Ann Arbor, Michigan Papers in Chinese Studies, no. 7, 1970. See also later version in Mark Elvin and G. William Skinner, eds., The Chinese City Between Two Worlds, Stanford, 1974.

Myers, Ramon H. The Chinese Peasant Economy: Agricultural Development in Hopei and Shantung, 1890–1949. Cambridge, Mass., 1970.

Nakahama Yoshihisa. Kitsurin-shō no zaisei (The finances of Kirin province). Dairen, 1928. Mantetsu chōsa shiryō, no. 82.

Nangō Tatsune. Hōten hyō to Tōsanshō no kin-yū (The Fengtien p'iao and the finances of the Three Eastern Provinces). Mantetsu chōsa shiryō, no. 56. Dairen, 1926.

Nathan, Andrew J. Peking Politics, 1918–1923: Factionalism and the Failure of Constitutionalism. Berkeley, Calif., 1976.

Nezu Masashi. "Shidahara gaikō no sai hyōka" (A reappraisal of Shidehara diplomacy), in Hihan Nihon gendai shi (A critical modern Japanese history). Tokyo, 1958, pp. 101–17.

Nihon kokusai seiji gakkai (Japan Society for the Study of International Politics). Nihon gaikōshi kenkyū: gaikō to yoron (Studies in Japanese diplomatic history: foreign policy and public opinion). Tokyo, 1970.

————. Nihon gaikōshi kenkyū: Nitchū kankei no tenkai (Studies in Japanese diplomatic history: the evolution of Sino-Japanese relations). Tokyo, 1961.

————. Nihon gaikōshi kenkyū: Taishō jidai (Studies in Japanese diplomatic history: the Taisho Period). Tokyo, 1958.

————. Nihon gaikōshi no sho-mondai (Various problems in Japanese diplomatic history). Tokyo, 1964.

————. Taiheiyō sensō e no michi: kaisen gaikō-shi (The path to the Pacific war: diplomatic history of the opening of the war): 8 vols. Tokyo, 1962–63. Vol. 1, Manshū jihen zenya (The eve of the Manchurian Incident).

Ning Wu. "Tung-pei hsin-hai ko-ming chien-shu" (A short account of the 1911 Revolution in the Northeast). In Chung-kuo jen-min cheng-chih hsieh-shang hui-i ch'üan-kuo wen-shih tzu-liao yen-chiu wei-yüan-hui (The Research Committee on Literary and Historical Materials, National Committee of the Chinese People's Political Consultative Conference), Hsin-hai ko-ming hui-i-lu (Reminiscences of the 1911 Revolution), 5 vols., Peking, 1963. Vol. 5.

————. "Tung-pei ko-ming yün-tung" (The revolutionary movement in the Northeast), in Chung-hua min-kuo k'ai-kuo wu-shih nien wen-hsien (Documents on the 50th anniversary of the founding of the Chinese Republic). Vol. 5, Kosheng kuang-fu (Revolution province by province). Taipei, 1962, pp. 372–88.

Nishimura Shigeo. "Dai kakumei-ki ni okeru Tōsanshō, rōdō mondai o chūshin ni" (The Three Eastern Provinces during the Great Revolution, centering on the labor problem), Ajia seiji gakkai, ed., *Ajia kenkyū*, Oct. 1972, pp. 29–63.

———. "1920 nendai Tōsanshō chihō kenryoku no hōkai katei" (The process of collapse of regional power in the Three Eastern Provinces in the 1920's), *Osaka gaikokugo daigaku gakuhō* (Bulletin of the Osaka Foreign Languages University), no. 25, July 1971, pp. 131–51.

———. "Tōsanshō ni okeru Shingai kakumei" (The 1911 Revolution in the Three Eastern Provinces), *Rekishigaku kenkyū* (Historical studies), no. 358, March 1970, pp. 12–30.

Nomura Kōichi. "Manshū jihen chokuzen no Tōsanshō mondai" (The problem of the Three Eastern Provinces on the eve of the Manchurian Incident), Nihon kokusai seiji gakkai, Nihon gaikōshi kenkyū: Nitchū kankei no tenkai, pp. 71–86.

Offner, C. B., and H. Van Straelin. Modern Japanese Religions. Tokyo, 1963.

Oshibuchi Hajime. Hōten to Ryōyō (Mukden and Liao-yang). Tokyo, 1940.

Otsuka Reizō. Manshū ni okeru genron kikan no gensei (The present state of organs of public opinion in Manchuria). Dairen, Mantetsu chōsa shiryō, no. 61, 1926.

People's Revolutionary Movement, *see under* Chung-kuo k'o-hsüeh-yüan.

Powell, Ralph L. The Rise of Chinese Military Power, 1895–1912. Princeton, N.J., 1955.

Pye, Lucien W. Warlord Politics: Conflict and Coalition in the Modernization of Republican China. New York, 1971.

Roberts, John. Mitsui: Three Centuries of Japanese Business. New York and Tokyo, 1973.

Sada Kōjirō. Hōten-shō no zaisei (The finances of Fengtien province). 2 vols. Vol. 1, Dairen, Mantetsu chōsa shiryō, no. 74, 1928.

Saeki Yūichi. Chūgoku no rekishi. 8, Kindai Chūgoku (History of China. 8, Modern China). Tokyo, 1974.

Sakurai Chūon. Taishō Shirakawa (General Shirakawa). Tokyo, 1933.

Sasaki Kōzaburō. Hōten keizai sanjū-nen shi (A thirty-year history of the economy of Fengtien). Mukden, 1940.

Sasaki Tōichi. Aru gunjin no jiden (Autobiography of an army man). Tokyo, 1967.

Sheridan, James L. Chinese Warlord: The Career of Feng Yü-hsiang. Stanford, 1966.

Shidehara heiwa zaidan (Shidehara Peace Foundation). Shidehara Kijūrō. Tokyo, 1955.

Shidehara Kijūrō. Gaikō gojū-nen (Fifty years of diplomacy). Tokyo, 1951.

Shimada Toshihiko. Kantōgun (The Kwantung Army). Tokyo, 1965.

Shinobu Junpei. Taishō gaikō jūgo-nen (Diplomacy of fifteen years of the Taishō era). Tokyo, 1927.

Snow, Edgar. Far Eastern Front. New York, 1933.

Sokolsky, George. The Story of the Chinese Eastern Railway. Shanghai, 1929.

Sonoda Kazuki. Hōten-ha no shinjin to kyūjin (New men and old men in the Mukden clique). Mukden, 1923.

———. Kaiketsu Chō Sakurin (The prodigious Chang Tso-lin). Tokyo, 1922.

———. "Kokuryūkōshō seikyoku no kaibō" (An analysis of the political situation in Heilungkiang province), July 15, 1924, JFMA 1614 6, pp. 9218–43.

———. Shina shinjin kokki (Biographies of the new men of China). Osaka, 1927.
———. Tōsanshō no seiji to gaikō (Politics and foreign relations of the Three Eastern Provinces). Mukden, 1925.
South Manchuria Railway, *see* Mantetsu. For other works published by the company, see the following listings: Amano, Dazai, Funahashi, Gotō, Itō, Nakahama, Nangō, Otsuka, Sada, Takahisa, Yen.
Stauffer, Robert B. "Manchuria as a Political Entity: Government and Politics of a Major Region of China, Including Its Relations to China Proper." Doctoral dissertation, University of Minnesota, 1954.
Stephan, John J. "The Tanaka Memorial (1927): Authentic or Spurious?" *Modern Asian Studies*, 7, no. 4 (1973): 733–45.
Suleski, Ronald Stanley. "Manchuria under Chang Tso-lin." Doctoral dissertation, University of Michigan, 1974.
Sun, Kungtu C. The Economic Development of Manchuria in the First Half of the Twentieth Century. Harvard East Asian Monographs, no. 28. Cambridge, Mass., 1969.
Suzuki Teiichi. "Hokubatsu to Shō-Tanaka mitsuyaku" (The Northern Expedition and the secret agreement of Chiang Kai-shek and Tanaka), Bessatsu *Chisei* (Special issue of *Chisei*), 1956, no. 5. Himerareta Shōwashi (Neglected Shōwa history), pp. 20–25.
Taga Muneyuki. Shina no gunjō (The military situation in China). Tokyo, 1931.
Taiheiyō sensō, *see under* Nihon kokusai seiji gakkai.
Tajima Tomiho. "O Eikō o kataru" (Speaking about Wang Yung-chiang), Manshū kaikoshū kankōkai (Reminiscences of Manchuria Publications Committee), A Manshū (Oh, Manchuria). Tokyo, 1963.
Takahashi Reisen. Mantetsu chihō gyōsei-shi (A history of regional administration by the South Manchurian Railway Company). Dairen, 1936.
Takahisa Hajime. Tōsanshō kanken no shisei naijō (The facts about administration by the officials of the Three Eastern Provinces). Mantetsu shomubu chōsaka, Dairen, Sept. 15, 1928.
Tanabe Tanejirō. Tōsanshō kanshinroku (Records of officials of the Three Eastern Provinces). Dairen, 1924.
Tanaka Giichi denki kankōkai. Tanaka Giichi denki (A biography of Tanaka Giichi). 3 vols. Tokyo, 1958.
Tang, Peter S. H. Russian and Soviet Policy in Manchuria and Outer Mongolia, 1911–1931. Durham, N.C., 1959.
T'ao Chü-yin. Pei-yang chün-fa t'ung-chih shih-ch'i shih-hua (Historical tales of the period of rule by the Peiyang warlords). 6 vols. Peking, 1957–61.
———. Tu-chün-t'uan chuan (Biographies of tuchün). Peking, 1948.
Tao Shing-chang. International Controversies over the Chinese Eastern Railway. Shanghai, 1936. Reprinted, Taipei, 1971.
T'ien Pu-i teng (T'ien Pu-i and others). Hsien-hua chün-fa (Discussion about warlords). Taipei, 1967.
Tōa dōbunkai (East Asia Common Culture Society). Taishi kaikoroku (Reminiscences about China). 4 vols. Tokyo, 1936.
———. Zoku taishi kaikoroku (Reminiscences about China: a continuation). 2 vols. Tokyo, 1941. Reprinted, Hara Shobō, 1973.
Tōa Keizai Chōsakyoku (East Asian Economic Research Bureau). Manchuria Year Book, 1932–33. Dairen, 1932.

————. Manmō seiji keizai teiyō (Handbook of the politics and economy of Manchuria and Mongolia). Dairen, 1932.

Ts'ao Te-hsuan. "Wo so chih-tao te Chang Tso-lin" (The Chang Tso-lin I knew), *Ch'üan-chi wen-hsüeh* (Biographical literature), vol. 5, no. 6. Taipei, 1964, pp. 24–28.

Ts'en Hsüeh-lü. San-shui Liang Yen-sun hsien-sheng nien-p'u (A chronological biography of Liang Shih-i). Chung-kuo hsien-tai shih-liao ts'ung-shu (Collected source materials on modern Chinese history). 2 vols. Taipei, 1962.

Tung Chien-chih. Chang Tso-lin chih ch'i-mou ch'üan-shu (A complete account of the clever stratagems of Chang Tso-lin). Shanghai, 1921.

Tung-san-sheng chin-yung cheng-li wei-yüan-hui pao-kao-shu (Report of the Three Eastern Provinces Currency Reorganization Committee), May 1931. Japanese text in *MCG*, Nov. 1932, pp. 113–74.

Ugaki Kazushige (Kazunari). Ugaki nikki (Ugaki diary). Tokyo, 1954.

Usui Katsumi. "Chō Sakurin bakushi no shinsō" (The truth about the assassination of Chang Tso-lin), Bessatsu *Chisei* (Special issue of *Chisei*), 1956, no. 5. Himerareta Shōwashi (Neglected Shōwa history), pp. 26–38.

————. Nihon to Chūgoku: Taishō jidai (Japan and China: the Taisho Period). Tokyo, 1972.

————. Nitchū gaikōshi: hokubatsu no jidai (History of Sino-Japanese relations: the period of the Northern Expedition). Tokyo, 1971.

————. "Sen kyūhyaku jūkyū nen no Nitchū kankei" (Sino-Japanese relations in 1919), *Shirin*, vol. 43, no. 3 (May 1960), pp. 61–80.

————. "Shidehara gaikō oboegaki" (A note about Shidehara diplomacy), *Nihon rekishi*, no. 126, Dec. 1958, pp. 62–68.

————. "Shōwa shoki no Chū-Nichi kankei: hokubatsu e no kanshō" (Sino-Japanese relations in the early Shōwa Period: intervention in the Northern Expedition), *Kokushi ronshū* (Essays in Japanese history), vol. 2, Kyoto, 1959, pp. 1657–72.

————. "Tanaka gaikō ni tsuite no oboegaki" (A note on Tanaka diplomacy). Nihon kokusai seiji gakkai, Nihon gaikōshi kenkyū: Shōwa jidai (Studies in Japanese diplomatic history: the Shōwa period). Tokyo, 1959.

Uyehara, Cecil H. Checklist of Archives in the Japanese Ministry of Foreign Affairs, Tokyo, Japan, 1868–1945. Washington, D.C., 1954.

Valliant, Robert B. "Japanese Involvement in Mongol Independence Movements, 1912–1919," *Mongolia Society Bulletin*, vol. 11, no. 2 (Fall 1972).

Vespa, Amleto. Secret Agent of Japan: A Handbook to Japanese Imperialism. London, 1938.

Wang T'ieh-han. "Chang Yü-t'ing hsien-sheng chang-wo tung-san-sheng chün-cheng ch'uan te ching-kuo" (The process of Chang Yü-t'ing's seizure of political and military power in the Three Eastern Provinces), *Ch'üan-chi wen-hsüeh* (Biographical literature), vol. 5, no. 3. Taipei, 1964, pp. 31–34.

————. Tung-pei chün-shih shih-lüeh (Outline history of military affairs in the Northeast). Taipei, 1972.

Watanabe Ryūsaku. Bazoku: Nitchū sensō-shi no sokumen (Mounted bandits: A sidelight on the war between Japan and China). Tokyo, 1963.

Weale, Putnam (Bertram Lennox Simpson). Chang Tso-lin's Struggle Against the Communist Menace. Shanghai, 1927.

————. The Vanished Empire. London, 1926.

————. Why China Sees Red. New York, 1925.

Weigh, Ken Shen. Russo-Chinese Diplomacy, 1689–1924. University Prints and Reprints, Russian Series, vol. 3. Bangor, Maine, 1958.

Wen Kung-chih. Tsui-chin sa nien Chung-kuo chun-shih shih (Military history of China over the past thirty years). Shanghai, 1930. Reprinted in Chung-kuo hsien-tai shih-liao ts'ung-shu (Collected source materials on modern Chinese history). 4th series. 2 vols. Taipei, 1962.

Whiting, Allen S. Soviet Policies in China, 1917–1924. New York, 1954.

Wieger, Léon. Chine moderne. Vol. 5, Nationalisme, xénophobie, anti-Christianisme. Hien-hien (Hsien-hsien), 1924.

Wilbur, C. Martin. "Military Separatism and the Process of Reunification under the Nationalist Regime, 1922–1937," in Ho Ping-ti and Tsou Tang, eds., China in Crisis, vol. 1, book 1. Chicago, 1968, pp. 203–63.

Wilson, David Clive. "Britain and the Kuomintang, 1924–1928: A Study of the Interaction of Official Policies and Perceptions in Britain and China." Doctoral dissertation, London University, 1973.

Wou, Odoric Ying-kwong. "Militarism in Modern China as Exemplified in the Career of Wu P'ei-fu, 1916–1928." Doctoral dissertation, Columbia University, 1970.

Yamamoto Jōtarō denki hensankai. Yamamoto Jōtarō denki (A biography of Yamamoto Jōtarō). Tokyo, 1942.

Yanaihara Tadao. Manshū mondai (The Manchurian problem). Tokyo, 1934.

Yen Ch'uan-fu. "Hōten-shō no tochi seido to chizei seido" (The land system and land tax system of Fengtien province), first reproduced in mimeographed form in Jan. 1929; published in four parts between June and September, 1932, in MCG.

Young, C. Walter. The International Relations of Manchuria. Chicago, 1929.

————. Japanese Jurisdiction in the South Manchurian Railway Areas. Baltimore, 1931.

————. Japan's Special Position in Manchuria: Its Assertion, Legal Interpretation and Present Meaning. Baltimore, 1931.

Young, John W. "The Hara Cabinet and Chang Tso-lin, 1920–1," Monumenta Nipponica, vol. 27, pt. 2, Summer, 1972, pp. 125–42.

————. The Research Activities of the South Manchurian Railway Company, 1907–1945: A History and Bibliography. Columbia University, The East Asian Institute, New York, 1966.

Yü Ming. Chang Tso-lin wai-chuan (An unofficial biography of Chang Tso-lin). 3 vols. Hong Kong, vol. 1, 1965; vol. 2, 1967.

Index

Index

"warlord lit."
see p 269 n. 26

changed mother
neg.